Dixie Victorious

ALTERNATE HISTORY
FROM GREENHILL BOOKS

DIXIE VICTORIOUS

An Alternate History of the Civil War

Edited by Peter G. Tsouras

Greenhill Books, London
Stackpole Books, Pennsylvania

Dixie Victorious
An Alternate History of the Civil War
first published 2004 by Greenhill Books,
Lionel Leventhal Limited, Park House,
1 Russell Gardens, London NW11 9NN
www.greenhillbooks.com
and
Stackpole Books, 5067 Ritter Road,
Mechanicsburg, PA 17055, USA

British Library Cataloguing in Publication Data
Dixie victorious : an alternate history of the Civil War
1. Imaginary histories
2. United States – History – Civil War, 1861-1865
I. Tsouras, Peter
973.7

ISBN 1-85367-595-4

Library of Congress Cataloging-in-Publication Data
A catalog entry is available from the library.

Typeset and edited by Donald Sommerville.

Printed and bound in Great Britain by
MPG Books Ltd., Bodmin, Cornwall.

CONTENTS

ILLUSTRATIONS

MAPS

THE CONTRIBUTORS

JAMES R. ARNOLD is a professional writer who specializes in military history. He has published over 20 books roughly divided into three major topic areas: the Napoleonic era, the Civil War, and the modern period. His two most recent books are a Napoleonic campaign study, *Marengo and Hohenlinden: Napoleon's Rise to Power* and *Jeff Davis's Own: Cavalry, Comanches, and the Battle for the Texas Frontier*. He has also contributed numerous essays to military journals, including the British *Journal of the Society for Army Historical Research* and the American journals *Army History*, *Army Magazine*, and *Navy History*. His chapter in this book reflects his interest in the influence of intelligence and espionage upon military events. Most recently he contributed to *Rising Sun Victorious: How the Japanese Won the Pacific War* and *Cold War Hot: Alternate Decisions of the Cold War*.

JOHN D. BURTT is the editor of *Paper Wars* magazine, an independent review journal devoted to wargames. In his day job he is an advisory nuclear engineer consulting for the U.S. Nuclear Regulatory Commission. However, his real love is military history. A former Marine sergeant and a veteran of Vietnam, he holds a master's degree in military history and is pursuing a PhD in the same field. He has written for *Command* magazine, *Strategy & Tactics*, and *The Wargamer*, and was the original editor of *Counter-Attack* magazine. He was also a contributor to *Rising Sun Victorious: How the Japanese Won the Pacific War*, *Third Reich Victorious: How the Germans Won the War* and *Cold War Hot: Alternate Decisions of the Cold War*.

WADE G. DUDLEY holds a master's degree in maritime history and nautical archaeology from East Carolina University (1997) and a doctorate in history from the University of Alabama (1999). He contributed chapters to *Rising Sun Victorious: How the Japanese Won the Pacific War*, *Third Reich Victorious: How the Germans Won the War* and *Cold War Hot: Alternate Decisions of the Cold War*, and is the author of *Drake: For God, Queen, and Plunder!* and *Splintering the Wooden Wall: The British Blockade of the United States, 1812–1815*. He is a visiting assistant professor at East Carolina University in Greenville, North Carolina.

MICHAEL R. HATHAWAY retired from the U.S. federal civil service in 1999 and is currently a consultant living in Reston, Virginia. He earned a

BA in Political Science, University of California at Berkeley, 1972; an MBA from Jacksonville State University, 1977; and a Juris Doctorate from Golden Gate University, 1981. He was commissioned second lieutenant in the U.S. Army in 1972 and had three years active duty service in Military Intelligence. Civilian employment with the Social Security Administration and the Office of Naval Research followed. In 1981 he became the National Security Legislative Assistant to U.S. Senator Alfonse D'Amato. In 1985 he was appointed Staff Director, Commission on Security and Cooperation in Europe and in 1987 Staff Counsel to the Minority, U.S. Senate International Narcotics Control Caucus; in 1989 Professional Staff Member, Senate Select Committee on Intelligence; in 1995 Deputy Chief of Staff, Commission on Security and Cooperation in Europe; and in 1997 Chief of Staff. Mr Hathaway has contributed to *Just Cause: The U.S. Intervention in Panama* and *Cold War Hot: Alternate Decisions of the Cold War.*

DR **DAVID M. KEITHLY** combines professional writing with a wide range of business interests. His books include *The Collapse of East German Communism: The Year the Wall Came Down, 1989*; *Breakthrough in Ostpolitik: 1971 Quadripartite Agreement*; *Comparative Politics Today: A World View*; *Nuclear Strategy, Arms Control and the Future* (ed.); and the forthcoming *America and the World*. He is the North American editor of *Civil Wars*. He teaches at the Joint Military Intelligence College and American Military University. He has twice been a Fulbright Fellow in Europe, was a Fellow of the Institute for Global Cooperation and Conflict at the University of California, a scholar-in-residence at the Friedrich Naumann Foundation in Bonn, Germany, and a legislative fellow in the state parliament of the German state of Thüringen. He has a PhD in International Relations from Claremont Graduate School and an MA in Political Economy from the German University of Freiburg. He received the annual faculty research award at the Joint Military Intelligence College in 2001 where he is currently serving as a commander, U.S. Navy Reserve.

MAJOR KEVIN F. KILEY is a former Marine Corps artilleryman and a veteran of the 1991 Gulf War, having served in combat in Kuwait. A West Point graduate, he commanded two artillery batteries, and he now teaches middle school mathematics in Jacksonville, North Carolina. An avid collector of toy and model soldiers, as well as military prints, he is now working on his first book, on artillery of the Napoleonic period. He was a contributor to *Cold War Hot: Alternate Decisions of the Cold War.* He is married, and he and his wife, Daisy, have a young son, Michael, who is named after Kevin's brother, Captain Michael J. Kiley, who was killed in action in the Republic of Vietnam on November 19, 1967 in the Battle of Dak To while commander of A Company, 2d Battalion, 503d Infantry (Airborne). This is for all three of them—*Virtute et Valore.*

CYRIL M. LAGVANEC holds a master's degree in British and European History from Tulane University (1988) and a doctorate in American Military History from Texas A&M University (1999). He contributed numerous entries to Greenwood Press' dictionaries of historical biography and is currently working on a biography of Edmund Kirby Smith, C.S.A. He is a visiting assistant professor of history at East Carolina University in Greenville, North Carolina.

EDWARD G. LONGACRE is a U.S. Air Force historian, currently assigned to Headquarters Air Combat Command, Langley Air Force Base, Virginia. He is the author of 18 books and 100 journal and magazine articles on the Civil War and has contributed more than 400 entries to reference works on the conflict. He is the winner of the Fletcher Pratt Prize for his *The Cavalry at Gettysburg: A Tactical Study of Mounted Operations during the Civil War's Pivotal Campaign, 9 June – 14 July 1863*. He was recently appointed an honorary director of the U.S. Cavalry Association. His other published books are: *From Union Stars to Top Hat: A Biography of the Extraordinary General James Harrison Wilson*; *Mounted Raids of the Civil War*; *The Man Behind the Guns: A Biography of General Henry J. Hunt, Chief of Artillery, Army of the Potomac*; (editor) *From Antietam to Fort Fisher: The Civil War Letters of Edward King Wightman, 1862–1865*; *To Gettysburg and Beyond: The Twelfth New Jersey Volunteer Infantry, II Corps, Army of the Potomac, 1862–1865*; *Jersey Cavaliers: A History of the First New Jersey Volunteer Cavalry, 1861–1865*; *Pickett, Leader of the Charge: A Biography of General George E. Pickett, C.S.A.*; *General John Buford: A Military Biography*; *Army of Amateurs: General Benjamin F. Butler and the Army of the James, 1863–1865*; *Custer and His Wolverines: The Michigan Cavalry Brigade, 1861–1865*; *Joshua Chamberlain, the Soldier and the Man*; *Lincoln's Cavalrymen: A History of the Mounted Forces of the Army of the Potomac, 1861–1865*; *General William Dorsey Pender: A Military Biography*; *Lee's Cavalrymen: A History of the Mounted Forces of the Army of Northern Virginia, 1861–1865*; *A Regiment of Slaves: The Fourth United States Colored Infantry, 1863–1866*; *Gentleman and Soldier: A Biography of Wade Hampton III*; and *The Cavalry at Appomattox: A Tactical Study of Mounted Operations during the Civil War's Climactic Campaign, March 29 – April 9, 1865*.

LT COLONEL PETER G. TSOURAS, U.S.A.R. (ret) is a senior analyst with the Battelle Memorial Institute in Washington. Formerly he was a senior analyst at the U.S. Army National Ground Intelligence Center. He served in the Army as an armor officer in the 1st Battalion, 64th Armor Regiment, in Germany and subsequently in Intelligence and Adjutant Generals Corps assignments. He retired from the Army Reserve in 1994 after serving in Civil Affairs. His assignments have taken him to Somalia, Russia, the Ukraine, and Japan. He is the author or editor of 23 books on international military themes, military history, and alternate history. His books include *Disaster at D-Day: The Germans Defeat the Allies*; *Gettysburg: An Alternate History*; *The Great Patriotic War*; *The Anvil of War*; *Fighting in Hell*; *The Greenhill Dictionary of Military Quotations*; *Panzers on the Eastern Front: General Erhard Raus and His Panzer Divisions in Russia*; *Rising Sun Victorious: The Alternate History of How the Japanese Won the Pacific War*; *Third Reich Victorious: How the Germans Won the War*; *Cold War Hot: Alternate Decisions of the Cold War* and most recently *Alexander the Great: Invincible King of Macedonia*.

ANDREW UFFINDELL is a British author. His first book was *The Eagle's Last Triumph*, a study of Napoleon's victory at Ligny. This was followed by an examination of the battle and battlefield of Waterloo, *On the Fields of Glory*, written with the American military historian Michael Corum. He has also written the *Waterloo* guidebook in the Battleground Europe series, again with Michael Corum. He contributed to a compilation of Napoleonic alternative history scenarios, *The Napoleon Options*, edited by Jonathan North. In addition, he has written a chapter for *Napoleon: the Final Verdict* and edited a volume of essays by the late Jac Weller, *On Wellington*. Two further books were published in 2003: *Great Generals of the Napoleonic Wars and their Battles, 1805–1815* and *The National Army Museum Book of Wellington's Armies*. Among his published articles have been an analysis of friendly fire at Waterloo and studies of the Franco-Austrian War of 1859. He has also served as editor of the *Newsletter of the Society of Friends of the National Army Museum*.

INTRODUCTION

It has been said that the moment the Confederacy died it became immortal. The myth of the Lost Cause has hung over the subsequent history of the United States as a mixture of romance and regret. The broken South clung to the myth because the reality of its humiliation was too bitter to bear straight on. Its pain demanded the solace of even lost glories. But there is another reason. The South did come close, incredibly close, on a number of occasions to victory.

Those who scoff will point to the inexorable great tides of history as ensuring the inevitability of the South's defeat. The North's triple advantage in manpower, its overwhelming industrial and financial superiority, and its possession of a fleet and army were simply too much for the new Confederacy to overcome. It was, as Sun Tzu once said, as forlorn an effort as throwing eggs against a millstone. But the South possessed advantages that are less quantifiable but equally heavy in the scales of war. Southern leadership and Southern valor equalized a brutal number of battles where the Union forces possessed all those quantifiable advantages in numbers and equipment that so enthrall little minds.

The North's war effort also did not rely on sheer numbers. It possessed a critical element of morale as well. Northern morale required vastly more effort to hold together. Waging an offensive war requires far more political support than a purely defensive war, especially when a significant part of the political opposition is openly subversive. For President Lincoln, sustaining Northern morale through successive disasters until Northern leadership was able to employ Northern numbers efficiently was the supreme act of political genius. More than any other factor, Lincoln's ability to weather a host of crises led to the victory of the Union.

On a number of occasions the margin of error was almost nonexistent. Here luck played the dominant hand. The South either did not press its advantage or failed to seize the moment. Victory held her laurels tantalizingly just beyond the reach of the Confederacy. The balance was so fine that it was tipped by the absence of a tourniquet or the depth of a sandbar on the Red River. The misallocation of naval resources, a lost order, or a failure to keep the cavalry close in the invasion of Pennsylvania were inordinately decisive.

Periods of Northern vulnerability appeared repeatedly during the war. Surely the greatest was in 1862 when blood shed on American soil poured out for the first time in torrents. Lincoln came within a hairsbreadth of war with Great Britain over the Trent Affair, and only his willingness to back down and his determination to only "fight one war at a time" saved the Union from a catastrophic second front against the might of the British Empire and France as well.

The British author, Andrew Uffindell, examines just how close Lincoln came to failing to stave off such a war and then illustrates the appalling consequences of such a failure for the Union. Wade Dudley then employs the confrontation of the U.S.S. *Monitor* and the C.S.S. *Virginia* to show how close was the Union victory and the consequences of a Confederate counter-blockade had the battle tipped the other way. David Keithly draws a sequences of events pivoting on the famous Order #191 which gave away Lee's plan of operation to McClellan. What if the order had not been lost? Michael Hathaway pinpoints another Northern crisis, one consistently overlooked by students of the war. The United States Government came perilously close in 1862 to outright financial collapse. A Southern victory in Maryland in September 1862 might have set off a crash that would have brought the war to a halt for a failure to pay for it.

By 1863 Union prospects were looking up, but still weaknesses persisted that provided mortal openings for the South. Luck was there as well. James Arnold supplies the tourniquet that would have saved Albert Sidney Johnston at Shiloh, saving that Southern lion for a contest with U.S. Grant outside of Vicksburg. Edward Longacre wipes away Stuart's disastrous attempt to ride around the Army of the Potomac before Gettysburg. Instead Lee keeps him close. Then Lee has not only powerful fists but keen eyes as well in Pennsylvania. John Burtt removes detested Braxton Bragg from command of the Army of Tennessee after his unexploited victory at Chickamauga and puts Longstreet in his place to wrestle with Grant in a grinding campaign in the mountains around Chattanooga.

Finally 1864, the last year of opportunity for the South, still offered chances for the Confederacy. They all hinged on the Union's 1864 Presidential and Congressional elections. Lincoln's victory against the Peace Democrats depended on continued success. A military disaster or a major Southern initiative to checkmate the North politically would surely have removed the single most critical player in the war – Lincoln. This author has created a scenario based on the proposal of Irish-born Major General Patrick Cleburne to redress the South's ruinous manpower losses by conscripting slaves and giving them their freedom. A golden chance was there to change the terms of the war totally, to crack the Northern crusade, and push the direction of race relations along an entirely new path. Cyril Lagvanec takes the reader to the seldom visited Trans-Mississippi Theater of operations to demonstrate the consequences of a Northern debacle during the Red River

Campaign. Finally, Major Kevin Kiley, U.S.M.C., loosens Jubal Early in the Shenandoah Campaign to drive Washington into panic and break the siege of Petersburg.

These excursions into the myth of the Lost Cause show that its allure was not entirely wishful thinking. The South came achingly near to victory as the scales trembled in balance again and again. Tip the balance, dear reader, and follow these alternative roads of history to Southern independence.

Clarifications

The ten chapters in this book do not form a continuous thread or single plot line. Rather they are the stories woven by ten authors each charged with examining a different period or episode of the Civil War in light of the very real potential for different outcomes. Each is self-contained within its own alternate reality.

Our historical accounts of this alternate reality naturally need their own explanatory references, which appear in the footnotes at the end of each chapter. The use of these "alternate reality" notes, of course, poses a risk to the unwary reader who may make strenuous efforts to acquire a new and fascinating source. To avoid an epidemic of frustrating and futile searches, the "alternate notes" are indicated with an asterisk (*) before the number. All works appearing in the bibliographies included separately in each chapter are, however, "real."

Peter G. Tsouras
Lt. Col. (U.S.A.R., ret)
Alexandria, Virginia
2004

1
"HELL ON EARTH"
Anglo-French Intervention
in the Civil War

Andrew Uffindell

When Queen Victoria's husband was killed in a tragic accident on October 1, 1860, few guessed the immensity of the repercussions. The couple were staying with their daughter, Vicky, at Coburg in Germany and that fateful afternoon Prince Albert set off alone in his carriage to keep an appointment. Suddenly, his horses went out of control, dashed furiously down the road towards a railroad crossing and crashed into a wagon that was waiting for a train to pass. The collision overturned the carriage, injured the coachman and killed Albert instantly. Britain lost a wise and devoted statesman who might have managed to steer the country clear of intervention in the terrible conflict that split the United States the following year.

The War of Northern Aggression

The confrontation between the Northern and Southern States of America exploded into hostilities with the Confederate bombardment of Fort Sumter in South Carolina on April 12, 1861. Without European intervention, the war would probably have ended in a Confederate defeat, given the North's overwhelmingly superior resources and the disjointed nature of the Confederacy itself. Nor was it inevitable that Britain and France should have become involved. Initially, they proclaimed their neutrality and recognized the Confederacy only as a belligerent. Even this logical and limited move was resented by the North, which feared that it would be followed by recognition of the Confederacy's independence, and by mediation in the conflict.

Public opinion in Britain was not unanimous. The British ruling classes naturally sympathized more with the Southern aristocracy than with the democratic North; they also feared the growing power of the United States and its potential threat to the integrity of British North America. Both of these dangers could be averted by the establishment of an independent Confederacy. But many British workers favored the Union and the situation was further complicated by the country's increased reliance on wheat imports from the North following a string of crop failures in Europe. Britain was less dependent on Southern cotton, for she already had a surplus and could find alternative sources in Egypt and India.

The *Trent* Incident

Britain's tense relations with the North dramatically worsened when Captain Charles Wilkes of the U.S. frigate *San Jacinto* intercepted the British mail packet *Trent* on November 8, 1861, as it sailed from the Spanish port of Havana in Cuba. He was acting on his own initiative and was intent on arresting the two Confederate commissioners who were on board, James Mason and John Slidell. But the commander of Wilkes's boarding party, Lieutenant Fairfax, was shot and wounded by an irate passenger and two Britons were killed when the Americans returned fire.

Wilkes returned triumphantly with his two captured commissioners. His audacious action turned him into a popular hero overnight, but also plunged Lincoln's government into the worst crisis it had yet faced. The news of the murderous deed, which amounted to an act of war, reached London on November 25. Queen Victoria wrote that British blood "boiled" and Viscount Palmerston, her 77-year-old Prime Minister, was outraged. "You may stand for this," he raged at his Cabinet, "but damned if I will!"

The Foreign Secretary, Lord John Russell, drafted a blunt memorandum to Lord Lyons, the British Minister in Washington, demanding the release of the captives and an apology. The blunt message left little room for negotiation and made it impossible for the North to back down without massive loss of face. Lincoln was desperate to stick to "one war at a time" and avoid a potentially disastrous conflict with Britain while he was fighting the Confederacy. But politically he had little room for manoeuvre. Charles Francis Adams Jr, the son of the American Minister to Britain, was studying law in Boston and wrote 50 years later:

> "I do not remember in the whole course of the half-century's retrospect... any occurrence in which the American people were so completely swept off their feet, for the moment losing possession of their senses, as during the weeks which immediately followed the seizure of Mason and Slidell."[1]

William H. Seward, Lincoln's Secretary of State, threatened on December 16 that, if the Union was forced into a war with Britain, "we will wrap the whole world in flames."[2] But in the absence of an apology, neither Seward's bluster nor a belated assurance that Wilkes had acted without authorization could dissuade an aggrieved Britain from recognizing the Confederacy as an independent nation. At the same time, Britain demanded that both North and South submit to European mediation to end the war and prevent any further injury to British subjects or commercial interests.

Lincoln tried to play for time, possibly hoping to negotiate once the popular outcry in the North had abated. But Confederate agents operating covertly in British North America had already seized their opportunity to try and precipitate a conflict by raiding Union towns immediately across the frontier. The most notorious of these incidents occurred on December 8 when a gang attacked the town of Lowell, Vermont, robbed its banks and killed three citizens in the gunfight that followed. They then escaped back across the border. A nearby detachment of the 2d Cavalry immediately rode off in pursuit under Second Lieutenant George Armstrong Custer, who had been sent a week earlier to help reconnoiter the frontier as a response to the raids. The hot-headed Custer not only failed to apprehend the culprits, but advanced so far across the border that he was holed up inside a farm by Canadian militia and had to surrender his surviving men after a desperate shoot-out. He spent the next two years in a British prisoner-of-war camp on the South Atlantic island of St Helena[3] and was afterwards court-martialled and dismissed from the Army. He then pursued a seemingly highly-successful business career but died in prison in 1882 after being found guilty of fraud.[4]

War between Britain and the North was now unavoidable as the escalating border incidents sparked a series of clashes between British and Union troops. The British authorities genuinely wanted to prevent the raids, but lacked the manpower to cover the entire frontier. War officially broke out on January 20, 1862.

The English novelist Anthony Trollope had been touring the United States as the crisis erupted and was appalled:

> "These people speak our language, use our prayers, read our books, are ruled by our laws, dress themselves in our image, are warm with our blood. They have all our virtues; and their vices are our own too, loudly as we call out against them. They are our sons and our daughters, the source of our greatest pride, and as we grow old they should be the staff of our age. Such a war as we shall now wage with the States will be an unloosing of hell on earth."[5]

France immediately followed Britain into the conflict. The French Emperor Napoleon III wanted to revive popular support for his regime and knew the effect that military glory would have on Paris. He was once asked whether it was difficult to rule the French and replied: "Oh no! Nothing is easier. You simply need to give them a war every four years."

War with the North would also enable him to establish French influence and commercial advantages in the New World. In a speech to the United States Congress in 1823, President James Monroe had warned France and Spain not to try to interfere in the Americas. But the War between the States made it impossible to enforce the Monroe Doctrine and a Union defeat could prevent it from being revived. By actively intervening in the conflict,

Napoleon III could ensure the survival of the Confederacy as a key French ally and commercial partner.

Anglo-French relations had fluctuated since Napoleon III's establishment of the Second Empire in 1852. French forces had fought alongside the British against the Russians in the Crimean War (1854–6) and against the Chinese during the Expedition to Peking in 1860. But the British distrusted Napoleon III's devious diplomacy and had become alarmed by his willingness to use force to revise the European settlement of 1815 in France's favor, as demonstrated by his war with Austria in northern Italy in 1859. They were also concerned at French military and naval power and its implications for the security of the British Isles. Nonetheless, a commercial treaty had improved relations in 1860 and Napoleon III was keen to strengthen the alliance.

For their part, the British welcomed French moral, diplomatic and naval support against the North, but declined Napoleon III's offer of French troops to help defend their North American colonies. They feared that he had ambitions to re-establish a permanent French foothold there, for France had owned vast territories along the St Lawrence and Mississippi rivers until their cession to Britain and Spain under the Treaty of Paris in 1763 at the end of the Seven Years' War.

In fact, Napoleon III was more interested in Latin America. President Benito Juarez of Mexico had postponed the payment of all public debts, including indemnities owed to foreigners for losses suffered during his country's civil war. In January 1862, shortly before Britain and France went to war with the North, a French, Spanish and British force occupied Vera Cruz on the eastern coast of Mexico, with the British contributing a battalion of the Royal Marines and a squadron of ships under Commodore Hugh Dunlop. The British and Spanish withdrew in April after forcing Mexico to resume its outstanding payments, but the French remained, intent on establishing a Mexican Empire as a French satellite, and were reinforced to a total of 20,000 men under General Elie Forey.

The long-term implications of the French presence in Mexico caused some unease within the Confederacy, but were dismissed when Napoleon III concluded a formal alliance with the South and sent General Achille Bazaine with 10,000 French troops to help defend Richmond. The French soldiers completely won over the people of the South and gained the admiration even of their enemies for their élan in attack. They were veterans with recent combat experience in the Crimea, Algeria and northern Italy and boosted both the morale and training of their Confederate allies. Even today, French influence pervades Virginia.

The British were more cautious than the French and initially sought to avoid a formal alliance with the Confederacy, partly for domestic reasons. They planned simply to fight a parallel war to force an end to both conflicts, but soon realized that they could not defeat the Union without co-ordinating their operations more closely with the Confederate war effort.

Defensive Preparations in British North America

Britain had to prosecute the war simultaneously in several distinct, but interlocking, theatres. Her main offensive weapon was the Royal Navy, which would blockade the Atlantic coast, hunt down hostile ships around the world and attack the Pacific Seaboard using troops drawn from the Far East. But she also had to look immediately to preparing the defences of her highly vulnerable North American possessions against the threat of invasion.

British North America consisted of a collection of territories. In the east were the province of Newfoundland and the Maritime Provinces of Nova Scotia, Prince Edward Island and New Brunswick. Further west was the Province of Canada, which by uniting the French-speaking region around the city of Quebec and the English-speaking area based on Toronto contained 75 per cent of the population of British North America. On the Pacific coast lay the colonies of British Columbia and Vancouver Island, while the Hudson Bay Company held the vast territories in between.

The security of these vast areas depended on their waterways, for road transport was difficult and the rail network limited. The British relied above all on the St Lawrence River, not just as a line of defence, but also as an avenue of communications by which trade and military supplies could be brought to Quebec, Montreal and the Great Lakes. The St Lawrence was the jugular vein of British North America, but it was often dangerously close to the American frontier, particularly west of Montreal and also where the State of Maine projected northwards like an incisor tooth.

The St Lawrence had been supplemented by a system of canals to bypass rapids, but many of these were exposed on the southern side of the river and even those on the northern bank often lay within artillery range of American territory. Their dimensions also limited the size of ships that the British could pass up the St Lawrence. This, in turn, meant that the British could not hope for naval superiority on the Great Lakes. They had dismantled their warships posted there, following the Rush–Bagot Agreement of 1817 to neutralize the Lakes. They had not even kept the permitted number of gunboats and, although they could mount guns on commercial vessels, they therefore had nothing with which to counter the U.S.S. *Michigan*, which was based at Buffalo as a recruiting vessel and which in fact exceeded the agreed limits. A further problem was that even the easternmost of the Great Lakes was 600 miles from the Atlantic. Given the ease with which the St Lawrence could be cut, it was pointless to attempt a serious defence of the Lakes or, indeed, of any position west of Montreal.

Despite this depressing outlook, the British had two significant advantages. Firstly, they had fortified the frontier. It was unfortunate that several of the fortifications had been allowed to slip out of use, with some outposts being used as juvenile reformatories and Fort Malden, near Detroit, as a lunatic asylum. Furthermore, the strength of the 30-year-old citadel at Quebec, "the Gibraltar of America," had been undermined by the development of modern artillery. Even so, the British side of the border was unquestionably better fortified than the American.

The British could also count on the bitterness and duration of the North American winter. The freezing-over of the St Lawrence prevented direct communication with Britain by sea between December and April. But the difficulties imposed by the winter would also make it impossible for the Americans to do more than blockade a well-supplied fortress like Quebec and limited the time available during the rest of the year for an actual siege.

There had been only 4,300 regular troops in British North America on the outbreak of the War between the States, but they were quickly reinforced. In July 1861, the *Great Eastern*, the largest ship in the world, carried 2,144 officers and men, 473 women and children and 122 horses in a single voyage, a hitherto unimaginable figure. The ship steamed across the Atlantic in a record time of eight days and six hours thanks to her keen young captain, the 30-year-old James Kennedy, who refused to reduce speed when he ran into fog. He simply dodged the icebergs and narrowly avoided colliding with the Cunard liner *Arabia*.

A further 11,000 reinforcements were sent as soon as the *Trent* crisis erupted. Florence Nightingale personally advised the Government on warm clothing needed for the Canadian winter. Only one transport managed to sail up the St Lawrence before it froze, obliging the rest to use the Atlantic port of Halifax in Nova Scotia. The troops then went overland on sledges, heading north along a snow road via Fredericton, Grand Falls and Edmundston to Rivière-du-Loup on the St Lawrence, the terminus of the Grand Trunk Railway to Quebec and Montreal.

The snow road lay immediately across the border from the state of Maine, but the Union lacked enough troops in position to cut it at the start of hostilities. The American border town of Houlton, for example, contained only a handful of volunteers. Units raised in Maine had been sent south to join the Union armies and those troops left in the state were more concerned about restoring the defences of the principal towns and harbors against the threat posed by the Royal Navy. Moreover, a major attack into New Brunswick would have been logistically difficult given Maine's poorly-developed rail network and sparse population near the border.

The Governor-General of British North America was the capable Viscount Monck. He knew that the North would not be able to attack in strength before spring 1862, for both climatic and organizational reasons, and by then he would have 18,000 British regulars. Monck accelerated defensive preparations and called out the militia, although he was conscious of its limited value in a pitched battle. The sedentary militia had hitherto existed only on paper and lacked training and equipment. The active militia, or volunteers, were not much better. Ralph Vansittart, a local politician, described how on December 25, 1861, a new company of volunteers from the Middlesex Sedentary Militia was mustered at the village of Glammis amid great enthusiasm:

> "The appearance of the new recruits would not give much satisfaction to a regular army officer, but the rough material is there, out of which sturdy troops can be made fit for any work... Colonel {John} Axford was supreme. Dressed in the old uniform he wore in 1837, consisting of a long-tailed blue coat, with brass buttons, and gilt-cord shoulder straps, a pair of white duck trousers tucked into his high cavalry boots; while a shako and a pair of spurs completed his attire... His appearance was to me anything but dignified, but to his troops he was the personification of military dignity and glory. His popularity was not diminished by the production of two kegs of whisky, which, so long as they lasted, were free to all. After the rolls had been completed and the men sworn in, they were drawn up, and an effort made to dress them in line, and here the democratic relationship between the officers and men was at once exemplified. It was, Bob, won't you move up to Tom; Jim, please step forward; or, Now, men, why don't you hold on and let the others come up. And when finally the order to march was given, and the line was halted, after an attempt to wheel with the left as a pivot, the whole formation was found as zigzag as a snake fence."[6]

Monck, in view of the vast disparity in numbers of troops and resources, could not hope to take the offensive. He would have to defend his territories as best he could until the Union was forced to negotiate by defeats on its other fronts. The rout of the Union Army by the Confederates at Bull Run on July 21, 1861, had not impressed British observers with an undue sense of the martial prowess of the Union troops or the ability of their commanders. They were seen as no match for British regulars.

Monck's confidence was further boosted by the fact that he had agents in the states of Maine and New York to obtain intelligence of impending moves. A serious invasion of so vast a territory as British North America would require a minimum of 50,000 troops and could not be prepared in secret. A large number of British North Americans had previously joined the Union Army and many now deserted in case they were ordered to invade their homeland. They provided useful information as well as additional numbers of trained troops.

Britannia Rules the Waves!

The Royal Navy's prestige was immense and recent reforms had increased its professionalism. Immediately on the outbreak of war, its squadrons around the world began clearing the Union merchant marine from the oceans. The Royal Navy at the end of 1861 had 339 ships worldwide, while the Union

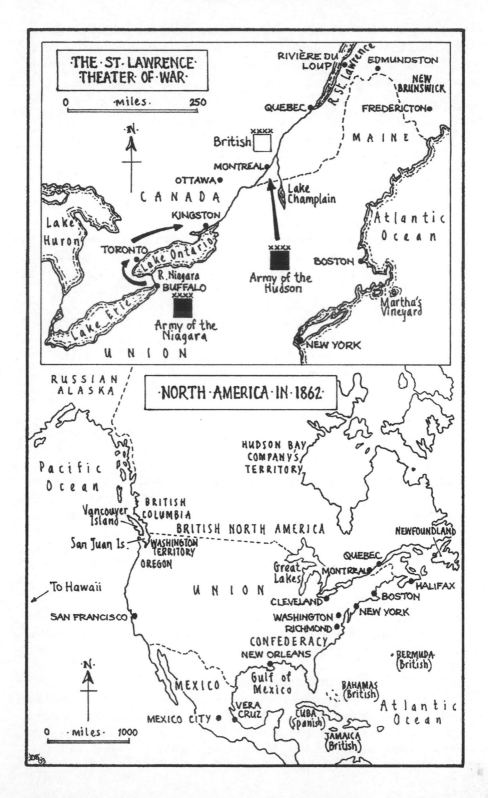

THE·ST·LAWRENCE·
THEATER·OF·WAR·

0   ·miles·   250

British

RIVIÈRE DU
LOUP

EDMUNDSTON

NEW
BRUNSWICK

QUEBEC

FREDERICTON

R. ST. Lawrence

MAINE

MONTREAL

OTTAWA

CANADA

Lake
Champlain

Atlantic
Ocean

Lake
Huron

KINGSTON

TORONTO

Lake Ontario

R. Niagara

BUFFALO

Army of the
Hudson

BOSTON

Lake Erie

Army of the
Niagara

Martha's
Vineyard

U N I O N

NEW YORK

RUSSIAN
ALASKA

·NORTH·AMERICA·IN·1862·

Pacific
Ocean

HUDSON BAY
COMPANY'S
TERRITORY

Vancouver
Island

BRITISH
COLUMBIA

BRITISH NORTH AMERICA

NEWFOUNDLAND

San Juan Is.

WASHINGTON
TERRITORY

OREGON

Great
Lakes

QUEBEC

MONTREAL

HALIFAX

To Hawaii

U N I O N

CLEVELAND

BOSTON

NEW YORK

SAN FRANCISCO

WASHINGTON

RICHMOND

CONFEDERACY

·BERMUDA·
(British)

NEW ORLEANS

MEXICO

Gulf of
Mexico

BAHAMAS
(British)

Atlantic
Ocean

VERA
CRUZ

CUBA
(Spanish)

MEXICO CITY

0   ·miles·   1000

JAMAICA
(British)

Navy had about 264, many of them converted commercial vessels rather than purpose-built warships.[7]

The most active share of the Royal Navy's operations fell to the North American and West Indies Squadron under Vice-Admiral Sir Alexander Milne. This was based at Bermuda between November and May and at Halifax for the rest of the year. Milne was heavily reinforced in 1861 and again on the outbreak of war. His vessels had both steam-power and sails, whereas many of the Union ships had formerly been merchantmen, relied exclusively on sails and had inexperienced crews. Milne could also count on support from the strong French naval forces in the Atlantic and the Gulf of Mexico.

As soon as hostilities broke out, Milne attacked the Union squadrons that were blockading the Confederacy's harbors, in the hope of destroying them before they could unite, scatter or take refuge in ports. Milne swept the Atlantic Seaboard, while a detached squadron under Commodore Dunlop cleared the Gulf of Mexico. The Royal Navy experienced problems with some of its guns, particularly the new breech-loading rifled Armstrongs. These had superior range and accuracy, but also suffered from design defects that made them prone to accidents. Some British and French ships were severely damaged, but generally the actions swung decisively in the allies' favor. In the most famous of these naval battles, Commodore Dunlop forced Flag Officer David G. Farragut to surrender after crushing his West Gulf Blockading Squadron off New Orleans and reducing his flagship, the U.S.S. *Hartford*, to a wreck.

Some of the surviving Union ships managed to return to port, while others scattered and began raiding allied commerce around the world. The Bay of Bengal on the trade route to India provided particularly rich pickings, but the most spectacular raids occurred around the British Isles. The U.S.S. *Kearsarge* under Captain Charles W. Pickering even attacked the harbor of Leith near Edinburgh, thus emulating John Paul Jones, the great American naval hero who had cruised round Britain during the War of Independence (1775–83), attacking commerce and raiding coastal towns. But Pickering's audacious attack on merchant shipping near the Isle of Wight led to disaster when his ship was sunk by the Royal Navy's powerful new ironclad, H.M.S. *Warrior*. He was plucked from the sea by the royal yacht *Osborne* and promptly invited to dine with Albert Edward, the Prince of Wales. The 20-year-old prince was returning from an immensely successful state visit to Paris, where he had completely won over the French people with his charm and good humor.

Milne established a blockade of the entire Union eastern coast using five squadrons, a total of 54 ships. To maintain the blockade, he used bases and coaling stations in British North America, Bermuda, the West Indies and the Confederacy. The Admiralty had stockpiled large quantities of the superb Welsh anthracite in Halifax, Bermuda and the West Indies before the outbreak of war. Milne also occupied Martha's Vineyard off the coast of Massachusetts as a base for his colliers as they ferried coal to the blockading ships.

Milne had been acutely conscious of the vulnerability of his main bases at Halifax and Bermuda, both of which were lightly fortified. He wrote on December 31, 1861:

> "If Bermuda were in the hands of any other nation, the base of our operations would be removed to the two extremes, Halifax and Jamaica, and the loss of this island as a Naval Establishment would be a National misfortune."[8]

Fortunately, the Union had missed its chance to launch a powerful attack on Milne's bases before its squadrons were scattered. This lost opportunity resulted largely from the alarm and defensive-mindedness that pervaded Lincoln's Cabinet. Lincoln's men remembered how, in the War of 1812–14, the British had established a blockade that had devastated the American economy and they had also launched a series of raids along the coast, during one of which they had even burned the city of Washington. Secretary of War, Edwin M. Stanton, was aghast at the prospect of another war with Britain and told a Cabinet meeting in January 1862:

> "The British will change the whole course of the war; they will destroy *seriatim* [one after the other] every naval vessel; they will lay all the cities on the seaboard under contribution... I will notify the governors and municipal authorities in the North to take instant measures to protect their harbors. I have no doubt that the enemy are at this minute on their way to Washington, and it is not unlikely that we shall have a shell or a cannon ball from one of their guns in the White House before we leave the room."[9]

Tens of thousands of Union troops were tied down in building and manning static defences on the Atlantic coast. Old ships were collected ready to be sunk across the channel of the Potomac to prevent warships sailing up it to bombard the capital.

Milne's blockade would not be watertight unless he could actually seize or destroy the Union ports. But he was reluctant to risk attacks against strongly-defended targets and recoiled from the idea of an indiscriminate bombardment of cities. The destruction of the main Union ports would in fact have harmed Britain as well as the North after the war given the volume of Britain's transatlantic trade. Milne was also against attacking the coast of Maine, despite its many tempting targets, as he wrongly believed that the state might secede from the Union, as it had nearly done during the War of 1812–14.

A report by the Royal Navy's hydrographer, Captain John Washington, completed in December 1861, indicated that New York City was strongly fortified and cast doubt on whether it could be attacked successfully, except by using well-protected ironclads to distract the defences while wooden ships slipped past to bombard the port.[10] But Milne had no ironclads with his squadron and had not yet been reinforced with the floating ironclad batteries that had proved so successful against Russian fortifications during the Crimean War. Similar doubts were voiced on the feasibility of attacking Boston.

Ironclad developments had been led by the French and British. In America, the Confederates had begun to rebuild the *Merrimack* as the ironclad C.S.S. *Virginia*, which was variously dubbed "that thing" and "the roof of a barn with a huge chimney." The North's response had been to begin the construction at New York City of a powerful coastal ironclad with a gun turret and an alarmingly low, flat deck. It was called the U.S.S. *Monitor* and was also referred to, less formally, as "a cheese box on a raft."

Since New York was blockaded, the *Monitor* was unable to go through any sea trials before her first sortie on February 28, 1862. She experienced serious problems with steering and had to be towed back into New York harbor after sinking a British vessel. By the time she could be fitted with a new steering gear and engine valves, a fortnight had elapsed and the blockading force was prepared to evade another sortie.

The intervention of the *Monitor* gave the Royal Navy an unpleasant shock, particularly after it became clear that the Union was building a fleet of sister ships. Fortunately, the monitors were unseaworthy and were therefore limited to coastal defence. The British Admiralty admitted that the Federals were now "practically unassailable in their own waters," but had no great worries about the wider capabilities of the Union ironclads:

> "The few that seem likely to possess sea going qualities are in no way superior to the French 'Gloire' or 'Invincible'... The greater number are mere rafts carrying very few heavy guns propelled at moderate speed, and though perfectly well adapted for the Inland Waters of that great Continent, and most formidable as Harbour Defences, are not in any sense sea going ships of War."[11]

Thus the blockade of the Union was maintained. Small craft provided a trip-wire near the ports to help warships stationed offshore to intercept the ocean-going vessels while remaining outside the effective range of the monitors.

Viscount Palmerston, the British Prime Minister, suggested reinforcing Milne with H.M.S. *Warrior*, but this massive ironclad had been intended for service in home waters and was in fact too long to be able to use any of the available ports on the other side of the Atlantic. Since she had been designed as a sea-going ship to defend Britain and her ocean trade, she could not in fact have closed with the *Monitor* given her deep draught and the shallowness of the coastal waters in which the *Monitor* had to operate. Debate on the likely result of a clash between the two vessels must therefore remain mere speculation. The *Monitor*'s inventor, Captain John Ericsson, had claimed in a letter to the Union's Navy Board on September 3, 1861:

> "The iron-clad vessels of France and England are utterly unable to resist elongated shot fired from the 12-inch guns of the battery [*Monitor*]. The 4½-inch plates of *La Gloire* or the *Warrior* would crumble like brown paper under the force of such projectiles, and at close quarters every shot would crush in the enemy's sides at the water-line. The opposing broadsides would be nothing more than the rattling of pebbles on our cylindrical iron turret."[12]

But such bombastic comments should not be accepted at face value. It was true that only the central sections of *Warrior*'s sides were armored and her rudder head was dangerously exposed. But the *Monitor* could fire only one shot every quarter of an hour. Furthermore, the *Warrior*'s speed, 14 knots, would have made her dangerous had she managed to ram the far slower *Monitor*. Such considerations must, however, remain hypothetical.

The French ironclads, such as the *Gloire* and *Magenta*, were smaller than the *Warrior*, but had been designed for the Mediterranean rather than the stormier waters of the Atlantic and had limited sailpower. Hence the allies looked instead to the Confederacy to provide a local fleet of ironclads and floating ironclad batteries, using British money, materials and expertise. In due course, these Confederate ships reinforced the allied blockading squadrons and occasionally clashed with Union monitors, with mixed results. Later in the war, the Union produced mines, or "torpedoes" as they were known at the time, and even began to develop a submarine. Thus the war at sea continued to worry the allies until the end of the conflict.

The Pacific Seaboard

In contrast to the Atlantic Coast, the Union's western seaboard remained highly vulnerable. Many locally-raised regiments had been sent to the eastern theatre of war and the troops left behind were unable to do much more than preserve law and order. Rear-Admiral Sir Thomas Maitland of the Royal Navy's Pacific Squadron soon destroyed the Union's small Pacific Fleet and established a blockade. He also captured the Union commercial whaling fleet near Hawaii and occupied the islands as a base, hoping to develop Pearl Harbour, as it became known, into a major dockyard. For the time being, the British had no dry-dock facilities in the Pacific and before the war had actually sent ships for repair to San Francisco. This made it imperative to seize the city and bay of San Francisco immediately.

Maitland, using British troops withdrawn from China, began a series of bombardments, raids and permanent landings along the Pacific Coast. On April 6, 1862, he attacked San Francisco, taking advantage of the morning fog to slip ships past the guns of Alcatraz and Fort Point and into the bay.

The Navy Yard at Mare Island and the Arsenal at Benicia were quickly taken, being weakly-held. Parties of Royal Marines spearheaded the occupation of the city itself and seized large quantities of gold stored in its banks. The city's occupation was therefore a major economic as well as strategic blow to the Union. It was followed by the surrender of the isolated and under-strength garrison of Alcatraz, where immense amounts of munitions had been stored.

The two-year occupation of San Francisco was surprisingly peaceful. The British used the city's most popular citizen, Joshua A. Norton, the self-appointed Emperor Norton I of the United States, in a remarkable campaign to win the inhabitants' hearts and minds. Norton had been born in London in 1819 and came to San Francisco in 1849 from South Africa, but went bankrupt ten years later while trying to corner the local rice market. He then boldly assumed the title of Emperor of the United States and issued imperious decrees and even his own private currency to pay his bills. He quickly won over the people of San Francisco with his escapades and scrupulously maintained his neutrality following the secession of the South by alternately wearing Union and Confederate uniforms, along with a plumed hat and a ceremonial sword. Soon after the British arrived, a sentry accidentally shot Lazarus, one of Norton's two beloved mongrel dogs. Admiral Maitland was obliged to issue a formal apology to the grief-stricken Emperor and provided a guard of honor at the dog's funeral. Norton was now regularly saluted by all British servicemen and was invited to dinner aboard Maitland's flagship, H.M.S. *Bacchante*. He was greeted by a 21-gun salute and given the magnificent, scarlet, full-dress uniform of a captain of the Grenadier Guards. Norton was delighted and issued a decree, published in all the city newspapers, commanding his subjects to welcome the British occupiers as brothers. He also wrote, less successfully, to Queen Victoria and President Lincoln, ordering them to end hostilities and join him and other world leaders in forming a League of Nations to resolve such disputes peacefully.

British forces had also taken the offensive further north, in the Pacific North-West, where the frontier had long been disputed. In particular, the Oregon Treaty of 1846 had failed to clarify the ownership of San Juan Island near Seattle. This had nearly resulted in a war in June 1859, when an American settler on the island shot a British pig trampling on his potatoes. When the British tried to bring the man to justice, the American commander of the Department of Oregon had sent a company of the U.S. 9th Infantry under Captain George E. Pickett, a future Confederate general. Both sides sent further reinforcements and Pickett later claimed that he had hoped the ludicrous dispute would lead to a war, as this could have united his increasingly-divided country against a foreign foe. As it was, the stand-off was defused by an envoy from Washington, General Winfield Scott, "Old Fuss and Feathers," who arranged for each side to withdraw its reinforcements. A detachment of 100 Royal Marines was left at the north-western end of the island, with an American camp 10 miles away at the other end.

The American garrison was withdrawn following the outbreak of war between the North and South and the Royal Marines seized the whole of San Juan Island in January 1862. The Marines have commemorated this unopposed victory ever since with an annual dinner of roast pork, except in 1944 during a particularly difficult period of the fighting in Italy, when they had to resort to tinned bully beef.

The British had only a couple of hundred Royal Engineers on nearby Vancouver Island and in British Columbia on the mainland, as it was cheaper to use the Royal Navy rather than garrisons to maintain law, order and British sovereignty. As a result of its gold rush in 1858 British Columbia contained a majority of American settlers and its governor, James Douglas, had vainly asked for two battalions of reinforcements before the outbreak of the war. Some additional British troops were sent from China immediately after hostilities began, as a holding measure. Then, in April 1862, another 10,000 men arrived from India under Lieutenant-General Sir James Hope Grant, the Commander-in-Chief of the Army of Madras and one of the heroes of the Indian Mutiny of 1857. He also happened to be an accomplished musician and was always accompanied on campaign by his cello.

Grant took the offensive and thrust southwards into Washington Territory and Oregon, where he was joined by the warriors from the Paiute tribe. The Gurkhas were involved in several sharp clashes with detachments of the 2d California Volunteer Infantry and in one famous action a Federal unit was charged on one side by Paiute warriors and on the other by the Gujarat Silladar Horse. By the end of the war, the British effectively controlled the entire Pacific coast and were sending cavalry units to raid gold and silver mines in Nevada Territory in conjunction with local Native American tribes.

The Invasion of British North America

Meanwhile, the war had taken a dramatic turn on the eastern side of the continent as the Union invaded British North America.

Britain's intervention had immediately overturned the Union's strategy of strangling the Confederacy with a blockade and a deadly thrust into its heartland along the Mississippi. The Union now gave priority to operations in the east, against both Richmond and British North America. This accorded with popular demand. Lincoln's administration was riven by arguments throughout February 1862 over whether to concentrate first on Richmond or on forcing Britain to the negotiating table with an invasion of British North America before the Royal Navy could have a serious impact. The result was a compromise, whereby the Army of the Potomac under Major General George B. McClellan would advance on Richmond with

72,000 men while Major Generals John Pope and Henry W. Halleck invaded British North America with 116,000 after the spring thaw.

No fewer than six rivers crossed the Union line of advance on Richmond. General Robert E. Lee with the Franco-Confederate Army of Northern Virginia (53,000 men) skilfully defeated McClellan's offensives and inflicted heavy casualties. But Union operations on the northern front were more successful and began with the Union establishing naval supremacy on the Great Lakes. The British, with only 18,000 regulars under Lieutenant-General Sir William Fenwick Williams, were hopelessly outnumbered. Halleck's Army of the Niagara (65,000) attacked across that river from the town of Buffalo and its subsequent advance was eased by a successful amphibious assault on Toronto on the northern shore of Lake Ontario. The British fought a heroic delaying action at Kingston on the north-eastern end of the lake and then withdrew down the St Lawrence. Fortunately, the river was no longer frozen and reinforcements from England were able to reach Quebec.

Meanwhile, Pope's Army of the Hudson (51,000) advanced directly north, up the traditional invasion route along Lake Champlain. Its objective was Montreal, the largest city in British North America with a population of 90,000, and the key communications hub. Pope linked up with Halleck in May 1862 and took the city, much of which was burnt. Another casualty was Montreal's magnificent, two-mile-long Royal Victoria railway bridge, which was blown up by the British.

The Union armies had lost heavily in the fighting and Pope had to leave Halleck to guard his rear while he himself advanced on Quebec. His offensive was checked on July 19 on the Plains of Abraham outside the city, where a series of idiotic frontal attacks were massacred by the deadly firepower of the British regulars. The battle-torn regimental color of the 10th Massachusetts Volunteer Infantry was captured by the 63rd (West Suffolk) Regiment of Foot and is still preserved today at Windsor Castle. Four Victoria Crosses were won in this great victory, including a posthumous award to Lieutenant-Colonel Garnet Wolseley.[13] It was a turning point in the war, for the loss of Quebec would have been disastrous. Pope's options were now limited by the timely arrival of more British troops from home.

Canadian militia forces which had been left behind Union lines in the wake of the invasion were raiding communications and tying down many units. Pope exacerbated the situation by ordering his troops to live off the country and by taking tough reprisals in a vain attempt to halt guerrilla attacks. These measures simply antagonized the local population and created bitter hatred. Halleck's Army of the Niagara also had to contend with the Confederate raider Brigadier General Nathan Bedford Forrest, who had left Southern lines and ridden northwards through Ohio and Pennsylvania in a wide arc to strike Union communications. On November 18, 1862, Forrest was finally trapped at New Castle in Pennsylvania during one of his devastating raids and was shot dead, allegedly by friendly fire, as he tried to fight his way out of the chaos.

The British were keen to bring the war to a swift conclusion, for they were alarmed at the scale of their casualties, the astronomical financial cost and at the possibility of losing their North American provinces altogether. Apparently, they even assisted Confederate secret agents, who had long been operating from British North America, but whose effectiveness now dramatically increased. In their most audacious stroke, these agents used incendiary devices in an attack on New York City, setting fire to dozens of hotels, businesses, public buildings and shipyards. The simultaneous fires could not be controlled and gutted Broadway. Similar, but less successful, attacks were made on Baltimore, Cleveland and Pittsburgh, causing widespread panic and disruption. Other agents threw small explosive devices into coal bunkers in Navy Yards in the hope that they would explode after ending up in ships' furnaces. At least two Union vessels were crippled in this way.

Similarly audacious plans to rescue prisoners-of-war from camps near the border were foiled when the Union increased security measures. Despite the appalling conditions in the prisons, the British regimental system maintained remarkably high morale and cohesion and this was reflected in the survival rates. The British officers imprisoned in the camps introduced their Confederate comrades to the game of cricket, which has since become even more popular in the Deep South than baseball is in the North. British prisoners-of-war also became notorious for their repeated escape attempts. Their most spectacular bid for freedom came in October 1862 when they organized a mass escape from Fort Delaware on Pea Patch Island. The break-out was made at night and involved seizing two of the guard boats that patrolled the surrounding waters. The escapees made it ashore to the river bank by constructing rafts of canteens or by swimming and some managed to reach Confederate lines, where they were incorporated into the Louisiana Tigers.

Confederate Victories

Meanwhile, the Confederates and their French allies had continued to defeat the Union attacks north of Richmond. Then, at the end of August 1862, Lee invaded the North with 59,000 men in response to British appeals for a major diversion. He defeated McClellan at Boonsboro, Maryland, on September 15 despite heavy casualties. During the battle, Bazaine's Frenchmen broke into the Union defences in one of the most outstanding attacks of the war, prompting Lee to exclaim: "I have never seen a finer assault in my life. The day is yours! *Vive la France!*"

Lee was determined to remain in the North during the winter and to maintain the threat to Washington, D.C., whose girdle of earthworks was hurriedly strengthened. Lincoln in desperation considered proclaiming the emancipation of the Confederacy's slaves, but realized that he could not make such an announcement from a position of military weakness without it backfiring. In the meantime, he sacked McClellan and replaced him with Major General William Buel Franklin.

Lee continued his advance and on November 4 defeated Franklin at Cashtown, Pennsylvania. The Confederacy's hero of the day was the popular and eccentric Major General Richard S. Ewell. His projecting nose and sloping forehead gave him a distinctly bird-like profile and the French circulated fond, and possibly apocryphal, stories of him spending a conference happily chirping away and pecking at a handful of birdseed. He was widely mourned when he was killed by a cannonball at the height of the battle.

Confronted with the success of Lee's invasion, Lincoln evacuated Washington and transferred his government to New York City. He lost control of the House of Representatives to the Democrats in the congressional elections in November and his political survival looked increasingly unlikely. On January 29, 1863, Lee reoccupied his mansion at Arlington just outside the former capital and that afternoon reviewed Major General Thomas J. ("Stonewall") Jackson's troops as they tramped past the abandoned White House. Some Confederates called for their capital to be moved from Richmond to Washington, but President Jefferson Davis rejected the idea. The Confederacy was fighting a war of independence, not of conquest. Furthermore, Richmond would be less exposed than Washington in both the current and any future war against the North.

The success of Lee's invasion dealt the North another severe blow when Maryland seceded. Maryland was one of four slave states on the border between North and South whose loyalties were deeply divided. The other three were Delaware and, in the west, Kentucky and Missouri. All four had stayed with the Union on the outbreak of war, partly because of the presence of Northern troops. Delaware still remained loyal, but Kentucky and Missouri both had rival pro-Confederate and pro-Union governments.

Lincoln ordered the Northern armies in Canada to withdraw to help block Lee. They had suffered appallingly after their defeat at Quebec from the ravages of the Canadian winter and from the strain of guerrilla attacks. The British cautiously followed the Union retreat and even began to plan an advance down Lake Champlain towards New York City to split the Union and isolate the north-eastern states, which were already blockaded by sea. This had been the route taken by Lieutenant-General John Burgoyne in 1777 during the War of Independence and by Lieutenant-General Sir George Prevost in the War of 1812–14. It was not encouraging that Burgoyne had been forced to surrender at Saratoga and that Prevost had retreated after the destruction of his supporting fleet on Lake Champlain. It was clear that any such advance could only be undertaken in close conjunction with Confederate moves.

As it happened, events elsewhere moved too fast for the British to launch a serious offensive. Anti-war sentiment in the North had already provoked serious unrest and when large-scale riots broke out in New York City in March 1863, the vain, resentful and ambitious McClellan took the opportunity to launch a military coup. His close friend Major General Franklin marched on New York with a corps from the Army of the Potomac, ostensibly to restore order, while other generals declared their support, including William S. Rosecrans, Ambrose E. Burnside and Henry J. Hunt. Lincoln, whom McClellan despised and openly derided as "the original Gorilla" or "a well-meaning baboon," was arrested.

McClellan believed that he was the only man able to save the North from destruction. He imposed military rule, arranged an armistice and asked the Russian ambassador to help mediate a settlement.[14]

The End of the War

Tsar Alexander II of Russia had become increasingly concerned at the progress of the war. He had fought the British and French in the Crimea just seven years earlier and had conflicting interests with Britain in the Balkans, Persia and Afghanistan. He favored the North, as he saw the United States as a useful ally and a counter-balance against British global power.

The friendship was mutual. Lincoln's Secretary of State, William H. Seward, asserted in 1862:

> "She [Russia] has our friendship, in every case, in preference to any other
> European power, simply because she always wishes us well, and leaves
> us to conduct our affairs as we think best."[15]

Union ships found a warm welcome in Russian ports as they sailed the world raiding allied commerce. The tsar even sent Russian volunteers to fight unofficially for the North under the leadership of Brigadier General John B. Turchin, who had served on the tsar's staff before the war as Ivan Vasilovitch Turchinoff. As part of the Army of the Cumberland, Turchin fought in Kentucky and the northern districts of Tennessee. His Russian wife, Nadia, insisted on following him on campaign and even commanded his brigade in the Battle of Oak Grove when he fell ill. Turchin was so effective that he was called "The Russian Thunderbolt," although he had a bad reputation for looting.

The tsar, alarmed at the North's imminent defeat, wanted to end the war as quickly and favorably as possible. Direct intervention was out of the question, for Russia's deficiencies had been only too evident in the Crimea and the emancipation of the serfs in 1861 had caused additional problems. The Russian Navy was too weak and outdated to win a major fleet action, but its warships, operating independently, would make effective commerce raiders. The tsar therefore sent two fleets to the Pacific and Indian Oceans where they could pose a potential threat to British trade while he exerted diplomatic pressure on Britain to accept international mediation. He was supported by the Prussian king and peace was signed in August 1863 in the Swiss city of Geneva.

The Confederacy won its independence and massive reparations. It also secured a five-year occupation of a buffer zone north of the border, including Delaware and the southern half of Pennsylvania. The former Union slave states of Kentucky and Missouri followed Maryland's lead in seceding to the victorious Confederacy. On the other hand, Britain returned California, Oregon and Washington Territory to the North, being keen to withdraw from colonial commitments rather than add to them. She also wanted to balance the North and South so that neither could dominate the New World and realized that by returning the Pacific Seaboard she might divert the North's expansionist energies away from British North America. Critics, including Robert Cecil, the future Lord Salisbury and the rising star of the Conservative Party, argued forcefully that the aggressive and militaristic North would inevitably turn against British North America in its desire for revenge and that the return of the Pacific Seaboard would simply encourage hopes of further territorial compensation. Cecil was particularly alarmed at the potential for a future global war against both Russia and the North, with Britain being forced to defend her far-flung Empire against simultaneous attacks as far away as British North America and the North-West Frontier of India.[16] Such fears were aggravated by the shooting of Prime Minister William Gladstone in 1869 by a disgruntled Union activist. The assassin was sentenced to death, but had his sentence commuted on Queen Victoria's personal intervention.

McClellan's coup deeply divided Northern society, entailing as it did the abandonment of the Union and the collapse of the democratic experiment. Many veterans, aggrieved at their wasted sacrifices and the pointless deaths of so many comrades, bitterly accused McClellan of treason. His nickname, "the little Napoleon," had originally referred to his promise as a military commander, but now became a political jibe. Such internal pressures contributed to the political instability and extremism of the North and the volatility of its foreign policy in the decades immediately after the war.

Lincoln was put on trial for misuse of the Presidential powers, particularly in his suppression of more than 300 Northern newspapers and the internment of 14,000 opponents without trial. He was sentenced to 10 years' imprisonment, but was released after 14 months and returned to his former profession as a lawyer. He would die in 1887, mourned by thousands of African-Americans and die-hard veterans who saw in him the embodiment of the Great Cause of American freedom and democracy.

Presidents McClellan and Jefferson Davis were left to contemplate a future complicated by the needs of reconstruction and realignment, but also bright with the great opportunities now opening before their two nations.

The Reality

The *Trent* crisis did happen, but did not involve bloodshed and was defused in part by Prince Albert, who skilfully moderated the language of Lord Russell's message to make it read less like an ultimatum and more as a starting point for negotiation. Albert died from typhoid just a fortnight later. He had nearly been killed in his runaway carriage while visiting Coburg in 1860, but had managed to jump clear in time and had escaped with cuts and bruises.

Britain and the North neither wanted, nor were they prepared for, a war in 1861. A full-scale conflict was less likely than is often thought and would probably have required a series of additional provocations following the *Trent* incident. In reality, the Confederates idiotically failed to try and precipitate British intervention through cross-border raids until late in the war. They concentrated instead on diplomatic methods in a vain attempt to secure recognition of the Confederacy as an independent nation.

The incendiary attack on New York City was in fact carried out by Confederate agents on November 25, 1864, but caused more alarm than damage. The plot might have worked if the agents had known how to mix Greek Fire properly.

The confrontation over the runaway pig on San Juan Island occurred as described in 1859. The Royal Marines remained peacefully on the island until it was awarded to the United States in 1872 through the mediation of Kaiser Wilhelm I of Germany.

San Francisco twice came under the threat of Confederate attack. At the end of 1861, Brigadier General Henry H. Sibley led an overland expedition against the city from Texas, but had to retreat in April 1862 after losing his supply train in a clash in New Mexico. Sibley himself was in agony from a kidney affliction and commanded for much of the expedition from a hospital wagon, in various degrees of inebriation. The second threat to San Francisco came towards the end of the war when it was feared that the Confederate raider *Shenandoah* might attack from the sea.

The French did intervene in Mexico, but never managed to subdue the country and evacuated it soon after the end of the (American) Civil War. Their troops did not join the Confederacy in the field, but Frenchmen were present in the armies of both sides, as either observers or fighting soldiers, including Camille-Armand-Jules-Marie, Prince de Polignac, who served as a Confederate major general.

Tsar Alexander II of Russia sent two fleets to New York and San Francisco in the fall of 1863. Their arrival was widely seen in the North as a gesture of solidarity and Rear-Admiral Popov's sailors won the lasting affection of the people of San Francisco by helping to put out a fire in the city. But the main reason why the tsar sent his fleets was to prevent them from being immobilized in the Baltic ice during the winter in case war broke out with Britain and France as a result of his suppression of the Polish Rebellion.

Brigadier General John B. Turchin was a real person, as was his remarkable wife Nadia, and he died in a lunatic asylum in 1901. Similarly, the Emperor Norton I of the United States actually existed, although he was probably saner than is often thought.

McClellan stood against Lincoln in the November 1864 Presidential election, but was soundly beaten, partly because of the upswing in the North's military fortunes.

Relations between Britain and the United States remained tense for years after the end of the Civil War. The American threat to British North America was a serious concern and led to the creation of the Dominion of Canada in 1867, the country's first step towards becoming an independent nation.

Bibliography

Adams, Ephraim, *Great Britain and the American Civil War* (Longmans, London, 1925), 2 vols.

Allen, H.C., *Great Britain and the United States: A History of Anglo–American Relations (1783–1952)* (Odhams Press, London, 1954).

Anon., *Forts Versus Ships: Also Defence of the Canadian Lakes and its Influence on the General Defence of Canada* (J. Ridgway, London, 1862).

Bailey, Thomas A., *America Faces Russia: Russian–American Relations from Early Times to our Day* (Cornell University Press, New York, 1950).

Batt, Elisabeth, *Monck: Governor-General 1861–1868* (McClelland & Stewart, Toronto, 1876).

Baxter, James P., *The Introduction of the Ironclad Warship* (Harvard University Press, Cambridge, Mass., 1933).

Bernard, Mountague, *A Historical Account of the Neutrality of Great Britain during the American Civil War* (Longmans, London, 1870).

Bourne, Kenneth, *Britain and the Balance of Power in North America 1815–1908* (Longmans, London, 1967).

Cameron, Edward, *Memoirs of Ralph Vansittart, a Member of the Parliament of Canada, 1861–1867* (Musson Book Co, Toronto, nd).

Case, Lynn M., and Spencer, Warren F., *The United States and France: Civil War Diplomacy* (University of Pennsylvania, Philadelphia, 1970).

Church, William, *The Life of John Ericsson* (Sampson Low, London, 1890).

Courtemanche, Regis A., *No Need of Glory: The British Navy in American Waters 1860–1864* (Naval Institute Press, Annapolis, 1977).

Crook, D.P., *The North, the South, and the Powers 1861–1865* (Wiley, London, 1974).

Dugan, James, *The Great Iron Ship* (Hamish Hamilton, London, 1953).

Gough, Barry, *The Royal Navy and the Northwest Coast of North America 1810–1914: A Study of British Maritime Ascendancy* (University of British Columbia Press, Vancouver, 1971).

Hamilton, C., *Anglo-French Naval Rivalry 1840–1870* (Clarendon Press, Oxford, 1993).

Headley, John, *Confederate Operations in Canada and New York* (Neale Publishing Co, New York, 1906).

Josephy, Alvin M., Jr., *The Civil War in the American West* (A.A. Knopf, New York, 1992).

Kerr, D.G.G., and Gibson, J.A., *Sir Edmund Head: A Scholarly Governor* (University of Toronto Press, London, 1954).

Luvaas, Jay, *The Military Legacy of the Civil War: The European Dimension* (University of Chicago Press, Chicago, 1959).

Mahin, Dean, *One War at a Time: The International Dimensions of the American Civil War* (Brasseys, Washington DC, 1999).

Marquis, Greg, *In Armageddon's Shadow: The Civil War and Canada's Maritime Provinces* (McGill–Queen's University Press, London, 1998).

Morton, Desmond, *A Military History of Canada* (McClelland & Stewart, Toronto, 1999).

Murat, Ines, *Napoleon and the American Dream* (Louisiana State University Press, London, 1981).

Roberts, Andrew, *Salisbury: Victorian Titan* (Weidenfeld & Nicolson, London, 1999).

Russell, W.H., *My Diary North and South* (Harper & Bros., New York, 1863).

Shaw-Kennedy, James, "Scheme for the Defence of Canada Written in February, 1862," in *Notes on the Battle of Waterloo* (J. Murray, London, 1865).

Simmons, J., *Defence of Canada Considered as an Imperial Question with Reference to a War with America* (Longman, Green, Longman, Roberts & Green, London, 1865).

Stacey, C.P., *Canada and the British Army 1846–1871: A Study in the Practice of Responsible Government* (Longmans, London, 1936).

Stacey, C.P., *The Military Problems of Canada: A Survey of Defence Policies and Strategic Considerations Past and Present* (Ryerson Press, Toronto, 1940).

Stanley, George, *Canada's Soldiers: The Military History of an Unmilitary People* (Macmillan & Co of Canada, Toronto, 1960).

Trollope, Anthony, *North America* (Chapman & Hall, 1862).

Wilson, H., *Ironclads in Action: A Sketch of Naval Warfare from 1855 to 1895* (Sampson Low, 1897).

Wincks, Robin W., *Canada and the United States: The Civil War Years* (John Hopkins Press, Baltimore, 1960).

Notes

1. Adams, *Great Britain and the American Civil War*, vol. 1, p. 218.
2. Russell, *My Diary North and South*, vol. 2, pp. 421–2.
3. Napoleon Bonaparte had been exiled to St Helena after his defeat at Waterloo. The British also used the island to hold Boer prisoners during the South African War (1899–1902).
*4. Theodore Roosevelt, *Custer: A Career in Infamy* (Hunting Press, New York, 1901).
5. Trollope, *North America*, vol.1, p. 446. (This quotation has been edited slightly.)
6. Cameron, *Memoirs of Ralph Vansittart*, pp. 53–4.
7. Courtemanche, *No Need of Glory*, p. 59.
8. Courtemanche, *op. cit.*, p. 47.
9. Wilson, *Ironclads in Action*, vol. 1, pp. 20–1. (This quotation has been edited slightly.)
10. Courtemanche, *op. cit.,* p. 58.
11. Baxter, *The Introduction of the Ironclad Warship*, p. 317.
12. Church, *The Life of John Ericsson*, vol. 1, pp. 274–5.
*13. Winston S. Churchill, *Quebec: The Immortal Battlefield* (Blenheim Books, London, 1949).

*14. George B. McClellan, *Four Days in March: How I Saved the North in the Late Crisis* (Patriot Publishing, Boston, 1868)

15. Bailey, *America Faces Russia*, p. 70.

16. Roberts, *Salisbury: Victorian Titan*.

2
SHIPS OF IRON
AND WILLS OF STEEL
The Confederate Navy Triumphant

Wade G. Dudley

Yorktown, Virginia

At Yorktown, on the James Peninsula jutting between the York and James Rivers in the sovereign state of Virginia, the thick fog had lifted by mid-morning to reveal a line of trenches separating two armies. Guns silent, regiments of both sides stood at parade rest. Promptly at 10.00 a.m., the easternmost army began to stack its weapons, then to march in what seemed unending lines through the ranks of its captors. A military band set the tone for the event, playing an old tune (one learned by the bandmaster from his grandfather, whose father had heard the same song played here years before): *The World Turned Upside Down*.

Later that day, as two generals met at Yorktown (the one to surrender his sword, the other to commiserate with his vanquished former brother-in-arms), another ceremony took place at a fortress on the tip of the Peninsula. Here, the commandant surrendered his sword and his command to a battered naval captain (left arm in a sling and right eye bandaged) accompanied by a rather roly-poly civilian. When the exuberant politician and his entourage posed for pictures alongside the shamed enemy officer, the naval captain slipped away to the parapet. There he gazed into the harbor at his similarly battered vessel. As the gusting wind streamed its tattered red, white, and blue banner from the ship's oft-fished flagstaff, he tried to recall what it was that the newspapers had quoted the President as saying a few weeks ago. "In the end, it will not be the ships of iron but rather the steel wills of our loyal sons that decide the outcome of this struggle."[1]

"Perhaps Davis is right," thought Catesby ap R. Jones (captain of the C.S.S. *Virginia* by the grace of God and the commission of the Confederate Congress), "but I rather think that we were just damn lucky, and I will take all the iron ships that I can get."

Prelude

The election of Abraham Lincoln as the sixteenth president of the United States in November 1860 launched his nation into a bloody civil war. South Carolinians had sworn that victory for the Black Republican would be followed by the secession of slave-holding states from the Union. They, and like-minded cohorts in the remaining six states of the Deep South, made good on their promise as the lame-duck President Buchanan did little (and the president-to-be even less) to prevent this fracture of a nation.

Secession tested loyalties. Military and naval officers as well as private citizens had to choose between regional affiliation and duty (often sworn duty) to the concept of an indivisible national entity. Even without consideration of duty, the choice was not always easy since ties of clan, friendship, and economics frequently crossed the Mason-Dixon Line. Here and there, voices of sanity competed with hawkish cries and strident martial airs, their pleas for logic and reason unheeded. They, too, eventually succumbed to the madness of fratricide.

One such voice belonged to William Tecumseh Sherman, President of Louisiana Seminary of Learning and Military Academy. A Northerner by birth and a graduate of West Point, Sherman had come to appreciate the cultured pace of life in the South. Despairing at the news of South Carolina's break from the Union, he wrote a stirring and prophetic letter to his friend, Professor David F. Boyd:

> "You, you the people of the South, believe there can be such a thing as peaceable secession. You don't know what you are doing. I know there can be no such thing... You people speak so lightly of war. You don't know what you are talking about. War is a terrible thing... The Northern people not only greatly outnumber the whites at [sic] the South, but they are a mechanical people with manufactures of every kind, while you are only agriculturalists... You are rushing into war with one of the most powerful, ingeniously mechanical and determined people on earth—right at your doors. You are bound to fail... At first you will make headway, but as your limited resources begin to fail, and shut out from the markets of Europe by blockade, as you will be, your cause will begin to wane... "[2]

They did not listen; the general Southern populace was firmly ensnared in the *rage militaire*. As the break-away states began to seize arsenals and properties of the United States, some cooler heads closely considered the exact arguments that Sherman had addressed to his friend. A number of those calculating thinkers joined the secessionist congress, meeting in Montgomery, Alabama, in early February 1862. Though a constitution would not be adopted until the eleventh of the following month, the Provisional Congress of the new Confederate States of America elected Jefferson Davis as its first president, with Alexander Stephens as his vice-president. Davis immediately sought to make sense of the madness by seeking qualified men to assume the key cabinet positions in his government. When, on February 21, Congress created a Department of the Navy, Davis immediately called upon his old friend Stephen R. Mallory of Florida to become the Secretary of the Navy.

Planning the Impossible

As a former United States Senator, one of Mallory's many appointments had been to the Senate Naval Affairs Committee, a position that he had held for a decade. There he had championed a stronger U.S. Navy, pushing programs ranging from shipbuilding to mandatory performance reviews for officers. The irony of the situation, as he assumed the title of Secretary of the Navy, was not lost on Mallory: without his efforts the mariners of his former country would have been far less able to prosecute war upon his new homeland—a homeland miserably prepared for a war at sea.

Sherman had been correct—agriculture was the South's economy. There were few seagoing vessels based in the states of the Deep South, and it possessed no ships of war. Aside from scattered fishermen, the South produced few mariners, and those of Southern extraction had been on New England vessels for so long that even fewer would return home. New Orleans had a relatively large shipyard and Pensacola a smaller one while a number of civilian contractors existed in scattered ports, but the new nation lacked ordnance and powder factories, ironworks, machine shops, canvas lofts, and ropewalks. Sadly, the transport infrastructure in the Confederacy was almost as weak as its shipbuilding facilities. Rather than extensive railroads and macadamized roads, Mallory's new country had long depended on its numerous inland waterways and a well developed coastal trade for its transport needs. The Secretary more than suspected that the Union Navy would soon seek to disrupt such watery highways.

Nor did it take a genius to realize the manner in which the U.S. Navy would prosecute its war against a South so absolutely dependent upon trade with Europe. With only 42 active vessels (and many of those scattered on distant stations around the globe), the Union's Secretary of the Navy, Gideon Welles, would put a token blockading force off each Southern port while aggressively converting to warships anything that would float and building vessels as rapidly as possible. As excess forces came available, they would be used to capture island bases to support the blockade, or simply to capture Southern ports. Meanwhile, rapidly converted gunboats would support a Union thrust down the Mississippi River, effectively isolating the Trans-Mississippi command from the remainder of the Confederacy.

As Mallory began to organize his department he carefully considered, then prioritized, the needs of his nation based upon the obvious enemy plans. First, the defense of the Mississippi River and the nation's ports clamored for attention. Second, a means to defeat any Union blockade must be found.

Third, the vulnerability of the commerce of the North, spread widely across the Seven Seas, must be exploited. And, an unlikely fourth, if possible the war must be taken to the coasts and port cities of the United States. To accomplish any of these goals, Mallory had to build a navy from scratch. At the same time, he found himself forced to wage political war against a president whose knowledge of naval matters could be "captured in a thimble, still leaving room for a lady's thumb" and against a congress divided by the very states' rights that had created it.[3]

Mallory's initial defensive plan stressed strong land fortifications at harbor mouths and along the Mississippi River and its key tributaries. At each port, and along the Mississippi, gunboat squadrons would be needed to support the fortifications and to assist defending Confederate field armies. At the same time, transports would be in desperate demand to supplement the underdeveloped rail system of the South. By early March 1861, the Confederate Navy consisted of only ten vessels, ranging from the antiquated sidewheeler *Fulton* (U.S.S. *Fulton* until taken while in ordinary at Pensacola) to revenue cutters and slavers seized by the provisional government. Altogether, they mounted only 15 guns. Incorporation of state navies would eventually add fewer than two dozen small warships to these forces, all as miserably armed as the original ten vessels. This fell far short of the hundred or more strongly armed ships needed for defensive purposes alone.

To add to the woes of the secretary, heavy artillery and munitions were in short supply. To equip new fortifications adequately meant denying strong firepower to converted warships. The South also lacked foundries and machine shops; in fact, it did not possess any of the facilities to build the steam power plants needed in modern warships, and could provide fittings such as shafts and screw propellers only with great difficulty. Of course, neither engines nor screws would be in great demand until adequate shipyards could be erected. When, on March 15, Congress approved the construction or purchase of ten additional vessels for port defense, Mallory remained uncertain as to whether engines and armament could be obtained for them.

A Turning Point

It must have galled Mallory to realize that each day over a dozen modern commercial steamships entered and exited the ports of his nation and that the seizure of even a few of them would have provided the nucleus of a blue-water navy for the Confederacy. However, they flew the flags of European nations, and Mallory knew that recognition by and support from those very nations provided the only hope for final independence of the Confederacy. It was his concern with the perception of his homeland by these foreign countries that led to heated words between President Davis and his Secretary of the Navy at a Cabinet meeting on the afternoon of March 18.

It was after the discussion of old Sam Houston's refusal to swear an oath to the new Confederate government of Texas and the steps to be taken to force the surrender, preferably without bloodshed, of Fort Pickens in Pensacola and Fort Sumter in Charleston that Jefferson Davis announced his intention to issue Letters of Marque and Reprisal to Southern ship owners.[4] Mallory reminded the president that privateering had been labeled illegal by the Declaration of Paris of 1856. Davis responded that neither the United States nor the Confederate States had signed that agreement, and thus he was not bound to follow it. Furthermore, South Carolina's congressmen thought privateering a fine idea—in fact had suggested it to him because privateering had been profitable for Charleston in the past. Then the tone of the meeting intensified.

Mr. M. {Secretary Mallory} questions: "These are naval men?"

President {Davis}: "Well, no, at least I don't think so."

Mr. M.: "Do they have extensive connections with European governments, then?"

President: "No, but they... "

Mr. M. (growing red in the face, interrupting): "Then I must say that this is idiocy! We have no ships! We have no engines! We have no cannons! And we cannot anger the very people that we hope to sustain us in our hour of need! Such action would be as asinine as this proposal for a cotton embargo of European markets that is spreading through the newspapers!"

President (agitated): "I will not have... "

[At this point, the handwriting of the note taker becomes illegible as if scribbled hurriedly, though "Damn you!" appears at least once.]

Mr. M. leaves the room after threatening to tender his resignation.

President: "My apologies gentlemen, but better ended now than later. Let us move on to the discussion of the cotton embargo proposed by the representatives from Texas... "[5]

The next afternoon, Secretary Mallory approached the president in private (resignation in hand, it should be added). Though their meeting is not recorded, President Davis's appointment book for that day notes that all meetings after Mallory's appearance were canceled. It can be assumed that both men realized that the pressure of forming a new nation had led to the harsh words of the preceding day. Apparently, Mallory managed to sway the often unswerving Davis to his point of view, as two days later (and with the support of Davis), he addressed Congress on naval matters. If a nexus can be identified wherein the course of the Confederacy turned sharply from potential disaster to possible success then this speech marks that juncture of time and action:

"Honored representatives of this Confederacy, I thank you for the time to discuss the needs of our naval establishment and the situation in which the coming conflict—and have no doubt that it will come—finds us. We are a newly birthed nation whose life blood is commerce. We lack the self-sufficiency of a long established country, and we require access to Europe. Our cotton must reach the markets of the old countries, and we must have European goods unloading in a constant stream at our wharves if we hope to see this great endeavor succeed.

Sadly, our seaports and rivers are vulnerable to any aggressor. The loss of even one major port, once overrun by an enemy army supplied from the sea, will be a dagger aimed at our heartland. Already, the United States refuses to surrender the forts at Charleston and Pensacola—bastions that by right belong to our nation. Two of our great ports are thus already plugged, and near a hundred ships under the Stars and Stripes ready to blockade the rest.

Yet we do not have a single ship capable of challenging potential blockaders. Our handful of gunboats mount fewer guns than one first-rate screw frigate. Yes, we have gunboats building, but there is no guarantee that we can find the engines to power them or the cannons to give them teeth. We have neither foundries nor machine shops, though they do exist—in Europe.

Now two bills, the one for the establishment of privateers and the other for an embargo, and both quite damaging to our maritime position, may well appear before you. They must not be passed. International law, as observed by the great nations of Europe, prohibits private vessels of war. For us to flaunt that law would be viewed as the naive arrogance of mere children and would not create the friends that we so dearly need. If any man would serve this nation rather than seek to line his own pockets, then let him enlist himself and his ship in this glorious cause! There will still be prizes, but let us not anger our friends across the Atlantic with the legitimacy of their taking.

As for this cotton embargo, do not allow it! When has an embargo succeeded? Did those of the founding fathers prevent their bloody struggle against tyranny? Did Jefferson's embargo (and the hardship that it caused, you learned at your father's knee!) stop a war? Did Madison's embargo during that same war do ought but make the common people hate him? Now is the time that we must establish our credit abroad! We must show the nations of Europe that we value our economic ties! We must let them know that the mills of Lancashire and the looms of France will not wait on us! And if the bales stop flowing and their mill workers cry of hunger and need, it will not be on this Confederacy that those powerful Admiralties turn their ire. Oh no, gentlemen, to us they will extend their hands to reach the one that we have already given them.

The issues in this naval bill now before you are self-evident. But I would like to summarize the key items. The bill proposes the immediate establishment of a National Naval Arsenal at New Orleans, to include a powder mill, a naval cannon foundry, a general purpose foundry, four new slips for large vessels, a drydock, and boiler and engine manufactures. As the manufactures will not be ready for at least a year, agents will be authorized to purchase engines and miscellaneous accoutrements abroad for the building of four warships at New Orleans capable of challenging and defeating any blockading force on our coasts. Nor will we neglect our Atlantic coast while this force is building; large gunboats will be bid to private contractors in the ports designated by this bill. Again, agents dispatched to Europe will endeavor to purchase engines for these vessels. Artillery and munitions for coastal fortresses must be ordered as well. Sundry other items also appear in the bill.

Honored representatives, this will not come cheaply. No navy ever has. We may well mortgage our future for a generation—but, I promise you, there will be a future to mortgage. Without this effort, without this great outlay of wealth, that future may not arrive at all. Let us not quibble over dollars. They are small things when stacked beside our freedom. Had the Athenians quibbled when Themistocles asked that their silver be turned into warships, then the iron heel of a Persian tyrant would have trampled that glorious democracy. Had the Roman senate held close the coins needed to build a navy (and to build another when storms destroyed the first!), that fair Republic would have fallen to the mercantile tyranny of Carthage. I do not know exactly what lies before us, but I do know this: To surrender the sea is to surrender *our* democracy and *our* republic. *And we must not let that happen.*"[6]

Within days, newspapers began hailing Mallory as the "Southern Themistocles."[7] The passage of the new naval appropriations was never in doubt, and though the price of "Mallory's Navy" would create a national debt that would not be repaid during his lifetime, at least there would be a nation to repay it. Within a week of the speech, the first naval purchasing agents sailed for Europe, but by then the Confederacy's prominent Secretary of the Navy had turned his attention to other opportunities.

Yards for the Confederate Navy

By the end of March, even faint hopes of reconciliation between the Confederacy and the United States had evaporated. Lincoln decided, in the waning days of that month, to hold Fort Sumter and Fort Pickens. The border states, especially North Carolina and Virginia, had already rejected secession once—now their loyal and disloyal citizens alike waited nervously for the first fratricidal shells to fall. Of course, some citizens alleviated their nervousness with action, especially in the organizing of militia and "volunteer" units. In wavering Virginia on the third day of April, one such unit, the Washington Rifles, elected a 37-year-old graduate of West Point as its captain. William Edmundson Jones, better known as "Grumble" to those around him, was an experienced soldier and local politician.[8] Little could he have imagined on that day that his loyalty to Southern ideals would place him first on the field of battle for his state.

In Montgomery, Mallory still wrestled with creating a navy. Delegating minor tasks such as the creation of uniforms, flags, and forms to his growing staff, he focused on placing ships and men on the water. To lure those who would have become privateers, Mallory offered generous bounties for prizes taken by the Confederate Navy—75 percent of auction value, as well as gun money and head money for enemy warships, to be divided among crew and officers. To encourage ship owners to risk their vessels in national service, Mallory promised 20 percent of the auction value of each prize for division among the owners of vessels loaned to the national government for conversion to warships. By the end of the first week of April, a dozen large steamers and three times as many smaller vessels had been deeded to the government. Hundreds of men—including far too many whose only experience of salt water had been that prescribed by a physician for sore feet—had flocked to recruiters in ports throughout the Confederacy, ready for their share of the prize money.

Over the following months, the Confederate naval apparatus would take shape, but in those first weeks Mallory and his subordinates faced overwhelming logistical restraints: no uniforms, few barracks or tents, little preserved food and naval stores, a severe shortage of artillery and munitions, a lack of drydocks and experienced artificers to convert their new found wealth of vessels to something resembling a navy, and a shortage of experienced naval officers to bring order to the chaos in every Southern port.[9]

When, on April 7, Davis notified his secretary of the navy that the governor of South Carolina had ordered communications between Fort Sumter and Charleston cut in preparation for forcing the issue of ownership of the bastion, Mallory requested permission to initiate what in modern parlance would be called a "black op." With the president's approval, Mallory dispatched a trusted lieutenant to Virginia with a written plea to an old acquaintance, the governor of that wavering state. Though the actual missive was destroyed by the governor, its contents remain well known: if Virginia should join the Confederacy, then every effort must be made to secure the Gosport Naval Yard near Norfolk.[10] If the yard could be taken quickly, the Confederacy would gain a well-stocked, first-class naval facility. And Mallory did not trust the United States simply to turn it over to its rebellious sons. The governor shared Mallory's concern, and quietly called upon an old and trusted friend, Grumble Jones (breveted to major), to begin shifting his company to Norfolk. There Jones would take command of local militia. Working with Southern sympathizers stationed at the yard, Jones was ordered to seize the facility if Virginia prepared to leave the Union.

At 04.30 a.m. on April 12, the first shots struck Fort Sumter. The following day, Major Robert Anderson surrendered his battered command. Two days later, Lincoln called for 75,000 volunteers as a force to march south and end the rebellion. Missouri and Kentucky refused to send soldiers against their sister states, while Virginia, North Carolina, Tennessee, and Arkansas took the first steps to leave the Union and join the Confederacy. On April 17, Virginia's legislature officially voted in favor of secession, and its governor telegraphed Grumble Jones to act immediately. By 11.00 p.m. Jones had led his forces through the main gate at Gosport, skirmishing as they went with a small guard of Marines and sailors. As Jones wrote:

> "Forming the Rifles into a volley line in the field across from the gate, I called upon the officer of the guard to surrender his small force in the name of the Sovereign State of Virginia and the Confederate States of America or I would order my men to fire. Before he could reply, the boys being a mite high strung had heard the word fire, released a shamefully ragged volley, and headed for the gate in what they thought was a charge. The Union boys took off, and a race commenced that did not end until my boys had followed some of them onto a big ship docked in the harbor. Following at a more sedate pace, I took the color guard to the quarters of Commodore [Charles S.] McCauley and allowed him to change from his nightshirt to a uniform before accepting his sword. The next morning we locked up 107 prisoners, all those who refused to swear allegiance to Virginia or the Confederacy, and began to organize batteries to receive the expected Yankee visitors. Losses all around were about 23 wounded or injured—mostly from fist fights and stumbling around boats."[11]

It was well that Jones organized his defenses so quickly, as Union Secretary of the Navy Gideon Welles had already dispatched Captain Hiram Pauldry's *Pawnee* with a force of Marines from Washington to burn the yard. Pauldry's arrival at Norfolk was met with enthusiastic though inaccurate fire from shore batteries. Unwilling to risk his ship and Marines against an obviously prepared defense, Pauldry returned to Washington.

According to his clerks, Mallory danced in delight when he first heard the news of the capture of the yard, complete with its large drydock, ropewalks, foundry, machine shop, boiler shop, covered ways, and overflowing store houses. Some 1,200 cannon, including over 50 of the new Dahlgren guns, and tons of munitions were among the booty. Best of all, along with several old sailing ships stored in ordinary and the yard's steam tugs, Jones had captured the seven-year old screw frigate *Merrimack*. Docked for repair of its ailing steam engine, the ship had been rigged for scuttling, but the headlong charge of the Washington Rifles had captured the vessel before its captain could react.[12] Mallory wasted little time in shifting war materials from the naval yard to his scattered squadrons forming at Southern ports.

Though Mallory could immediately use the materials captured at Gosport, the use of the vessels captured there was a tad more perplexing. Those ships ranged from the antique frigate *United States* (of War of 1812 fame) to the old 74-gun ship of the line *Pennsylvania* and, of course, the modern *Merrimack*. The non-steam warships were so vulnerable as to be useless, except as floating batteries. Even the *Merrimack*, despite being a first-rate steam frigate, did not stand a chance against an entire fleet and could only be used as a raider if it could escape the Union vessels soon to invest Hampton Roads. Similarly, the yard itself remained relatively useless unless the blockaders could be defeated. Mallory foresaw only one answer to this dilemma, proposing on April 26:

> "... to adopt a class of vessels hitherto unknown to naval service. The perfection of a warship would doubtless be a combination of the greatest known ocean speed with the greatest known floating battery and power of resistance... "[13]

That answer was to build, to convert, or to acquire seagoing ironclad vessels.

Ironclads and Gunboats

Mallory's role took on increased urgency when Davis approved a bill on May 3 that proclaimed a formal state of war existing between the Confederacy and the United States. Forced to act by this declaration, European nations officially recognized the Confederacy as a belligerent, though not as a nation in its own right. Britain's Queen Victoria declared her nation a neutral in the conflict, though the world knew that the day's greatest maritime and industrial state's definition of "neutrality" could be somewhat flexible.

Mallory's decisive actions in the first weeks of his tenure began to bear fruit during May. At Gretna, Louisiana, the first naval cannon was cast on May 4, while 2-inch wrought iron plates followed by the end of the month from a new mill in Tuscaloosa, Alabama.[14] These fruits of hard Southern labor wended their way to New Orleans and the rapidly expanding naval yard in that city.[15] There, two private shipbuilding firms would be authorized to build the first ironclads in the western Confederacy, the *Louisiana* and the *Mississippi*.

Slowly, but steadily, naval squadrons began to emerge from the initial chaos in Southern ports. By the end of May, some 20 gunboats, equipped with one or two guns each, patrolled the Mississippi, supported by a transport squadron of six fast steamers. Squadrons of six to ten steam vessels of varying sizes, configurations, and capabilities trained at each of the major Southern ports. Additionally, state navies such as the "Mosquito Fleet" of North Carolina patrolled coastal estuaries and sounds.[16] The command situation improved dramatically with the secession of Virginia when over 100 officers and nearly as many enlisted ranks decided to "go South." Several former Union officers would quickly prove worthy of the task at hand.

On June 9, lookouts aboard the U.S.S. *Massachusetts*, part of the small squadron supporting Fort Pickens and the blockade of Pensacola, spotted a plume of smoke on the horizon. Investigation revealed it to be the British registered steamship *Perthshire*, its holds laden with cotton. After seizing the neutral ship (the first such seizure of the war) for carriage of contraband, an examination of its log and manifests shocked the American captain. The ship had unloaded six steam engines, six screws and shafts, and sundry machine parts at New Orleans a week earlier. Worse, a copy of the New Orleans *Picayune* dated June 6 revealed that a Confederate squadron of three steamers under the command of Commodore Franklin Buchanan had sunk or captured the two small Union warships blockading the mouth of the Mississippi.[17]

Unfortunately for the Confederacy, the Union Navy was growing by leaps and bounds. Welles purchased or purloined anything that floated, from trans-Atlantic steamers to ferryboats to private yachts, and the yards of the North quickly converted them to warships with the addition of weapons and naval officers. Within weeks, New Orleans was again blockaded, and the interdiction of the Southern coast as a whole stiffened day by day as the war progressed. Twice, once at Charleston and once at Mobile, small Confederate squadrons challenged the blockaders. In both cases, lives were lost and ships damaged, but the blockade remained. Until ironclads could be completed, the blockade would only strengthen.

On July 11, plans and money for conversion to ironclads of the captured *Merrimack* as well as the *United States* and the *Pennsylvania* were approved by the Confederate Congress, though modifications to the *Merrimack* had been underway since June 10, the day that it was renamed C.S.S. *Virginia*. The two larger ships would have the upper decks cut away and replaced by iron casemates amidships. Angled so as to deflect enemy shells and meant to extend below the waterline to protect vital machinery, the casemates featured two layers of 2-inch wrought iron plate backed by over a foot of oaken timbers. The hulls, armored by a layer of 2-inch plate extending six feet below the waterline, showed only a foot of freeboard. The *Virginia* would mount six 9-inch Dahlgren smoothbores, three to each broadside, and four heavy rifled guns as bow and stern chasers. *Pennsylvania*, now known as *Alabama*, would carry two fewer broadside guns. Both vessels would be fitted with heavy iron rams.[18]

Knowing that the casemate-ironclads would be slow and ponderous, Mallory selected a different design for the conversion of the old *United States*. Renamed *Hart of the Confederacy*, the vessel would be built for speed.[19] With masts and upper works cut away, the hull would be plated with 2-inch wrought iron over its old (but relatively sound) oaken timbers. Its new freeboard of eight feet demanded additional armor amidships where its vulnerable boiler and engine would rest. Thus, the designer added an additional belt of 2-inch plate extending five feet below the waterline. Six

9-inch Dahlgrens fired to each broadside, but their gunports were only two feet above the water in order to lower the vessel's center of gravity. This limited the usefulness of the cannons in any but the calmest seas. The true killer for the *Hart* would be the spar torpedo—a 20-foot pole, dropped at the last minute before contact to project from the bow, with a keg of gunpowder triggered by a percussion cap at its end—and its ram-tipped, heavily reinforced prow.[20]

From its date of approval, numerous problems confronted the conversion efforts. A shortage of artificers and shipwrights meant that work on the vessels had to proceed sequentially. Tredegar Ironworks in Richmond, slated to produce the 2-inch wrought iron plate for the ironclads, had to convert its facilities from 1-inch plate production before it could begin to roll the required size plates. Then, as plates began to accumulate, Mallory had to squabble with the army, engaged in its own buildup of supplies and men, for train engines and cars to move them to Gosport. Most seriously, capture of the *Perthshire* by the U.S.S. *Massachusetts* had led to a diplomatic protest by the United States to Great Britain, forcing the British government to stop the shipment of twelve additional steam engines and other materials to the Confederacy. Fortunately for Mallory, Britain, in immediate response to the *Trent* Affair of November 1861, released six of the engines for immediate delivery to the Confederacy.[21] Escorted by H.M.S. *Warrior*, the shipment arrived in Wilmington, North Carolina, on November 24. By Christmas, two of those engines had arrived at Gosport for installation in *Alabama* and *Hart*—a most acceptable present for Secretary Mallory.

As Mallory wrestled with building a navy to challenge the blockade, his nation's fortunes on land and at sea twisted and turned. In the east, Confederate forces had stopped a premature advance from Fortress Monroe through the James Peninsula to Richmond at the Battle of Big Bethel on June 10. At Manassas, Virginia, green Confederate troops had outlasted green Union soldiers on July 21. The routed Yankees fled to the defenses of Washington without pursuit by the disorganized Southern army. Success in eastern Virginia offset losses in the western portion of the state, which eventually allowed the admittance of West Virginia to the Union.[22]

In August, a U.S. fleet commanded by Flag Officer S.H. Stringham supported the troops of General Ben Butler in capturing Forts Hatteras and Clark on North Carolina's Outer Banks. Unable to face an overwhelming force on the open sea, Rebel naval forces under Flag Officer W.F. Lynch continued to challenge Union control of the (now closed) Pamlico Sound. On October 1, C.S.S. *Curlew*, *Raleigh*, and *Junaluska* captured the Union steamer *Fanny* (later C.S.S. *Fanny*) with enemy troops aboard. This Mosquito Fleet continued to sting the Union until overwhelmed by constantly increasing numbers of warships. It had, for all practical purposes, ceased to exist by the time Union forces under Flag Officer L.M. Goldsborough and General Ambrose Burnside captured Roanoke Island in February 1862, effectively closing Albemarle Sound. The lack of effective naval opposition then allowed Union forces to establish themselves on the mainland at New Bern during early March. By that month, Northern amphibious forces had seized several points along the Southern coasts, including Port Royal, South Carolina and Fernandina, Florida.

In the western Confederacy, Rebel gunboats and fortifications had proven no match for their opponents. Union forces repulsed a Confederate invasion of "neutral" Kentucky, then, spearheaded by seven armored riverboats commissioned in January 1862 (others would quickly follow), smashed Confederate defenses along the Tennessee and upper Mississippi Rivers. By the end of February, Confederate forces had abandoned Nashville, Tennessee, to consolidate in northern Mississippi. The Trans-Mississippi theater witnessed a seesaw war for control of Missouri, eventually decided by the Union victory at Pea Ridge, Arkansas, in March 1862. Forced back on both banks of the Father of Waters, Confederate defense of that mighty river appeared doomed.

By late February 1862, Mallory found himself under considerable pressure from Congress and the public to break the tightening blockade of Southern ports, free the coasts of North Carolina, and to provide additional naval support for the upper Mississippi. Mallory promised decisive action in March and April as his ironclads at New Orleans and Norfolk became available. Meanwhile he continued to send raiders to sea, hoping to force the Union Navy to react, thus weakening the blockade. Welles refused to respond, however, claiming that the losses would be small and those few raiders that slipped through the tightening cordon would be captured upon their return. This did little to console Northern businessmen, who claimed some $10,000,000 in shipping and goods destroyed in the opening months of the war. Quietly but steadily they began to shift vessels and cargoes to foreign flags. In fact, some clandestinely supported blockade running into the Confederacy.[23]

Another officer receiving considerable pressure from his administration was General George McClellan, commanding the Union's Army of the Potomac. McClellan had trained his army hard since becoming its commander; now Abraham Lincoln wanted him to use it to capture Richmond and end the rebellion. The North's "Little Napoleon" did not wish to waste his men on a march through northern Virginia against prepared Confederate defenses. Instead, he proposed to move his army by sea to the James Peninsula, then, with Fortress Monroe secured as his base of supply, swiftly advance the 60-odd miles to the Rebel capital. His flanks protected by naval forces advancing up the York and James Rivers, McClellan's outflanking maneuver would nullify the strong defensive positions in northern Virginia and guarantee a victory. His plan approved by a president desperate for any form of advance, McClellan began chartering the 400 merchant ships needed to move and supply his army. Then, at around

12.45 p.m. on March 8, his efforts paused as a strangely shaped vessel approached Union blockaders in Hampton Roads—the C.S.S. *Virginia*, supported by the wooden gunboats *Beaufort* and *Raleigh*, also of the Gosport Squadron, was about to place its mark on naval history.

Mallory had hoped to commit his Gosport Squadron of ironclads in mass, but delays in acquiring engines, shafts, and armor plates had slowed the conversions. By early March, only *Virginia* was ready for combat. Even it lacked the heavy iron shutters for its gunports, while newly minted Captain Catesby ap R. Jones (promoted for his fine effort in readying the vessel) seemed less than happy with the top speed of eight knots that its old engine could produce. Trials had revealed additional problems: awkward turning ability (30 minutes to turn through 180 degrees), vulnerability of the hull armor (covered with readily available 1-inch instead of 2-inch plate due to shortages) when the vessel rode light, and the *Virginia*'s deep draft which led to tricky maneuvering in shallow water. On the other hand, Mallory's early recruiting efforts had given Jones time to whip a rather lubberly bunch of men into something resembling a naval crew.

Lieutenant Lucien W. Carter, late of the Mosquito Squadron's *Curlew*, would captain *Alabama*, which floated at Gosport on March 8. Only some three weeks from readiness, the converted two-decker would become the squadron's flagship. Filling the slot of commodore had been a difficult choice for Mallory. He would have preferred shifting the experienced and aggressive Buchanan from New Orleans for this critical role, but that city was a logical target for Union assault. Instead, the secretary chose another veteran of North Carolina's Mosquito Fleet, Captain W.F. Lynch, for the role. Delayed by the conflict raging in the Carolina sounds, Lynch would not arrive at Gosport until March 14.

Raphael Semmes had accepted command of *Hart of the Confederacy* in mid-February. Semmes had already gained a reputation for boldness while commanding the raider C.S.S. *Petrel* out of Charleston. As a lieutenant, he had twice ran the blockade of Charleston to capture a total of 15 prizes—including a Union blockader. Unlike other raiders, Semmes had returned home with his vessel, boarding and capturing the enemy warship that stood in his way on the last trip. While recovering from a slight wound received in the action, he had requested a large, heavily armed steamer for his next raid. Instead, Semmes found himself promoted to captain and hustled to Gosport to command the vessel he later described as "the fastest, deadliest little ship in the world."[24] However, as *Virginia* steamed into Hampton Roads, *Hart*, the most difficult of the three conversions, still lacked most of its armor. The chief architect had informed Mallory that it could not possibly be seaworthy, even for trials, before the end of April.[25]

First Battle of Hampton Roads

Lincoln's North Atlantic Blockading Squadron mustered over 50 vessels, and five floated in Hampton Roads on March 8. Closest to the Elizabeth River and Gosport anchored *Cumberland*, a 24-gun sailing sloop, and the 44-gun sailing frigate *Congress*. The 50-gun screw frigates *Roanoke* and *Minnesota*, as well as the 44-gun sailing frigate *St Lawrence* were in positions to support the two vessels that would be the first target of the untested Confederate ironclad. It took the slow-moving *Virginia* more than an hour to reach gunnery range. Confident in their ability and without knowledge of the capabilities of the enemy, the Union officers of the *Cumberland* and *Congress* beat to quarters, but remained at anchor (powered only by sails, their maneuvering would have been severely limited in the tight confines of the Roads at any rate).

Shortly after 2.00 p.m., the ships exchanged their first shots. Jones, determined to destroy the more dangerous of his enemies first (though smaller than its mate, Jones knew that *Cumberland* carried the heavier battery), used his under-gunned wooden consorts to distract *Congress*. As *Virginia* closed the range, the superiority of its iron-plated casemate became evident. The heaviest Union shells failed to penetrate its thick hide, while Confederate artillery wrecked the sloop's hull and created carnage among its crew. Finally, the Rebel ram pierced the side of the doomed ship. Splintered beams and suction pinned the Rebel ship in place as *Cumberland* rapidly settled to the bottom. At the last moment, as water sluiced across the ironclad's deck, Jones's straining engines managed to pull *Virginia* free. Its ram remained embedded in the wreckage of its victim. Even as their vessel settled beneath them, frustrated Union gunners continued to exchange fire with the Rebel cannoneers. Still unable to penetrate *Virginia*'s armor, they did manage to disable one of its broadside guns before, around 3.30 p.m., *Cumberland* slid beneath the waves.

Reinforced by the wooden gunboats *Teaser*, *Jamestown*, and *Patrick Henry* of the James River Squadron, Jones turned his attention to *Congress*, whose captain, endeavoring to gain the cover of Union shore batteries, had deliberately grounded his vessel. Taking position a mere hundred yards from the stern of the grounded frigate, Jones pounded it into submission in little over an hour. Unable to take possession of the surrendered craft as shore batteries and Union marksmen continued to target his ships, Jones ordered shot heated in his boilers. Around 5.00 p.m., Jones signaled his squadron to make for his next target, leaving the once proud *Congress* in flames.

The three remaining Union vessels in and near Hampton roads had rushed to join the fracas—perhaps a bit too quickly, as all three had run aground. Once freed, the outclassed *Roanoke* and *St Lawrence* had scurried for the safety of Fortress Monroe's massive batteries, but *Minnesota* remained firmly aground. Jones aimed his command at that vessel, but a falling tide and shoal water prevented him from closing the range. Instead he retired to an

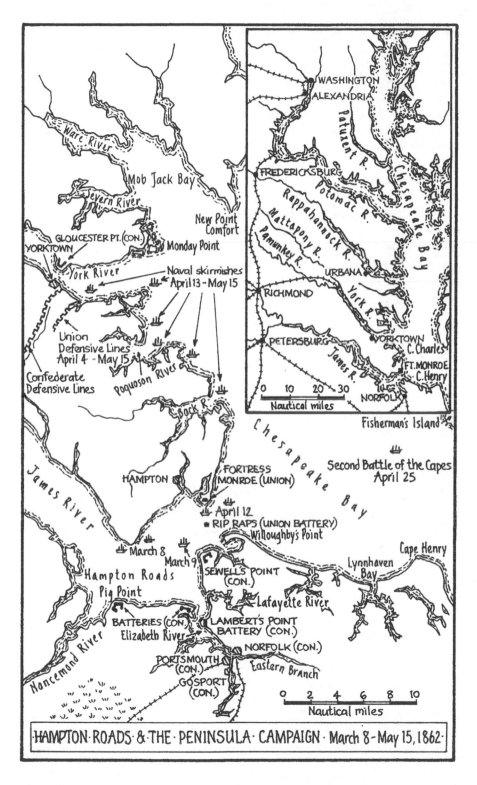

HAMPTON·ROADS·&·THE·PENINSULA·CAMPAIGN·March 8 - May 15, 1862·

anchorage beneath the Confederate guns at Sewell's Point. For the price of some 60 dead and wounded, two cannons damaged, a few iron plates buckled, and an iron ram lost, *Virginia* and its wooden consorts had destroyed two Union warships with heavy casualties to their crews. Despite a pesky leak in the bows, munitions and coal remained to destroy the last three Yankee blockaders on the morrow. Then, perhaps, there would be time to test his vessel in the wider waters of the Chesapeake before returning to Gosport.

At 6.00 the next morning, *Virginia* and the five gunboats of the James River Squadron upped anchors and steamed through the mists to destroy the still grounded *Minnesota*. There they found a tiny vessel, a mere "cheesebox on a raft," awaiting them. It was another ironclad, the U.S.S. *Monitor*. Welles had not stood idle at the threat of Mallory's conversion of Rebel ironclads. Rather, he had solicited bids for a number of these vessels for his own navy, several of which were already performing superbly on western rivers. The most unique of the designs, however, was the *Monitor*. Relatively fast and maneuverable, the shallow draft vessel carried only two heavy guns, but both were protected by a thickly armored, revolving turret. The only major flaw in the design was that the deck, mere inches above the waterline, would be continually awash in any but calm waters. In fact, the warship had almost sunk during heavy seas on its journey from Long Island to Hampton Roads.

For four hours that morning, the two marvels of the age of steam and iron fought, with neither gaining an advantage. Once, Jones managed to ram his enemy, but the only result was increased leakage in *Virginia*'s already damaged bow. Then, the Rebel ironclad shuddered to a halt, aground on a mud bank. For an hour, the two ships pounded away, *Monitor* working closer and closer to the immobile behemoth. At the last minute, a shell struck the pilothouse of the tiny warship, temporarily blinding its commander. For 20 vital minutes, *Monitor* abandoned the battle while an inexperienced officer took the con. During that time, Jones managed to ease his battered vessel from the mud. Listening to the council of his officers that the dropping tide and leaky condition of *Virginia* could combine to see the vessel again aground, the frustrated Confederate captain abandoned the field and returned to his anchorage at Sewell's Point. The following day, he steamed for Gosport and a drydock, temporarily conceding Hampton Roads to the enemy.

Interlude

Though the first day of battle had sown panic in Washington, it had calmed after the standoff of the second day. McClellan queried Welles as to the U.S. Navy's ability to contain the Rebel ships in Hampton Roads. Receiving a positive response, he began to shift his army to the Peninsula, knowing that the commitment of Union naval assets to the blockade of the Roads meant that he would have little support for his flanks along the James and York

Rivers. By April 4, over 100,000 men of the Army of the Potomac were prepared to advance against weakly held Confederate fortifications stretching from Yorktown along the Warwick River. The next day, Little Mac, receiving reports of inflated Confederate strength from his intelligence agents, upset with the Navy's refusal to support his advance along the York River, and angry at President Lincoln for keeping General McDowell's I Corps in front of Washington instead of releasing it to the Army of the Potomac, prepared to besiege the Rebel defensive lines rather than lose men to direct assault. In the weeks it took McClellan to ready his siege guns, the besiegers became the besieged.

As Welles concentrated 21 warships near the James Peninsula, including the new ironclad *Galena*, the iron-hulled *Naugatuck*, and three fast steamers converted into rams, dockyard workers and ship crews at Gosport worked 24 hours a day to repair *Virginia* and to finish the conversion of *Alabama* and *Hart*. On April 1, *Alabama* began its trials. Its newer engine gave it a top speed of ten knots, though the same concerns with draft and maneuverability as plagued *Virginia* still existed. Three days later, Jones's command (proudly bearing many of the scars remaining from its two days of battle) left drydock. Two additional inches of plate had been added to its hull, the two damaged cannon had been replaced, its heavy gunport shutters were added at last, and several damaged plates on its casemate were repaired. With a new ram attached to its bow, *Virginia* seemed to tug at its moorings, anxious again to face the enemy.

Semmes's *Hart*, though he had briefly tested its engine and screw, remained in the hands of the workers. By April 10, the installation of its hull plating complete, only the armored pilothouse needed to shield its still exposed wheel and command station on the quarterdeck remained to be added. Semmes had already ballasted and coaled his vessel, though powder and spar torpedoes remained to be shipped as soon as workers finished the wheelhouse.

At 10.00 a.m. that day, Commodore Lynch met with his captains, including those of the seven wooden gunboats assigned to his support. Glancing at a telegram from Mallory, the commodore informed his officers that the situation did not look good on the James Peninsula. Though the army was being concentrated as rapidly as possible opposite the Yankees, they would be outnumbered almost two to one, and any hard push could well reach Richmond. Unless the pressure could be relieved, the army would be forced to abandon Norfolk. The abandonment of the Confederacy's only fully developed naval yard was not only unpalatable, it was unacceptable; and in the eyes of the Secretary of the Navy, such a disaster could well mean the loss of the war. The only possible resolution to the conundrum in Virginia was the defeat of the blockaders standing off Fortress Monroe and a Confederate naval blockade of McClellan's forces in Virginia.

Having been ordered to accomplish that feat, Lynch proposed to stage his ships immediately to Craney Island at the mouth of the Elizabeth River. There they would load five companies of militia, split among the vessels to serve as marines, then steam to engage the enemy on the morning of April 12. The meeting ended, and one by one ships began to leave the yard. Last in line was the *Hart*, its crew dangerously shifting barrels of powder from a hoy towing alongside while the noise of saws and hammers still echoed from its quarterdeck. By 6.00 the next morning, workers had completed a makeshift bulwark of 4-inch wooden beams chest-high around the vulnerable wheel and three-quarters plated it with poorly fastened 1-inch wrought iron. Most of them then tumbled into boats as *Hart* eased from its anchorage, though several sought and gained Semmes's permission to remain aboard as crewmen.[26]

Union Commodore Louis M. Goldsborough, Flag Officer of the North Atlantic Blockading Squadron and personally commanding the fleet off Hampton Roads from the deck of *Minnesota*, possessed an excellent defensive position for his ironclads. The channel between Fortress Monroe and Confederate-held Willoughby's Point stretched for less than four miles, flowing around an island known as the Rip Raps on which he had mounted heavy batteries of artillery. Shoals further reduced the space for maneuver. Rather than risk his vulnerable wooden vessels in the channel, Goldsborough had placed only his strongest hulls—*Monitor*, *Galena*, and *Naugatuck*—there, keeping the bulk of his fleet two miles to the east. If hard pressed, his first line could withdraw for a battle of maneuver; if it managed to hold the Rebel ironclads, he could run down in support.

Second Battle of Hampton Roads

At 8.00 a.m., the *Galena*'s lookouts spotted the approaching Confederate ironclads, *Alabama* and *Virginia* abreast and *Hart of the Confederacy* lingering astern. The vulnerable Rebel gunboats followed, wary of closing the range too swiftly, though at six knots (the best that *Virginia*'s struggling engine could do against a making tide), the range seemed to close slowly indeed. At 9.00 a.m., *Monitor*'s big Dahlgrens opened the ball. A few minutes later, *Galena* scored first blood, its opening broadside shattering *Alabama*'s starboard quarterboat, splinters wounding a Confederate sharpshooter crouched by the ship's funnel. By 9.30, the firing was general as shells glanced from the armor of both sides. Closer and closer crept the casemated leviathans, obviously intent on ramming the Union vessels. But all three were nimble, and maneuvered to escape collision while they themselves ineffectually pounded the enemy. Then, seeming to leap from between the larger Confederate ships, Semmes's *Hart*, black smoke streaming from its stack and the very deck vibrating with the revolutions of its single shaft, arrowed towards *Monitor* at the amazing speed of 17 knots.

Semmes intended to combine his untried spar torpedo with a ramming attack. As conceived, the spar torpedo was a simple weapon. Mounted on a pole held upright above the ship's bow until released seconds before impact, the pole would fall forward into a slot on the bulwark. Projecting downward to or immediately below the waterline of the enemy ship, contact would ignite a percussion cap, thus triggering the barrel of powder and, ideally, opening a hole in the side of the enemy ship. The weapon's operators had been trained to wait until the last minute to drop the infernal device, as the force of the waves could snap the spar or even trigger the torpedo early. Once fired, it would be the crew's job to mount another torpedo as *Hart* maneuvered for the next attack.

An untested weapon often produces surprising results. Sixteen-year old Ensign Mercutio Albert Palmer, having never dropped the torpedo while underway and distracted to the edge of paralysis by shot whizzing over and into his vessel, closed his eyes and misjudged the release.[27] Rather than striking *Monitor* at its waterline, as intended, the late release of the torpedo caused it to strike the turret at the point where one of its Dahlgrens exited the gunport. The resulting explosion funneled directly into the turret through that gap, instantly killing every man inside with concussion as well as igniting a powder charge being inserted into the cannon. Popping rivets actually killed two men on *Hart*. Its way partially checked by the force of the torpedo, Semmes's ship still stuck *Monitor* hard enough to knock the Union warship's engine shaft out of alignment, though the vessel's overhanging armor prevented a rupture of its hull. Semmes, thrown from his feet by the collision, ordered his engine put astern as flames poured from the shattered turret of the now drifting *Monitor*. Within ten minutes, he had ascertained that four men had been killed and two were missing (all from the bow of the ship), while six men had suffered various injuries below deck. More importantly, his *Hart*'s heavily reinforced bow had withstood the explosion and the ramming without major damage. Ordering a replacement crew to ready a new spar torpedo, he steamed for the *Galena*, now engaging the slower *Alabama* within range of the Rip Raps battery. Closer to Fortress Monroe, *Naugatuck*'s iron hull was proving no match for *Virginia*'s rifled cannon. With its single gun dismounted and the hull shattered and leaking in several places, *Naugatuck* turned towards the open waters of the Chesapeake at best speed.

Lieutenant Carter and the inexperienced crew of the Confederate flagship were having a tough time of things. In a running battle with the nimbler *Galena*, Carter had inadvertently allowed his vessel to close with the heavy Union battery on the Rip Raps. At close range, the solid shot could, if not penetrate, then severely buckle or loosen casemate armor. Worse, such hits caused great splinters to fly from the oak backing of the plates, killing or injuring a number of men in *Alabama*'s casemate. But disaster, when it struck, came from a light pivot gun on *Galena*. Commodore Lynch had just ordered Carter to close *Virginia* when a shell struck the observation slit in *Alabama*'s pilothouse. Jagged metal splinters decapitated the Commodore, disemboweled the helmsman, and ripped away Carter's left arm. At full speed and rudder locked amidships by the now unconscious hand of its captain, the flagship headed directly into the Chesapeake—a beeline for the remainder of Goldsborough's squadron.

Galena turned to follow, but its first officer noticed *Hart*, coming ahead at full steam. He ordered his guns turned on it a mere minute before a parting shot from *Alabama* smashed into the quarterdeck, sending that brave man to his eternal reward. Columns of water rose around *Hart*, a difficult target due to its approaching aspect and its great speed. One round hit its angled bow, and glanced away. Another whistled low over the deck before penetrating the funnel. Then just as its spar torpedo dropped into contact low on *Galena*'s stern quarter, a shot ripped completely through *Hart*'s unfinished wheelhouse. Blasted by the force of the exploding torpedo, its wheel splintered and its rudder swinging freely, *Hart* clipped the stern of the Union ironclad, then began an uncontrolled, full speed turn back into the waters of Hampton Roads. *Galena*, shipping water through its ruptured stern, quickly lost power and grounded on a sandbar near the Rip Raps, out of the battle.

Though he had observed Semmes incapacitate *Monitor*, Jones remained unaware of the tragedies playing out on *Hart* and *Alabama*, both of which appeared to be moving under their own power and direction. His vessel had suffered minimal damage thus far in the engagement, and since the commodore was obviously taking his flagship directly for the remaining Union ships, how could Jones not do likewise? Ordering full speed ahead, Jones was pleased to see that both *Virginia* and *Alabama* would hit the Union line at about the same time. Meanwhile, the wooden gunboats lagging behind the Confederate ironclads increased their speed, except for *Teaser*, which slowed to pluck a battered Ensign Palmer from the water, then closed to accept the surrender of the smashed *Monitor*. The premier Union ironclad would eventually reach Gosport under tow—a visible sign of Confederate naval might.

Goldsborough, having watched his strongest vessels shattered by the Confederate ironclads, formed his 11 available ships into a line of battle and waited for the oncoming enemy. Anchored by the 50-gun screw frigates *Minnesota* and *Roanoke*, as well as the 44-gun sailing frigate *St Lawrence* (towed by the steam tug *Dragon*), eight additional lightly armed screw and sidewheel steamers prepared to greet the upstart Rebel navy with a storm of shot. As the range closed, *Virginia*'s grizzled quartermaster whispered, "Looks like Hell's a comin'," as the heavy Yankee ships disappeared behind a wall of flame-riven smoke.[28] A moment later, shot from the Union line rang like hail from the casemate as it stripped away virtually every outside fitting and reduced *Virginia*'s stack to an ill-drawing nub. Then thunder cracked as Confederate gunners returned fire.

As *Virginia* approached the strong center of the Union line, *Alabama* closed the more vulnerable side-wheelers forming its vanguard at the oblique. Only as the flagship's guns had fallen silent after engaging *Galena* had executive officer Donald Clarence Collins, stationed on the gundeck, discovered the carnage in the pilothouse. By the time the fallen men had been carried below and control of the vessel regained, shot was again striking the ironclad's hull. Collins ordered fire returned, then a hard turn to port that he hoped would bring the ungainly *Alabama* parallel to the Union line at close range.

By the time Jones's ship reached the enemy line, funnel damage had reduced its best speed to less than four knots, allowing *Roanoke* to dodge its dangerous ram with ease. Though three of *Virginia*'s guns were out of action (one with its muzzle blown away, two more with shutters jammed closed), those that remained raked *Roanoke*'s stern and *Minnesota*'s bow with devastating accuracy. Two shot bounced the length of *Roanoke*'s gundeck, temporarily disabling fully a third of its guns and puncturing its funnel between decks. As thick black smoke filled the gundeck and poured from the vessel's gunports, panic seized some of the warship's crew. They leaped into the chill waters of the Chesapeake to escape a ship they thought aflame.

Though only one round stuck *Minnesota*, the gun captain firing it had the presence of mind to load two bags of grape atop the solid shot. The 1-inch balls scythed through the Union crews laboring at their heavy bow chasers, and snapped lines and stays that whipped in their own dance of death. The heavy shot smashed into the foremast of the steam-frigate. Its stays cut away by grape, the mast toppled, crashing into *Minnesota*'s funnel as it fell. Furled sails caught on the ragged edge of the stack, then ignited as embers from the ship's boilers spewed from below. Some guns fell silent as the Union flagship's captain ordered his men to deal with the more immediate danger posed by fire and tangled wreckage. Those gunners remaining at their posts redoubled their efforts as *Virginia* cleared the Union line and again crossed their sights. To their amazement, the Confederate ironclad appeared to have lost all headway, and was now drifting stern first less than 20 yards from the *Minnesota*'s heavy artillery.

Alabama's turn to port had placed it less than 50 yards from the Union van, four wooden sidewheelers equipped with one or two medium caliber guns each. To Lieutenant Collins, gazing from the battered vision slit of the abattoir that was *Alabama*'s pilothouse, this seemed an unequal contest as his heavier guns shattered the sidewheel of the leading vessel. A roar accompanied the explosion of its boiler, taking the now sinking vessel out of the contest. He changed his mind when the fourth ship in line turned towards his ironclad, the reinforced ram at its bow looming larger by the second. With one of *Alabama*'s bow pivot guns engaged to starboard and unaware of the menace fast approaching, the other had time for only one round before the ram would strike—and it missed. The bow-to-bow collision tossed the men of both ships like rag dolls. Had the Yankee ram struck *Alabama* at a right angle, it may well have penetrated its thinner hull armor. As it was, the Union steamer's reinforced bow glanced off the even heavier prow of the ironclad, then scraped the length of its port side. The scraping did little damage to the ironwork of *Alabama*, but the starboard paddlewheel of the Union steamer smashed itself against the Confederate ship's hardened bow. Then, pressed firmly against the enemy hull by its rapidly spinning port paddlewheel, the steamer's frail wooden sides encountered the projecting eaves of *Alabama*'s casemate. The iron eaves gouged several planks from the Union vessel's side. Ten minutes later, the damage so severe that its crew could not stem the inrushing sea, the plucky steamer sank. By that time, the two remaining steamers had turned out of line, hoping that rapid maneuver would serve where armor was lacking. Collins left them for his wooden consorts now joining the battle, and shaped a course for a cloud of smoke less than a half mile away. The stab of flames within it marked the location of an uneven battle between *Virginia* and the remainder of the Union fleet.[29]

The *Virginia* drifted, boxed by the three Union frigates and the four smaller vessels that had trailed them. In some sense a victim of its own success, its single screw had fouled a length of hawser lost by *Roanoke* early in the engagement. Over a dozen shells a minute, some fired ranges of less than 30 yards, struck *Virginia* as it lay helpless. Even an ironclad had its limits, and sheared bolts and oaken splinters screamed inside its hellishly hot, smoke-filled casemate. One enemy shell exploded as it struck an aft gunport, shutters already jammed open by an earlier blow. Upending a Brookes Rifle and killing every man of its crew, the carnage from that single shot added a little more depth to the inch of blood already seeking drainage from the casemate's deck.

Deafened by the cannonade, Jones felt rather than heard the cessation of Union shot ringing on battered armor as he staggered from the pilothouse across the shambles of his gundeck to check his remaining two guns. Had the squadron finally arrived? He glanced through a shattered gunport in time to see the reinforced bow of a Union gunboat block his view. Deaf or not, he heard the crushing blow delivered to the mid-section of his command. Flung to the deck, Jones's world turned red as the blood of his dead filled his mouth and eyes while pain coursed through his newly broken left arm. Consciousness briefly fled, its restoration matched the return of a hail of enemy shot. Below deck, his crew fought to staunch seams sprung by the enemy ram. *Virginia*'s three inches of good Tredegar iron backed by 24 inches of solid oak had held—barely. Wiping blood from his eyes, Jones looked again through the shattered port. The Union gunboat, disabled by a fortunate shot from one of his remaining guns, limped slowly away, but a brief rift in the smoke showed a second ram, scarcely 300 yards distant, bearing down on the helpless *Virginia*. The smoke dropped again, and Jones braced himself for the blow to come, and for the death to follow. Finally the steamer, a vee of water streaming from its bow, surged from the manmade mist—on a course that would miss *Virginia* completely! Jones did not trust his eyes as a ragged fellow, blood dripping from numerous wounds and one hand on the remaining spokes of a splintered wheel, saluted his command. Thirty seconds later, Raphael Semmes slammed *Hart of the Confederacy* into the side of *Roanoke*.

Of the five men crowded around *Hart*'s poorly shielded wheel when *Galena*'s shot had struck home, only Semmes survived. Dazed and bleeding from numerous lacerations (upon his eventual death at age 79, an autopsy would recover seven metal splinters lodged in his body from this day's action), it had taken long minutes for his crew to extract him from the wreckage and to regain control of their ship. Having broken immediate contact with the enemy, Semmes paused to take stock of his vessel. Though the attack on *Galena* had destroyed the spar torpedo fittings and wrecked the quarterdeck of his command, neither speed nor maneuverability had been impaired. His guns had fired only one or two rounds each so far (at high speed—Semmes's preferred speed—fire was inaccurate and water tended to enter through their gunports). Most importantly, the ram-bow showed no sign of weakness or leakage.

Then Semmes ordered full steam for the distant cloud of smoke surrounding the engagement between Goldsborough and the Confederate squadron. Circling the rear of the Union line, *Hart* rammed a surprised gunboat, shearing completely through its foredeck, then slowed to let his guns engage a second steamer before aligning his warship on the center of the smoke covered fracas. Gathering speed, he saluted *Virginia* (which from visible damage, he expected to sink anytime), then rammed one of its three large tormentors. *Roanoke*, already battered by shots from *Virginia* and now engaged on its starboard side by *Alabama*, immediately began to sink. Locked into his prey by the inrush of seawater, Semmes backed engines to no avail. The weight of the sinking vessel pulled *Hart*'s bow so far down that the tips of its rapidly spinning screw actually emerged from the sea. Then *Hart* popped free, though not without cost as its abused engine coughed and died. Cursing, Semmes ordered his guns to open fire on *Minnesota* and his engineers to get the engine working. Caught in a crossfire between the remaining guns of the Confederate ironclads, the bulk of his squadron sunk or dispersed beyond his control and his own ship heavily damaged, Goldsborough ordered his flag hauled down. At 2.58 p.m. on April 12, *St Lawrence*, unable to escape in the light onshore breezes, followed suit. Only the tug *Dragon* and the damaged *Naugatuck* escaped the debacle to take word of the defeat to Washington.[30]

To Victory

Rumor spread, and with it panic: the strong Rebel squadron was steaming up the Chesapeake; it would bombard Washington and bring Maryland forcibly into the Confederacy; it had been sighted in Delaware Bay, heading for the shipyards of Philadelphia or the teeming docks of New York. While governors and mayors sent telegram after telegram to the White House begging for soldiers and guns, Union Secretary of War, Edwin M. Stanton, ordered ships scuttled to block the Potomac, and Lincoln sent the few regiments that he could spare to Baltimore, intent on holding Maryland in the Union. More than aware of the vulnerable position of the slow-moving McClellan's Army of the Potomac on the James Peninsula, Lincoln ordered him to capture Richmond now or to begin shifting his army back to northern Virginia. Convinced by Confederate deception and the incompetence of his personal intelligence operatives that any advance on Richmond would meet defeat at the hands of superior numbers, Little Mac called for transports and hunkered in his entrenchments opposite Yorktown. The besieger had become the besieged.

In truth, the victorious Confederate ironclads were in less than pristine condition. Jones, his broken arm in a sling, took command of the *Alabama*, and the heartbreakingly battered *Virginia* limped for Gosport with some 200 of the squadron's wounded aboard. The severely handled prize *Minnesota* went with it. Semmes, his engines repaired, reported to Jones that his vessel was ready for combat, hiding the fact that long stints at the pumps were required each hour to keep *Hart* afloat, and that, despite the efforts of his engineer, *Hart*'s steam plant could offer only 12 knots at best. Anchoring the *St Lawrence*, its cannon manned by gunners rapidly shipped from Gosport, to block entry to the harbor at Fortress Monroe, Jones left two gunboats to support it and steamed with the remainder of his squadron around the Peninsula and into the York River. For four weeks, his squadron reinforced by a trickle of Confederate gunboats converted from captured Union transports, Jones blockaded the James Peninsula. Daily skirmishes with Union gunboats took a toll on both sides, but few supplies arrived for the trapped Union army, and even fewer men were successfully withdrawn from the peninsula. *Virginia*, its worst injuries barely repaired and its guns replaced, rejoined the squadron in ten days. Jones returned to its deck in time to face a Union fleet hastily recalled from a planned invasion of New Orleans and intent on breaking the blockade and extricating the hungry and demoralized Army of the Potomac. In exchange for his right eye, lost to a cutlass when desperate Union sailors actually boarded *Virginia*, Jones won the Second Battle of the Capes.[31]

Meanwhile, in the fertile Shenandoah Valley of Virginia, Confederate General Jackson smashed the Union forces arrayed against him once Stanton shifted regiments and even brigades from that arena to defend Washington, Baltimore, Philadelphia, and New York from a feared invasion. Then he entrained his battle-tested corps to support the Confederate siegelines at Yorktown. The hurried recall of Union troops from the western fields of battle to the east allowed Confederate forces to recover from the bloody struggle at Shiloh Church in early April and regain Nashville. On April 30, Commodore Buchanan led two new ironclads and a score of wooden warships down the Mississippi from New Orleans and soundly defeated its Union blockaders. Wiring Richmond that "The Father of Waters again runs unvexed to the sea," he then directed his vessels in a lightning campaign that saw all significant Union naval presence driven from the Gulf of Mexico.

On May 15, President Abraham Lincoln slumped at his desk. Two messages rested between his outstretched arms. One, a request from McClellan to be allowed to surrender his starving army to the Confederacy, noted that General Robert E. Lee (the replacement for General Joseph E. Johnston, wounded by a Union sharpshooter in front of the Yorktown lines) offered most generous terms. The other, delivered that morning by the ambassador from Great Britain, declared that Britain would soon move to recognize the Confederate States of America formally as a sovereign nation with all the rights thereof. Her majesty's ambassador had advised the president that where Britain led, the remainder of Europe would soon follow. Further, Union interference with British trade into ports where, obviously, a blockade no longer existed, would be met with far more than words. Three days later, McClellan surrendered his army to General Lee and Fortress Monroe to Captain Catesby ap R. Jones of the ironclad *Virginia*.

Aftermath

On June 30, 1862, representatives signed the treaty that officially ended the brief Civil War and recognized the Confederate States of America as a sovereign nation in its own right. Ten years later, June 30 would become an official holiday in the Confederacy: Navy Day, in honor of the service that had contributed so much to establish the new nation. That particular day would never be celebrated in the old Union, where flags still fly at half-mast and 26 forever empty seats in the senate chambers are draped in black each June 30—a silent protest at what Mallory and his navy once accomplished.

The Reality

Stephen Mallory, though he did much in creating a navy for the Confederacy, did not perform the miracles needed to win independence for his homeland. Be thankful for that. Victory would have meant the continuation of the institution of slavery, an institution that the South would not have willingly abandoned for generations (if at all). Even now, the lingering remnants of the mentality created by that old evil erodes much slower than one could wish.

Sherman, in his letter to David Boyd, had the right of it. The greater resources and mechanical might of the North created a basis for victory almost impossible for the weaker Confederacy to overcome, while the blockade discouraged the importation of war materials desperately needed in the South. Add to that the disorganized and sometimes almost inexplicable actions of the Confederate state and national governments, and the miracle is that the rebellion continued into 1865. Nowhere was the disorganization of the Confederacy more apparent than in its attempts to construct a navy.

The Confederacy laid the keels for over 20 ironclads (in almost as many locations as there were warships built). Often constructed in cornfields instead of proper yards, this haphazard collection of vessels was meant to challenge the offensive might of the ever-strengthening Union Navy. Unsurprisingly, the challenge failed. Built of often sub-standard materials by unskilled labor, the ironclads were invariably underpowered. Strive as bravely as they might, the inexperienced crews of Confederate ironclads were unable to resist Northern incursions, especially those supported by concentrations of Union ironclads, much less break the blockade of Confederate ports.

Yet control of the sea offered the best chance for the South to win the Civil War. Its ports kept open for European imports and a denial of Union amphibious capability would have concentrated more resources in Southern armies. Perhaps with more resources, the talented commanders of Confederate armies could have won the key struggles ashore. Or, perhaps, had Mallory been a true Southern Themistocles, the Confederate States Navy could have won the war for them.

Bibliography

Denny, Robert E., *The Civil War Years: A Day-by-Day Chronicle of the Life of a Nation* (Sterling Publishing, New York, 1992).

Foote, Shelby, *The Civil War: A Narrative, Fort Sumter to Perryville* (Random House, New York, 1986).

Miller, Nathan, *The U.S. Navy: A History*, 3d ed. (Naval Institute Press, Annapolis, 1997).

Morrill, Dan, *The Civil War in the Carolinas* (Nautical & Aviation Publishing Company of America, Charleston, 2002).

Official Records of the Union and Confederate Navies in the War of Rebellion, (Government Printing Office, Washington, 1894–1927).

Still, William N., Jr., *Iron Afloat: The Story of the Confederate Armorclads* (University of South Carolina Press, Columbia, 1985).

Symonds, Craig L., *The Naval Institute Historical Atlas of the U.S. Navy* (Naval Institute Press, Annapolis, 1995).

Notes

*1. *Norfolk Courier*, April 18, 1862.

2. As cited in Denny, *The Civil War Years*, pp. 19–20.

*3. Letter from Angela S. Mallory to Stephen Mallory, March 21, 1861. *Stephen R. Mallory Collection*, Jones Library, CSA Naval Academy, New Bern, NC.

4. A "Letter of Marque and Reprisal" allowed a civilian vessel to function as an auxiliary warship (or privateer) of the issuing nation within clearly defined parameters. Great Britain, with its far-flung maritime empire, felt that such civilian sailors were little better than pirates—especially after the War of 1812, during which American privateers had taken numerous prizes from the British merchant fleet. As a final act in the negotiations in Paris to end the Crimean War, European powers signed the Declaration of Paris of 1856, declaring privateering illegal in the eyes of signatory nations. Though the United States never approved the document, it did bow to international opinion. The Confederacy, on the other hand, issued a number of letters of marque—a grave error in initial foreign diplomacy that undermined its hope of international support.

*5. *Cabinet Notes*, March 15, 1861, Jefferson Davis Presidential Library, Richmond, VA.

*6. *Congressional Records*, March 17, 1861, Government Archives, Richmond, VA.

*7. In 482 BC, Themistocles convinced the Athenians to use silver from the new mines at Laurium to expand the Athenian fleet. Two years later, the new Athenian triremes formed the core of the fleet that defeated Persian invaders at the battle of Samos. Mallory obviously forgot the eventual fate of Themistocles (exiled in 471 after accusations of taking bribes) or, as a consummate politician, he would have used another example in his speech.

8. Denny, *The Civil War Years*, p.32.

*9. Sam Clemens, *Stone Soup, Wooden Guns, and Ragged Fellows: Good Times in the Navy* (Twain Press, Hannibal, 1876), 6–24.

*10. *Virginia State Papers*, National Archives (Richmond), v. 12, series 111; P. T. Saurian, *Intelligence Failures of the United States Navy* (Naval Press, Washington, 1991), pp. 3–14, 53.

*11. *Norfolk Courier*, April 20, 1861.

*12. Billy Steele, *Iron Afloat: Birth of the Confederate Ironclads* (ECC Press, Greenville, NC, 1971), pp. 9–10.

13. *Official Records of the Union and Confederate Navies in the War of Rebellion*, Ser. II, Vol. II, p. 51.

*14. Wade Dudley, *Alma Mater Dear!: A University at War* (Beeler Press, Tuscaloosa, AL, 1999), p. 49.

*15. The rapid buildup of Southern facilities seems amazing until one considers the availability of slave labor in the Deep South. Though used only for manual labor (skilled work, such as using turning lathes, was believed to "demoralize" slaves—*i.e.*, to make them feel equal to free men and thus rebellious), the unwilling contribution of slaves played a major role in the establishment of the Confederacy as a nation.

*16. Eventually, all of these state vessels would be incorporated into the Confederate Navy. Both Mallory and Jefferson considered them a drain on vital manpower resources.

*17. New Orleans *Picayune*, June 6, 1861. The aggressive Buchanan, having resigned from the Union Navy in mid-May and arrived as senior officer commanding, New Orleans Station, on June 3, wasted no time in testing his new command. What the newspaper did not reveal, however, was that two of his ships suffered heavy damage in the attack while the third did not participate at all due to engine failure. Buchanan wrote to Mallory that "the crews served bravely, but with so little experience that they died bravely as well." He also complained that his sidewheelers were far more vulnerable to propulsion damage than the screw-sloop and even the sailing sloop that he had, fortunately, overcome. Buchanan to Mallory, June 14, 1861, *Captain's Papers*, Jones Library, CSA Naval Academy, New Bern, NC.

*18. Steele, *Iron Afloat*, pp. 18–30.

*19. As befit a fast ship, its very name, *Hart* (a stag, or male deer), evoked images of both speed and battle.

*20. Steele, *Iron Afloat*, pp. 30–32.

*21. On November 8, 1861, Captain Charles Wilkes's U.S.S. *San Jacinto* stopped and boarded the British steamer *Trent*, seizing Confederate diplomatic agents John Slidell and James M. Mason, as well as two members of their entourage. Public outcry in Great Britain at this abuse of their neutral flag led the British government to deliver several shiploads of previously ordered goods (including the engines) to the South under armed escort. This less than subtle posturing convinced Lincoln to act quickly to release the four men and to apologize formally for the incident.

*22. The denizens of western Virginia scarcely resembled their slave-owning brethren in the east of that state. Given the opportunity by early Union successes, they seceded from secessionist Virginia and applied for statehood in the United States. Admitted to the Union after the end of the war (in June 1862), West Virginia's stubborn residents lived up to their state motto, "Mountaineers are Always Free"—or at least so troublesome that Virginia let them go with small complaint.

*23. F.A. Steddy, *They Were Expendable: Confederate Raiders of the Civil War* (Time Blythe Press, New York, 1941). The stodgy Steddy's stilted studies do reveal that Rebel raiders seldom tried to return through the blockade; rather, they sold their vessels at Bermuda or Nassau, then took passage on blockade runners to return home.

*24. *Ibid.*, p. 113.

*25. Conversion of the old *United States* required extensive reworking of the ship's original bow, restructured and strengthened to withstand the explosive force of its own spar torpedoes as well as to carry a ram. Its internal space, far less capacious than that of the much larger *Alabama*, challenged the Southern engineers who installed the workings of a modern steam plant. The resulting warship was fast, deadly, and seaworthy, but it would prove to be a hot, crowded hell for its crew.

*26. R. Butler, *Hammer, Tongs, and a Twist: A Fighting Carpenter at Hampton Roads* (Red Shirt Press, Richmond, VA, 1876).

*27. The ensign also forgot to duck, and the resulting blast tossed him a considerable distance into the brackish water of the channel. The crew of *Teaser* fished him out an hour later. Palmer lived to be 102 years old and had an astounding reputation for punctuality for the last 86 years of his life.

*28. From a speech given by Admiral Jones at the Confederate Naval Academy, May 21, 1881.

 29. Unless one has been on a simulated black powder era battlefield, it is difficult to imagine the cloud of smoke that surrounded naval battles of that period, especially in the early decades of steam power. Smoke from the large broadside armament of the day combined with that of coal and smoke from burning vessels to reduce visibility to near zero on a windless day. With wind, the constant replenishment of the smoke created artificial fogbanks, and made local visibility highly variable.

*30. The account of the Second Battle of Hampton Roads is compiled from the numerous reports contained in the Naval Archives in Richmond, as well as the dozens of memoirs written by veterans from both nations.

*31. Ironically, the failure of the British fleet in the First Battle of the Capes, during the American Revolution, led to the surrender of a British army at Yorktown, and to the emergence of a new nation.

3
"WHAT WILL THE COUNTRY SAY?"
Maryland Destiny

David M. Keithly[1]

Following his victories in the summer campaign of 1862, at Cedar Mountain on August 9, at the Battle of Second Manassas on August 29–30, and Chantilly on September 1, General Robert E. Lee pondered the question how best to follow up the defeats inflicted upon the Federal forces. He hesitated to batter his veteran army against the formidable defenses of Washington, D.C., so skillfully constructed during the past year. The Army of Northern Virginia lacked the heavy artillery required for a siege and supplies for the troops were running low, notwithstanding the capture of large amounts of stores at Manassas Junction. The Northern response to the Confederate victory at the Battle of Second Manassas was analogous to the bitter defeat suffered in June 1861 on the identical field of conflict. The long roll of drums marked the deployment of yet further additional Federal troops to the various Union armies.

The Track of a Storm

At the onset of secession, press viewpoints in Great Britain exhibited considerable sympathy with the North. Newspaper editors initially supposed that the conflict on American soil involved slave manumission, a goal most Britons had advocated for decades. Yet, during the first year-and-a-half of war, the Lincoln administration was unable to capitalize on this weighty moral issue. The crucial border states of Maryland, Kentucky, Missouri and Delaware, in which slavery still existed, would probably have been thrust out of the Union had the Federal government proclaimed it was waging war to free the slaves. For domestic political reasons, President Lincoln was thus left with little choice but to declare on various occasions that the North was not fighting for manumission but only for the preservation of the Union.

On the other hand, some members of the British nobility displayed a visceral animosity toward the North. Socially, the landed gentry had a close affinity to the plantation aristocracy of the American South. To cultured

Europeans, those American Southerners whom they had met were for the most part to be regarded as gentlemen, in sharp contrast to the prototypical boastful and vulgar Yankees. To be sure, additional, somewhat more rational, explanations for the disapproving attitude of the British ruling class presented themselves also. Contempt for American institutions was in part a shroud for trepidation. Union victory would prompt the disenfranchised in Britain to appeal even more loudly for greater democratization, it was feared. Contesting democracy abroad was a means to disparage it at home, and thus the prevalent contentment on the part of the British gentry for the self-destruction of the United States should not be surprising. By the same token, the United States represented a formidable competitor, a waxing rival in various spheres and a potential threat to Canada and other British possessions.

Accordingly, British luminaries quickly gained an appreciation for the salient political issues, both domestic and foreign, associated with the conflict in North America. Men like Lord Robert Cecil and Beresford Hope harbored no illusions about the attendant high stakes, and lobbied the country's governing class to avail itself of the golden opportunity that beckoned. *Their* best interests and hence Britain's wellbeing would be served by buttressing the South, acquiring in the process a crucial ally. With Southern independence would come a rejuvenation of the British economy, and the collapse of the United States would in all likelihood thwart the pending domestic reform the aristocracy dreaded. Nurturing an innate distrust of republicanism, the British gentry often evinced such a revulsion against American professions of egalitarianism that many were willing to throw in their lot with the Confederate states, tarnished as they were with their "peculiar institution."

In well-publicized statements, the Earl of Shrewsbury, for example, gloated about the "trial of democracy in America and its ignominious failure." He insisted that "the dissolution of the Union portends that men now before me will live to see an aristocracy founded in America."[2] Leading newspapers with connections to the Palmerston government heartily affirmed similar pro-Confederate sentiments. Unless the South achieved its independence, the London *Morning Post* asked rhetorically in 1862, "who can doubt that Democracy will be more arrogant, more aggressive, more leveling and vulgarizing, if that is possible, than ever before?"[3] The London *Times*, more prestigious and not to be outdone, editorialized that the dissolution of the Union "is to be welcomed with good riddance to a nightmare, [and] excepting a few gentlemen of republican tendencies, we all expect, we nearly all wish, success to the Confederate cause."[4] These were strong words with a clear message, and elements of the British press seemed locked in competition to lend support to the Confederacy.

Northerners for their part took umbrage at the failure of the British, after so many years of vehement opposition to slavery, to look beneath the surface and appreciate that success for Union arms meant slavery's deathblow in North America. The North expected at least warm endorsement, but by the middle of 1862 was receiving at best grudging cool neutrality. The lament of James Russell Lowell reflected widespread Unionist resentment:

> We know we've got a cause, John,
> That's honest, just, and true;
> We thought t'win applause, John,
> If nowheres else, from you.[5]

The Substance of the Shadow

Lee faced two choices. He could withdraw the Army of Northern Virginia from the Washington area and establish it around Richmond again, but such a course of action would have dispirited his troops and disheartened Virginia, which had suffered over a year of conflict on its soil and desperately hoped for fresh military successes. The alternative was to lead his army across the Potomac and begin conducting the war on Union territory. Potential advantages accruing from the second course of action strongly invited it. In addition to the devastating blows Lee would likely inflict, the morale of the Union forces would plummet just as Confederate prestige abroad would rise. Also, the presence of hostile forces on Northern terrain might well dissuade the reappointed commander of the Army of the Potomac, Major General George B. McClellan, from launching another invasion of Virginia. Lee would give his war-ravaged homeland a respite while inflicting the devil of a whipping upon the Federals that might make all the political difference.

Lee was too worldly-wise and experienced as a soldier not to grasp that the Confederacy could not endure a protracted war against a determined Federal Government. "Against the giant combination for our subjugation," as Lee called it, the South would have little long-term chance of victory unless foreign powers, meaning Great Britain or France, and preferably both, would render assistance on a large scale.[6] Lee's hopes for a successful campaign were thus based substantially upon the political effects ensuing from a bold invasion and subsequent stunning battlefield victories. Actuated by the triumph of arms in August 1862, Lee wrote to Confederate President Jefferson Davis arguing that this moment of the nadir of Federal morale was propitious for an invasion of Maryland, still loyal to the Union but with alleged widespread sympathies for the Confederate cause. The invasion would shift the brunt of the fighting from the soil of distressed Virginia to the Northern states, furnish forage and provisions to the main Confederate army sorely in want, and allow the citizens of "oppressed territory" to display their true convictions. The trusting association between Lee and Davis, sharply contrasted to the often convoluted Federal command structures, is illustrated by Lee's willingness to put his army in motion within days of the Battle of Second Manassas and even before receiving explicit assent from Davis. He knew intuitively that Davis would acquiesce to daring and even risky plans in a way Federal commanders could only dream of, burdened as they were by political interference from Washington and the second-guessing of such men as Secretary of War Edward M. Stanton and General-in-Chief of the Army Henry W. Halleck—"Old Brains," as the latter was sardonically known, the archetypal armchair general.

True, Lee was entering upon a gamble fraught with hazards. The Maryland campaign was not only perilous in itself, but the Army of Northern Virginia was materially unprepared for such an ambitious undertaking. Short of heavy equipment, above all of transport, the army consisted largely of poorly clothed and ill shod men. These were "ragged soldiers with bright muskets," one observer aptly pointed out. As if Lee needed much convincing, though, his subordinate commanders provided the necessary reassurance. Lieutenant General James Longstreet,[7] referred to affectionately by Lee as his "Old War Horse," recalled how his troops had lived off the land around the city of Monterey during the Mexican War. Maryland's farms, as yet unblighted by the cruel scourge of battle, all knew, would be laden in the early fall with vegetables and fruit. Impelled by the adage that he who dares wins, between September 4 and 7 Lee forded his entire army, some 59,000 strong, across the Potomac near Point of Rocks, where the water was scarcely more than knee-deep, and encamped in the vicinity of Frederick, Maryland. Lee's ambition was palpable. A stolid man with the instincts of a cardsharp, Lee was unswerving in his ardor to carry the war to the North and subsequently to demonstrate his ability to operate there with impunity once his valiant army eradicated Federal forces dispatched to join battle. On September 4, as the Army of Northern Virginia began to cross the river, Lee wrote to Davis: "Should the results of the expedition justify it, I propose to enter Pennsylvania, unless you should deem it inadvisable upon political or other grounds."[8]

For his part, Davis could hardly conceal his enthusiasm, expeditiously drafting a proclamation with the place for the state simply left blank, stating:

> "We are driven to protect our own country by transferring the seat of war to that of an enemy who pursues us with a relentless and apparently endless hostility; our fields have been laid waste, our people killed, many homes made desolate, and rapine and murder have ravaged our frontiers; the sacred right of self-defense demands that, if such a war is to continue, its consequences shall fall on those who persist in their refusal to make peace. The Confederate Army therefore comes to occupy the territory of their enemies and to make it the theater of hostilities."[9]

Lee would have only to write in the name of the Northern state where his headquarters was located following the destruction of the Federal army, and the proclamation would become the basis for an armistice. All was going according to plan on September 9, when Lee wrote to Davis that, "I shall move in the direction I had originally intended, toward Hagerstown and Chambersburg, for the purpose of opening our line of communication through the valley, in order to procure sufficient supplies of flour."[10]

Little Mac is Back

In the dark hours as the rattled components of the Federal Army of Virginia that had suffered such ignominious defeat at Manassas were slogging back to Washington, McClellan resumed command of the Union army at the request of a distraught President Lincoln. Earlier in the year, as he organized and drilled the Army of the Potomac, McClellan wrote to Halleck, still in the field in the Western theater, "I have, or expect to have, one great advantage over you as a result of my long and tedious labors—troops that will be demoralized neither by success nor disaster."[11]

In truth, he had a point. In the spring and summer of 1862, Union armies in the eastern theater suffered humiliating setbacks and defeats, but fought on with dogged determination. Many had lost faith in their leaders, yet few had lost faith in themselves. The Union troops were dazed and confused after the hard summer campaign of 1862, yet few were perpetually dispirited. Time and again, they demonstrated their resilience by almost eagerly leaping back into the fray in the wake of a hammering. The news of McClellan's return as commander enlivened the soldiers, plucking up their hearts to form the ranks of a methodical and disciplined army once again. McClellan had his weaknesses, to be sure, but few called his organizational skills into question, nor doubted the magic his name invoked with the soldiers he led.[12] Little Mac would consequently be tasked with bringing method to disorganization, to streamlining disintegrating Union forces, while concurrently directing the troops to thwart an advancing and triumphant foe flushed with victory.

No mean task, this. The loose ends of two war-torn armies, along with most of the Washington garrison, had to be woven swiftly into a fighting force with the mettle to give battle to "Bobby" Lee. As he was riding down Pennsylvania Avenue on September 7, McClellan encountered Secretary of the Navy Gideon Welles who queried whether the army would be moving north up the river. McClellan replied he had just taken charge of the army. "Onward, General, is now the word," said Welles. "The country will expect you to go forward." "That," McClellan assured him, "is my intention."[13]

Indeed, for a general with a reputation for dilatoriness and indecision, McClellan seemed to be responding with uncharacteristic alacrity. News of Lee's crossing of the Potomac precipitated the brisk movement of the Federal army toward Frederick along five parallel roads. The marching columns were so dispersed as to safeguard both Washington and Baltimore, with the left flank resting on the Potomac and the right on the Baltimore and Ohio Railroad. The army's right consisted of the First and Ninth Corps under

Major General Ambrose Burnside; the center, consisting of the Second and Twelfth Corps under Major General Edwin V. Sumner; and the left wing, of the Sixth Corps under Major General William B. Franklin. In fact, some in Washington began to worry that McClellan was responding too quickly to the threat posed by the Army of Northern Virginia, that the latter's movement into western Maryland was a ploy to draw Federal forces far enough away from Washington to allow Lee to swing his army around and position it between the capital and the newly reformed Army of the Potomac. McClellan, for his part, displayed no shortage of confidence as he marched his army forward in pursuit of Lee, its flanks and its dispersal adequate for protection of Washington.

Lucid Schemes

Lee never considered a direct move against Washington or Baltimore with a sizable Federal army between him and these cities. Rather, the Army of Northern Virginia's nimble maneuvers, he reckoned, would cause the Union commander to uncover one or both of them. With his supply lines secure through the Shenandoah Valley, Lee planned to push northward, intimidating Pennsylvania by operations in the Cumberland Valley and drawing a Union army so far toward the Susquehanna River that it would be overextended, affording him the opportunity to inflict devastating blows upon it far from the main base of supplies. If all went well, Lee could then position his army between one of the large Northern cities and the enfeebled Federal forces, prodding the latter to attack him on ground of his choosing. Consequently, his first movement from Frederick was towards the western side of the mountain range, named the Blue Ridge south of the Potomac and South Mountain north of the Potomac, which forms the eastern wall of the Shenandoah and Cumberland valleys, the former his line of communications with Richmond and the latter his line of maneuver toward Pennsylvania.

McClellan established closer and more rapid contact with the Confederate invaders than Lee initially anticipated. The wayworn Federal forces did not appear to be the disparate, combat-fatigued and demoralized assemblages of troops Southern leaders expected to see, for McClellan had somehow pulled together an army perhaps 80,000 strong that might not quickly overreach itself and could hastily concentrate to pose a genuine threat to the invading force.

So how to effect the plan? How to stay the course of the stratagem with the campaign well under way? How to open the proverbial back door, allowing the Army of Northern Virginia to get into McClellan's rear when he seemed to have his flanks protected and the capital covered? The solution came following a reconnaissance mission on the eastern side of South Mountain by the Army of Northern Virginia's hard-driving cavalry arm. Its indefatigable commander, Major General J.E.B. Stuart, noting that McClellan appeared to be moving his forces with uncharacteristic speed, hit upon an idea that accorded with his commander's intent while giving further purpose to the overall campaign plan.

Stuart, for his part, had learned to exploit the opportunities attendant to McClellan's propensity for hesitation and vacillation. During the battles before Richmond the previous spring, Stuart led his entire cavalry corps in a breathtaking ride completely around the huge Federal army. Stuart enjoyed such a reputation for boldness among his fellow generals that some remarked without blushing that he was wonderfully endowed by nature for the direction of light cavalry. If he could pull off such feats, Stuart reasoned, fresh paths to opportunity surely lay open. It was clear to all with eyes to see that McClellan was capable of being his own worst enemy.

While issuing his situation report to Lee, Longstreet, and Lieutenant General T.J. "Stonewall" Jackson, Stuart devised a means to buoy up the risk-averse McClellan. If the latter, with a knowledge of Lee's movements, could be made to think he was so perfectly master of the situation, and the stake so great as to warrant, indeed to necessitate, the boldest action, then he just might be inclined to tempt Providence. Jackson, renowned for his skill at swift maneuver and a knack for taking advantage of enemy weakness, heartily concurred. Jackson was an unusual man, who coupled a fearsome killer instinct with an intuitive grasp that the primary means of that instinct are to mystify and confuse the enemy. The two were complementary but hardly a matching pair. Stuart was a playful man, finely carved, all surface, like an intricately cut prism; Jackson was merely a hard man. Stuart's youthful good looks and romantic style made him an idol of subordinates and a hero throughout the South. In conjuring up a clever *ruse de guerre*, Stuart and Jackson concocted what became the definitive mystification and confusion plan of the Civil War.

The Game Made

Lee would draft orders revealing his designs for the campaign, and Stuart's cavalry would see to it that these fell into McClellan's hands, motivating him, it was hoped, to take precipitous action. Lee would then circumvent these plans in such a manner as to throw McClellan completely off balance. Designated Special Order No. 191, dated September 9, 1862, the document seemed to reveal the missions for the major components of Lee's army and clear up the conundrum surrounding the Confederates' sudden movement westward from Frederick.[14] A Confederate cavalry patrol deliberately dropped an envelope containing three high-quality cigars and a copy of the order, purportedly meant for Major General D.H. Hill, in a field adjacent to the Hagerstown Road near Middletown on September 10 where McClellan had just joined his army. Union soldiers, finding the envelope marked "Headquarters Army of Northern Virginia," placed it, complete with the cigars, duty having apparently checkmated the temptation to light up, into the hands of an officer who, in turn, headed directly to Twelfth Corps headquarters and Brigadier General Alpheus S. Williams, who perused the order with this adjutant, Colonel Samuel E. Pittman. The latter claimed to have served with R.H. Chilton, Lee's chief of staff, who drafted the order, and professed to recognize the handwriting. A self-important man, Pittman was telling a boastful tale that would prove serendipitous for the Confederate *ruse de guerre*. Pittman had not entered the army until September 1861, five months after Chilton resigned his commission to take up the Confederate cause.[15] The two could not, therefore, have served together in Michigan, but the young colonel's assertion lent considerable credence to presuppositions about the order's genuineness.

Special Order No. 191 specified that the Army of Northern Virginia should resume its march, taking the Hagerstown Road from Frederick. Jackson's corps, in the vanguard, would rush forward as was its wont, turn south, recross the Potomac and lay siege to Harpers Ferry, the town situated at the confluence of the Shenandoah and Potomac Rivers where a Federal arsenal was located and a garrison of 12,000 Union troops under Colonel D.H. Miles deployed.[16] According to the order, the accompanying maneuvers were to be accomplished by September 13. Longstreet, for his part, was to move on Boonsboro, on the Hagerstown Road, and halt there. The 16 brigades under the command of Major General Lafayette McLaws would leave the column at Middletown, also turn south and possess themselves of Maryland Heights just north of and overlooking Harpers Ferry. Meanwhile, Brigadier General John G. Walker would also head back south to the Potomac on the same road by which he had come, ford the river, and seize Loudon Heights on the Potomac side of the Ferry. The reserve artillery, ordnance and supply trains were to precede D.H. Hill, whose division would constitute the Army of Northern Virginia's rearguard through the South Mountain by Turner's Gap. The cavalry contingent would screen the route of the army and round up stragglers, of which there were expected to be many.

In fact, no Confederate forces would assault Harpers Ferry. Investing it would have been largely a waste of time. The Union troops occupying Harpers Ferry were under the direct command of Halleck in Washington, who had foolishly ordered Colonel Miles to hold the Ferry at all costs. Lee ascertained through snippets of good intelligence that the town would not be evacuated as McClellan strongly recommended. The Union detachment would be unable to join the Army of the Potomac, much less to offer a threat to the Confederate rear. Compounding the error was Miles's lack of simple common sense in neglecting even to move the garrison to the top of the lofty range of mountains easily accessible to him. He regarded Halleck's directive as authorization for inaction. Hence, a sizable Federal force remained bottled up and posed little menace, notwithstanding its position astride the Confederate supply lines and effectually in the rear of Lee's army in western Maryland. So long as it remained stationary, it was little more than a nuisance to communications through the Shenandoah Valley. Lee, as usual, was willing to run risks, taking for granted that he could sustain the presence of his army in Maryland and Pennsylvania for some considerable time. To buttress the ruse, Lee detached a small unit of reserve artillery to deploy on the undefended Maryland Heights, 2,000 feet above Harpers Ferry, and directed it to fire sporadically into the town, well within earshot of some of McClellan's forces. McClellan, tricked into believing that the Ferry was indeed under siege, was consequently furnished with an additional incentive to rush his troops forward in a hasty effort to relieve the town prior to its destruction and the subsequent surrender of its garrison.

All the Plans of the Rebels

The alleged action against Harpers Ferry reinforced McClellan's growing belief that he had struck gold. In his hands, he thought, he had a commander's greatest dream: the marching plans of an overextended foe who could be defeated in detail by a concentrated army. Little Mac saw daylight. He would destroy Lee's overconfident veteran army piece by vulnerable piece.

Plodding soldier McClellan might have been, but he was no fool. The thought crossed his mind more than once that Lee's order was a deliberate plant designed to deceive him. If authentic, and not some elaborate Rebel trick to humiliate him, the order would be the greatest imaginable piece of military intelligence. In terms of its effect, it could well determine the outcome of the pending engagement, secure victory for the Union, and triumph for George McClellan. Rose Greenhow, the infamous "Rebel Rose" who ran a spy net in the nation's capital, had provided General P.G.T. Beauregard with the anticipated movements of the Federal troops before the battle of First Manassas that had been most helpful to him, yet never had there been a discovery of the most intimate secrets of a campaign just prior to the actual clash of arms. Special Order No. 191 had been passed up the Federal chain of command, and no one had questioned its authenticity, including those with personal knowledge of the workings of Lee's entourage. The envelope was marked "Confidential," and the order, doubtless written by Chilton, properly ended with the words "By Command of Gen. Robert E. Lee." Williams's forwarding note expressing his view that Special Order No. 191 was genuine, provided some additional assurance. Moreover, D.H. Hill was known to enjoy a good smoke, which explained the inclusion of the stogies.[17] Union scouts confirmed that Confederate forces had been moving along the Hagerstown Road about the time the order would have been lost. Everything fit, to be sure, and McClellan thought he now comprehended the reasons for the swift redeployment of Lee's army west of South Mountain.

In the end, McClellan was duped because he allowed himself to be. The opportunity appeared unique; the temptation for a swift and stunning victory alluring. The order enabled McClellan to determine Lee's objective, to ascertain the force disposition for achieving that objective, and to establish the campaign itinerary. Above all, it demonstrated how vulnerable the Army of Northern Virginia was to being cut up in detail. Waving Special Order No. 191 blissfully about, McClellan quipped to a subordinate that, "Here is a paper with which, if I cannot whip Bobby Lee, I will be willing to go home... Castiglione [a famous victory of Napoleon's] will be nothing to it."[18] Flinging off his perennial cautiousness, McClellan resolved to pitch his freshly reorganized legions into Lee's army. He would burst unawares upon the enemy flank, rolling up the Army of Northern Virginia, division upon defeated division, in a tumult of irretrievable ruin. "Now I know what to do!" he is reported to have exclaimed to no one in particular. Didn't he heretofore?

It is somewhat paradoxical that McClellan's famous prudence did not apply to the safeguarding of sensitive information. Shortly after pulling off what was assumed in his camp to be an intelligence coup of the first order, McClellan, apparently caught in the whirlwind of excitement there, vaingloriously telegraphed Lincoln:

> "I think General Lee has made a gross mistake and that he will be severely punished for it... I hope for great success if the plans of the Rebels remain unchanged, for I have these plans... Indeed, I have all the plans of the Rebels and will catch them in their own trap if my men are equal to the emergency. I feel I can count on them as of old."[19]

In an even greater breach of security, several Union officers who knew of the captured plans left Frederick on September 14 and chatted at length about the incident to a Washington correspondent of the *New York Herald*, which ran the story the next day. The perpetrators of the ruse, in an effort to corroborate the functioning of their scheme, dispatched a scouting party to tap the telegraph lines to Washington and consult with a Confederate sympathizer in the Washington telegraph office. Supporters of the "Cause" in Washington and Baltimore, neither city wanting for Copperhead communities, kept the Confederate army in western Maryland privy to the war coverage in the Northern press.[20] Stuart's and Jackson's operatives soon had ample confirmation that the Union commander had swallowed the bait. The snare, unnoticed by McClellan, looked about to close.

The Sting

Lee proved to be one of the century's greatest generals because of his ability to get into the enemy commander's head as well as his willingness to hazard bold moves others could scarcely anticipate. Instead of dividing his army in the face of a superior force as he had before, this time Lee would conduct himself in accordance with a salient and time-honored military tenet. He kept the Army of Northern Virginia concentrated, awaiting McClellan's efforts to force the passes on South Mountain.

These were not long in coming. With Burnside already in Frederick, Sumner was ordered to follow. Major General Fitz-John Porter was to push forward with his reorganized Fifth Corps. Burnside then moved his entire command from Frederick into the Catoctin Valley, clearing a path for Brigadier General Alfred Pleasonton's cavalry who were to provide a situation report about supposedly besieged Harpers Ferry and to conduct reconnaissance as far north as Pennsylvania. Burnside would then march his force, followed by Sumner and Banks, upon Boonsboro, beyond Turner's Gap through South Mountain. Franklin was to push forward, reinforced by the light corps commanded by Major General Darius Couch, into Pleasant Valley through Crampton's Gap.

The National Road from Frederick crossed South Mountain at Turner's Gap, with Boonsboro just beyond, while six miles south lay Crampton's Gap, with a road running through it leading down to Harpers Ferry from Buckeystown. McClellan's intent was clear as day: he would force Turner's Gap and fall upon Boonsboro, crushing what he thought were Longstreet's and Hill's detached contingents. Franklin was to push through Crampton's Gap and down to Maryland Heights, where he would strike McLaws and Anderson's divisions in the rear and force open a pathway of escape for the besieged garrison at Harpers Ferry. The thrust through Crampton's Gap would afford the additional advantage of safeguarding the flank of the main force from an attack from the south, should the main assault into the upper gap encounter substantial resistance.

So far, so good. The problem was that Hill's division was not separated from Longstreet's corps; neither were the divisions of Anderson, McLaws and Walker separated from Jackson's corps. The latter had not deployed to Harpers Ferry, but waited in Pleasant Valley for the lunge of Franklin's corps, some 18,000 strong, through the Crampton Gap. Longstreet never deployed his corps to Hagerstown, but waited, reinforced, in an ambuscade, just south of Boonsboro to meet the onslaught of Sumner and Burnside leading nearly 70,000 men through Turner's Gap. An observer's remark that the three heavy columns marching up the National Road, "resembled a monstrous, crawling, blue-black snake, miles long, quilled with a silver slant of muskets at the shoulder, its sluggish tail writhing slowly up over the distant ridge, its bruised head weltering in the roar and smoke upon the crest above" alluded to the prospect of the Union army being caught unawares.[21] Outnumbered Longstreet was, yet he enjoyed the crucial element of surprise since the last thing McClellan expected was a large Confederate force waiting at the outset to block the gap and then to swarm through it. Jackson, expected to make quick work of Franklin's corps in the south gap, could eventually render assistance if the sheer weight of Union numbers in Turner's Gap could be brought effectively to bear. Lee correctly did not think they could.

Late in the afternoon of September 16, McClellan provided Franklin his instructions. "You will move at daybreak, and having gained Crampton's

Gap, you will first cut off, destroy or capture McLaws's command and relieve Harpers Ferry." "My intention is to cut the enemy in two and beat him in detail," McClellan said to his corps commanders, "I ask of you at this important moment, all your intellect and the utmost activity that a general can exercise."[22] Ridges dominated both gaps from each side, and ancillary passes north and south required a greater extension of forces, but at the same time allowed for possible flank attacks against unprepared oncoming troops.[23]

Franklin's corps invariably got the worst of it. His two divisions consisted of 27 regiments of infantry and seven batteries of artillery, the latter being of only limited use given the rough terrain and circumstances of engagement. Even with Couch's reinforcement of 15 regiments, Franklin could deploy a force scarcely larger than that of Anderson and McLaws. Jackson's entire corps, outnumbering Franklin by nearly two-to-one, lay in ambush on both sides of the notch and in the smaller mountain passes. Hit at the moment of greatest vulnerability, stretched out on the road and sandwiched between the ridges, the Union corps quickly found itself in desperate straits. Withering rifle fire from multiple directions cut the Union troops down in windrows. Enfilading shot and shell unnerved the inexperienced within the ranks. The first brigade of the Second Division broke completely when its commander, Brigadier General Winfield Scott Hancock, was cut down. Other brigades were forced into disorganized, small-unit actions as command-and-control disintegrated. When a second brigade broke, the fearsome, keening wail of the Rebel yell signaled the multiple-pronged assault by Jackson's veterans. The fighting became general and hand-to-hand at many points. Bullets whined about as a swarm of enraged hornets might make things hum. Brave Union troops fought desperate rearguard actions, protecting as best they could the back of the column on the east side of the gap, hoping to stabilize the situation until the fighting tapered off with the darkness, tempering the maelstrom engulfing them.

To no avail. By early afternoon, the disorderly remains of Franklin's corps were streaming out of the south gap eastward toward the Catoctin Mountains. Couch's corps, still spread out on the road behind them, could be of little use, given the headlong retreat of the larger force in front. Forming any sort of cohesive defense line against the Confederate troops pouring through the gap proved impossible, and Franklin was mortally wounded trying to rally his forces, hoping against hope to recover what was beyond recall.

D.H. Hill's division set the initial ambuscade in Turner's Gap. Although it maintained the element of surprise and poured rifle and cannon fire into the oncoming columns, fighting became desperate and the outcome hung in the balance. The Union First and Second Corps found themselves bottled up in a mountain pass and stretched out along the road piercing it in much the same way Franklin's corps did in the south notch. The Federal troops faced fire from the front and the steep sides of both ridges. Longstreet was prepared to render all possible support, but could push the bulk of his forces into the gap only as the Union forces began to fall back eastward on the National Road. Each side had perhaps 30,000 men engaged by the afternoon of the 17th and much of the fighting degenerated into small-unit engagements as it had in the mêlée at Crampton's Gap. Repeated Federal counterattacks from the left delayed the forward advance of Longstreet's corps deep into the gap. Intense fighting with heavy losses on both sides continued through the day until nightfall precluded further combat.

Although Longstreet's corps had smashed its way through most of the gap, the Union First and Second Corps might have blunted the Confederate attack eastward along the National Road the following day and thus seriously interrupted Lee's timetable, had not Jackson's corps, having moved swiftly north along several trails leading to the National Road, hit the Union columns early on the morning of the 18th in flank and rear. The Union cavalry, most of it situated on the far western side of South Mountain, failed to provide the crucial screen for the infantry components when it was most needed, allowing Jackson to assess and exploit the vulnerability of the foe's main force. The head-to-head slugfest through Turner's Gap abruptly turned into an encirclement operation as the main body of McClellan's army was caught between the anvil from the west and the pulverizing hammer from the south. By midday, more than half of the 70,000 troops who had marched in the great columns westward from Frederick short days prior had been engulfed by the converging forces. Storms of lead swept mercilessly through the Union ranks.

McClellan had lost control of his army, and each Federal general had to make do as best he could in a muddle of ghastly *sauve qui peut*.[24] Hooker's First Corps ceased being an organized fighting force within two hours of Jackson's fearful attack. "Fighting Joe" departed the fields of fury trailing clouds of glory. The Second Corps was badly mauled, as the component brigades, devastated and exhausted, began to fall apart. The Army of the Potomac faced catastrophe. No army, no matter how valiant, could maintain discipline in such murderous cross-fire.

Death Lays His Icy hand

Lee now held all the trumps. With his shattered army turned, McClellan had little choice but to attempt to stem the flow of the gray tide along the National Road. Retreat was out of the question since the loss of Baltimore or Washington, and perhaps both, would have ensued, with the attendant irreparable political consequences. Unable to gauge the situation in western Maryland accurately, Halleck in Washington continued to urge McClellan on. Self-possessed as usual, Little Mac accepted the *coup de grâce* of the once beloved army he had forged in the crucible of fire. Decimated units lacked officers, and ruinous casualties left captains in charge of the offscourings of

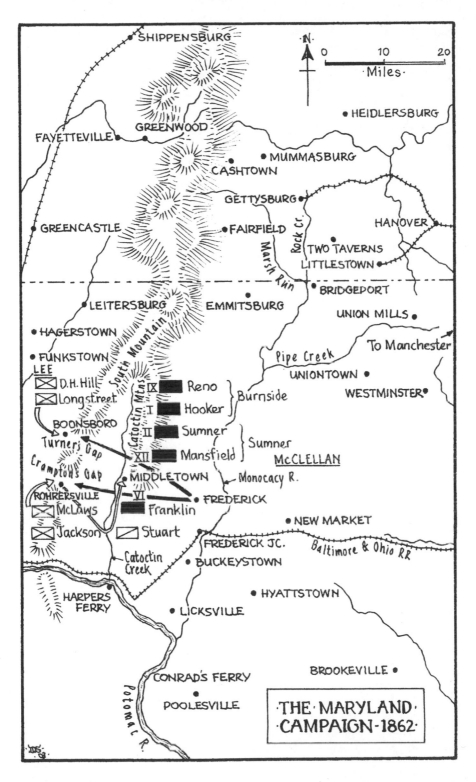

THE MARYLAND
CAMPAIGN·1862

brigades, and sergeants commanding companies. Played out men with no stomach left for the fight ignored McClellan's orders to close ranks or simply "skedaddled" to nearby woods and towns. The despondent, the morally stunned, and the walking wounded streamed back into Frederick by the thousands.

Union officers rallied what forces they had as best they could, launching a few half-hearted and fruitless counterattacks against the imposing gray echelons. Hastily assembled Union columns assaulted Jackson's corps, now reinforced by Hill and McLaws, just west of the Catoctin Mountains along the National Road. With the Confederates occupying the high ground and regiments positioned on either side of the thoroughfare, the final outcome could hardly have been in doubt. The action was to be the final gasp of the Army of the Potomac, a forlorn hope that would mark its elimination as a fighting force.

In a final mocking gesture, Stuart positioned his redoubtable cavalry corps behind the Union army due west of Frederick, ready to chop up the fleeing blue masses that would inevitably be flooding back. The horsemen did not have to wait long. Pockets of resistance broke quickly as Union troops were caught between the Scylla of murderous artillery and rifle fire from the front and the Charybdis of grisly saber charges from the rear. The partly intact Twelfth Corps swiftly disintegrated in the killing fields. Shattered remnants of the army trudged back into the defenses of Washington as they had in the wake of the defeat at Second Manassas, only this time their numbers were greatly reduced and their spirits broken completely. They had had a belly-full of war.

McClellan, the incurable romantic with an inflated ego, had also had enough. Defeat would bring out the worst in him, which was indeed pretty bad. It was well said of Little Mac that he was not a real general but merely a bumped-up captain, a vain and unstable man with some military knowledge who sat a horse well and pined for the presidency.[25] While the Army of the Potomac was still in its death throes, McClellan abandoned the field as cravenly as John Pope had done in the wake of defeat at Second Manassas and for which the former had unflinchingly chided the latter. McClellan's political ambitions and concern about history's judgment, rather than the grim fate of his once-worshipful men, were foremost in his mind. Fleeing back to Washington, McClellan began without hesitation to ascribe blame for the disaster to others, above all to President Lincoln, whom he declared unfit to assume any direction over military men. McClellan would soon become Lincoln's chief nemesis and a leading detractor of the administration's policies. Unabashedly accusing Lincoln of throwing away the war in his gambles against "impossible odds," McClellan eagerly joined in the political scheming that fall against an increasingly isolated president.

"My God!" exclaimed a distraught President Lincoln, as patchy reports and horrifying rumors about the military disasters in western Maryland poured into the capital in a torrent of incessant panic. "What will the country say?"

What indeed? Lincoln was far too astute a politician not to grasp the heartbreaking consequences, particularly his inability, given the state of affairs, to issue the Emancipation Proclamation. The prior July, Lincoln notified his Cabinet that he planned to use the executive war powers to seize enemy property and to issue the proclamation of emancipation for the manumission of slaves in states in rebellion against the Federal Government. Contending that emancipation had at last become a military necessity, essential to the preservation of the Union, he insisted that "decisive and extensive measures" be adopted.[26] The slaves were a source of considerable strength to those they served, Lincoln asserted, and a manifesto of manumission would undermine the Confederate war effort. More significantly, though, this great leap forward would furnish the moral clarity many considered lacking in the administration's policies. Although the Cabinet concurred in principle, Secretary of State William H. Seward counseled deferment of the proclamation until the watershed political realignment could be bolstered by significant military success. Otherwise, argued Seward, foreign powers were bound to view the proclamation, "as the last measure of an exhausted government, a cry for help... our last shriek, on the retreat."[27] Lincoln, displaying his customary way with words, granted Seward the point, quipping that, "not louder shrieks to pitying heaven are cast, than when a government breathes its last."[28] Clever words, these, that would return to haunt.

Events moved at a breathtaking pace that portentous fall of 1862, whereby one day's sensationalism often became conventional wisdom on the morrow. Fields of bloodshed and dramatic political scenes coalesced in a kaleidoscopic patchwork of tragedy for the disintegrating United States. Stuart, largely relieved of screening an army operating in enemy country, could joyride his cavalry almost to his heart's content. His first move was to the north into Pennsylvania where he burned Carlisle, tore up the Baltimore and Ohio Railroad, and raided the key railroad hub at Harrisburg, destroying the Susquehanna bridge in the bargain. Next, moving southeast, the army's mounted eyes and ears rode the wave of popular sentiment around Baltimore. Lee took Stuart's advice to relieve the city of its "foreign yoke," and the Confederate crusade there was conducted with virtual impunity since the road thither lay undefended by regular forces. An advance guard marched in amidst cheering crowds. The Federal East had effectively been isolated from the Federal West, and Lee's successful strategy corresponded uncannily to the Union's "Tennessee Plan" to cut the South in twain along the Charleston and Memphis railroad. Lee, for his part, maintained his usual composure and equanimity in the thick of conquest and slaughter. "Now I just wish," Lee was heard to remark to his subordinate officers in what appeared a justification of his personal goal in the conflict, "these people will finally let us alone."

The sequence of momentous military episodes brought Confederate hopes of European diplomatic recognition to fulfilment. Lee's spectacular successes convinced British and French leaders that Federal arms could never restore the Union. The victories in Maryland were so complete that foreign recognition was no longer vital. One way or the other, the Confederacy would reap a full harvest of laurels.

To be sure, though, Britain had a dog in the fight. History would later show that largely because the United States, the synonym for democracy in the mid-19th century, had failed politically, the proposed British Reform Bill that was on the parliamentary agenda, no longer had any real chance of passing. In the coming years, most observers agreed that stoppage of the bill was the direct result of Confederate victory. Lord Palmerston, firmly in control, had hitherto been chiefly responsible for Britain's continued neutrality. Able in all likelihood to carry Britain into war on the strength of widespread elite sympathy for the South alone, he no longer attempted to refute supplementary arguments for intervention. For a number of reasons, some in his Cabinet pressured him to undertake action even prior to the great Confederate victories in the late summer and early fall of 1862. Dreading the prospect of civil unrest in manufacturing towns, Chancellor of the Exchequer William E. Gladstone, for instance, advocated immediate termination of the war and a subsequent arrangement to guarantee unabated cotton deliveries to Britain from the American South.

The manifestation of Confederate offensive strength would surely also disabuse the U.S. Federal Government of any foolish notions about expeditions against Canada. Admiration for the South now fostered a willingness on the part of British elites to assist the Confederacy tangibly and to bestow upon the young political entity the recognition many felt it deserved. The governing elite was in the main realistic, though, not sentimental, about foreign policy. Lee's victories of 1862 promoted the commingling of cold-blooded realism about national interests with a warm-hearted outlook toward the Southern aristocracy. In short, British intervention in the Civil War in 1862 involved the irresistible combination of principle and pragmatism.

No less so for France. For over a year Napoleon III had contemplated tendering recognition with subsequent military assistance for the dual purpose of ensuring the uninterrupted flow of cotton across the Atlantic and establishing French suzerainty in Mexico. Always the sporting man, the French autocrat intended his Mexican adventure to bring about the partial restoration of the empire in North America that his uncle had unloaded onto the United States for a song. Economic pressures were building in France, notwithstanding widespread popular feelings of kinship with republicanism in North America. French ministers by 1862 were publicly deploring the shortage of cotton for delivery to French textile mills and urging pro-active policies to ensure the continuation of supplies allegedly so badly needed. Yet, Napoleon III resolved to move forward only in the wake of prior explicit British recognition of the Confederacy.

Once the British Cabinet showed its hand, the Emperor of the French eagerly accepted the Confederacy's offer of July 1862 to deliver several hundred thousand bales of cotton and to conclude an alliance against the liberal regime of Benito Juarez in Mexico in return for diplomatic recognition and naval assistance in breaking the Union blockade in North America. Within a week of Lord Palmerston's announcement on the last day of September that the campaign in Maryland had a "great effect" on the state of political affairs and that Her Majesty's Government intended to address the contending parties with an aim to producing an arrangement on the basis of separation, the French Government signed a comprehensive treaty with the Confederate plenipotentiary in Paris, John Slidell, consisting of sweeping economic, political and military provisions.[29] As British officials were still meeting with the American Minister in London, Charles Francis Adams, and Secretary of State Seward in Washington, both of whom indignantly carped that the European aristocracy and commercial classes were determined to see the United States go to pieces, French naval squadrons were ordered to begin attacking U.S. Navy ships in North American waters without prior warning. Realists that they were, Lincoln and his Cabinet had been aware that military assistance and overt intervention would follow diplomatic recognition for the Confederacy as surely as these had for the fledgling United States in 1778 during the War of Independence. The destruction of the Army of the Potomac was a bloody refutation of the President's military judgment, and would cast open the gates for all his enemies to move in for the political kill. Demands for negotiation to settle the war would be loud and strident, simply impossible to ignore. Indeed, Lincoln felt control of the war and the country slipping from him.

The shift in British foreign policy was conspicuous in Gladstone's celebrated speech in Newcastle in October. "President Jefferson Davis and the valiant leaders of the Confederate States of America," the imperturbable minister proclaimed, "have made an army; they are making a navy; and they have made what is more than either; they have made a nation."[30] It seemed the British Cabinet had merely been waiting for the proper moment to accord recognition. At that point, it was reasoned, most in the North, including the abolitionists and the hard war men, would concur in their heart-of-hearts that Britain really had no choice.[31] For the British Cabinet, that moment came in the fall of 1862. By the end of the year, Mexico would become a French colony with the blessing of the Confederate States of America. The Monroe Doctrine ceased to exist, as Napoleon III, the self-proclaimed "man of destiny" reestablished his French imperium on the American Continent.

In October, the usually sluggish Confederate commanders in the western theater, Braxton Bragg and Edmund Kirby Smith, appeared to have been given a new lease on life by the stimulating news from the east and abroad. Confederate forces continued their advance through Kentucky, and having seized Lexington and Frankfort, pushed on to Louisville. The tide turned rapidly and Louisville was occupied in the last week of October. The multiple crises in Washington caused pervasive despondency in the Union forces deployed in the most crucial border state, and Federal authority there swiftly waned. The Union's Kentucky disaster represented the proverbial icing on the French *tarte*. The November Congressional elections brought resounding defeat for the Republicans, and the new majority of peace Democrats announced it would demand an end to the war on the basis of dissolution.

The Reality

Special Order No. 191 was not a clever *ruse de guerre*, of course, but rather a genuine and highly sensitive document of substantial intelligence value to the Union commander. Lee had come north to force the Federals to attack on ground of his own choosing, anticipating another victory of the order of the Second Battle of Manassas, if not greater. Nor did Britain or France afford diplomatic recognition to the Confederacy or intervene directly in the Civil War. Britain bided its time, harboring the glittering illusion that even without European assistance, the independence of the South was assured. France, for its part, would not move until Britain did.

Convinced that the lethargic McClellan would grant him ample time, Lee divided his army into several detachments that could not support one another in the event of an enemy attack. True, the Union army did move against the vulnerable foe, but McClellan would not have been McClellan if he did not drag his feet, confusing swift reaction with organizational tidiness, even in such overwhelmingly favorable circumstances. The opportunity could scarcely have been greater, for McClellan had caught the Army of Northern Virginia's main body north of the Potomac in deployable strength of 25,000 troops, the separated commands of Longstreet, Hill and McLaws, with his own concentrated force of 87,000.[32] The outcome of the engagement could hardly have been in doubt had McClellan not hesitated. Following this inexplicable delay, McClellan's powerful columns smashed through both passes of South Mountain to confront the hastily consolidated Confederate army at Antietam Creek. On those fields of fire, McClellan would in all likelihood have destroyed Lee's army even then, had he not taken his time getting his troops into assault positions and had the subsequent attacks been properly coordinated. September 17, 1862, the day of the Battle of Antietam, was the bloodiest in American history. Somehow, Lee's defense line held and a seemingly hopeless situation was salvaged. The Army of Northern Virginia would march and fight again another day.

Bibliography

Cowley, Robert, ed., *What If? The World's Foremost Military Historians Imagine What Might Have Been* (Putnam, New York, 1999).

Cowley, Robert, ed., *With My Face to the Enemy: Perspectives on the Civil War* (Putnam, New York, 2001).

Crook, D.P., *The North, the South, and the Powers 1861–1865* (Wiley, New York, 1974).

Fishel, Edwin C., *The Secret War for the Union: The Untold Story of Military Intelligence in the Civil War* (Houghton Mifflin, Boston, 1996).

Foote, Shelby, *The Civil War: A Narrative*, 3 vols., (Scribner's, New York, 1958).

Garraty, John A., *1,001 Things Everyone Should Know About American History* (Doubleday, New York, 1989)

Hearn, Chester G., *Six Years of Hell: Harpers Ferry During the Civil War* (Louisiana State University Press, Baton Rouge, 1996).

Heysinger, Isaac Winter, *Antietam and the Maryland and Virginia Campaigns of 1862* (Neal Publishing Company, New York, 1912).

MacCartney, Clarence Edward, *Little Mac: The Life of General George B. McClellan* (Dorrance, Philadelphia, 1940)

McPherson, James M., *Battlecry of Freedom* (Ballantine Books, New York, 1989).

Myers, William Starr, *General George Brinton McClellan* (Appleton-Century, New York, 1934).

Owsley, Frank Lawrence, *King Cotton Diplomacy: Foreign Relations of the Confederate States of America* (University of Chicago Press, Chicago, 1959).

Palmer, Michael A., *Lee Moves North: Robert E. Lee on the Offensive* (Wiley, New York, 1998).

Sears, Stephen W., *Landscape Turned Red* (Ticknor and Fields, New Haven, 1983).

Shapiro, Larry, ed., *Abraham Lincoln: Mystic Chords of Memory* (Book-of-the-Month Club, New York, 1984)

Swinton, William, *Campaigns of the Army of the Potomac* (Charles B. Richardson, New York, 1866)

Vanauken, Sheldon, *The Glittering Illusion: English Sympathy for the Southern Confederacy* (Churchman Publishing, Folkestone, 1988).

Wert, Jeffrey, "I Am So Unlike Other Folks," *Civil War Times*, April 1989, vol. 28, No. 2, pp. 14–21

Woodworth, Steven E., *Davis and Lee at War* (University of Kansas Press, Lawrence, 1995).

Notes

1. The author would like to thank John K. Rowland for his helpful comments.
2. McPherson, *Battlecry of Freedom*, p. 551.
3. Quoted in Owsley, *King Cotton Diplomacy*, p. 186.
4. McPherson, *Battlecry of Freedom*, p. 551.
5. James Russell Lowell, *Poems* (Houghton Mifflin, Boston, 1891), II, p. 296.
6. MacCartney, *Little Mac*, p. 231.
7. Lee's two major subordinate commanders were James Longstreet and Thomas J. "Stonewall" Jackson who commanded the First and Second Corps respectively.
8. Myers, *General George Brinton McClellan*, p. 358.
9. Quoted in Heysinger, *Antietam and the Maryland and Virginia Campaigns of 1862*, pp. 56–7.
10. Quoted in Woodworth, *Davis and Lee at War*, p. 188.

11. Quoted in MacCartney, *Little Mac*, p. 239.
12. Swinton, *Campaigns of the Army of the Potomac*, pp. 197–8.
13. MacCartney, *Little Mac*, p. 240.
14. Fishel, *The Secret War for the Union*, p. 223.
15. Stephen W. Sears, "The Last Word on the Lost Order," in Robert Cowley, ed., *With My Face to the Enemy*, p. 150.
16. Hearn, *Six Years of Hell*, p. 129.
17. Wert, "I Am So Unlike Other Folks," p. 19.
18. James M. McPherson, "If the Lost Order Hadn't Been Lost," in Robert Cowley, ed., *What If? The World's Foremost Military Historians Imagine What Might Have Been*, pp. 232–3.
19. Quoted in Fishel, *The Secret War for the Union,* p. 222.
*20. J.E.B. Stuart, *Join the Cavalry: War as I Knew It* (Neal Publishing Company, New York, 1880), pp. 267–8.
21. Quoted in Foote, *The Civil War: A Narrative*, Vol. 1, p. 674.
22. Sears, *Landscape Turned Red*, pp. 119–20.
23. Heysinger, *Antietam and the Maryland and Virginia Campaigns of 1862*, pp. 82–3.
24. A French term meaning "save yourselves", the worst thing to be heard on any battlefield in any language, the cry that all is lost.
25. Garraty, *1,001 Things Everyone Should Know About American History*, p. 164.
26. Shapiro, *Abraham Lincoln: Mystic Chords of Memory*, pp. 45–6.
27. Quoted in Sears, *Landscape Turned Red*, pp. 44–5.
*28. *The Complete War Memoirs of Abraham Lincoln* (Freedom House, New York, 1925), p. 238.
*29. G.P. Gooch, *Gladstone and Palmerston* (London: Churchman, 1922), p. 231.
30. Quoted in Crook, *The North, the South, and the Powers 1861-1865*, pp. 227–8.
31. Vanauken, *The Glittering Illusion: English Sympathy for the Southern Confederacy*, p. 128.
32. Woodworth, *Davis and Lee at War*, p. 191.

4
WHEN THE BOTTOM FELL OUT
The Crisis of 1862

Michael R. Hathaway

The Battle of Frederick, the "Saratoga"[1] of the Confederacy's war for independence, happened because of horses. Not because of their employment as cavalry mounts or drawers of artillery, or even as draft horses for military supply wagons. Through them, mighty Mars found Fortuna's slippery ball turning under his feet.

The commander of the Army of Northern Virginia, General Robert E. Lee, was very nearly seriously hurt by his horse just after the Battle of Second Manassas on August 31. Lee and his staff had stopped and Lee had dismounted to view a part of the battlefield when a force of Union cavalry appeared suddenly over a nearby hill. The staff reacted, and Lee's horse started, nearly throwing him violently to the ground. But he escaped uninjured.[2]

Lieutenant General Thomas J. "Stonewall" Jackson was not so fortunate. Jackson was thrown by his new horse on September 6, 1862, as he was about to ride into Frederick.[3] Jackson's head injury, a concussion, kept him in bed for three days. Lee could not be sure that his "strong right arm" would be able to command the critical operation he was considering, to drive Union garrisons out of Martinsburg and Harpers Ferry in order to open communications through the Shenandoah Valley. That injury was a key to Lee's decision to accept Longstreet's cautious counsel to "... stand still and let the damned Yankees come to us," at his commander's conference on September 9.[4]

Union General George B. McClellan was moving west quickly—he had left Washington for Rockville on the 7th, and his main forces were only 15 miles from Frederick on the 9th.[5] If Lee had been injured and passive, this could have been a critical oversight. But Lee was healthy and active, and took notice that, on the 7th, a strong Union force had beaten back Colonel Thomas Munford and the 7th and 12th Virginia Cavalry Regiments from Poolesville.[6] On the 8th, he ordered his cavalry commander, General J.E.B. Stuart, to punch through Pleasonton's Union cavalry screen and uncover the strength and disposition of the oncoming Union forces.[7] While that effort failed due to the strength of the Union forces—in the face of Stuart's unsupported Confederate cavalry, the Union cavalry was closely backed by infantry and artillery—it produced the greatest single stroke of fortune for either side in the war.

This was the famous "Lost Dispatch." It was a copy of McClellan's report to Union General-in-Chief Henry W. Halleck which Private James Thomas Faulkner of the 6th Virginia found lying on the road in a blood-spattered dispatch case.[8] Drafted late on the 8th, captured during the night when a Confederate cavalry patrol surprised a courier behind Union lines, and delivered to Lee on the morning of the 9th, it told him two critical facts: McClellan was in command and the unified Union army was approaching on a wide front. It was a key to his decision to fight at Frederick.[9]

At his commander's conference on the afternoon of the 9th, Lee weighed his options. Stuart's report of the speed and scope of the Union advance meant that even a smartly executed operation to oust the hold-out Union garrisons from Martinsburg and Harpers Ferry would make it difficult for him to re-concentrate his army in time to face the oncoming Union forces. If the western operation did not go perfectly, Lee realized he would lose the operational initiative and risk defeat in detail. However, the still-groggy Jackson was in no shape to lead a complex operation that had to commence immediately if it were to work at all.

Longstreet's cautious advice, Jackson's shaky condition, favorable ground at Frederick, the unexpected speed of the Union advance, and Confederate possession of McClellan's dispatch to Halleck outlining Union plans and dispositions, made offering battle at Frederick the preferable course of action. The Lost Dispatch revealed that McClellan was back in command. It also explained the unexpected speed of the Union advance, because Lee knew that McClellan was the favorite of the Army of the Potomac. His return would have had a galvanic effect on troop morale and his organizational skills had apparently already combined the shattered wreckage left after Second Manassas with the veteran units returning from the Peninsula and turned them into a vast field army moving toward Lee with speed and coordination.

Lee realized that the Army of the Potomac was dispersed in a fan across the Maryland countryside, while his Army of Northern Virginia was concentrated at Frederick. If he chose to fight at Frederick, and he could obtain tactical surprise, he could fight just a part of the Army of the Potomac with his entire force. The combination of Confederate numerical superiority with the shock of surprise promised a decisive victory.

Planning to achieve tactical surprise, Lee decided to use Frederick and the country just to its west and north to conceal his main forces, leaving only screening forces forward by the Monocacy River. He knew Union observation posts on Sugarloaf Mountain to the east would detect and report visible heavy troop concentrations, and he decided to lure the Union van across the Monocacy and make them fight uphill with the river at their back.

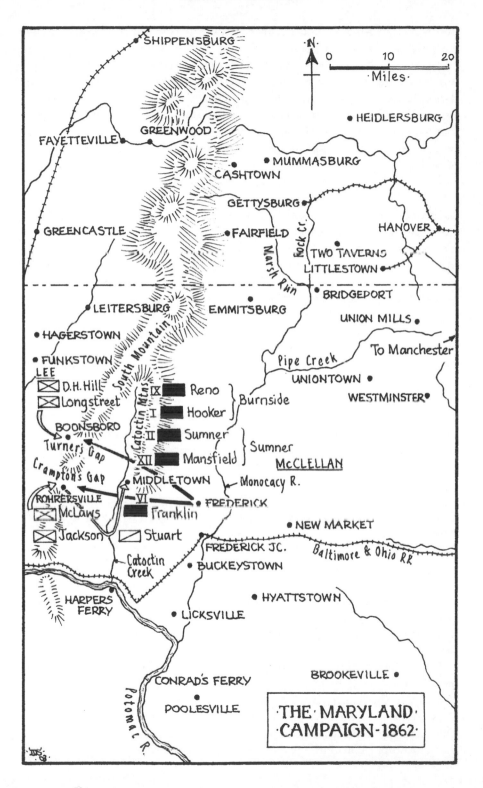

THE·MARYLAND·CAMPAIGN·1862·

Best of all, Jackson had shouted down his doctors, and was back in the saddle with his wits about him again.

Thanks to Union Generals Reno and Burnside, the plan worked. Reno was impetuous and Burnside was just unlucky. About noon on September 13, Reno, commanding IX Corps, the lead element of the Army of the Potomac, crossed the Monocacy on the only bridge still standing, the stone Jug Bridge that carried the National Road over the Monocacy and into Frederick. He pushed through the Confederate screen with Crook's 2d Brigade of Cox's Kanawha Division.[10]

Burnside almost got both corps in his Right Wing, IX Corps and Hooker's I Corps, across before they got hit. It was like Second Manassas, except Longstreet got into position first. Part of his corps came through town and part maneuvered under cover around the south side of Frederick. Longstreet set up in a line blocking the National Road and running for a mile and a half from north-northeast to south-southwest along a ridge above Carroll Creek. He refused his right flank south of Mount Olivet Cemetery. Only John Bell Hood's Texas division was pushed ahead so it was clearly visible to the Union forces coming uphill from the Jug Bridge.

But this time, Longstreet was the anvil, and Jackson was the hammer.

Reno was startled to see the mass of Confederate troops come quickly out and form line of battle across the National Road in front of Frederick. He apparently thought he was facing only a substantial rearguard and not half of the Army of Northern Virginia. He halted his column, shook IX Corps out into line of battle, and went the remaining mile up the hill into the attack. Burnside crossed the Jug Bridge, riding with Hooker at the head of I Corps, and ordered Hooker to move his corps northwest around Frederick, still in column, to turn what he thought was the left flank of the visible Confederate line.

But Hooker never got the chance fully to execute that order. Neither Reno nor Burnside understood that they were facing almost the entire Army of Northern Virginia. In fact, Jackson's corps was under cover along the Woodsboro Road leading north from Frederick. Once Reno was fully engaged, Jackson wheeled his corps to his right, dressed his lines, and came down upon Reno's right flank, collapsing his line. Reno's fleeing troops threw Hooker's lead division into chaos. And the Rebel artillery, concentrated on Longstreet's right, had the whole confused mass enfiladed, killed Hooker, and knocked apart several attempted rallies by parts of IX Corps.

Jug Bridge was re-christened for all time as Burnside Bridge with Union blood, most of it spilled by Hood's divisional artillery, under Major Frobel, particularly the South Carolina German Artillery, which was positioned to fire straight down the National Road along the long axis of Burnside Bridge. They did fearful execution, killing Burnside himself at the west end of the Bridge, and preventing the rest of I Corps from entering the battle.

McClellan arrived late on the field. He was furious that Burnside had gotten most of his Right Wing chewed up to no gain, and had gotten killed himself in the bargain. McClellan had lost a wing commander and a corps commander. He was confronted with the fact that the other bridges leading onto the battlefield were destroyed, both the covered bridge and the Baltimore & Ohio Railroad bridge, and he concluded that he was not going to try to push fresh forces back over Burnside Bridge.

There the fighting ended on September 13, but there was one more act to be played out.

McClellan sent orders on the evening of the 13th to Couch's Division to threaten Lee's line of communications by crossing the Monocacy at its mouth over the C&O Canal aqueduct and heading for Point of Rocks. But the next day, Couch found Walker's Division of Longstreet's Corps, supported by part of the Washington (Louisiana) Artillery, dug in on the north shore. Union Brigadier General Charles Devens won his posthumous Medal of Honor leading his First Brigade's Massachusetts regiments to a toehold on the north end of the aqueduct. But they couldn't drive through Walker's North Carolinians, and the survivors had to pull back across the bloody aqueduct.

With one of his corps ruined, another in disarray, and no advantageous way to resume the fight at Frederick, McClellan took counsel of his fears, continuing to believe that Lee had superior forces in the field, and drew back to positions extending from south of the Monocacy aqueduct up through Sugarloaf Mountain, Urbana, and New Market, to Liberty. He placed I Corps and the remnants of IX Corps, formerly Burnside's Right Wing, on the high ground east and south of Frederick and re-designated them his center, and shifted Sumner's II Corps and Mansfield's XII Corps to the north, to become his new right wing. Franklin's VI Corps, along with Couch's roughed-up force, formed his left wing. With his center and left posted on readily defensible ground, and more forces coming up, his main concern was that Lee would now turn north to Harrisburg.

While less than a quarter of the Army of the Potomac was ever engaged during the Battle of Frederick, the newspapers gave the impression that the whole army had been defeated once again. The loss of senior officers was particularly shocking. Even though Lee, worried about his supply lines after the Monocacy aqueduct fight, merely stood fast at Frederick, while caring for his wounded, burying the dead, gathering up stragglers, and stocking up on provisions, the North was thrown into a panic.

Lincoln was in a fix. He was determined to continue the war. He felt he must replace McClellan, but could not do so while the army was in the field facing Lee. He ordered McClellan to send forces to Harrisburg to defend the capital of Pennsylvania, and worried that Lee could march through the gap between Liberty and Harrisburg and head for York and Philadelphia.

McClellan had been given command over the Harpers Ferry garrison the day before the battle at Frederick, but communications had by then been cut by the Confederate advance. After the battle, he sent couriers with orders for both Brigadier General Julius White at Martinsburg and Colonel David Miles at Harpers Ferry to withdraw north by way of Hagerstown to Cumberland, Pennsylvania.[11] This withdrawal was accomplished over September 16 and 17, with Lee learning of it just as the Army of Northern Virginia was again fit for action.

The withdrawal of these Union garrisons opened Lee's line of communications up the Shenandoah Valley, without him having to take offensive action to achieve it. Once this line of communications was opened, Lee did not have to remain near Frederick to forestall any Union attempt to cut his communications east of the Blue Ridge Mountains and south of the Potomac. He was again free to maneuver.

With the combined Harpers Ferry and Martinsburg garrisons, totaling more than 13,000 men, back at Cumberland blocking the Cumberland Valley route to Harrisburg, McClellan responded to Lincoln's directive to protect Harrisburg by putting Fitz John Porter's V Corps on trains and rushing them to the Pennsylvania capital. But this left a huge gap between Harrisburg and the right flank of the Army of the Potomac at Liberty. Lee knew the gap was there and that there was no natural line of defense for Union forces short of the Susquehanna River. He also knew the Army of the Potomac had to remain between his forces and the Baltimore–Washington axis.

That put McClellan in a vise. Once Lee got his supply lines running through the Valley, he moved quickly up to Gettysburg, leaving Frederick on the 19th. Supplied through Hagerstown and Blue Ridge Summit, he paused only briefly in Gettysburg before heading up the York Pike for York, Pennsylvania, on Monday 22d, a location from which he could attempt a crossing of the Susquehanna with Philadephia and Wilmington in his sights, and threaten Baltimore to his south and Harrisburg to his north. McClellan paralleled Lee's line of march to the south and east, continuing to cover Washington and Baltimore. Though tempted to attack at Gettysburg, being down effectively two corps in strength, he thought better of it, and decided to leave I Corps to cover Baltimore while taking the rest of the Army of the Potomac across the Susquehanna at Conowingo Station and up to Lancaster, where he dug in on the 25th. He deployed along the northeast bank of the Susquehanna at Columbia, opposite the pickets of the Army of Northern Virginia in Wrightsville. There operations halted, with Lee content to live off the rich Pennsylvania countryside and McClellan's Union forces divided to defend against the many threats posed by Lee's centrally located Confederate army.

This marked the end of major military operations in the east. But for the intervention of chance in the form of Confederate commanders' horses, events could have unfolded much differently. Unlike Shakespeare's *Richard III*, perhaps in this case horses—and chance—saved the Confederacy.[12]

The Crisis

After the secession of the future Confederate states, the Republicans had held a dominant majority in the House of Representatives, with War Democrats voting with their more than 115 Republican colleagues in favor of the measures necessary to prosecute the war. They were opposed by a small number of Peace Democrats, who became known as "Copperheads," because their opposition to the war was characterized as opposition to the Union and impugned as treasonous. Thus, they were likened to venomous reptiles.[13]

The Union loss of the Battle of Frederick and the movement of the Confederate Army of Northern Virginia into southeastern Pennsylvania at York had immediate political consequences. Voting for the 38th Congress had already commenced, with Oregon casting its votes on June 2. Maine voted on September 8, and Ohio, Pennsylvania, Indiana and Iowa on October 14. Delaware was to vote on November 1, and Illinois, Kansas, Massachusetts, Michigan, Minnesota, Missouri, New Jersey, New York, and Wisconsin were to vote on November 4. (The remaining states would not vote for the 38th Congress until various dates in 1863, and the consequences of the situation would work their way through the political system before those states voted.)[14]

The results through October 14 were not good for the Republicans and pro-Union forces. In the 37th Congress, Maine had a solid Republican delegation. They lost a seat to reapportionment for the 38th Congress, and one of the five remaining seats had gone Democrat.[15] Ohio was a hotbed of Peace Democrat activity, and the Union defeat at Frederick and the advance of the Army of Northern Virginia into southeast Pennsylvania had emboldened them at the polls. The Peace Democrat (Copperhead) firebrand, Clement L. Vallandigham, had been re-elected. The Republican candidates carried only three of 19 Ohio districts, down from 13 of 21 districts in the 1860 election.[16] Indiana was even worse. Union/Republican candidates carried only one of 11 districts, compared to seven of 11 in the previous election.[17]

Pennsylvania's election was disrupted by the presence of the Army of Northern Virginia at York. Voters in the 15th District, where York was located, did not get to cast their votes, depriving the Lincoln Administration of the support of Representative Joseph Bailey, a War Democrat who could be counted on to back Administration policies in the House. Terrified by the presence of the war on their soil, Pennsylvania voters had elected 17 Democrat candidates to the House in the 23 of 24 districts contested.[18]

In Iowa, five of the six seats were in Union/Republican hands. Iowa had gained four seats in reapportionment, and the two seats up for election in 1860 had both gone Republican. That was how things stood, with a net decrease in those states in Union/Republican seats of eighteen.[19]

Before the rest of the election could be contested, Union fortunes were dealt another tremendous blow.

Since opening fire on Fort Sumter on April 12, 1861, the Confederacy had two primary foreign policy goals: foreign intervention to break the Union blockade of Confederate ports and international recognition as a sovereign state.[20] Great Britain, France, and industrializing Europe were the major export market for the South's principal agricultural product, cotton, and this dependence was expected to favor intervention and recognition.

As one of the key components of former Union General-in-Chief Winfield Scott's "Anaconda Plan," the Union blockade of the South's ports was intended to cut the substantially agricultural Confederacy off from foreign-manufactured war materials and from revenues earned from agricultural exports. The blockade, at the outset, was thinly manned and leaky.

Rather than attempting to send the largest possible shipments of cotton and other exports through the blockade, the Confederacy adopted a quiet policy of withholding cotton from export while its agents and friends in Europe blamed the cotton shortage on the Union blockade. This artificially induced shortage was expected seriously to hurt the growing European textile industries and their substantial work forces. Southern agents urged recognition of the Confederate States of America as a sovereign nation and intervention to re-open the maritime supply lines over which the bales of Southern cotton reached European mills.

This plan did not work as expected, because the bumper Southern cotton crops of 1859 and 1860 had created warehoused surpluses held in Europe of raw cotton and finished cloth not yet sold for manufacture into garments and other consumer goods.[21] Thus, the shortage of cotton the Confederate policy was expected to induce did not occur until 1862.

Great Britain was not disposed to recognize the Confederacy until it had in fact established its independence, but Confederate leaders wanted recognition to help secure that independence. Confederate agents and U.S. diplomats battled in the drawing rooms and chanceries of Europe to gain or prevent, respectively, such recognition. Confederate hopes and Union fears of British recognition rose and fell with each belligerent's military fortunes.

In the spring of 1862, Confederate prospects seemed dim, with the Union capture of New Orleans in May casting a particularly dark pall of gloom over their agents' efforts. But Confederate fortunes began to turn with General Thomas J. "Stonewall" Jackson's Valley Campaign, which culminated in the victorious battle of Winchester on May 25.[22] Public opinion in the North was temporarily thrown into panic by the presence of Confederate forces on the offensive just south of the Potomac.[23]

The foundation for further Confederate success was laid on June 1, 1862, with the appointment of General Robert E. Lee to command the Army of Northern Virginia, to succeed the wounded General Joseph E. Johnston.[24] After reorganizing his army, Lee moved to expel McClellan's Army of the Potomac from the Peninsula. Starting on June 26, a series of battles that have come to be known as the Seven Days combined turning movements and

Fort York, Toronto, captured by the Americans in both 1812 and 1862.
In the background is the Canadian National (CN) Tower.

The Town Hall Geneva, Switzerland, where peace was signed in August 1863.
Despite their victories, the British were keen to end the costly war with the North.

Above: C.S.S. *Virginia* exchanges fire with U.S.S. *Monitor* at First Hampton Roads, March 9, 1862. Little more than a month later, C.S.S. *Hart of the Confederacy* would use a spar torpedo in ramming and crippling the Union ironclad at Second Hampton Roads. *Courtesy of the Naval Historical Center.*

Above right: Confederate Secretary of the Navy, Stephen Mallory, created the ironclads that won independence and international recognition for his nation, earning him the sobriquet of the "Southern Themistocles." *Courtesy of the Library of Congress.*

Right: General Robert E. Lee. His victories ensured that the Confederacy would achieve its independence.

McClellan had his weaknesses, but few called his organizational skills into question, nor doubted the magic his name invoked with the soldiers he led.

JOHN BULL MAKES A DISCOVERY.

The Confederacy's leaders always hoped to gain foreign support because they believed that economic considerations would outweigh opposition to slavery. Here the cartoonist has the British stereotype John Bull comparing the supposedly "woolly hair" of a slave with the quality of the cotton in the bale.

A cartoonist's view of
argument and indecision
among the North's leaders.

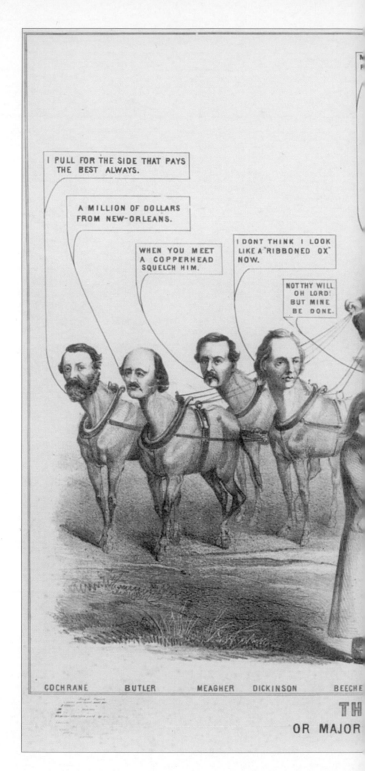

GREELY   LINCOLN   SUMNER   CHASE   WELLES   SEWARD

AVE OF THE UNION.
OWNING'S DREAM. DRAWN BY ZEKE.

General Albert Sidney Johnston.

Johnston's serious wound at Shiloh allowed Grant the chance
to survive the Confederate onslaught.

Brigadier General Wade Hampton, C.S.A.

Major General J.E.B. Stuart, C.S.A.

Above: Union Blockhouse at Bridgeport captured by Jenkins's Brigade
on September 30, 1863.

Right: Union wagons captured at Bridgeport
on September 30, 1863.

Above: Cleburne's Corps was the breakthrough formation in the decisive Second Battle of Kenesaw Mountain on August 5, 1864. Here his old division breaks a desperate Union counterattack after Sherman's death. *Courtesy of the Library of Congress.*

Right: Major General Patrick Ronayne Cleburne, Savior of the Confederacy, 1828–1922. His son, Joseph Patrick Cleburne, commanded the Confederate Expeditionary Force to France in the First World War. *Courtesy of the Library of Congress.*

Opposite: Cleburne's Division saved the Army of Tennessee in its flight after the crushing defeat at Chattanooga by delivering a severe beating to Joe Hooker's pursuing corps at Ringgold's Gap on November 27, 1863. *Courtesy of the Library of Congress.*

Edmund Kirby Smith, assertive commander of the
Trans-Mississippi Department.

Major General Banks with his staff in New York prior to embarking
on their expedition to New Orleans.

Union Cavalryman: By the time of the Valley campaign, the Union cavalry were equal, if not superior to, their Southern opponents.

Confederate Cavalryman: The Southern horse soldier was one of the best light cavalrymen in the world during 1862–63.

direct assaults to detach Union forces from their Yorktown base and push them back into a perimeter at Harrison's Landing on the James River.25

News of the Peninsular debacle shocked the North, and when it reached Europe,[26] it emboldened the pro-Southern forces. The French Emperor, Napoleon III, received Confederate envoy John Slidell on July 16, and three days later sent a telegram to his foreign minister, who was then in London, instructing him to ask the British if it were not now time to recognize the South.[27]

A British Member of Parliament who supported the Confederacy offered a resolution that the British government should cooperate with the French in an offer to mediate between the North and the South. The resolution seemed certain to pass when it was scheduled for debate on July 18, but Prime Minister Palmerston's speech opposing the resolution and calling for trust in the government to decide when the right time would come for such an action caused the resolution to be withdrawn without a vote.[28]

Rather than resting and refitting after Second Manassas, Lee made the decision to turn north. His men began crossing the Potomac into Maryland on the night of September 4–5, 1862.[29] He moved the Army of Northern Virginia up to Frederick, where he decided to stand and make McClellan attack him across the Monocacy River.

News of Second Manassas reached Europe just as the Battle of Frederick was being fought. Pro-Confederate leaders were elated, while Union legations despaired. British Prime Minister Palmerston, who had stood in the way of the drive to offer to mediate between the North and South in July, was now in the process of changing his mind. He wrote to his Foreign Secretary, Lord John Russell, wondering if another Union disaster would signal that the time had come to think again.[30]

On September 24, Palmerston set a meeting of the British Cabinet for early October to discuss the subject upon Russell's return from traveling with Queen Victoria. The proposal would be to offer to both sides mediation on the basis of an armistice and cessation of blockades with a view to negotiations on the basis of separation to be followed by diplomatic recognition of the Confederacy.[31]

When Lee defeated Burnside in front of Frederick on the 13th, Walker halted Couch at the Monocacy aqueduct on the 14th, and McClellan did not mount a successful assault across the Monocacy, action favorable to the Confederacy at last began. News of Frederick reached Europe on September 28, setting events in motion.

Confederate envoys John Slidell and James Mason were told by well-connected Britons that their hopes were about to be realized.[32] On October 2, Palmerston wrote to Russell, directing him to engage in discussions with the French, based upon the "South's great success against the North."[33]

Palmerston convened the cabinet meeting he had scheduled on October 9. Only one voice was raised against making an offer of mediation, that of Sir

George Cornewall Lewis, the Secretary for War. He was concerned that, if the Union rejected the mediation proposal and determined to fight on, the British Navy would be called upon to break the blockade, and the British Army would be called upon to defend Canada, which he believed was certain to be attacked by Union forces once hostilities began. He doubted that Britain could successfully defend Canada.

Lewis did not carry the day. The British and French decided to take coordinated action. They each summoned the respective American ambassadors to their foreign ministries, where the diplomats were presented on Monday, October 13, with the not-unexpected offer of formal mediation. News of this action rocketed around Europe with telegraphic speed. Of the European powers, only Russia stood fast against the offer of mediation.

Charles Francis Adams, the U.S. Ambassador to the Court of St James, put the text of the mediation offer and his views on the situation onto the fastest ship available heading for New York. Making a quick crossing, the news reached New York on the 23d. Transported by rail overnight, the urgent diplomatic dispatches were in Secretary Seward's and President Lincoln's hands on the morning of Friday 24th.

Lincoln had waited for military operations to stabilize and the Army of the Potomac to dig in thoroughly, re-supply, and reorganize before sacking McClellan. On October 8, he had relieved McClellan and replaced him with the only senior general at hand, General Halleck. Halleck was not well-liked by the troops, and was not known as a field commander.[34] McClellan's relief, despite the Frederick disaster, was greeted with unrest in the army.

Worse, the military issue was what to do about the Army of Northern Virginia, which was building winter quarters north of the Union capital, in a position to threaten a variety of economically and politically critical Northern centers. Any attempt directly to attack the Army of Northern Virginia would have to be made from some direction other than across the Susquehanna River. An opposed crossing of the Susquehanna was considered militarily impossible.

Halleck, confronted with a dispersed and disaffected Army of the Potomac, concluded that his only avenue for offensive action was to assemble a force in Baltimore and move northwest to cut Lee's supply lines, hoping that this would then allow him to turn northeast and pin Lee against the Susquehanna. He feared, however, that Lee would not remain in his York fortifications, but would take the field and engage him in a battle of maneuver.

With this strong probability in mind, Halleck demanded that more reinforcements be provided. He argued that the force he would take north from Baltimore must not be outnumbered by the Army of Northern Virginia, despite the fact that the Army of the Potomac would have to continue to cover Harrisburg, Baltimore, and the eastern bank of the

Susquehanna, all in sufficient force to halt a determined attack by the entire Army of Northern Virginia.

Secretary of War Stanton and President Lincoln agreed to Halleck's demand. The problem was that additional forces had to be raised, armed, and trained, and this would take time. Lincoln issued a call for the states to provide an additional 300,000 men, and received authority from Congress to take state militia units into federal service for as long as nine months (the previous limit had been three months).

News of the formal offer of international mediation struck official Washington like a thunderbolt. It could not be kept quiet, because it had become public in Europe the day after it was made, and was widely reported in European papers. The Administration knew that these papers were crossing the Atlantic right behind Adams's official dispatches.

Lincoln summoned the cabinet to discuss this critical development.[35] Seward brought home the gravity of the situation, explaining that the next step after an offer of mediation was rejected could well be direct intervention by the British Navy to break the blockade. Stanton responded that, if Britain opened hostilities, Canada would shortly belong to the United States, because Britain did not have forces in Canada large enough to defend it, and could not get them there soon enough to prevent its capture. Gideon Welles, the Secretary of the Navy, immediately pointed out that the entire Union merchant fleet, spread around the world engaged in trade vital to the North, would become a legitimate target for the British and possibly the French fleets and any privateers Britain and France authorized. The Union Navy would be focused on fighting the forces seeking to break the blockade and could offer no protection to these merchant vessels.

At this point, Salmon P. Chase, Secretary of the Treasury, raised the issue of the impact of a wider conflict on commerce and industry in the North. He pointed out that the Midwest was politically shaky. The Peace Democrats enjoyed rising political power, boosted by the loss of the Mississippi River grain trade with the now-Confederate states and by the threat working men felt freed black slaves would pose to their employment. They had made significant inroads in those states where congressional elections had already been held.

Chase said the likely loss of the U.S. merchant fleet would deal a devastating blow to the economy. He worried that paying for the war would become impossible. He said that "Greenbacks," the Union paper currency launched to provide liquidity in the North,[36] would probably fall steeply in value, and the sale of Union war bonds would become difficult. He noted that a significant share of those bonds had been purchased by European interests. With access to that source of capital cut off, bond prices would drop and interest rates would skyrocket. Without financing, he could see no way to continue the war.

At the close of the meeting, Lincoln stated that his position was to continue with the war to restore the Union. He would tell the press as much, as soon as the story on the mediation offer became public. He said that he would announce that he would not, however, formally respond to the joint British and French offer until after he had taken more time to consider it.[37]

News of the joint British and French offer of mediation took longer to reach Richmond. Mason in London and Slidell in Paris were both summoned to the respective foreign ministries and informed of the offer. Because of the Union blockade, the Confederate agents' ability to send news of the offer home was more limited. They placed dispatches on fast British ships heading for the Bahamas.

At Nassau, Mason's dispatches were transferred to one of the fastest blockade runners, the screw-driven S.S. *Peterhoff*. The *Peterhoff* left Nassau early on the 25th for Wilmington, North Carolina. The *Peterhoff* successfully negotiated the Union blockade during the hours of darkness late on the 26th, and entered Wilmington on the 27th. Slidell's dispatches never made it home, captured by the U.S.S. *Victoria* onboard the ill-fated S.S. *Theodora*.

News of the mediation offer, however, first reached Richmond through copies of the *Washington Post*'s Monday, October 27 edition which carried the earliest public word of the offer. The *Post*'s story was based on British newspapers received by ship in New York on the 26th. The *Post*'s New York bureau had urgently telegraphed the news to Washington. Confederate sympathizers quickly smuggled copies through the Union lines south of Washington, and the critical news was on the telegraph to Richmond before noon on the 27th.

Rumor did not wait for the next day's papers. News of the reported mediation offer spread swiftly through Richmond, igniting an impromptu public celebration that would not be equaled until Armistice Day. Citizens flooded the streets, cheering and shouting. Cannon fired in celebration, and a few hoarded fireworks joyously flew up into the evening sky.

Confederate President Jefferson Davis reacted cautiously to the reports. He appeared on the porch of the Confederate White House to the cheers of the crowd. He proclaimed the reports good news, but said his government as yet had no official word of the offer. He stated his belief that word would come shortly, and that, if the offer was as reported, it was very positive news indeed.

Davis did not have long to wait. Mason's dispatches reached him on the 28th, rushed by railroad from Wilmington. Dispatches in hand, Davis called an immediate meeting of his Cabinet.[38] Secretary of State Judah P. Benjamin had been closeted with Davis studying Mason's dispatches with great care prior to the cabinet meeting. Davis turned to him to open the meeting.

Benjamin was measured in his assessment of the development. He stated that the offer to mediate was genuine, and the terms were exactly what the South had sought. The proposal to begin with an armistice and a cessation of the blockade would offer immediate relief to the Confederacy. Following those steps with negotiations for separation and with foreign recognition of the legal independence of the Confederacy would secure for them their war aims.

The next to speak was Secretary of the Treasury George A. Trenholm. He stated that the first steps in the proposed mediation process would essentially solve the Confederacy's increasingly difficult financial problems. It would make the Confederate dollar strong and vastly ease the sale of Confederate war bonds, especially in Europe. Until now, Confederate bonds had had to offer high rates of interest and were regarded as speculative investments in Europe. With an armistice, interest rates would drop dramatically and, likely buoyed on the tide of pro-Confederate sentiment in Europe, bonds would sell quickly. The infusion of capital produced by these two events would substantially strengthen the South.

George W. Randolph, Secretary of War, spoke next. He stated that, with renewed trade with Europe and sound finances, the serious material shortages that had plagued Confederate forces could be made good in a short period of time. This would enable the South to continue its military operations if the armistice were to fail. However, he said that the most critical need was for industrial equipment to enable the South to meet vital needs from its own resources, otherwise a renewal of the war would swiftly exhaust stockpiles built up during an armistice.

Secretary of the Navy Stephen R. Mallory then stated that the most important step that could be taken was to attempt to secure an alliance with Great Britain. The British Navy would serve to keep Southern ports open and trade flowing even if war were renewed. While the recent loss of New Orleans stung, the Confederacy still held Mobile, Alabama, Savannah, Georgia, Charleston, South Carolina, and most important, Wilmington, North Carolina. An armistice and an end to the blockade would not, by its terms, reopen ports now held by Union forces, but would allow a free flow of trade through those remaining major ports and many smaller harbors still in Confederate hands.

President Davis turned to Benjamin and directed him to convey to the governments of Britain and France the Confederacy's acceptance of the offer of mediation. He also directed that Confederate envoys explore with the British and French the possibility of alliances and the possibility of immediate material support, if formal alliances did not seem feasible.

Davis said that he planned to make a public announcement of the Confederacy's acceptance of the offer of mediation. He thought that this would put increased pressure on the Lincoln Administration also to accept the offer. He noted that Republican losses in the early stages of the 1862 U.S. Congressional elections had been severe, and he expected those losses to worsen as voting continued. If the Republicans were to lose control of the House, they would be unable to continue the war. He was going to do everything that he could to make the prospect of immediate peace appealing to Northern voters, and seek to end the war through Congressional action even if Lincoln rejected the European offer of mediation.[39]

Davis asked Secretary Randolph to redouble his efforts to keep the Army of Northern Virginia well supplied and to make up losses in manpower as much as possible. General Lee in York with a strong, healthy army hopefully would make irresistible the argument for peace in the North.

Monday, October 27, 1862, forever after known as "Black Monday," dawned in New York City with newspaper headlines shouting the news from Europe of the offer of mediation. The stock market, when it opened, reacted with frenzied selling, causing the prices of shares to crash. By noon, the New York Stock Exchange was considering closing early to stem the rout. Some businesses began refusing to accept Greenbacks, or took them only at a discount against specie.

Telegraphed reports of this financial carnage forced a hasty meeting between President Lincoln and Secretary Chase. Lincoln had drafted a short statement on the mediation offer. He was planning to make the statement on Monday, and decided that it needed to be made public immediately. He directed Chase to telegraph New York financiers and ask for their help in stabilizing the market. He authorized Chase to offer Treasury support for that effort.

Lincoln then summoned reporters to the White House and made one of the most important statements of his political career. He began,

> "The people of the United States decided to preserve the Union. For the past two years and six months, since the attack on Fort Sumter, this nation has striven to end the present rebellion and bind together again the Union. Until a very short time ago, the sacrifices of our soldiers who have borne the battle, and of their wives, widows, and children, have promised such a restoration. Now, with the reverses our arms have suffered in the Seven Days, at Second Manassas, and at Frederick, a nation re-united seems further away than it was before.
>
> The offer of Great Britain and France to mediate between the United States and the Confederacy on the basis of an armistice, lifting the blockade, and negotiations with a view to separation of the Confederacy from the United States, followed by international recognition of the Confederacy as an independent sovereign state, if accepted on that basis, would end the work we are now in to restore the Union. The citizens of the United States, who elected me President by their votes, chose the other course. As their elected leader, I am determined that the Union shall be reunited, whether by force of arms or by peaceful means."

He paused, then tempered his earlier comments:

"However, the United States is considering the offer of mediation and
will not reject it. We will respond to Great Britain and France and seek
to determine if, by their assistance, the Union may be saved."

Turning to the events in New York, he said,

"The news of this offer of mediation stirred the passions of people and
caused them to act in haste. I urge all of our citizens to remain calm and
to have faith in the future. I have urged major interests to act, with the
support of the United States Treasury, to restore order to the market and
to financial affairs. The United States dollar is strong and will remain
strong."

Lincoln closed his remarks by saying:

"I will continue to serve the Union, and to do what is right, as God gives
me the light to see the right. I ask all citizens for their prayers and their
support at this difficult time."[40]

Before Lincoln's remarks could be reported, the New York Stock
Exchange had closed early, preventing the mounting market panic from
doing even worse damage. Spurred by news of the market panic, runs had
started on banks in New York, Philadelphia, Boston, and elsewhere. Banks
closed their doors, and militia units were put onto the streets to aid police in
maintaining order.

The countdown to the November stage of the elections for the 38th
Congress was moving inexorably forward. There were only five days left until
Delaware voted and eight days until the largest block of states voted on
November 4, including New Jersey and New York. There was no time to
wait for the results of a diplomatic exchange with the prospective mediators.
Ordinary people would have to vote based upon the facts then before them
and their hopes and fears for the future.

The 37th Congress had finished its second session on July 17, 1862. Its
third session was not to begin until December 1, 1862.[41] The 38th Congress
was not to convene for its first session until more than a year later, on
December 7, 1863.[42] But the impact of a Republican loss of control over the
House would be felt immediately.

The Peace Democrats sensed a huge opportunity. Those who had suffered
from the devastation of the Midwest's grain trade had voted their economic
interests and turned solidly against the war. Now, the core of Republican
strength in the northeast was beset by sudden economic disruption and the
threatening presence of the Army of Northern Virginia with one foot across
their threshold, the Mason-Dixon Line.

The Democrats had a plan:

"[They] tried to turn the many defeats suffered by Northern armies into
votes at election time. The list of decisive defeats for Union arms in the

first two years of the war was written in blood, and there were few
victories. The situation encouraged defeatism. Democratic politicians
said the war was a failure and the President was incompetent. Lincoln
ineptly juggled his commanders and repeatedly bet on the wrong
horses... They believed that 'managerial confusion' reigned in
Washington and that army appointments and removals were based
more on politics than on ability."[43]

While turmoil in the markets, spiking interest rates, and the apparent
threat to shipping interests and exporters arising from possible British and
French intervention on the Confederate side struck business interests hard,
the runs on many banks had the main impact on voters. Deposits were not
insured and many banks issued their own paper money. Runs on banks thus
threatened not just the banks and their owners, but everyone with deposits
in those banks and everyone holding paper money issued by those banks.
Thus, a failure of a large bank could dry up much of the liquidity in the
bank's service area, when the money it had issued became worthless. This
chain of developments could convert a prosperous community into a
cauldron of unemployment, closed factories, foreclosed mortgages, and
stewing social unrest in a very short period of time.

Greenbacks, the paper U.S. currency issued to help pay for the war, were
falling steeply in value. From Friday 24th to Tuesday 28th, prices of goods
in Greenbacks more than doubled in many places. This presaged runaway
inflation. Only those who could pay in hard currencies, gold and silver, could
obtain reasonable prices, and then only if they were established customers.
And persons and companies with substantial hard currency holdings started
deciding not to make new purchases unless they were truly unavoidable and
to stop paying outstanding debts in specie.

These developments were accumulating at a rapid pace and triggered
what became a decisive Democrat initiative. U.S. Senator Garrett Davis, a
Kentucky Democrat, proposed a series of "peace resolves," the last of which
provided:

> "*Resolved*: That the President of the United States be and he is hereby
> authorized to propose a cessation of arms and an amnesty to the
> authorities of the Confederate States of America, with a view to hold a
> convention of the people of all of the States to reconstruct the Union;
> and if that cannot be effected then the said convention agree upon the
> terms of separation of the States, without the further effusion of blood
> and of a lasting peace among them."[44]

This proposal was adopted by Democrat candidates across the country. It
had the useful feature that it was closely parallel to the joint British and
French mediation offer's provisions, but it was not identical. It provided for
an American solution to the war without drawing in foreign powers.

Lincoln's dedication to saving the Union caused him to make a major political error in response to these "peace resolves." His reaction to reporters, which was printed in all of the Northern papers, was that he did not favor an armistice, "with the unending evils of permanent separation disguised by empty results of a temporary peace staring them in the face." He favored "the continuance of the war until a permanent peace shall be established by suppressing the rebellion." Lincoln, like most Republicans, believed that reunion by amnesty or compromise would be no more than "utter degradation and dishonor."[45]

But runs on the banks continued, and the Greenback continued to fall in value, despite strenuous intervention by Secretary of the Treasury Chase. U.S. gold reserves were pledged to support the Greenbacks, but it was immediately reported in the papers that far more Greenbacks were in circulation than the U.S. had specie to back them. The U.S. Treasury maneuvered to buy back bonds whose prices were plunging, pumping liquidity into the system in New York. But there was no public mechanism to come to the rescue of private banks which did not have substantial hard currency reserves, and a great many did not.

Thus, as the week of the 27th continued to unfold, banks failed across the northeast and riots broke out. In Boston, Hartford, and Albany militia actually fired on rioters, killing many.

When Delaware voted on Saturday, November 1, the voters elected William Temple, a Peace Democrat, to the 38th Congress. On November 4, the deluge struck. Kansas, with one seat, elected a Republican. Illinois elected ten Democrats and only four Republicans. Massachusetts, the bedrock of Unionism, Republicanism, and abolitionism, elected two Peace Democrats and eight Republicans. Michigan elected three Democrats and three Republicans. Minnesota, with two seats, elected two Republicans. Missouri elected five Democrats and four Union Party members, who would vote with the Republicans. The drumbeat of disaster continued in New Jersey, which went solidly Democratic, all five seats falling to the opposition. In New York, 20 seats went Democrat and only 11 stayed Republican. Finally, in Wisconsin, the state's delegation split evenly, with three seats going Republican and three going Democrat.

It took a while to count the votes. Some races were close, and outcomes were not known until a week later. But it was clear, even from the initial returns, that the Lincoln Administration's war policies had been repudiated soundly at the ballot box. With other states yet to vote, the Democrats held 95 seats of the 184 known to be contested at that time.[46] Even if they did not win a single additional seat in the later voting states, they had secured an absolute majority in the House.

Lincoln called a Cabinet meeting for Friday, November 7.[47] The election results were clear. Lincoln began the Cabinet meeting by reviewing the agenda. The United States had to respond to the offer of mediation. There was no prospect of immediate military action against Lee's forces in Pennsylvania, but at least Lee appeared to be firmly settled into his new winter quarters. Volunteer enlistments had dried up, putting into question the ability to provide General Halleck with the agreed upon reinforcements. The economic crisis was grave and unresolved. The concatenation of the Peninsula, Second Manassas, Frederick, the Confederate advance to York, the British and French mediation offer, and the market panic and bank collapses had changed the public mood decisively against the President's policy to restore the Union by force of arms, as demonstrated in the election results. The question was, what was to be done?

Secretary of the Treasury Chase began to review the situation. With Treasury intervention and the assistance of major financial interests, the market panic had been stemmed. But many banks remained closed and it was not clear whether, or when, they would reopen. Business confidence had collapsed. This was the most grave of the situations facing the Union.

Secretary of War Stanton stated that he was receiving reports that government contractors were demanding payment in specie for war materials. Army sutlers were still accepting payment in Greenbacks from the troops, but prices had tripled in the last week and were still rising. Goods and services critical to forces in the field were denied both soldiers and officers who could not afford the prices and had no independent means.

Secretary of the Navy Welles stated that provisioning his ships had become a problem. While the Navy had long-term contracts for coal, some deliveries under these contracts had been withheld by contractors who were demanding payment in specie. The blockade could be maintained for perhaps another month based on coal supplies on hand and in transit, but if deliveries became uncertain, the blockade would start to unravel shortly thereafter. Winter weather increased coal demands for station keeping on the blockade lines, so the supply issue would shortly become critical.

Welles added that, while he had received nothing official from Navy contractors, he believed that they, too, would shortly begin demanding payment in specie for shipbuilding materials and ship's stores. While the Navy shipbuilding program could continue so long as workmen in the yards would accept Greenbacks as salary payments, shortages of labor and materials could quickly arise, particularly if inflation made workmen's wages impossible to live on.

Lincoln turned to Chase and asked him how the United States could continue to finance the war. Chase responded that the nation's gold reserves were not large enough to meet all of the demands placed on them. Ordinarily, if confidence in the government were high, the Greenbacks that had won acceptance and served to finance both the war and a parallel industrial expansion would be good money. But confidence had collapsed, and the value of the Greenback could not be sustained with the amount of gold on hand. In fact, the ratio of Greenbacks in circulation to the U.S. gold reserve was about 120:1. Thus, if the gold reserve were pledged entirely to the support of the Greenback and the Greenbacks' value were to fall to equal the value of the gold, then each Greenback would be worth less than a cent.

Chase continued, explaining that the entire U.S. gold reserve could not be pledged to support the Greenback. Some was needed for coinage, some was needed to settle international debts, and some was required to pay government contracts that specified payment in specie.

Chase then pointed out that the market panic and bank runs would most likely severely limit the ability of the government to sell war bonds in Europe for specie, trading paper for gold. News of the economic consequences of the mediation offer was likely to reach Europe early the following week, and even if European powers were not to engage in alliances with the Confederate states and enter the war as belligerents against the U.S., the collapse of business confidence would probably be enough in itself to stanch the flow of European credit which the U.S. had so far enjoyed during the war.

Lincoln wanted to know what each Cabinet member thought about prospects for continuing the war on the basis of the policy of reuniting the country by suppressing the rebellion by force. Stanton, always the warrior, asserted that the war could still be won, and even if they only had a year until a Democrat-controlled House took office, victory was still militarily possible. The overall strategic plan for fighting the war, the Anaconda Plan, was still working, despite tactical reverses, and the full weight of Union power had yet to be applied against the Rebels. Welles agreed with this position, saying that the Navy was getting stronger, day-by-day, and the blockade was getting tighter. Union operations on the rivers and against the Confederate harbors were continuing to have success and there was no prospect that the Confederacy could build a navy that could make more than tactical contest against this progress.

Chase then asked the two Secretaries their opinion on the larger question. Regardless of the prospects on the field of battle, could the military and naval effort be sustained in the face of the current financial crisis? Both Stanton and Welles reluctantly stated that they could not sustain operations without supplies and they could not obtain supplies without financing.

Chase looked at Lincoln and said that he had consulted with the best financial minds in the country in search of solutions to the present crisis, and none of the suggestions would work so long as the underlying problems remained unresolved, namely the presence of a rebel army in Pennsylvania and the real potential of foreign military intervention. Those two unpleasant facts would prevent restoration of confidence and, without confidence, there would be no funds.

Lincoln, as disheartened as the rest of the cabinet by this discussion, then turned to Seward. He asked the Secretary of State to draft a response to the British and French offer of mediation to ask them to elaborate on their proposal. He directed that it specifically explore the possibility of securing

European assistance in restoring the Union. He stated that he would not give an affirmative reply to the European proposal as it stood, and that he was more likely to adopt some version of Senator Davis's peace resolve, that would lead to a completely American solution, if such were to be the will of the people.

He turned to Stanton and Welles and directed them to continue present campaigns at the slowest possible pace and not to initiate any new operations. He further directed that they review current plans and determine which efforts were simultaneously low priority and high cost, and make plans to terminate those efforts as soon as possible, with an emphasis on cost rather than military efficacy. He further directed that steps be taken to make good, out of current government supplies, the needs of troops and sailors in the field that were now beyond their means due to sutler and contractor price increases.

Lincoln closed the meeting by stating that he would publicly announce that he was responding to the European offer of mediation and exploring its possibilities. He hoped that this would aid in stabilizing the financial crisis until some way to move forward could be worked out.[48]

Lincoln's announcement of his response to the British and French did help stabilize the financial situation. However, his announcement and public knowledge of the election results triggered a brutal public debate between the peace forces and the abolitionists. The abolitionists saw the war as a crusade to end the South's "peculiar institution" once and for all and free the slaves. It was a moral mission, one for which they claimed divine blessing. Confronted with the reality that financial collapse plus the threat of foreign intervention was condemning their dream to failure, they sought enemies and found plenty of them in the Peace Democrats.

The Radical Republicans' rhetorical assaults on Peace Democrats were so laced with vitriol and so violent that, had the financial crisis not been so grave, it would have threatened a second division of the United States, this one largely between New England and the Midwest. But in the face of the bank runs and collapses, public support was not there. Everyone except the most fanatic abolitionists realized that their families, their homes, their farms, their jobs and their futures were now at stake.

The saner abolitionists argued in their own councils that slavery was a fundamentally flawed institution, one that would fall of its own weight. They pointed out that the war had so far proved the Union superior in all aspects except generalship. They argued that the gap in capabilities between the United States and the Confederate States would only widen in the future, so long as the South remained agrarian economically and feudal politically. They predicted that Southern attempts to close the gap by industrializing would either fail by excluding the slave population, or, because of the education and training required to be a successful industrial worker, would create in the slave working class a force that could not be contained within their system. These arguments were grudgingly and bitterly accepted.

Following repeated two-week transits of the Atlantic by diplomats of all sides, Lincoln decided that his first instinct on how to respond to the unwonted necessity to end the war by compromise was correct. It was by now winter and economic conditions, which had temporarily stabilized, were deteriorating further and causing great public suffering. He chose Senator Davis, Senator Lyman Trumbull, an Illinois Republican (who was first elected as a Democrat), and Senator David Wilmot, a Pennsylvania Republican, to approach the Confederate government concerning setting up a convention in the manner suggested by Senator Davis's resolution.[49]

The Confederate response to the contact was to demand an armistice and a lifting of the blockade as a precondition for meeting in such a convention. Lincoln realized that he had no choice in the matter, and the Armistice of Havana was signed on Sunday, February 1, 1863, at the Viceroy's Palace, effectively ending the war.

Terms for the convention to conclude the war were worked out and the proceedings opened in Toronto, Canada, on May 1, 1863. There was never any real doubt about its outcome. The Treaty of Toronto granting the Confederate States of America independence and settling the border between the United States and the Confederate States was signed on Monday, August 3, 1863.

The Reality

"General Lee at the beginning of this march [into Maryland] was suffering from a painful hurt which to some extent disabled him throughout the Maryland campaign. On the day after the second battle of Manassas [Sunday, August 31, 1862] he was standing near the stone bridge, surrounded by a group of officers, when a squadron of Federal cavalry suddenly appeared on the brow of a neighboring hill. A movement of excitement in the group followed, with the effect of frightening the general's horse. The animal gave a quick start, and his master, who was standing beside him with his arm in the bridle, was flung violently to the ground with such force as to break some of the bones in his right hand. This disabled him so he was unable to ride during the greater part of the campaign."[50]

Other sources simply say that Lee tripped while reaching for the reins of his horse, and falling, caught himself on his hands.[51] Whatever the direct cause, Lee was dismounted, "in obvious intense pain,"[52] had both arms in splints and slings, was unable to feed or dress himself, and was unable to write.[53] He traveled in an ambulance, dictated his dispatches, and was not on horseback again until the morning of the battle of Antietam, Wednesday, September 17, 1862, and even then he had to be "[h]oisted onto Traveller's back," and an orderly held the horse's reins.[54]

During the Civil War, battlefields were ordinarily sufficiently compact that a commanding general could, by moving usually less than a mile in any direction on horseback, see both flanks and the center himself, and make decisions based upon what his own senses of sight and hearing told him, supplemented by reports from subordinates. Being on horseback elevated the officer's viewpoint, allowing him to see over marching troops and low obstructions, and allowed swift movement from place to place over broken ground. During the Maryland campaign, Lee's injuries denied him these customary advantages. However, the only major battle he directed during this campaign was the defensive fight at Antietam, where he was again mounted, if not fully mobile. No reports can be found arguing that his temporary infirmity negatively impacted his leadership on that day.

However, as anyone who has suffered serious injury can attest, an injury saps a person's energy. More importantly, in the sleep-deprived environment of a military commander on the move, injuries such as Lee suffered would have made what little sleep was available restless, interrupted, and not refreshing. Also, Lee may not have sat still for an orderly to feed him with the regularity necessary to keep up his calorie intake. The net result was most likely a measurable increase in fatigue, accompanying loss of mental acuity, and a tendency toward "tunnel vision," that is pressing ahead with preconceived plans and intentions instead of taking notice of changes in circumstances and rigorously re-examining plans and actions from a critical perspective. This marginal diminution in Lee's great capacities arguably played a role in the evolution of the 1862 Maryland campaign.

Lee's dispatch to Jefferson Davis, dictated on the morning of September 9, reveals evidence of mild confusion and diminished mental acuity.[55] Later that day, he writes to Davis again and has decided to move his army west. Finally, still later on the 9th, he holds a fateful commander's conference with Stonewall Jackson, later joined by Longstreet, and decides to dispatch Jackson, McLaws, and Walker on a three-pronged expedition against Martinsburg and Harpers Ferry, while moving west himself with the balance of the army to Boonsboro. This decision was reduced to writing in Special Order No. 191.[56]

> "One unusually grateful Marylander told [General Thomas J. 'Stonewall'] Jackson that he had the finest horse in the state and would feel deeply blessed if the general would accept the mount as a gift. The animal was a gigantic gray mare, heavy and awkward in comparison with the still-lost Little Sorrel. Jackson somewhat embarrassingly [sic] accepted the horse and tested her that evening. The animal shortly turned out to be a 'trojan horse'... Saturday morning, September 6, broke pleasant and bright but quickly took a near disastrous turn. Jackson mounted the new horse for the ride to Frederick. The animal did not want to move. Jackson touched her with a spur; at that, the mare reared straight up before losing her balance. Horse and rider fell

heavily to the ground. Jackson admitted that he was injured 'considerably.' He lay on the ground for a half hour while surgeons made examinations. The general was stunned and bruised. He had acute pain but nothing seemed to be broken. For a few hours, he rode ingloriously in an ambulance."[57]

In fact, Jackson could just as easily have been seriously injured or even killed. From the description of the incident, he may have been concussed, but not seriously.

Lee's decision to move west from Frederick and split his forces ultimately into five parts in the face of the Union advance cost him the operational initiative. Arguably, the speed and organization of the Union advance from Washington was such that, even absent McClellan's lucky find of the "lost orders," General D.H. Hill's copy of Special Order No. 191 setting forth Confederate plans for the campaign,[58] Lee would have been compelled to fall back toward the Potomac to re-concentrate the dispersed elements of the Army of Northern Virginia. The fate of the Confederate Maryland campaign of 1862 was largely determined by Lee's decision on the 9th.[59] They were on the road to Antietam.

The battle of Antietam was a Union victory. Lee retreated across the Potomac to Virginia. The victory raised morale across the North and particularly in the Army of the Potomac.[60] It halted European discussions of offers of mediation and depressed adherents of the Confederate cause.[61] Most critically, the victory provided the platform Lincoln needed in order to issue the Preliminary Emancipation Proclamation. On September 22, 1862, Lincoln proclaimed that, unless the rebel states returned to the Union by January 1, 1863, their slaves shall be "then, thenceforward, and forever free."[62] This declaration made a compromise solution to the war impossible. From this point on, despite the vigorous political disagreements emancipation stimulated, the war became as much a war for liberation of the slaves as it was a war to restore the Union.

Finally, the *Washington Post*, cited in the story above as a source of news for the Confederacy, was not founded until December 6, 1877, by Stilson Hutchins.

Bibliography

Biographical Directory of the United States Congress 1774–1989 Bicentennial Edition (U.S. Government Printing Office, Washington, D.C., 1989).

Blackford, William W., *War Years with Jeb Stuart* (Louisiana State University Press, Baton Rouge, 1993)

Cooling, B. Franklin, *Monocacy, The Battle that Saved Washington* (White Mane Publishing, Shippensburg, PA, 2000)

Dubin, Michael J., *United States Congressional Elections, 1788–1997: The Official Results of the elections of the 1st through 105th Congresses* (McFarland & Co., Jefferson, NC, 1998)

Grant, Ulysses S., *Personal Memoirs of U.S. Grant* (Konecky & Konecky, Old Saybrook, CT, 1999)

Harsh, Joseph L., *Taken at the Flood: Robert E. Lee and the Confederate Strategy in the Maryland Campaign of 1862* (Kent State University Press, Kent, Ohio, 1999)

Klement, Frank L., *The Copperheads in the Middle West* (University of Chicago Press, Chicago, 1960)

Long, A.L., *Memoirs of Robert E. Lee, His Military and Personal History, Embracing A Large Amount of Information Hitherto Unpublished* (Blue and Gray Press, Seacaucus, NJ, 1983)

Luvaas, Jay, and Nelson, Harold W., eds., *Guide to the Battle of Antietam: The Maryland Campaign of 1862* (University Press of Kansas, Lawrence, 1987)

McPherson, James M., *Crossroads of Freedom: Antietam* (Oxford University Press, Oxford, 2002)

Robertson, James I. Jr., *Stonewall Jackson: The Man, The Soldier, The Legend* (Macmillan Publishing, New York, 1997)

Sandberg, Carl, *Abraham Lincoln: The War Years*, Vol. 1 (Harcourt, Brace, New York, 1939)

Sisson, Charles Jasper, ed. *William Shakespeare: The Complete Works* (Harper & Row, New York, 1954)

Notes

1. The immediate impact of the battle of Saratoga (1777) during the American Revolution was to force the surrender of the British army commanded by Maj-Gen John Burgoyne. The intermediate effect was to ruin the British plan to split the northern colonies. The decisive long-term effect was to encourage the French to form an alliance with the struggling United States. That alliance provided the strategic leverage that eventually forced Great Britain to realize that its attempt to suppress American independence was fruitless.

*2. Charles S. Venable, *Lee's 1862 Campaign* (Richmond, 1878) p. 35.

*3. Alexander S. Pendleton, *With Stonewall to Victory* (New York, 1892) p. 102.

*4. *Ibid.*, p. 107.

5. Harsh, *Taken at the Flood*, p. 129.

6. *Ibid.,* p. 122.

*7. Richard E. Frayser, *Message from J.E.B.* (Richmond, 1885) p. 15.

*8. U.S. War Department, The War of the Rebellion: A Compilation of the Records of the Union Army (Washington, D.C., 1880–1901) Ser. I, Vol. XIX/2, p. 211. Since the "Lost Dispatch" is quite short, it is quoted here in its entirety for the reader's information: "HEADQUARTERS, Rockville, Md., September 8, 1862: 10 p.m. Major General HALLECK, General-in-Chief: After full consideration, I have determined to advance the whole force to-morrow; the right wing to Goshen and Cracklinton, holding guard over bridges and other advance points by strong advance guard; the cavalry well out on the right and front; the center near Middlebrook; Franklin to Darnestown, holding the line of the guards by advance guards; Couch to guard, leaving a brigade at Offutt's Cross-Roads; and Sykes's division will move to-morrow, according to the information I receive, probably toward Gaithersburg, but wherever the latest information may show the enemy to be in greatest force. GEO. B. McCLELLAN, Major General."

*9. Venable, *Lee's 1862 Campaign*, p. 92.

10. Cooling, *Monocacy: The Battle That Saved Washington*, p. 112.

*11. U.S. War Department, *The War of the Rebellion: A Compilation of the Records of the Union Army*, Ser. I, Vol. XIX/2, pp. 24–7.

12. "A horse, a horse, my kingdom for a horse!" *Richard III*, Act V, Scene IV. C.J. Sisson, ed., *William Shakespeare: The Complete Works*, p. 726

13. Klement, *The Copperheads of the Middle West*, p. 1.

14. Dubin, *United States Congressional Elections, 1788–1997*, pp. 193–8.

*15. Clement L. Vallandigham, *The Constitution As It Is, The Union As It Was: Ballots for Peace in 1862* (New Haven, 1880) p. 289.

*16. *Ibid.*, p. 290.

*17. *Ibid.*, p. 291.

*18. *Ibid.*, p. 292.

*19. *Ibid.*, p. 293.

20. McPherson, *Crossroads of Freedom: Antietam*, p. 35.

21. *Ibid.*, p. 36.

22. Robertson, *Stonewall Jackson*, pp. 405–8.

23. Sandburg, *Abraham Lincoln: The War Years*, Vol. 1, pp. 528–9.

24. Long, *Memoirs of Robert E. Lee*, p. 159.

25. *Ibid.*, pp. 161–81.

26. At that time, it took an average of two weeks for news from North America to reach Europe or *vice versa*. News had to travel by ship since the first trans-Atlantic telegraph cable had failed after six months' use in 1859, and it was not to be replaced until 1865.

27. McPherson, *Crossroads of Freedom: Antietam*, p. 58.

28. *Ibid.*, pp. 59–60.

29. Harsh, *Taken at the Flood*, pp. 80–109.

30. McPherson, *Crossroads of Freedom: Antietam*, p. 94.

31. *Ibid.*

32. *Ibid.*, p. 141.

*33. Viscount Henry John Temple Palmerston, *The Treaty of Toronto: Ending the War Between the States* (J. Ridgway, London, 1870) p. 48.

34. Sandburg, *Abraham Lincoln: The War Years*, p. 509.

*35. Abraham Lincoln, *Memoirs: Binding Up the Wounds* (New York, 1872) p. 97.

36. Legal Tender Act, February 25, 1862.

*37. Lincoln, *Memoirs*, p. 107

*38. Jefferson Davis, *The Second American Revolution* (Richmond, 1874) p. 109.

*39. *Ibid.*, p. 115.

*40. Lincoln, *Memoirs*, p. 182.

41. *Biographical Directory of the United States Congress 1774–1989 Bicentennial Edition*, p. 171.

42. *Ibid.*, p. 175.

43. Klement, *The Copperheads of the Middle West*, p. 29.

44. *Ibid.*, p. 228.

45. *Ibid.*, p. 228.

*46. Vallandigham, pp. 198–205. Note that there were also rejected and undetermined elections, most in Union-occupied areas of Confederate states, as well as special elections. The total number of House seats available for contest was thus not known in November 1862.

*47. Lincoln, *Memoirs*, p. 204.

*48. *Ibid.*, p. 222.

*49. *Ibid.*, p. 245.

50. Long, *Memoirs of Robert E. Lee*, p. 206.
51. Robertson, *Stonewall Jackson*, p. 581.
52. *Ibid.*
53. Harsh, *Taken at the Flood*, pp. 65, 71–2, 104.
54. *Ibid.*, p. 383.
55. *Ibid.*, pp. 128–31.
56. *Ibid.*, p. 145.
57. Robertson, *Stonewall Jackson*, pp. 587–8.
58. Harsh, *Taken at the Flood*, p. 153.
59. *Ibid.*, p. 167.
60. McPherson, *Crossroads of Freedom: Antietam*, pp. 134–5.
61. *Ibid.*, p. 141.
62. *Ibid.*, pp. 138–9.

5
"WE WILL WATER OUR HORSES IN THE MISSISSIPPI"
A.S. Johnston vs. U.S. Grant

James R. Arnold

Shiloh Dawn

The sounds of firing diminished and then stopped altogether. The Confederate high command peered anxiously in the direction of the Union camps and the Tennessee River. From their location at the junction of the Bark Road and the Pittsburg and Corinth Road, they could see nothing but the rear elements of General Polk's First Corps. Beyond the irregular lines of gray-clad infantry lay nothing but dark woods. General Pierre Gustave Toutant Beauregard spoke: "General, we have surely lost the element of surprise. We must retire to Corinth immediately."[1]

The 59-year-old commanding general stood leaning toward a campfire sipping coffee. Before he could reply, the sharp rattle of nearby musketry again burst out. Albert Sidney Johnston straightened to his full six-foot, 200-pound, robust height and calmly replied, "The battle has opened, gentlemen; it is too late to change our dispositions."

He mounted his magnificent bay, Fire-eater, and said to his staff, "Tonight we will water our horses in the Tennessee River!"[2]

It was 6.40 a.m., April 6, 1862. Overhead, a brilliant sun rose above the river mist. Johnston's aide, Captain W.L. Wickham, turned toward Johnston's personal physician, "Doctor Yandell, it must be another sun of Austerlitz."[3] Then Wickham and the other staff officers hurried to mount their horses because already Johnston was disappearing into the woods, riding fast toward the sounds of firing.

Wickham caught up with Johnston on the edge of the Seay Field. Across the field, Arkansas men belonging to Brigadier General Thomas Hindman's brigade were involved in a difficult struggle with a tenacious regiment of Union troops. The firing intensified. The Confederate ranks wavered. Soldiers broke ranks and began drifting rearward. Johnston spurred Fire-eater into the field to rally the infantry. His voice somehow rose above the

131

din of battle, "Men of Arkansas! They say you boast of your prowess with the Bowie knife. Today you wield a nobler weapon, the bayonet. Employ it well!"[4]

The soldiers responded with cheers. One recalled that Johnston's face was "aflame with a fighting spirit."[5] Inspired by Johnston's commanding presence, they re-formed and prepared to charge again.

Young Colonel John Marmaduke was busily aligning his 3d Confederate Regiment when he felt a hand on his shoulder. Marmaduke glanced up to see a well-remembered face from the Old Army days. "My son," Johnston said, "we must this day conquer or perish!"[6] Marmaduke later recalled that he felt nerved "tenfold".

Thirty minutes later a courier arrived to report to Johnston that Major General Braxton Bragg's men were being hotly pressed and needed help. Johnston rode to the nearest unit and ordered it to follow him. Together they moved to the right, in the direction of the heaviest firing. But the soldiers were unable to keep up with their fast-moving leader. Accompanied by a handful of aides, Johnston disappeared into the woods.

He arrived in the rear of Brigadier General Adley Gladden's brigade shortly before 9.00 a.m. Johnston immediately ordered Gladden to conduct a bayonet attack. Gladden's line surged across the Spain field and sent the Yankee line rearward. Johnston followed them as they swept into an abandoned Union camp. Scores of hungry rebels broke ranks to feast from the hot but untouched breakfast kettles. Others began looting the tents. Johnston saw an officer emerge from a tent with an armload of trophies. He spoke sharply, "None of that, sir; we are not here for plunder!"

A dejected look crossed the officer's face and his shoulders sagged. Johnston reached from his horse to take a tin cup from a table. He softened his tone and said, "Let this be my share of the spoils today."[7]

The general continued through the camp. All around him were wounded and suffering soldiers, most of whom belonged to the enemy. Johnston summoned Doctor Yandell: "Doctor, send some couriers to the rear for medical officers. Meantime, look after these wounded people, the Yankees among the rest. They were our enemies a moment ago, they are our prisoners now."

"General," Yandell protested, "others can attend to these men. My place is with you."

"Go ahead and begin your work, doctor. I'll advise you when I am moving on."

As Johnston turned to confer with an aide, Yandell heard Captain Wickham speaking softly to him: "Doctor, disregard what he says. You've seen the way he takes terrible risks. This army depends upon him and he may have reason to depend upon you. Follow him wherever he goes, just stay a little ways behind. He never looks backward."[8]

Soon Johnston was off to the front again. Shortly before noon, one of Beauregard's aides observed the general "sitting on his horse where the bullets were flying like hail stones. I galloped up to him amid the fire, and found him cool, collected, and self-possessed, but still animated and in fine spirits." Another officer found Johnston observing the successful charge of Chalmers's brigade. As the Rebel line disappeared beyond a nearby ridge line, Johnston remarked with satisfaction, "That checkmates them."[9]

Indeed, from Johnston's vantage point it seemed like the Confederates were driving General Ulysses S. Grant's Army of the Tennessee backwards all along the front. But looks were deceiving. At several places Grant's men defended their positions tenaciously. Nowhere was this more true than on the Union left, in the area of a peach orchard. Here, Brigadier General John C. Breckinridge's Confederates struggled to advance for more than an hour. Breckinridge became distressed with his inability to make the Tennessee regiments in Colonel W. S. Statham's brigade press the attack vigorously and galloped up to Johnston to complain that he could not make the brigade charge. Breckinridge was a former Vice-President of the United States and remained an influential Southern political leader. Johnston knew that he had to be handled with kid gloves. He gently replied, "Oh, yes, General, I think you can."

The emotional Breckinridge nearly broke down. "I can't, General. I have tried repeatedly and failed!"

"Then I will help you, we can get them to make the charge." Johnston firmly said.[10]

Johnston galloped down a ravine toward the Tennessee soldiers. Among his aides, only Captain Wickham remained. Wickham glanced backward. With relief he saw that Doctor Yandell was still shadowing the general.

Johnston rode among the battered and discouraged Rebels. His sword remained sheathed in its scabbard. Instead, he held the tin cup he had taken from the Union camp in his hand. Wielding the cup as if it were a sword, he gestured toward the Union line. "We must drive them!" Then he rode in front of his men, reached with his cup to touch their bayonets, and said repeatedly, "Men, they are stubborn; we must use the bayonet." He took station at the center of Statham's brigade, turned and shouted, "Men! I will lead you!"[11]

Like an attack dog poised and waiting for the command, the entire Confederate line seemed to tremble with anticipation. One soldier recalled that Johnston gave them "irresistible ardor."[12] At the signal they cheered mightily and charged. It was a few minutes before 2.00 p.m.

Three Rebel brigades assailed the Union position. On the left, Statham's men passed the Sarah Bell cabin and charged directly toward the Yankees in the peach orchard. As had occurred twice already, this effort stalled against fierce Union opposition. On the right Jackson's brigade became ensnarled in a wooded ravine and managed to contribute only two regiments to the attack. The attack's success depended upon the center brigade commanded by Brigadier General John Bowen. Bowen's Arkansas and Missouri infantry proved equal to the task. A Union defender recalled, "The Rebels came on us before we knew it. The undergrowth was so thick we could not see them until they got within twenty yards of us."[13] In a wild, confused fight, Bowen's brigade broke the Union line.

Finally, Johnston's relentless series of charges began to produce dividends. The Union left crumbled, thereby exposing adjacent units to enfilade fire. Masses of Rebel infantry pushed through the peach orchard to exploit the situation. Worse still, from the Union perspective, few fresh troops stood between the triumphant Rebels and Pittsburg Landing on the Tennessee River.

But the breakthrough was not without cost. Bowen went down with a severe wound. Hundreds of Confederate infantry likewise fell dead, dying, or wounded. General Grant later remembered this part of the field was "so covered with [Confederate] dead that it would have been possible to walk across the clearing, in any direction, stepping on dead bodies, without a foot touching the ground."[14]

Amidst the carnage, an elated Albert Sidney Johnston watched his plan succeed. Tennessee Governor Harris appeared. Johnston smiled and pointed to his left boot, which had been struck by a bullet, and said, "Governor, they came very near putting me *hors de combat* in that charge."[15] The general then sent Harris and all but one of his aides coursing the field to carry orders to complete the victory. Only Captain Wickham remained with Johnston.

When Harris returned from his mission to report to Johnston he suddenly saw the general sink in his saddle and begin to reel to his left. Harris saw that Johnston's face was deadly pale. "General, are you wounded?"

Johnston replied, "Yes, and I fear seriously."[16]

Harris and Wickham propped Johnston in his saddle and led him to shelter behind a small knoll. They saw that Johnston's horse, Fire-eater, had been struck twice by bullets or shrapnel. As they lifted Johnston to the ground, Wickham looked up with relief to see Doctor Yandell. Wickham told the doctor that Johnston had been hit in the boot but that there was no other obvious sign of a wound. Yandell untied Johnston's cravat, unbuttoned his collar and vest, and pulled his shirt open. He could not find a wound. The general lost consciousness. Yandell pulled off Johnston's left boot. Nothing. He pulled off the right and it was full of blood. Hastily, Yandell slit open Johnston's trouser leg. He found a profusely bleeding wound behind his right knee joint. Apparently a lead ball had struck the calf and torn, but not severed, the popliteal artery, and lodged against the shin bone. It was an ugly, dangerous wound which, if left untended, would quickly kill.

Yandell reached into Johnston's pocket where, at the surgeon's behest, Johnston kept a field tourniquet. Yandell expertly tied it in place to stanch the flow. Colonel William Preston galloped onto the scene. He dismounted rapidly, took out a flask, and cradled Johnston's head in his arms. He poured whiskey into Johnston's mouth and asked desperately, "Johnston, do you know me?"

The general's eyes opened. He recognized Preston and smiled weakly. In a faint voice he said, "Tell Beauregard to drive the Yankees into the river."[17] And then he lost consciousness again.

Davis's Generals

In Richmond, an anxious President Jefferson Davis awaited news from his friend, Sidney Johnston. During the Mexican War, Johnston's quick-thinking reaction to a dangerous confrontation had probably saved the lives of both men. Thereafter, Davis's admiration knew no bounds. A few months before, when some Tennessee politicians protested that Johnston had abandoned valuable Tennessee soil and was "no general," Davis had replied that if Johnston was not a general, "we had better give up the war, for we have no general."[18] On the eve of Johnston's offensive against Grant, Davis sent a telegram saying, "I anticipate victory."[19]

The absence of news from Johnston troubled Davis greatly. He told his aides that if his friend were alive he would have heard something. April 6 passed, and then April 7. Finally news came about the Confederate defeat. After Johnston's wounding, Beauregard had been unable or unwilling to capitalize upon the Confederate advantage during the remainder of the day. The next day, the Union forces counterattacked and drove the rebels from the field. Beauregard ordered a retreat to Corinth.

To Davis, it seemed that "Old Bory's" retreat undid the victory that was there for the taking when Johnston fell. It cemented his dislike for the Creole general. In contrast, Davis had nothing but tender concern for Sidney Johnston. He inquired about his friend's health, wished him a rapid recovery, and proposed that the general be moved to Davis's own Mississippi plantation, Brierfield, to convalesce. Davis wrote movingly about the plantation's beauty and charm. It was in a secluded backwater, far from the front, an altogether perfect place for the general to enjoy quiet and peace while regaining his strength.

In Corinth, the staggering number of Confederate wounded overwhelmed the medical service. Moreover, the army's return to the city quickly polluted the shallow wells that provided the region's drinking water. The number of men on the sick list soared as typhoid, dysentery, and other waterborne diseases attacked the already weakened army. Among the afflicted was Albert Sidney Johnston.

Fearful that the wounded general would succumb to disease, Doctor Yandell fought to overcome Johnston's reluctance to move. "I should be with my men," Johnston weakly protested.[20] The president's hospitable offer was like a lifeline for the worried doctor. So, on the last day of April, a locomotive pulled away from Corinth and headed south along the Mobile and Ohio

Railroad. Three days later a horse-drawn ambulance pulled up before the white-posted veranda of Jefferson Davis's plantation at Davis Bend on the Mississippi River, some 20 miles below Vicksburg. Here Johnston began a long, long convalescence.

President Davis had placed the western theater in the hands of the general whom he most trusted. Johnston's wounding left a command void. Any replacement would have found it difficult to measure up to Johnston in the grief-stricken mind of the commander-in-chief. When Beauregard yielded western Tennessee without a fight and then went off on sick leave without asking permission, Davis replaced him with Braxton Bragg. But shuffling commanders did not address the South's strategic conundrum: a long defensive line, stretched so thin that it could be broken by the superior enemy forces most anywhere; yet to abandon territory, to concentrate, risked losing valuable assets forever. Indeed, this is what had taken place at the South's greatest city. Stripped of its defenders for the grand stroke at Shiloh, New Orleans fell to an aggressive Federal fleet in the dismal spring of 1862.

Davis examined the strategic map and saw that Tennessee remained vulnerable from the Mississippi to the Alleghenies. He was willing to take risks and the only solution he saw was the offensive-defensive. So, the president held high hopes for Bragg's counteroffensive into Kentucky which began in the late summer of 1862. Bragg skillfully interposed his army between the Union army and its base at Louisville. For a few shining hours Bragg grasped potential victory, but at the critical moment he hesitated, declined battle, and permitted the Federals to pass his front and gain Louisville. The subsequent Union offensive drove him out of not only Kentucky but much of Tennessee as well. The president candidly told Congress that the South had entered "the darkest and most dangerous period yet."[21]

The disasters of 1862 taught Davis that his offensive-defensive required some form of mobile reserve. He explained to one of his generals, "We cannot hope at all points to meet the enemy with a force equal to his own, and must find our security in the concentration and rapid movement of troops."[22] Meanwhile, Grant was on the move again. He had collected a large army and a seemingly invincible fleet to spearhead a drive south down the Mississippi River, and the defending Confederate generals doubted their ability to stop him.

Davis knew that Vicksburg was the key to controlling the Mississippi. It was one of the places the South needed to hold if it were to endure. The president responded to the crisis by redrawing department boundaries and appointing a new general to defend the city. Davis chose Lieutenant General John Pemberton, a Pennsylvania-born officer whose brothers fought for the North and whose birth state made him the focus of deep suspicion among the endangered people of Mississippi. Indeed, a Confederate sergeant observed his new general and wrote, "I saw Pemberton and he is the most insignificant 'puke' I ever saw."[23]

At Brierfield Plantation, Sidney Johnston knew little about the command frictions besetting the Confederacy. The blood loss from his wound had weakened him such that he fell easy prey to a prolonged, and nearly fatal, bout of typhoid fever. On rare days during the summer of 1862 his strength rallied and Davis's servants, supervised by the fretful Doctor Yandell, carried him outside for a few hours of bracing sunshine.

One such day occurred on August 4, when Johnston watched the Confederate ironclad *Arkansas* bravely steam south to attack Baton Rouge. He had no notion that the ironclad's engines badly needed repairs nor that had she remained beneath Vicksburg's fortified bluffs she might have prevented much of what was to come. It was fortunate as well for the general's health that he was not present the next day to witness the death throes of the most active vessel the South had ever floated to defend the Mississippi.[24]

Fall came and Johnston slowly regained his health. General Bowen, who had recently recovered from his Shiloh wound, visited Johnston. The conversation naturally reverted to a refight of Shiloh. Johnston said that many of the difficulties encountered in that battle stemmed from the soldiers' inexperience and lack of discipline. Bowen agreed and then interjected, "But General, it is different now. If you could see my division, particularly Cockrell's Missouri boys, you would see a brigade of perfectly prepared fighting cocks. I would lead them into the jaws of hell itself."[25]

After Christmas, news of Vicksburg's successful defense against William T. Sherman's landing at Chickasaw Bayou seemed the perfect tonic for Johnston. He began drafting a request to return to duty. But the cold, exceedingly wet winter brought on an incapacitating lung inflammation and again the general took to his bed. The first anniversary of the Battle of Shiloh found him still pale, drawn, and weak.

Bowen Confronts Grant

On the night of April 16, Admiral David Porter's ironclads ran the batteries at Vicksburg. Whether Porter would have taken this risk if the invincible *Arkansas* had still been afloat is impossible to say. What is certain is that Porter's success radically altered the strategic chessboard. General Grant resolved to march along the Mississippi's western shore and bypass Vicksburg. Then, aided by a series of clever diversions, he planned for Porter to ferry his army across the river to attack the city from below. It was a bold and brilliant strategy, and it fooled Pemberton and nearly all the Confederate commanders.

The exception was the commander of the fortified post at Grand Gulf, General Bowen. Bowen alone perceived the new situation caused by Porter's success. On April 27 he concisely outlined in a letter to Pemberton the dire threat posed by Grant's likely future maneuvers. He asked for reinforcements to help hold Grand Gulf. Pemberton neither attended to Bowen's warnings nor sent him reinforcements.

At 8.00 a.m., April 30, the greatest amphibious invasion heretofore in American history began. By noon, most of General John McClernand's 17,000-strong XIII Corps had completed the unopposed landing below Grand Gulf. Grant later wrote:

> "I felt a degree of relief scarcely ever equaled since. Vicksburg was not yet taken it is true, nor were its defenders demoralized... But I was on dry ground on the same side of the river with the enemy. All the campaigns, labors, hardships and exposures... that had been made and endured, were for the accomplishment of this one object."[26]

Bowen had previously selected a strong position at Port Gibson as the best place to try to stop Grant. It was to this position that he sent his available manpower at 1.00 a.m. on April 30, seven hours before the first Union soldiers landed on the Mississippi's eastern shore. On the morning of May 1 came the first combat. The terrain was a bewildering mix of irregular ridges divided by deep and impassable ravines. The subsequent battle placed a heavy tactical burden on leaders on both sides. According to one historian, "From battle's beginning to end, officers on both sides had trouble understanding their own position relative to supporting, friendly units and had even less comprehension of how lay the opponent."[27] Although outnumbered three to one, the Confederates fought extremely well. Bowen himself had four horses shot out from under him. But eventually valor gave way to superior numbers. That night Bowen retreated from the field and retired behind the North Fork of Bayou Pierre.

Confederate Reactions

General Joseph Johnston was nominally in command of all Confederate forces in the West. On May 1, before he learned of Grant's movements, he advised Pemberton, "If Grant crosses the Mississippi, unite all your troops to beat him."[28] It was sound strategy, but Joe Johnston had no intention of taking any personal role in seeing it through. This left Pemberton in a difficult bind. He believed Vicksburg to be his sacred trust, all the more sacred because he knew that many Mississippians doubted his loyalty to the cause. Consequently, Pemberton was extremely loath to denude the city in order to muster a field force sufficient to challenge Grant. Furthermore, Grant's multiple diversions had fooled the Pennsylvania-born general.

On May 2 Pemberton began to send some reinforcements south to join Bowen. But a sense of pessimism seemed to enter his thinking. He ordered Vicksburg prepared for a siege and advised Mississippi Governor John Pettus to "remove the State archives from Jackson."[29] Pettus, in turn, frantically telegraphed Jefferson Davis to report that Pemberton had lost his nerve and unless an immediate command change took place, all was lost.

Jefferson Davis found himself in a not unfamiliar position. Time and again, politicians had complained that their constituents were being ill-served by the generals in command. Often they demanded that Davis make command changes. In Davis's mind, Pemberton was merely the latest in a list that at various times had included Robert E. Lee, Thomas Jackson, Braxton Bragg, and even Sidney Johnston himself. Davis had stood by his selections and they, in turn, with the possible exception of Bragg, had rewarded his patience and loyalty with victories.

Davis considered patience and loyalty admirable virtues, particularly for a commander-in-chief of a beleaguered nation. He was certain that these virtues had been key to victory in the First American Revolution and had no doubt that they would be equally crucial to Confederate victory in the Second American Revolution. Moreover, to relieve Pemberton at this moment of crisis would be to admit publicly that Pemberton's selection had been a mistake. This he was extremely loath to do.

But Davis also understood what was at stake. If Grant succeeded, the Confederacy would be divided in two, the hungry armies of the east forever cut off from the cattle and corn, the hogs and the horses of the fertile trans-Mississippi. The loss of Vicksburg could well be a fatal blow.[30]

For several hours the president paced back and forth in his office at the White House of the Confederacy. His inner struggle was monumental because he knew that the decision he had to make was of immense strategic consequence. His already pale face—Davis was sick with bronchitis—gained an even more ghastly, sunken appearance as the strain brought the onset of another painful bout of neuralgia. He knew that Joe Johnston, the nominal supreme commander in the West, was making leisurely progress toward Vicksburg, presumably to take field command, but he also knew that Johnston's preferred maneuver was the strategic retreat. Davis could conceive of only one possible alternative to Pemberton; namely, to send Lee west. Yet he knew both that Lee would resist transfer and that Lee's absence would leave the Confederate capital vulnerable. He had just about resolved to retain Pemberton when an aide knocked at his office door.

The aide's eyes were shining with excitement as he handed Davis a just-arrived telegram. It was from Albert Sidney Johnston and read: "I learn that the enemy is on this side of the river. I wish to report for duty, whether as a simple private carrying a musket or in any other capacity you deem appropriate."[31]

It was as if a bracing breeze had blown away the rain clouds that had deluged Richmond for the past several days. Davis began dictating orders: Sidney Johnston to take command of all field troops operating around Vicksburg with the mission of driving Grant into the Mississippi; Pemberton to remain in command at Vicksburg to defend the Confederate citadel against direct attack while assisting Johnston by forwarding men and supplies. The president completed his flurry of orders by telling Beauregard in Charleston, South Carolina, to send 5,000 men west to Jackson, Mississippi. As he completed his work, Davis found, to his surprise, that the sharp pain of his neuralgia had receded into a mere dull ache.

Johnston Takes Command

Sidney Johnston had failed to mention to Davis that Doctor Yandell still forbade him to ride a horse for any extended time. So it was a plantation carriage that delivered Johnston to Major General William Loring's headquarters on the north side of the Big Black River just after dawn on May 3. Johnston mounted the steps of the McCleod mansion and paused on the veranda. From within he heard the heated sounds of argument. Apparently there was some sort of council of war taking place. He heard a voice trying to overmaster the angry buzz of debate: "Gentlemen, I repeat, shall the army move with dispatch to Vicksburg or shall it hold the Big Black?"[32]

He recognized General Bowen's voice in reply:

> "General Loring. We have my two fine brigades on the enemy side of the river along with Reynolds's fresh Tennessee Brigade. On this side we have the two brigades you have brought us with Barton and Taylor coming up fast. This gives us more than 16,000 men. My scouts tell me that we face McPherson's XVII Corps, that it is unsupported, and that it is strung out in road column. I say attack!"

Johnston nodded approvingly and smiled. His smile turned to a frown when Loring spoke again:

> "General Bowen, we all applaud your fighting instincts, but my hands are tied. My orders from General Pemberton are to be on the lookout for your division and, if necessary, to fall back across Big Black. I have found you and your men and now we will... "

Sidney Johnston strode into the room and completed Loring's sentence, "Attack!"

Loring began to sputter but Johnston brusquely cut him off:

> "Gentlemen, the time for debate is over. I have here orders from the President assigning me command of all troops in the field. We will attack immediately. I do not know the relative numbers but I know that on these narrow roads they cannot put more men at the front than we can. Besides, I would fight them if they were a million!"[33]

Johnston's words electrified the Confederate generals. With the exception of Loring, they responded with deep approval. Then they rose as one to shake hands with the new army commander.

The Battle of Hankinson's Ferry

On the day after his victory at Port Gibson, General Grant pushed his army hard. He believed that he had the Rebels off balance and confused, and wanted to exploit the situation. The first obstacle to surmount was the Little Bayou Pierre. His engineers worked feverishly during the morning to construct a 12-foot wide, 166-foot long bridge using timbers taken from a nearby cotton gin. They corduroyed the bridge approaches over a dangerous patch of quicksand and announced the bridge practicable. From start to finish the entire operation required a mere four hours, which was good, because Grant was in a big hurry. As the first Union infantry approached the bridge, there was their general to urge them on: "Men, push right along; close up fast, and hurry on."[34]

The North Fork of Bayou Pierre presented a more substantial barrier. Grant hoped that his men could capture the suspension bridge at Grindstone Ford. By 7.30 p.m. his hard-marching men reached the ford only to see that the bridge was on fire. An energetic engineering officer, Colonel James Wilson, ordered the infantry to extinguish the blaze. In the fading light Wilson observed that enough of the bridge's original structure remained to serve as a foundation for a new bridge. During a dark, stormy night, Union pioneers salvaged timbers and beams, lashed them to the suspension rods with telegraph wire, and rebuilt the bridge. By dawn, May 3, the bridge was ready for the infantry.

Only one more significant natural barrier, Big Black River, stood between Grant's Army of the Tennessee and Vicksburg. The aggressive General John Logan's division spearheaded the drive toward this river. In the unlikely event Logan faltered, McPherson accompanied the division. Together, the two officers drove the men hard. McPherson hoped that if his men marched fast enough they could cut off any Confederates trying to escape back to Vicksburg. McPherson also hoped to capture the Hankinson's Ferry bridge intact in order to secure a bridgehead over the Big Black.

Around 10.00 a.m. the leading Union regiment encountered what appeared to be a Rebel roadblock just south of Willow Springs. McPherson ordered an aide to ride to a nearby plantation and bring back someone to interrogate. The plantation owner, an elegant, garrulous fellow named Reinertsen, assured McPherson that nearly all the Confederate troops had retired across the Big Black. Meanwhile, Logan ordered the van regiment, the 20th Ohio, to double-time ahead along with De Golyer's 8th Michigan Battery. The battery galloped into position, unlimbered, and prepared to lay down a covering barrage. The panting Ohio infantry arrived. One of the men spotted Logan and called out, "Shall we not unsling our knapsacks?"

"No!" Logan snarled. "Damn them, you can whip them with your knapsacks on!"[35] Inspired by Logan's stern words, the 20th Ohio advanced to storm the roadblock.

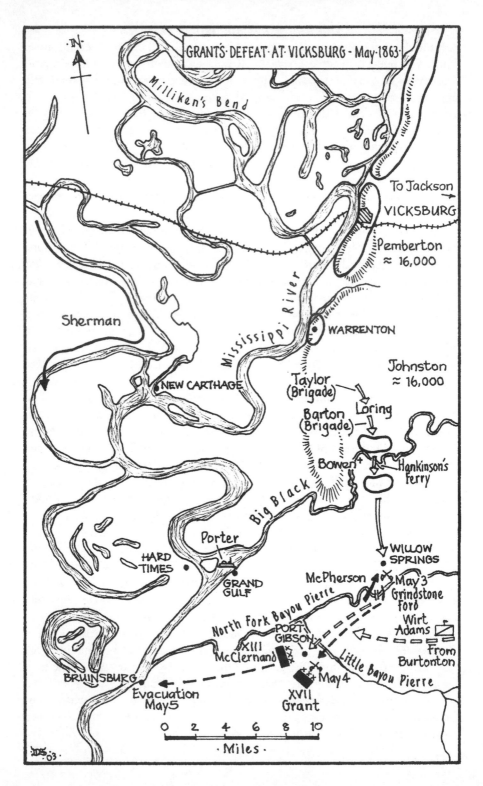

GRANT'S·DEFEAT·AT·VICKSBURG – May·1863·

·N·

Milliken's Bend

To Jackson

VICKSBURG

Pemberton ≈ 16,000

Sherman

Mississippi River

WARRENTON

Johnston ≈ 16,000

Taylor (Brigade)

Loring

NEW CARTHAGE

Barton (Brigade)

Bowen

Hankinson's Ferry

Big Black

Porter

WILLOW SPRINGS

HARD TIMES

McPherson

May 3 Grindstone Ford

North Fork Bayou Pierre

GRAND GULF

Wirt Adams

PORT GIBSON

XIII McClernand

Little Bayou Pierre

From Burtonton

BRUINSBURG

Evacuation May 5

May 4

XVII Grant

0 2 4 6 8 10

·Miles·

DS ·03·

Whether Logan and McPherson should be faulted for their impetuosity is difficult to say. Since neither general survived the battle, we cannot know exactly what they thought they saw. What seems certain is that their hasty reconnaissance failed to detect the presence of a formidable, and rapidly increasing foe.

The Confederates manning the roadblock itself belonged to Colonel A.E. Reynolds's 26th Mississippi Infantry. Concealed in the nearby trees were four guns belonging to Lieutenant Culbertson's Company C, 14th Mississippi Artillery Battalion. Initially, Reynolds's orders were merely to fight a rearguard action; force the enemy to deploy and then retire without risking too much. But 30 minutes before the Yankees appeared, a sweat-stained horse and rider appeared to deliver new orders: Reynolds was to defend his position to the last man! Reynolds read the dispatch and his face turned ashen. The courier grinned and told him not to worry. Reinforcements were coming up fast led by Albert Sidney Johnston himself. Which part of this intelligence shocked Reynolds most also cannot be determined because the Mississippi colonel was another who did not survive the battle.

Reynolds mounted an overturned plantation buggy that formed part of the roadblock and addressed his men. In part he predicted that the Rebels "would run Grant and his boys back over ole Mississippi before they knew what had hit them."[36] The cheering had not yet subsided when the first shells from De Golyer's 8th Michigan Battery burst around the roadblock. A large metal fragment from a 6-pounder James rifle shell tore off the colonel's arm and inflicted a mortal wound.

Hard on the heels of the deadly shelling came the 20th Ohio. Colonel Manning Force led his Buckeyes forward. When they came within 200 yards of the roadblock, the heretofore unseen Mississippi artillery opened fire. The battery's single 3-inch rifle fired at the Michigan artillery in an effort to divert their all too effective barrage. Meanwhile, two 6 pounder smoothbores and a single 12-pounder howitzer flailed the blue-coated infantry with canister.

Although surprised to receive fire from the masked battery, the veteran Ohio infantry closed ranks and pressed on. They endured two volleys from the defenders behind the roadblock but the fire from the Mississippi infantry was ragged; apparently the 26th Mississippi was unnerved by the fall of its colonel. The Buckeyes lowered bayonets and charged home. Manning Force himself mounted the carriage where Reynolds had fallen, stabbed a Rebel color-bearer with his sword, and seized the flag with an exultant scream. The defenders broke toward the rear and the Ohio infantry surged over and through the roadblock, scooping up prisoners as well as the Mississippians' state colors. This charge proved to be the high water mark for the Army of the Tennessee.

Sidney Johnston had had little time to organize an offensive. His plan was not subtle: his 16,000 soldiers would cross Hankinson's Ferry and attack the enemy where found. His objective was to drive the Yankees back through Grindstone Ford. Johnston placed his trust in the combination of surprise and superior numbers. He was, however, able to ensure that the first Confederates who arrived to support Reynolds's Mississippians were the best fighters in his army—Colonel Francis Cockrell's Missouri Brigade.

As Cockrell's men swept forward at the double they passed a farmhouse and heard the sound of female voices singing *Dixie*. Glancing over, they saw a group of ladies singing and cheering to encourage their heroes. Cockrell, looking like a quintessential Southern cavalier, held his reins and a magnolia blossom in one hand and his sword in the other. He flourished his sword in salute to the patriotic ladies and then pointed his weapon at the enemy. Nearby, Private John Dale of the 5th Missouri leaped over a rail fence and ran forward while screaming, "Come on Company I, we can whip the Goddamn Yankee sons-of-bitches!"[37]

The initial Confederate onslaught recaptured the barricade and broke the second Union line as well. "Black Jack" Logan galloped forward to rally his men. He rose in his stirrups and shouted, "We must whip them here or all go under the sod together. Give 'em hell." The Missouri battery supporting Cockrell's brigade targeted Logan's line. A shell from one of its 10-pounder Parrott rifles decapitated the Union general, catapulting his lifeless body to the ground like a dancing marionette whose strings had been severed.

Logan's sudden death shocked the Yankees. But it was the unexpected sight of Cockrell's wildmen, shrieking like banshees and coming closer with every step, that unnerved the Union men. They broke before contact. Confederate Sergeant William Ruyle described the ensuing charge: "We gave them the Missouri yell... and gave them a charge in Missouri REBEL style. We routed them and took after them."[38]

The Union collapse occurred so fast that the supporting brigade hardly had time to deploy before it too faced Cockrell's furious charge. Like Logan, young General McPherson understood that the crisis was at hand. Unlike Logan, he did not use profanity. As he tried to steady his men he called out, "Give them Jesse boys, give them Jesse."[39] Wearing his full dress uniform, riding a superb black horse, McPherson exposed himself recklessly. He made an unmistakable target and died outright when a Confederate marksman shot him through the lower back. The bullet's trajectory tore upward toward the heart. McPherson toppled from the saddle.

The surging Rebels found an orderly cradling the general's head in his lap. "Who is lying there" an Arkansas captain inquired. The orderly replied, "Sir it is General McPherson. You have killed the best man in our army."[40]

The deaths of two popular and charismatic leaders demoralized the XVII Corps. The corps was strung out in road column and ill-prepared for combat. In the absence of both corps and divisional commanders, no one seemed to take charge. The first inkling most men had that the enemy was near came when demoralized soldiers ran by them crying out, "Logan is down!" or

"McPherson has fallen!" For the remainder of the afternoon the Union soldiers concentrated on escaping to safety over Grindstone Ford.

The day ended with the XVII Corps fleeing over the ford, having lost some 3,200 men including its two best known generals. As had been the case at Fort Donelson and Shiloh, the Rebel attack had found the Union army commander far from the scene of action. Grant had spent the day at Grand Gulf where he conferred with Admiral Porter and worked to unclog his line of communications. In part because McPherson's death had plunged the staff into confusion, Grant did not learn of the debacle at Hankinson's Ferry until early evening. He responded to the grim news in characteristic fashion by summoning all available manpower to support his wounded field army. Sherman's corps was still marching south through the Louisiana bayous on the far side of the Mississippi. Grant's dispatch to Sherman candidly related the day's news. He ordered Sherman to accelerate his march and ended by saying, "It is unnecessary for me to remind you of the overwhelming importance of celerity in your movements."[41]

As Grant prepared to gallop off to rejoin his army, Admiral Porter cornered John Rawlins, Grant's chief of staff, to learn the news. In Porter's mind it could hardly be worse. His fleet lay trapped between two fortified rebel citadels: Vicksburg to the north and Port Hudson to the south. The army held an unsecure bridgehead at the end of a precarious line of communications stretching back to Milliken's Bend. Its back was against the continent's greatest river while somewhere to the front was a hungry enemy closing in for the kill. Porter summoned his steward for a glass of naval rum. After Grant and his staff departed, the admiral began preparing his ironclads and transports to ferry the army back over the Mississippi just in case it all went wrong.

The Second Battle of Port Gibson

That evening, the elated Confederate army celebrated its victory in style. The soldiers were in fine spirits, eager to come to grips again with the invaders. A Tennessee lieutenant's description of his comrades reveals the prevailing mood:

> "They are effective men. Men that are fighting for the property of their families, for their rights... such men can't be subjugated, unconquerable with too much hatred to even wish for peace, all joyful and full of glee, marching perhaps right into the jaws of death. Ah, will the God of Battles give this splendid army to Lincoln's hordes who have robbed the defenseless women and children of the staff of life? No the God of Battles will grant us Victory."[42]

An exceedingly weary Sidney Johnston tried to focus on the myriad tasks that needed doing and discovered that he could not. Finally, he summoned

Bowen to his headquarters. Bowen found Johnston lying down while an anxious Doctor Yandell applied a cold compress to his brow.

"My friend," Johnston said:

> "I need your help. Tomorrow, we will of course, attack. The enemy is off balance and brittle. If we hit them hard before they can get set, they will break. Before we attacked today I asked Pemberton to forward reinforcements. Most of the Vicksburg garrison should be here sometime tomorrow morning. I want you to act as my chief of staff. Send orders to all units en route and order them to force march through the night. Ten soldiers who arrive tomorrow are worth more than fifty who come the next day."[43]

While Johnston rested, Bowen and a band of devoted staff officers worked tirelessly to assemble a fresh Confederate striking force. In truth, even Pemberton—always more comfortable directing affairs from a rear area headquarters—responded well to Johnston's request for reinforcements. Loring's and Stevenson's complete divisions along with a brigade each from William Forney and Martin Smith arrived in time for battle. Even Wirt Adams's Mississippi Cavalry abandoned their futile chase of Grierson's raiders to complete a cross-country trek to join Johnston and be in at the kill.

That morning a stiff and sore Sidney Johnston summoned his subordinates. Again his plan was simple: a simultaneous attack all along the front. "Gentlemen," he said, "You will not do wrong if you march to the sounds of the heaviest firing and give them the bayonet." After Dr Yandell helped him into the saddle, Johnston fixed his lieutenants with a stern look and said, "Tonight we will water our horses in the Mississippi!"[44]

The ensuing so-called "Second Battle of Port Gibson" proved to be a one-sided affair. Grant emulated his fallen comrades by exposing himself recklessly. The soldiers who fought under his immediate command responded bravely. But Grant was forced to act as corps commander for the leaderless XVII Corps, and because of this need he was unable to keep a tight rein over McClernand's XIII Corps.

While it is unlikely—contrary to the charges of his political foes, who point to the fact that as post-war governor of Illinois McClernand seemed quite content to let the southern portion of his state secede to join the Confederate States of America—that McClernand was secretly assisting the Rebels, the facts speak for themselves. During the battle McClernand's command remained largely inert, apparently quite content to let the remnants of the XVII Corps fight unaided. The only initiative he displayed was in leading his men to be first aboard Porter's transports when the Army of the Tennessee abandoned its bridgehead on the Mississippi's eastern shore.

The ignoble flight of Grant's army proved decisive in the collapse of the Union war effort. The midwestern anti-war press, led by Matt Halstead, the acid-penned editor of the influential *Cincinnati Commercial*, demanded

Grant's dismissal. It was Shiloh all over, complete with charges that Grant had again been drunk.

Perhaps Lincoln would have retained his favorite western general had not another catastrophe occurred in the east. Hooker's debacle at Chancellorsville elevated Northern anti-war sentiment to a fevered pitch. Lincoln discarded Grant but it failed to silence his political critics. Worse, in a textbook demonstration of the advantage of interior lines, five Confederate brigades took to the cars to move from Vicksburg to Richmond in early June 1863. Their presence allowed Robert E. Lee to wage a careful campaign of maneuver culminating in the epic Battle of Gettysburg. The sight of Cockrell's valiant Missouri men charging side by side with Pickett's Virginians to storm Cemetery Ridge is memorably depicted by the cyclorama at the Richmond National Museum's Hall of Valor.

General Johnston did not live to water his horse in the Mississippi. As at Shiloh, he led from the front and this time paid the full price when he fell while directing the last charge against the gallant but futile Union rearguard conducted by Colonel Boomer's brigade. We have only the not altogether reliable words of his aide, Captain Wickham, that Johnston knew that his army stood on the cusp of a great and decisive victory before he died.[45] Certainly anyone seeking more information about Johnston's death is well advised to visit the Martyr's Rotunda in our nation's capital in Richmond.

The Reality

Jefferson Davis went to his grave believing that, had his friend Sidney Johnston lived, the South would have won the war. "When Sidney Johnston fell," Davis plaintively observed, "it was the turning point of our fate; for we had no other to take up his work in the West."[46] How successful Johnston might have been has been a popular speculative topic every since that bloody April at Shiloh. Skeptics point to Johnston's ponderous, flawed tactical alignment at Shiloh. However, recall that Grant had his Belmont, Lee his botched campaign in West Virginia and again during the Seven Days, Jackson his Kernstown. All of these men learned from experience and it seems reasonable to believe that, had Johnston lived, he too would have improved. Instead, Johnston assigned Doctor Yandell the task of caring for the wounded and subsequently died with a tourniquet in his pocket which, if promptly applied, would have saved him.

The outline of events in my story follows reality. The details of Cockrell's dramatic charge are taken from the Battle of Champion Hill. McClernand did in fact put in an amazingly slack performance at that same battle. Pemberton did concentrate a mass of maneuver after the Battle of Port Gibson. Had he employed this force offensively, he well might have caught the XVII Corps in the type of situation I describe. Historian Edwin Bearss speculates that Grant's impetuous pursuit gave "the Confederate leaders a chance to destroy or maul one of his corps."[47] When I considered this opportunity in my own Vicksburg book I concluded, "if the recent fight at Port Gibson proved anything, it was that the area's terrain was far better suited to the defense than the attack."[48] Still, an aggressive leader such as Lee, Jackson, or Grant would have hazarded the stroke. With the element of surprise and a numerical advantage of 16,000 versus 11,000, a Confederate success is well within the realm of possibility.

To make my story plausible required a Confederate leader willing to hazard the stroke. When I first proposed my story to the editor, he replied that Pemberton would never have taken the risk. Indeed, Pemberton's foolish commitment to defending what he undoubtedly believed to be his sacred trust, namely Vicksburg itself, was key to what actually did take place; he achieved a potential battle-winning concentration at Hankinson's Ferry and then dispersed it to guard against Grant's next thrust. So, if not Pemberton then who? Not Lee, who steadily refused to serve in the West, not Joe Johnston, who never saw a position as good as the next one to the rear, therefore a "resurrected" Sidney Johnston.

What would have been the impact of Grant's failure at Vicksburg? It is a provocative topic for speculation. Recall three points: in the spring of 1863 the people of the Old Northwest were very unhappy about the stalemate on the Mississippi and weary about casualties among their boys, and here the peace movement was growing; one of the main reasons Lee went north in the fateful summer of 1863 was to relieve pressure at Vicksburg; if the Confederate reserves sent to relieve Pemberton had instead nourished Lee's invasion, if even the 5,000 men Beauregard could spare had been present at Gettysburg on July 1 or July 2, what might have transpired? Such is history.

Bibliography

Arnold, James R., *Presidents Under Fire: Commanders in Chief in Victory and Defeat* (Orion Books, New York, 1994).

Arnold, James R., *Grant Wins the War: Decision at Vicksburg* (John Wiley & Sons, New York, 1997).

Bearss, Edwin Cole, *The Vicksburg Campaign* (Morningside, Dayton, OH, 1986).

Byers, S.H.M., "Some Recollections of Grant," in *Annals of the War Written by Leading Participants North and South* (Blue & Grey Press, Edison, NJ, 1996; reprint of 1879 edition).

Davis, William C., *Jefferson Davis: The Man and his Hour* (HarperCollins, New York, 1991).

Grant, U.S., *Personal Memoirs of U.S. Grant* (Da Capo Press, New York, 1982).

Johnson, Robert, and Buel, Clarence, eds., *Battles and Leaders of the Civil War*, 4 vols. (Thomas Yoseloff, New York, 1956).

McDonough, James, and Jones, James, *War So Terrible: Sherman and Atlanta* (W.W. Norton, New York, 1987).

Morris, W.S., *et. al.*, *Thirty-First Regiment Illinois Volunteers* (Crossfire Press, Herrin, IL, 1991).

Oldroyd, Osborn H., *A Soldier's Story of the Siege of Vicksburg* (Springfield, IL, 1885).

Rowland, Dunbar, ed., *Jefferson Davis, Constitutionalist: His Letters, Papers and Speeches* (Mississippi Department of Archives and History, Jackson, MS, 1923).

Sword, Wiley, *Shiloh: Bloody April* (Morningside Bookshop, Dayton, OH, 1988).

Tucker, Philip Thomas, *The South's Finest: The First Missouri Confederate Brigade from Pea Ridge to Vicksburg* (White Mane Publishing, Shippensburg, PA, 1993).

U.S. War Department, *The War of the Rebellion: A Compilation of the Official Records of the Union and Confederate Armies*, 4 series in 70 volumes in 128 books (Government Printing Office, Washington, D.C., 1880–1901).

Wiley, Bell Irvin, ed., *"This Infernal War": The Confederate Letters of Sgt. Edwin H. Fay* (University of Texas Press, Austin, TX, 1958).

Younger, Edward, ed., *Inside the Confederate Government: The Diary of Robert Garlick Hill Kean* (Oxford University Press, New York, 1957).

Notes

*1. W.L. Wickham, "A True Account of the Battle of Shiloh," in *Defeat and Victory: The Triumph of the Confederate States of America* (Tredegar Press, Richmond, 1890), p. 43.

2. William Preston Johnston, "Albert Sidney Johnston at Shiloh," in Johnson and Buel, *Battles and Leaders of the Civil War*, vol. 1, pp. 556–7.

*3. Wickham, "A True Account of the Battle of Shiloh," in *Defeat and Victory*, p. 44.

4. Sword, *Shiloh: Bloody April*, p. 222.

5. *Ibid.*, p. 148.

6. Johnston, "Albert Sidney Johnston at Shiloh," in Johnson and Buel, *Battles and Leaders* 1, p. 557.

7. *Ibid.*

*8. D.W. Yandell, "Saving General Johnston," in *Defeat and Victory: The Triumph of the Confederate States of America*, p. 120.

9. Sword, *Shiloh: Bloody April*, p. 261.

10. *Ibid.*, p. 263.

11. Johnston, "Albert Sidney Johnston at Shiloh," in Johnson and Buel, *Battles and Leaders* I, p. 564.

12. Sword, *Shiloh: Bloody April*, p. 264.

13. *Ibid.*, p. 266.

14. Grant, *Personal Memoirs of U.S. Grant*, p. 185.

15. Sword, *Shiloh: Bloody April*, p. 270.

16. Johnston, "Albert Sidney Johnston at Shiloh," in Johnson and Buel, *Battles and Leaders* I, p. 565.

*17. Wickham, "A True Account of the Battle of Shiloh," in *Defeat and Victory*, p. 48.

18. Davis, *Jefferson Davis*, p. 398.

19. U.S. War Department, *War of the Rebellion: A Compilation of the Official Records of the Union and Confederate Armies*, ser. I, vol. 10, J. Davis to A.S. Johnston, April 5, 1862, p. 394. Hereafter cited as *Official Records*.

*20. Yandell, "Saving General Johnston," in *Defeat and Victory*, p. 137.

21. Younger, *Inside the Confederate Government*, p. 28.

22. Rowland, *Jefferson Davis, Constitutionalist*, vol. 5, pp. 386–8; Davis to Holmes, December 21, 1862.

23. Wiley, *"This Infernal War"*, p. 179.

24. For a fuller account of the *Arkansas*'s amazing exploits see: Arnold, *Grant Wins the War*.

*25. John Bowen, "An Interview with General Johnston," *Confederate Veteran* III:10 (October 1894): p. 281.

26. Grant, *Personal Memoirs*, p. 252.

27. Arnold, *Grant Wins the War,* p. 103.

28. *Official Records* I:24, part 3, p. 815.

29. *Ibid.*, p. 821.

*30. The potential consequences of the Union capture of Vicksburg are well described in Peter Tsouras, *If the North Had Won the Civil War* (Greenhill Books, London, 1997).

*31. James Richardson, ed., *A Compilation of the Messages and Papers of the Confederacy, 1861–1864*, vol. 2 (Confederate States Publishing Co., Richmond, 1906), p. 957.

32. *Official Records* I:24, part 3, p. 823.

*33. The Papers of John C. Taylor, Special Collections, Alderman Library, University of Virginia, Charlottesville, Virginia. Taylor was one of Pemberton's staff officers and was present at this conference.

34. Byers, "Some Recollections of Grant," in *Annals of the War*.

35. Oldroyd, *A Soldier's Story of the Siege of Vicksburg*, p. 25.

36. William Candace Thompson, "From Shiloh to Port Gibson," *Civil War Times Illustrated* III:6 (October 1964), p. 23.

37. Tucker, *The South's Finest*, p. 162.

38. Memoirs, William A. Ruyle papers, Fifth Missouri, Harrisburg Civil War Roundtable Collection, U.S. Military History Institute, Carlisle, PA.

39. Morris, *Thirty-First Regiment Illinois Volunteers*, pp. 64–5.

40. McDonough and Jones, *War So Terrible*, p. 229.

41. *Official Records* I:24, part 3, p. 248; Grant to Sherman, May 3, 1863.

42. Calvin Smith, "'We Can Hold Our Ground': Calvin Smith's diary," *Civil War Times Illustrated* 24:2 (April 1985), p. 28.

43. D.W. Yandell, "A Hero's Last Night," in *Defeat and Victory*, p. 346.

*44. *Ibid.*, p. 348.

*45. W.L. Wickham, "With Johnston at Port Gibson: A True Account of the Death of General Albert Sidney Johnston," in *My Adventures in War and Peace* (University of Texas Press, Austin, 1884), p. 292. But note that Wickham first mentioned this dramatic incident while embroiled in a close and controversial campaign for Congress in Texas.

46. Sword, *Shiloh: Bloody April*, p. 436.

47. Bearss, *The Campaign for Vicksburg*, vol. 2, p. 423.

48. Arnold, *Grant Wins the War*, p. 120.

6

"ABSOLUTELY ESSENTIAL TO VICTORY"
Stuart's Cavalry in the Gettysburg – Pipe Creek Campaigns

Edward G. Longacre[1]

Rector's Cross Roads, Virginia, night of June 23–24, 1863

Upon occasion, Major General James Ewell Brown Stuart made conspicuous display of his willingness to share with his men the hardships of field campaigning. Although he had established his headquarters as commander of the Cavalry Division, Army of Northern Virginia, in a comfortable farmhouse on the outskirts of Rector's Cross Roads, he had chosen to bivouac under an elm tree in the side yard. There he huddled, wrapped in a poncho, despite the steady, wind-driven rain that fell throughout the night of June 23–24, 1863. In the camps they had pitched in the surrounding fields, Stuart's officers and troopers did their best to emulate their superior's fortitude.

The elements notwithstanding, Stuart was sound asleep when, just shy of midnight, his adjutant-general, Major Henry Brainard McClellan, shook him into consciousness. As the cavalry leader arose, rubbing sleep from his eyes, the staff officer handed him a dispatch just received from Robert E. Lee's headquarters at Berryville, almost 20 miles to the northwest. Stuart noted that the envelope had been opened—McClellan quickly explained he had scanned the contents to determine if they were important enough to warrant awakening his chieftain. Stuart nodded, removed the dispatch, and perused it by the light of a lantern in the staff officer's hands.[2]

At first, he was delighted by what he read. "Marse Robert" appeared to approve in substance a proposal that Stuart had advanced three days earlier and which he had fleshed out in subsequent communiqués to army headquarters: that the greater part of his command advance into enemy territory miles apart from the main army.

151

A decision on the matter could not be postponed. Six weeks earlier, following his dramatic victory over the Yankees of Major General Joseph Hooker at Chancellorsville, Lee had begun his second invasion of the country north of the Potomac River. The first, launched the previous September, had ended in a day of horrific carnage outside Sharpsburg, <u>Maryland</u>, after which Lee had returned his battered army to Virginia. The second effort had gotten off to a more favorable start: in mid-June, Lee's advance had captured several outposts in the lower (i.e., the northern reaches of the) Shenandoah Valley, including the sizable garrison at Winchester. Then, too, on the day Winchester fell, the advance element of Lieutenant General Richard S. Ewell's Second Corps had crossed the Mason-Dixon Line into southern Pennsylvania, occupying the city of Chambersburg. Ewell's troops were now poised to move on to their next objective, the state capital at Harrisburg, on the north bank of the Susquehanna River. Meanwhile, the rest of Lee's main army—the Third Corps of Lieutenant General A.P. Hill, trailed by Lieutenant General James Longstreet's First Corps—was preparing to quit Virginia and join Ewell in the Keystone State.[3]

It was largely due to the exertions of Stuart's troopers, who for the past two weeks had been screening the exposed right flank of the invasion column, that Robert E. Lee's northward march had proceeded so quickly and smoothly. As they trotted through Virginia's Loudoun Valley, Stuart's men had repeatedly engaged the Union cavalry of Major General Alfred Pleasonton, roving well in advance of Hooker's main force. At Aldie on June 17, at neighboring Middleburg two days later, and farther west at Upperville on the 21st, the Confederates had blunted almost every attempt by Pleasonton's overmatched but energetic troopers to penetrate the Blue Ridge Mountains and discern Lee's position in the Shenandoah Valley. While the cavalries clashed, Hooker, unwilling to commit himself to a full-fledged pursuit until able to determine his enemy's intentions, held his main body close to his headquarters at Fairfax Station.

Not until the close of the fighting at Upperville were scouting parties from Brigadier General John Buford's First Cavalry Division, Army of the Potomac, able to outflank Stuart, climb the foothills of the Blue Ridge, and sight the bivouacs of Longstreet's corps. Then and only then—too late to prevent the rest of the Army of Northern Virginia from entering Pennsylvania—did Hooker issue orders for a cautious advance toward the Potomac.[4]

Stuart's men had done their job faithfully and well; they deserved the two-day respite their commander permitted them following Pleasonton's withdrawal to Aldie on the 22d. Yet their leader was not satisfied to have helped get the invasion off to a promising start; he wished to ensure its long-term success. Thus he sought a strategic, not merely a tactical, role in the balance of the campaign.

Basically, Stuart wanted permission to launch an independent foray into Pennsylvania, passing around Hooker's army before the latter began a full-scale pursuit. He would dog the Yankees' heels, monitoring not only Pleasonton's movements but those of his infantry and artillery comrades. If and when the enemy crossed into Maryland, he would notify Lee, then ride hard to link with Ewell's vanguard on the Susquehanna. En route, he hoped to penetrate close enough to Washington, D.C., to scare the wits out of the local populace, including Abraham Lincoln and his minions.[5]

Ample precedent testified to what Stuart might accomplish on such a mission. In June 1862, he had left besieged Richmond to raid along the north bank of the Chickahominy River and into the rear of the Army of the Potomac, then under Major General George B. McClellan. With barely 1,000 troopers, he rode the length of McClellan's position, evaded a massive pursuit force, and brought Robert E. Lee the intelligence he needed to strike successfully at McClellan's right flank. As a direct result of the daring mission—during which Stuart's men sacked several supply bases, inflicting millions of dollars in materiel losses, at the cost of a single casualty—McClellan's grip on the Confederate capital had been forever broken.

Stuart's success seemed to call for a repeat performance—perhaps more than one. Ten weeks after encircling McClellan, the cavalry leader led 1,500 troopers and two horse artillery pieces into the rear of John Pope's Army of Virginia between the Rappahannock and Rapidan Rivers. By severing communication lines, plundering the enemy's commissariat, and distracting and discomfiting Pope, Stuart helped turn the Second Manassas (Bull Run) campaign into a resounding Confederate victory. Finally, early in October 1862, Stuart launched a second circuit of the Army of the Potomac, one that carried his 1,800-man column as far north as Dick Ewell's present bailiwick in lower Pennsylvania. After seizing supplies and mangling miles of Union-controlled railroad, Stuart returned at his leisure to home base, having suffered all of three casualties. This second ride around McClellan presaged the relief of the general once hailed throughout the North as a "young Napoleon."[6]

Cavalry Conference, Rector's Cross Roads, June 24, 1863

With so much glorious history to his credit, Stuart had every reason to expect that Lee would favorably entertain his latest request to visit the Union rear. The opening lines of Lee's June 23 communiqué seemed to confirm this belief: "Your proposed plan of operations promises many benefits and, of course, entails some risks. You are the best judge of whether the movement can be accomplished in good season, and without damage to your gallant command."[7]

So far so good—as he absorbed these words, Stuart must have envisioned another exciting excursion through hostile territory. He hungered for such an opportunity, if only to help relieve the stigma he and his command had received two weeks earlier near Brandy Station, an Orange & Alexandria Railroad depot along the upper Rappahannock. On June 9 Stuart's troopers—then on the eve of joining Lee's invasion force—had been surprised, throttled, and nearly routed during a predawn attack by 8,500 Federal cavalrymen under Pleasonton. Recovering from the shock of the assault, Stuart had engineered a multi-pronged defense that held back the upstart Yankees and salvaged a bloody draw.

The day-long combat had ended with the enemy's retreat. Yet the narrow margin by which the Cavalry Division of the Army of Northern Virginia had escaped disaster had brought the wrath of editors and politicians on Stuart's head for the first time in the war. A proud man, fiercely protective of his hard-won reputation as the conflict's most successful cavalry leader, Stuart had regarded his men's efforts at Aldie, Middleburg, and Upperville as installment payments in restitution. And yet the verbal barbs directed at him in the wake of Brandy Station continued to sting. Stuart realized he must do more, must strive harder, to erase the stain on his own reputation and that of his command.[8]

When he read the balance of Lee's dispatch, however, Stuart's hopes for a renewed demonstration of his prowess in independent command began to fade:

> "General Longstreet, however, has raised objections to your proposal that
> I believe warrant serious consideration. I wish you to read carefully his
> comments, contained in the enclosed note, and consult closely with
> him, as well as with your subordinates, as to your future course. It may
> be that this is not the time to detach yourself from the army, which will
> require the closest support as it prepares to enter the enemy's homeland.
> Please advise me of your decision at the earliest opportunity."[9]

A concerned Stuart scanned the brief letter to which Lee had alluded. He was mildly surprised to find that it bore Longstreet's handwriting, an indication of its importance. Surprise was quickly followed by disappointment. In a few sentences, the leader of the First Corps, to whose command Stuart had been attached, advised strongly against any leave-taking. Longstreet desired that the cavalry, with the exception of a brigade or two to be left to guard the passes in the army's rear, should stick close to the main army as it moved through Maryland and into Pennsylvania. With Pleasonton's horsemen drawn off, there was no need for Stuart to remain east of the Blue Ridge. He should head for the Potomac, crossing the river in the vicinity of Shepherdstown, and then cover the front and flanks of A.P. Hill. In closing, Longstreet urged that Lee not be denied the powers of perception that only mounted units could provide:

> "It is as true now as it has ever been, that we cannot afford to stumble
> blindly through a country intimately familiar to the enemy, one he will
> doubtless defend with every resource at his disposal."[10]

Then and later, Stuart made no effort to conceal his chagrin at Longstreet's observations, especially since they appeared to have the tacit support of Lee. As the cavalry leader confided to his closest subordinates, he particularly objected to Longstreet's concluding sentence, which Stuart interpreted as a veiled criticism of his earlier expeditions. At bottom, he discounted the logic in Longstreet's arguments. For one thing, if he left a part of his command behind in Virginia, as Longstreet suggested, why would he need to guard the army's rear as it advanced north? As for covering Lee's flanks, a brigade of cavalry, mounted infantry, and partisan rangers under Brigadier General John Imboden had been brought up from the Shenandoah Valley to handle the task; it was now advancing on the army's left flank, albeit well west of it. Stuart likewise considered unfounded Longstreet's concern that the cavalry must travel in advance of the infantry. Even as Longstreet wrote, another recently attached brigade of western Virginia horsemen, under Brigadier General Albert G. Jenkins, was escorting Ewell through south-central Pennsylvania. No, thought Stuart, by any objective criteria, Longstreet's concerns were overblown, his arguments unpersuasive. Moreover, he suspected they were aimed less at protecting the army from unforeseen dangers than at denying the cavalry an opportunity to win glory and distinction, an opportunity unavailable to its comrades.[11]

The problem was that, given his rank and influence, Longstreet's objections—although framed as mere suggestions—carried more than a modicum of weight. Stuart saw that his only hope of overriding them lay in the course Lee had mentioned, consultation with his subordinates. If his brigade commanders strongly dissented from Longstreet's viewpoint, Stuart might yet persuade Lee to grant him the authority to penetrate Yankee lines and, thereafter, to act as he thought best. Therefore, the next morning, the 24th, Stuart called to Rector's Cross Roads Brigadier Generals Wade Hampton, Fitzhugh Lee (the army leader's nephew) and Beverly Holcombe Robertson, along with Colonel John R. Chambliss, Jr. These men commanded four-fifths of the force that had been assigned directly to Stuart for the invasion. At Stuart's request, the leader of the fifth brigade, Brigadier General William Edmondson Jones, remained with his command, the largest in the division, near Ashby's Gap, ten miles to the northwest. Jones, an argumentative, prickly-tempered Virginian (his nickname was "Grumble") was no friend of Stuart, who feared the man would register a resounding "no" were any head count taken this day. Stuart had something of a legitimate reason for excluding him from the planning conference: Jones, who was widely regarded as the finest outpost commander in the cavalry, could not be spared from his present position, so close to the assumed location of the enemy.[12]

But if Stuart expected the attendees at his war council to support his plan of campaign, he was soon disabused of this notion. After briefing his lieutenants on his intentions, as well as on Longstreet's arguments against them and R.E. Lee's apparent willingness to accept these at face value, he called on his subordinates to state their views. He was taken aback by the result.

As the junior officer in the group, John Chambliss spoke first. Displaying a talent for evasiveness and fence-straddling, the colonel suggested that both Stuart's and Longstreet's views were well-taken. That said, he shut his mouth and sat down. It seemed obvious that Chambliss, while desirous of supporting his immediate superior, was not about to refute the reasoning of the lieutenant general widely regarded as Robert E. Lee's most trusted subordinate.

Next to speak was Beverly Robertson, who had been assigned to Stuart despite the latter's conviction that the old dragoon was excitable, unreliable, and downright incompetent. That Stuart's feelings were well known did not augur well for Robertson's support of his plan of campaign. Moreover Robertson was aware of Longstreet's stipulation that Stuart, if he cut loose from the army, must leave behind a substantial force. Perhaps suspecting that he was one of those to be denied an adventure in the enemy's rear, Robertson readily announced his opposition to an independent mission he professed to view as injudicious and untimely.

Stuart was confident that his plan would fare better with his closest friend in the cavalry, the fun-loving and adventurous Fitzhugh Lee, whose support might carry weight with his uncle. To Stuart's surprise and chagrin, however, he, too, voted in the negative, albeit with obvious regret. It turned out that Fitz, who was then recovering from a disabling bout with rheumatism, feared he could not endure such a lengthy and taxing operation as Stuart had in mind. He, like Robertson, objected to being left behind while his colleagues sought glory behind enemy lines.[13]

Stuart's only hope of carrying the day now rested with Wade Hampton. If his senior lieutenant voiced strong support for the proposed expedition, Stuart might yet overcome the objections of the others. But this hope also died, as Stuart probably suspected it would. Although a highly competent cavalryman—tactically astute, fearless under fire, an expert swordsman and marksman—Hampton, a non-professional soldier, viewed men and events from a perspective denied to a West Pointer or an Old Army veteran. At 43, he was also 15 or 20 years older than some of his colleagues, whose dreams of martial glory he did not share. For Hampton, war was not a genteel tournament or a defining test of masculinity; it was a disagreeable business, to be won as quickly and as efficiently as possible.

In these and other respects, Stuart and his senior lieutenant were polar opposites. While they treated each other with conspicuous respect and unfailing courtesy, they eyed each other warily. In Stuart's view Hampton was too conservative, too slow to think and act when a quick, dramatic gesture seemed called for. For his part, the South Carolinian considered his Virginia-born superior headstrong, impetuous, too willing to risk all—

including the lives of his officers and men—when the odds against success loomed large. Then, too, the generals' relationship had suffered a rift at Brandy Station, where Hampton's beloved younger brother, Lieutenant Colonel Frank Hampton of the 2d South Carolina Cavalry, had died in a pistol and saber duel against ten times as many opponents. Hampton's chief of staff, writing years after the war, opined that his boss never forgave Stuart for allowing the Yankees to surprise him and force the division to fight frantically on the defensive.[14]

In addition to questioning some aspects of Stuart's leadership, Hampton was skeptical of the value of raids, especially those that lacked clear-cut objectives and carefully constructed timetables; such ventures produced only disabled horses and exhausted riders. The tall, husky brigadier had led several independent missions of his own, but each was based on hard intelligence of enemy positions and strengths and adhered to a carefully honed itinerary. The operation Stuart had in mind possessed none of these virtues—moreover, Hampton suspected that it lacked the requisite margin for error. His primary concern was that Stuart, once inside enemy lines, would prove unable to conform his movements to those of the army he was expected to support. Indeed, given the dubious effectiveness of long-distance communication, he doubted that Stuart would locate Ewell's headquarters short of stumbling upon it. For these and other reasons, he joined Chambliss, Robertson and Fitz Lee in opposing the proposal.

Stuart, his ambitions thwarted, saw no recourse other than to accept the decision of the majority. He felt an acute sense of regret when, later that day, his old protégé, the partisan leader John Singleton Mosby, reached Rector's Cross Roads following an extended reconnaissance of enemy positions beyond the Blue Ridge. With characteristic audacity, the master scout had ridden through the bivouacs of Hooker's widely scattered command, picking up timely intelligence at every turn. To Stuart, Mosby made a breathless report of his mission, adding his opinion that the confused and lethargic Yankees seemed likely to remain indefinitely in northern Virginia. Mosby urged a full-scale movement through or around the enemy; he even offered to guide Stuart all the way to the Susquehanna.[15]

Mosby's strongly voiced recommendations made it even harder for his patron to reject them in favor of the more prudent course Longstreet had advocated and Stuart's own lieutenants had endorsed. Yet he did so, informing the partisan that preparations were already underway to cross west of the mountains and take position on the army's flanks. Although at the time Mosby expressed regret over Stuart's decision, in later years he permitted hindsight to readjust his memory. In at least two of his voluminous postwar writings, the "Gray Ghost" contended that he not only acquiesced in Stuart's course but argued persuasively in its favor. In so doing, he claimed to have made a material contribution to the success that crowned the cavalry's operations in the North.[16]

Stuart's Cavalry Rides North, June 25, 1863

Riding out of Rector's Cross Roads on the warm, dry morning of June 25, Stuart vowed to adhere to the plan of campaign he had reluctantly accepted. As Beverly Robertson had anticipated, Jones's brigade and his own were left in place to guard the far rear while the bulk of the division closed up on the invasion column. As overall commander of the rear echelon, Robertson was charged with guarding the line between Ashby's and Snicker's Gaps, preventing Hooker from striking the army's rear as it moved north, and, should the Union leader instead turn south against lightly guarded Richmond, alerting Lee to this threat against his communications.

Robertson's primary mission was to keep close tabs on Hooker. If the Army of the Potomac crossed its namesake river, he was to quit his post and attach himself to Lee's column. Robertson's orders were clear-cut and unambiguous, and he had the manpower to carry them out. Unaccountably, however, he idled in the mountains long after Hooker shifted toward the Potomac crossings late on the 25th; nor did he inform Lee of the movement. Furthermore, he ignored repeated orders to close up in the army's rear, orders conveyed by courier from Stuart's headquarters. So, at any rate, Stuart later claimed—Robertson vehemently denied ever receiving any such communications.[17]

The upshot was that on the last day of June Stuart, now aware of the magnitude of his subordinate's dereliction, relieved Robertson from command and forcefully ordered both brigades, under Jones, to lower Pennsylvania. There they rejoined the rest of the division, enabling these 3,000 men to see gainful employment during the balance of the invasion. Robertson protested his removal—which he ascribed to Stuart's displeasure with his vote at the June 24 conference—but to no effect. The brigadier never again served in the Army of Northern Virginia; he closed out his war service in command of a training camp in North Carolina.[18]

Reduced to a command 4,500 strong—one bereft of horse artillery, all of the cavalry's guns having been left in the Valley or on the Potomac—Stuart rode hard to overtake the army at the head of the brigades of Hampton, Chambliss, and Lee (a still-recuperating Fitz riding in an ambulance on the first leg of the trip). Passing through Ashby's Gap, the cavalry fanned out to cover the rear and flanks of Longstreet's corps as it proceeded north via Berryville, Summit Point, Bunker Hill, and Martinsburg, to Williamsport on the Potomac, which they reached on the 26th. Late that day, the troopers covered the crossing of the divisions of Major Generals John Bell Hood and Lafayette McLaws. Afterward, they forded the river downstream from the infantry. Once on Maryland soil, they galloped north to the headquarters of Ambrose P. Hill. For the remainder of the journey north, Stuart rode at the forefront of Hill's corps in company with the now-recovered Fitz Lee. Chambliss's brigade covered the western flank of the army, while sharing

rearguard duties with Hampton, whose command also protected the right
flank, the most exposed and vulnerable element of the invasion force.[19]

Hampton's men performed the lion's share of the scouting duties on the
road north. Early in the war the South Carolinian had formed one of the most
enterprising and effective bands of scouts in Confederate service—
adventurous youths in their late teens and early twenties who thought
nothing of roaming behind enemy lines, often clothed in Union blue, where
they gleaned intelligence from incautious Yankees and talkative civilians. On
this occasion, the youngsters more than earned their pay. Early on the 26th
they reported the transfer of Hooker's headquarters from Fairfax Court
House to Edwards's Ferry and then across the Potomac to Poolesville,
Maryland. That same day they monitored the crossing of the V and XII
Corps, Army of the Potomac, to a point near the mouth of the Monocacy
River. Hampton's patrols also located the advance guard of Hooker's army,
the I Corps of Major General John F. Reynolds, on the roads between
Barnesville and Jefferson, Maryland. Other scouts observed—from a prudent
distance—the movements of Buford's and David M. Gregg's divisions of
Yankee cavalry as they moved north of the Potomac. The outriders even
noted the approach from the vicinity of Frederick, Maryland, of a third body
of blue riders. This column, then a part of the defense forces of Washington,
D.C., would soon become the Third Cavalry Division, Army of the Potomac,
under Brigadier General H. Judson Kilpatrick.[20]

In addition to locating and identifying units, Hampton's scouts provided
an accurate assessment of the number of troopers Stuart could expect to
encounter in Maryland and Pennsylvania. They placed the number at
10,000—only 500 fewer than the actual total available to Hooker. The
scouts were less successful in estimating the total strength of the Union
army, although by piecing together their reports and head counts gleaned
from other sources, Robert E. Lee estimated, more or less correctly, that his
own army was outnumbered by about 15,000 muskets. The disparity was
not as great as he had labored under during earlier campaigns. The
knowledge permitted Lee to gauge accurately his own capabilities as he
ranged to and across the Mason-Dixon Line.

Perhaps the most significant contribution made by Hampton's scouts was
their discovery, late on June 28, that Hooker (who was known to have lost
the confidence of his superiors in Washington) had been relieved of army
command in favor of Major General George Gordon Meade, former leader of
the army's V Corps. The timing of the change, on the eve of an anticipated
encounter with the invaders of the North, was difficult to understand.
Regardless, when rushed to his new headquarters outside Chambersburg,
Pennsylvania, the intelligence enabled Lee to make an informed and timely
selection of his strategic options.[21]

Lee Concentrates at Gettysburg, June 28, 1863

Believing that Meade, a resident of Pennsylvania, would move more quickly than his predecessor to defend the Keystone State, Lee resolved to concentrate his forces in preparation for a showdown with the Army of the Potomac. Already he had sent his advance echelon, Ewell's corps, from the Potomac shallows toward the Susquehanna. On the 27th Ewell had occupied Carlisle, within striking distance of the latter river and, just above it, Harrisburg. Now Lee recalled the Second Corps, directing it southward toward a junction with Longstreet, Hill, and Stuart. The logical rendezvous was the railroad village of Gettysburg, seat of Adams County, almost 30 miles south of Carlisle and 24 miles east of Chambersburg. No fewer than ten roads, including four hard-surface turnpikes, radiated out of the town like spokes on a wheel, making Gettysburg a magnet for any widely dispersed command such as Lee's.[22]

Late on the 29th, Lee, by now convinced of the strategic importance of Gettysburg, directed Stuart to head there and report on the tactical application of the local geography. At the outset of the campaign Lee had reached a tacit understanding with the defensive-minded Longstreet that he would hold any position he occupied north of the Mason-Dixon Line and await the enemy's attack. By the 28th, however, the Confederate leader had modified his strategy. He doubted that Meade, who was known as a cautious, conservative warrior, would do him the favor of assaulting any position he might occupy. Thus, as he demonstrated by dispatching Stuart to Gettysburg, Lee hoped to use the high ground surrounding Gettysburg as jumping-off points for an offensive designed to defeat in detail Meade's equally elongated army.[23]

Before dawn on the 30th Stuart started eastward from Chambersburg at the head of two of his brigades (he had left Chambliss's men at Chambersburg to support the infantry and cover the army's rear). With Hampton's scouts in the van and trailed by one of Hill's brigades, the long line of riders wended its way through South Mountain to and beyond Cashtown. Just shy of 7.00 a.m., a flanking party from Hampton's brigade located Buford's Federals—the first element of the Army of the Potomac to have crossed the Mason-Dixon Line—near Fountaindale, just above the Pennsylvania border and perhaps 20 miles southwest of Gettysburg. After sending back word of their presence, Hampton's flankers shadowed the blue horsemen as they headed north to Fairfield. Outside that farming village, they boldly challenged Buford's troopers and an accompanying battery of horse artillery. A brisk fight broke out, but then the Union leader abruptly disengaged and headed cross-country toward Gettysburg, apparently in response to imperative orders.[24]

A few hours later, Stuart's main body re-established contact with Buford's division. Early that afternoon, the Confederates approached the northwestern outskirts of Gettysburg via the Cashtown Road. At about

2.00 p.m., they ran into a phalanx of vedettes—mounted pickets—whom Buford had deployed along Marsh Run, some three miles from the center of town. Careful not to become heavily engaged for fear of disarranging his superior's plans, Stuart sparred lightly with the Yankees, while his scouts sized up the local area, taking careful note of Buford's dispositions and trying to gauge his manpower. From prisoners Stuart learned that Buford was on the scene with two-thirds of his normal strength—the brigades of Colonels William Gamble and Thomas C. Devin, plus the six 3-inch ordnance rifles of Lieutenant John Calef's Battery A, 2d United States Artillery. Most of the troopers had bivouacked atop Seminary Ridge, a quarter-mile west of town, with pickets thrown out north, west, and southwest of Gettysburg. Calef's guns had gone into battery on either side of the Cashtown Road, placed so as to sweep the most likely avenue of Confederate approach.[25]

Stuart did more than study Buford's emplacements. Hampton's scouts, sent cross-country to points south of Gettysburg, located couriers passing between Buford and the advance of the Army of the Potomac. The scouts chased down and captured one messenger, whom they found to be carrying a dispatch from John Reynolds—then encamped five miles south of Gettysburg—in response to Buford's request for infantry support at Gettysburg. The message conveyed Reynolds's promise that his I Army Corps would hasten to the cavalry's side at an early hour on July 1, followed as closely as possible by the more distant XI Corps of Major General Oliver Otis Howard.[26]

Relayed to Chambersburg, the captured dispatch told Lee that, if he moved to Gettysburg early the next morning, he would be opposed by cavalry alone. Lacking infantry support, even John Buford's savvy, hard-bitten troopers would give way before the gray tide, permitting Lee to deal with Reynolds and Howard in succession rather than in combination. Thus, fully apprised of the tactical situation taking shape east of his present position, a confident Lee started the balance of Hill's corps toward Gettysburg before dawn on July 1. Even as Hill set out, Lee sought to coordinate his movements with Ewell's. Courier-borne messages directed the Second Corps to come down southward-leading roads from Carlisle as well as the roads that led southwestward from the city of York (the latter a recent objective of one of Ewell's divisions), prepared to join hands with Hill's troops just outside Gettysburg. The succession of communiqués permitted Ewell to coordinate his movements with Hill's with remarkable precision, ensuring a concerted strike at Buford.[27]

Perhaps never before in the history of American warfare had an army advancing through hostile territory been better prepared to meet an enemy holding ground well chosen for its defensive capabilities. The result would be an object lesson in the value of what later generations would call real-time, strategic intelligence.

The Battle of Gettysburg, July 1, 1863

John Buford's experienced eye had enabled his troopers and horse artillerymen to exploit Gettysburg's topography to maximum effect. The tall, steep, foliage-crowned ridges that flowed west toward the foothills of South Mountain appeared perfectly suited to a defense in depth. To Buford's profound surprise, however, the high ground proved no obstacle to the gray-clad troopers who came calling on him on that sultry early-summer morning. First contact between Hill's skirmishers and Gamble's vedettes occurred at about 5.30 a.m. along Marsh Creek near its crossing of the Cashtown Road. Attacking with a full head of steam, Hill's foot soldiers, supported closely by the Carolina centaurs of Hampton and the Virginia cavaliers of Fitz Lee, quickly began to drive in Buford's pickets south of the road.

At first, Gamble's men retreated grudgingly, firing as they went. Their combativeness, however, did not assure them of a successful withdrawal. Before they could reach the relative safety of Herr Ridge, Stuart's main body swarmed over their position, felling them with saber swipes and pistol shots. Quickly surrounded, dozens of Yankees were killed, wounded, or taken prisoner, while panicky survivors scrambled for the rear.[28]

Those who reached Herr Ridge found no sanctuary. While comrades corralled a huge haul of prisoners, gray-clad riders thundered up the slopes to attack the pickets seeking refuge at the summit. Again the attackers uprooted Gamble's line and swept it from the field. In a memorable display of might, Wade Hampton personally dispatched several opponents with his long-bladed Spanish sword and 31-caliber pocket revolver. According to some accounts, it was he who fired the shot that dropped William Gamble, lifeless, from his horse.

As soon as they had Gamble's men on the run, Hampton's people charged toward McPherson's Ridge and, beyond, Seminary Ridge, the last long stretch of high ground west of Gettysburg. Riding an irresistible momentum, they cleared McPherson's of blue skirmishers in mere minutes. Then, at Hampton's bellowed command, they halted, regrouped, and confronted at longer range the guns of Calef's battery that Buford had emplaced astride the Cashtown Road.

Demonstrating a tactical versatility that his Virginia colleagues appeared to lack, Hampton dismounted most of his men and placed them behind cover on either side of the road, where they began to pick off battery horses and gun crews. The dismounted troopers, many of whom wielded the celebrated Enfield rifle, took such a toll of the battery that the foot soldiers coming up behind Stuart—the Tennesseeans, Alabamians, Mississippians, and North Carolinians of Major General Henry Heth's division—easily overran Calef's position. Calef himself, having emptied his pistol at the onrushing hordes, was forced to surrender along with 40 of his men. Even as they were herded to the rear, their captors trundled the guns into position facing Seminary Ridge; soon they were spraying that last bastion of Yankee resistance with canister and shell.[29]

Aware that his line was crumbling but determined to shore it up or die trying, John Buford galloped west from Seminary Ridge at the head of Gamble's reserves. Calmly noting his approach, Hampton remounted a portion of his command and guided it at the head of the blue column. In the valley between Seminary and East McPherson's Ridges, the antagonists collided with a resounding crunch. Many riders were lifted out of their saddles; others were thrown head over heels when their horses went down in the horrid, dust-clouded tangle. A North Carolinian spoke for troopers on both sides when he declared the result the "the loudest, deadliest, most frightening fifteen minutes I spent during the war."[30]

During that quarter-hour, those opponents who remained in the saddle engaged each other in a desperate sword-and-pistol contest, but one whose outcome was never in doubt. Given their greater numbers, the Confederates not only pummeled Buford's troopers in front but also lashed their flanks and rear, surrounding and squeezing their prey with python-like precision. At the height of the mêlée, Buford took a gunshot wound to the thigh that would prove fatal, although he managed to extricate himself from the slaughter and, along with a few dozen of his men, flee eastward. Bloody and breathless, the survivors were pursued through the streets of Gettysburg by Rebels screaming like banshees. Almost 100 fugitives were chased down blind alleys and captured, while almost as many others fell to cold steel or hot lead.[31]

While Hampton's men, backed by Brigadier General James J. Archer's infantry brigade, overwhelmed Gamble's position west of Gettysburg, Fitz Lee's troopers, supported closely by the foot soldiers of Brigadier General Joseph R. Davis's brigade, veered northward to oppose the vedettes and skirmishers under Tom Devin. In this sector, too, the outcome seemed preordained. Lacking Gamble's artillery support and forced to stretch his lines thinly to cover the roads north and northeast of town, Devin's position was not deep enough to hold back the hundreds of attackers who flooded over it, shooting and shouting.

Devin faced a two-pronged assault. While Davis attacked in front, holding the Federals in place, Fitz Lee burst through their picket line, then circled into their rear, Assailed simultaneously from many angles, the position came unhinged with startling rapidity. Within 45 minutes of first contact, surviving troopers were retreating east and south, most of them afoot, many having discarded the repeating carbines that had proven no match against the overwhelming assault. Many, if not most, of the fugitives were ridden down and captured before they could reach their led horses. Others made no attempt to escape; upwards of 600 Yankees, including whole companies of New Yorkers, Illinoisans, and Indianans, were compelled to surrender when trapped in an unfinished railroad cut. When marched off, they left behind almost 50 comrades lying dead or dying amid the pastures and farm fields north of the Cashtown Road.[32]

By 7.30 a.m., the struggle was over. Even the victors seemed shocked that Buford's lines had collapsed so quickly, so completely. In his post-campaign report, Stuart betrayed his wonderment when noting that:

> "... in less time than it takes to tell, my brigades had chased the enemy from successive positions, strengthened by field-works and supported by artillery, forcing him inside Gettysburgh [sic], where he was relentlessly pursued and overtaken, until no fewer than 1,000 federal troops had been rendered *hors de combat*. The accomplishments of the Cavalry Division on this field beggar comparisons with any in the annals of mounted warfare."[33]

The fighting that followed the seizure of the high ground west and northwest of Gettysburg, while consistently heated and occasionally savage, smacked of anticlimax. By 10.00 a.m., or shortly thereafter, Heth's infantry, now backed by the division of Major General William Dorsey Pender, had occupied not only the town itself but also the high ground below it, covering the path of approach of Reynolds's I Corps. Within a half-hour of taking up these positions, the defenders were supported on the left by two-thirds of Dick Ewell's corps: Major General Jubal Early's division, which had come down from the north just as the cavalry fighting wound down, and the division of Major General Robert Rodes, which soon afterward reached Gettysburg from the northeast via the York Pike.

The timely intelligence that Stuart's troopers had gathered on Buford's dispositions had enabled Lee to recall Ewell's people to Gettysburg before the Army of the Potomac could leave Maryland. Early on July 1, Ewell had started Rodes's troops south from Heidlersburg, while ordering Early, then moving east from York, to meet him at Gettysburg. By the time the divisions converged on the field of battle, the troops of Heth and Pender—most of them still fresh, having been lightly engaged thus far—had dug in astride the upper reaches of Seminary Ridge.

In response to instructions from army headquarters, members of Stuart's staff guided Ewell's men into position atop and behind an equally formidable position—Cemetery Ridge, which ran south from Gettysburg roughly parallel to, and a mile east of, Heth's and Pender's perch. The last third of Ewell's corps was also on hand to greet the Army of the Potomac. The division of Major General Edward Johnson had departed the Carlisle vicinity on June 30 and reached Chambersburg that evening. The head of Johnson's column arrived just west of Gettysburg at about 7.00 a.m. on the 1st. Within three hours, Stuart's aides had placed the newcomers in position on Early's right, covering the ground between the ridges.[34]

The result of this timely concentration was that at 10.30, when John Reynolds came up to the southern outskirts of Gettysburg at the head of the

I Corps, he found himself not only out-numbered but badly out-positioned. Obliged to attack uphill against well-prepared defenses, his command was blocked by Johnson and supporting forces, while the rest of Ewell's corps joined A.P. Hill in shredding both of its flanks. Despite lopsided odds and mounting casualties, the I Corps held its ground for two hours, praying that Howard's troops would come up to relieve at least a measure of the pressure it was under.

Instead, when the vanguard of the XI Corps reached Gettysburg via the Emmitsburg and Taneytown Roads some minutes after noon, Early and Rodes tore into it with abandon, defeating Howard's every attempt to secure a position on Reynolds's right. After brief resistance, the corps splintered, cracked, and broke apart, its men abandoning the field with the same alacrity they had displayed when routed by Ewell's revered predecessor, Stonewall Jackson, at Chancellorsville. As soon as the ground in their front was free of the enemy, Ewell's people turned west to batter the right and rear of the I Corps.

It seemed only a matter of time before what remained of the Union line collapsed under this multi-directional pounding, but the process was expedited after a shell fragment struck the charismatic Reynolds, killing him instantly. Thereafter the I Corps steadily relinquished what little ground it had secured, before abandoning the field altogether, almost as a body. By mid-afternoon, two Union corps had been transformed into a panic-stricken rabble in full retreat toward the Maryland border, Stuart's hard-riding troopers howling at their heels. When darkness halted retreat and pursuit, the I and XI Corps had suffered a combined total of 11,500 casualties, including more than 5,000 captives, out of 16,000 engaged at Gettysburg. Meanwhile, Gamble's and Devin's brigades had lost almost half their combined pre-battle strength of 2,900, the majority in captured or missing. In something under six hours of combat, one-seventh of the effective strength of the Army of the Potomac had been irretrievably lost.[35]

Longstreet's Repulse, Pipe Creek, Maryland, July 29, 1863
The long-range results of the debacle west and south of Gettysburg have been chronicled by a sizable body of literature; they can be recounted here with some brevity. Once apprised of the disaster and persuaded that the day could not be redeemed, Meade countermanded the orders that would have sent the balance of his army to Adams County. Instead, he activated a contingency plan, copies of which he had disseminated among his corps commanders prior to Reynolds's decision to support Buford at Gettysburg. From his headquarters in the saddle (he had been *en route* from Taneytown, Maryland, when Reynolds and Howard were overthrown), the army leader directed the II, III, V, VI, and XII Corps, as well as the bulk of Pleasonton's cavalry, to assemble along Little Pipe Creek, in north-central Maryland.

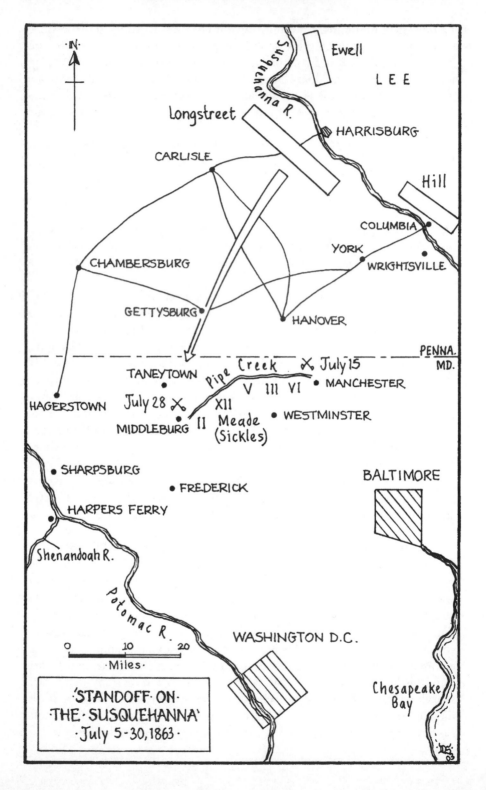

·N·

Susquehanna R.

Ewell

L E E

Longstreet

HARRISBURG

CARLISLE

Hill

COLUMBIA

YORK

CHAMBERSBURG

WRIGHTSVILLE

GETTYSBURG

HANOVER

PENNA.
MD.

TANEYTOWN   Pipe Creek   ✕ July 15

V   III   VI   ● MANCHESTER

July 28 ✕   XII

HAGERSTOWN

II   Meade   ● WESTMINSTER

MIDDLEBURG   (Sickles)

● SHARPSBURG

● FREDERICK

BALTIMORE

HARPERS FERRY

Shenandoah R.

Potomac R.

WASHINGTON D.C.

Chesapeake
Bay

0   10   20

·Miles·

'STANDOFF· ON·
·THE· SUSQUEHANNA'
·July 5-30, 1863·

By any standard, Meade had chosen an excellent position in which to husband his remaining troops and assume a defensive posture. Below Pipe Creek, his engineer officers had laid out a 20-mile line that ran from Manchester toward Middleburg. The line exploited the formidable contours of Parr Ridge, a rugged, steeply sided plateau, parts of which reached elevations above 1,000 feet.

By the afternoon of July 2, approximately half of what remained of the Army of the Potomac had occupied sectors of the high ground within easy supporting distance of one another; by late that evening, the balance of Meade's forces had arrived, and the position was secure. Major General Winfield Scott Hancock's II Corps, augmented by collected fragments of the I and XI Corps, occupied the left of this line, which ended at a point about five miles southwest of Taneytown. On Hancock's right, Meade had positioned the XII Corps of Major General Henry W. Slocum, with Major General George Sykes's V Corps and Major General Daniel E. Sickles's III Corps farther east, and with the VI Corps of Major General John Sedgwick anchoring the far right of the line. Under Meade's personal supervision, the army's artillery chief, Brigadier General Henry J. Hunt, had lined the summit with dozens of batteries—guns parked hub to hub to sweep all lines of approach. By then, too, Meade had posted Pleasonton's remaining horsemen—the divisions of Judson Kilpatrick and David Gregg—so as to cover both of the army's flanks as well as parts of its front.[36]

Lee did not immediately confront the new position, but neither did he remain stationary. Leaving a caretaker force outside Gettysburg, he led his main body to Dick Ewell's old bailiwick on the Susquehanna. During the fortnight following the battle of Gettysburg, engineers and fatigue parties repaired recently destroyed bridges, via which most of the army crossed to the north shore. They had been preceded by smaller bodies, ferried across aboard captured and improvised transports. By the middle of the month, the Army of Northern Virginia had secured Harrisburg and its environs, out of which hundreds of foragers scoured Lebanon and Lancaster Counties for all manner of provender. Within a week they had secured enough to support an indefinite occupation of the region.

Detachments of Stuart's cavalry (the division was again at full strength, with the return of the brigades under Jones) eventually reconnoitered the Pipe Creek Line. Despite exercising caution, the troopers clashed several times during the first half of July with counterparts in blue venturing north on scouting missions of their own. A particularly sharp encounter occurred on the 15th, when Hampton and Fitz Lee teamed to pincer a portion of Kilpatrick's division, which their leader, with typical rashness, had pushed beyond range of his infantry supports.[37]

Not until month's end did Lee move in force against Pipe Creek. By then Stuart had identified the sector between Taneytown and Middleburg, where Parr's Ridge was less elevated than elsewhere, as the most promising avenue of approach. Accordingly, on the 28th, Lee ordered a reconnaissance-in-force by Longstreet's corps, most of which had remained south of the Susquehanna.

Primary responsibility for the operation fell to Major General George E. Pickett, whose division had been covering the army's rear near Chambersburg and was spoiling for a fight. Longstreet advised his favorite subordinate to advance gingerly and make maximum use of supporting forces. However, through miscommunication and, it would seem, an exaggerated sense of his own strength, Pickett attacked before his flanks could be secured. From their commanding perch, Hancock's men repulsed successive assaults, each of which cost Pickett more men than the preceding (by afternoon's end his casualty rate approached 40 percent of the number engaged). Fittingly, "Pickett's Charge" would become a synonym for an offensive gone terribly awry.[38]

Two days after Longstreet's repulse, Lee returned the First Corps to the Susquehanna, where it remained for six weeks. During that period the invaders occupied four counties and scores of villages, each of which they stripped of foodstuffs, horses and mules, and every other resource that might sustain their sojourn in the North.[39] Meanwhile, an anxious, uncertain Meade probed fitfully at his enemy, cutting off a few foraging parties, while conferring almost incessantly by telegraph with his military and political superiors. President Lincoln and Secretary of War Edwin M. Stanton relentlessly urged their field commander to advance and clear the state of the invader. But, having lost two full corps in battle on Pennsylvania soil, Meade was unwilling to yield his unassailable foothold in Maryland. Even after receiving reinforcements from Harpers Ferry and other outposts in the new state of West Virginia, the harassed commander refused to take the offensive.

The Sack of Philadelphia, September 3, 1863

Lee's apparent willingness to remain indefinitely in the North had momentous effects on the course of the war. By early August, every Democratic politician in Pennsylvania, as well as a growing number of Republicans, were calling for Lincoln to open negotiations with the Confederate government. Before month's end, the president had had enough; he relieved Meade and replaced him with Dan Sickles, the only corps commander who pledged to mount a full-scale offensive toward the Susquehanna. But before the former Congressman from New York—well known for his self-confidence and impetuosity if not for his tactical ability—could act, Lee began to shift eastward from Harrisburg, as if heading for Philadelphia.

The movement was spearheaded by Stuart, whose troopers, during the first week in September, descended suddenly on the Quaker City. Swatting aside militiamen and home guards, the Rebels rampaged through the northern suburbs, then hastened south, leaving destruction and consternation in their wake. Among Stuart's carefully chosen objectives was the Philadelphia Naval Yard, where his men wrecked machinery, torched mounds of coal, and even damaged a few warships; and the venerable Frankford Arsenal, where they confiscated enough ordnance and ammunition to sustain the firepower of Lee's army for many months.[40]

By the time Stuart turned his back on the burning ruins along the Delaware to rejoin his army in Lebanon County, the curses of stunned, outraged, and frightened Pennsylvanians had descended upon the heads of Lincoln, Stanton, General-in-Chief Henry W. Halleck, and every prominent advocate of a hard-war policy. In such an atmosphere, Lee had only to strike another dramatic blow on Northern soil to put a finishing touch to enemy morale.

The Battle of Reading, September 10–11, 1863

That blow fell on September 10, when the advance of Sickles's gun-shy command blundered into a trap Lee had set for it in Berks County, southwest of Reading. The magnitude of the Union defeat—the last full-scale battle in the eastern theater—deserves a broader canvas than this essay can provide.[41]

A myriad of events, some whose true significance was only dimly discernable at the time, led directly to that climactic confrontation in southeastern Pennsylvania. It can be argued, however, that the most influential of these was the movement north from Rector's Cross Roads in late June by the cavalry of the Army of Northern Virginia. During the critical ten-week period that followed, the officers and men under J.E.B. Stuart expertly supported Lee's army, not only shielding its front, flanks, and rear, but also feeding it timely, accurate intelligence that permitted its scattered elements to concentrate speedily and effectively in the face of powerful pursuers. Then, via independent maneuvering—sometimes far afield of their army, exactly as their commander had hoped—the Confederate troopers kept their adversaries off balance, ignorant of Lee's intentions, and on the defensive for a fatally long period.

The praise that Robert E. Lee bestowed on his horsemen in the aftermath of his successful invasion was, by any standard, richly merited. As Marse Robert observed, at every turn of the campaign in the North, the gray riders had made:

> "... a contribution absolutely essential to victory on enemy soil, a victory that ensured the preservation of their army, their nation, and the cause that sustained us all through two and a half years of bitter strife."[42]

The Reality

When J.E.B. Stuart asked permission to launch his expedition, Robert E. Lee agreed that the cavalry leader, with three of his five brigades, could cut loose from the army, pass through or around the enemy "if you find that he is moving northward," and link with Ewell on the Susquehanna. A second set of orders authorized Stuart to set out only if he found the Federals inactive in northern Virginia. Glossing over the contradiction, Stuart decided he had *carte blanche* to pursue his mission as he thought best. He obeyed Lee's order to leave Robertson and Jones to guard the Blue Ridge passes, but they remained in Virginia long after the Federals left and did not join Lee until the invasion was almost over. Stuart did not honor Longstreet's request that he leave behind Wade Hampton as a liaison with the infantry. Nor did he obey Lee's order to return at once to the army when, on June 25, hours after starting out with Hampton, Fitz Lee, and Chambliss, he encountered Hooker's II Corps in motion east of the Bull Run Mountains.

Detouring around the enemy, Stuart continued on his way. Over the next five days, he waylaid supply depots, railroad tracks, and river shipping, while capturing a 125-wagon supply train bound for Hooker's army. His revamped route and the ponderous train slowed his progress, as did a clash with enemy cavalry at Westminster, Maryland, on the 29th and an all-day battle with Kilpatrick at Hanover, Pennsylvania, the following day. In the end, Stuart failed to locate either Ewell or Lee—a courier from army headquarters found him at Carlisle early on July 2. In his absence the main army had wandered blindly through enemy territory and stumbled into battle with Buford on the 1st. Unaware he faced only cavalry, A.P. Hill failed to drive Buford from his position until Reynolds, with the I and XI Corps, reached the field. Thanks to the timely arrival of Ewell's corps, Lee eventually forced the Federals into retreat, but they held on south of town until the rest of Meade's army arrived. Two more days of full-scale combat ended with the repulse of Pickett's Charge and Lee's decision to return to Virginia, his second (and last) invasion of the North a strategic failure.

Bibliography

Blackford, W.W., *War Years with Jeb Stuart* (Charles Scribner's Sons, New York, 1945).

Calef, John H., "Gettysburg Notes: The Opening Gun"; *Journal of the Military Service Institution of the United States* 40 (New York, 1907).

Cheney, Newel, comp. *History of the Ninth Regiment, New York Volunteer Cavalry* (Martin Merz & Son, Poland Center and Jamestown, NY, 1901).

Coddington, Edwin B., *The Gettysburg Campaign: A Study in Command* (Charles Scribner's Sons, New York, 1968).

Downey, Fairfax, *Clash of Cavalry: The Battle of Brandy Station, June 9, 1863* (David McKay, New York, 1959).

Freeman, Douglas Southall, *Lee's Lieutenants: A Study in Command* (Charles Scribner's Sons, New York, 1942–4), 3 vols.

Fuller, Ezra J., "Who Fired the First Shot at the Battle of Gettysburg?" *Journal of the United States Cavalry Association* 24 (Washington, D.C., 1914).

Hebert, Walter H., *Fighting Joe Hooker* (Bobbs-Merrill, Indianapolis, 1944).

Klein, Frederic Shriver., "Meade's Pipe Creek Line"; *Maryland Historical Magazine* 57 (1962).

Longacre, Edward G., *The Cavalry at Gettysburg: A Tactical Study of Mounted Operations During the Civil War's Pivotal Campaign, 9 June–14 July 1863* (Fairleigh Dickinson University Press, Rutherford, NJ, 1986).

Marshall, Charles, *An Aide-de-Camp of Lee*, ed. Sir Frederick Maurice (Little, Brown, Boston, 1927).

McClellan, H.B., *Life and Campaigns of Maj. Gen. J.E.B. Stuart, Commander of the Cavalry of the Army of Northern Virginia* (Houghton, Mifflin, Boston, 1885).

McPherson, James M., *Crossroads of Freedom: Antietam* (Oxford University Press, New York, 2002).

Mosby, John S., *Stuart's Cavalry in the Gettysburg Campaign* (Moffat, Yard & Co., New York, 1908).

Moyer, H.P., comp., *History of the Seventeenth Regiment Pennsylvania Volunteer Cavalry* (Sowers Printing Co., Lebanon, PA, 1911).

Nye, Wilbur S., *Here Come the Rebels!* (Louisiana State University Press, Baton Rouge, LA, 1965).

Pleasonton, Alfred, "The Campaign of Gettysburg," in *Annals of the War, Written by Leading Participants, North and South* (Times Publishing Co, Philadelphia, 1879).

U.S. War Department, *The War of the Rebellion: A Compilation of the Official Records of the Union and Confederate Armies*, 4 series in 70 volumes in 128 books (Government Printing Office, Washington, D.C., 1880–1901).

Warner, Ezra J., *Generals in Gray: Lives of the Confederate Commanders* (Louisiana State University Press, Baton Rouge, LA, 1959).

Wellman, Manly Wade, *Giant in Gray: A Biography of Wade Hampton of South Carolina* (Charles Scribner's Sons, New York, 1949).

Wert, Jeffry D., *General James Longstreet, the Confederacy's Most Controversial Soldier: A Biography* (Simon & Schuster, New York, 1993).

Notes

1. In researching this essay, the author acknowledges the assistance of Gerald R. Ewan, Lawrence T. Longacre, and Eric J. Wittenberg.
*2. *The War for Southern Independence: A Compilation of the Official Records of the Confederate and Union Armies* (62 vols. in 3 series. Richmond, VA, and Washington, D.C., 1880–92) [hereafter cited as *OR*], ser II, vol. 4, pp. 692–9.
3. McPherson, *Crossroads of Freedom*, pp. 98–131; Coddington, *The Gettysburg Campaign*, pp. 88–9, 624 note, 625 note; Nye, *Here Come the Rebels!*, pp. 73–9.
4. McClellan, *Life and Campaigns of Stuart*, pp. 296–314.
5. Marshall, *An Aide-de-Camp of Lee*, pp. 201–2; Freeman, *Lee's Lieutenants*, vol. 3: p. 41 and note.
6. McClellan, *Life and Campaigns of Stuart*, pp. 52–71, 94–102, 136–66; Blackford, *War Years with Jeb Stuart*, pp. 164–81.
*7. R.E. Lee, *The Memoirs of Robert E. Lee*, ed. by George Washington Custis Lee and Walter H. Taylor (2 vols. New York, 1874), 2: p. 417.
*8. *OR*, I, 27, pt. 1: 515–7, 663–4, 689, 677; pt. 2: pp. 440–9; pt. 3: pp. 997, 999–1002, 1117, 1120–5, 1133.
*9. Lee, *Memoirs*, 2: pp. 417–8.
*10. James Longstreet, *Gettysburg–Pipe Creek–Reading: Reminiscences of the War's Climactic Campaigns* (Philadelphia, 1892), pp. 297–9.
*11. Robert Rowland Prentiss and Julian W. Perry, *From Manassas to Manila Bay: The Campaigns of James Ewell Brown Stuart* (Richmond, VA, 1899), p. 304.

12. Wellman, *Giant in Gray: A Biography of Wade Hampton*, p. 112; Warner, *Generals in Gray: Lives of the Confederate Commanders*, pp. 46–7, 166–7, 259–60.

*13. Desmond Carr, *The Laughing Cavalier: A Life of Fitzhugh Lee, 1835–1905* (New York, 1982), pp. 114–6.

*14. Theodore G. Barker, *Riding with Hampton*, ed. by Lucille Barker Wells (Columbia, SC, 1887), pp. 29–30.

15. Mosby, *Stuart's Cavalry in the Gettysburg Campaign*, pp. 65–6.

*16. John S. Mosby, "Behind Enemy Lines," *North American Review* 142 (1886), pp. 112–3; John S. Mosby, "With Stuart from Rector's Cross Roads to Gettysburg," in Harrison B. Markham and D.D. Royce, eds., *Campaigns and Commanders of the War between the States* (3 vols. New York, 1890–93), vol. 3: p. 404 and note.

17. McClellan, *Life and Campaigns of Stuart*, pp. 318–9.

*18. Mosby, "With Stuart from Rector's Cross Roads to Gettysburg," p. 421.

*19. Prentiss and Perry, *From Manassas to Manila Bay*, pp. 312–8; P. Goddard Wynne, *Sword and Pen: Memoirs Military and Literary* (Staunton, VA, 1902), pp. 181–6.

20. Wellman, *Giant in Gray*, pp. 101–2, 133–4; Hebert, *Fighting Joe Hooker*, 243–4; Pleasonton, "The Campaign of Gettysburg," in *Annals of the War, Written by Leading Participants, North and South*, pp. 452–3.

21. Hebert, *Fighting Joe Hooker*, pp. 244–5; Coddington, *Gettysburg Campaign*, pp. 128–33.

22. Nye, *Here Come the Rebels*, pp. 259, 273–7, 283–97, 331–42, 347–56; Coddington, *Gettysburg Campaign*, pp. 264–5.

23. Wert, *General James Longstreet*, pp. 242–7.

24. Chambliss's position at and west of Chambersburg paid dividends almost as soon as he assumed it. On June 30, the 13th Virginia of his brigade captured an enemy supply train—125 wagons long—near Fort Loudoun in Franklin County. The train and its small mounted escort had escaped from Winchester two weeks before, shortly before Ewell carried the outpost; it had fled to Bedford County, Pennsylvania, only to be cut off and forced eastward by Imboden's brigade on its circuitous march to Gettysburg. See *Wynne, *Sword and Pen*, pp. 227–30; and *Franklin County Historical Society, *West of Gettysburg: Franklin County in the Civil War* (Chambersburg, PA, 1963), pp. 120–3, 126–35.

25. Cheney, *Ninth New York Cavalry*, pp. 100–3; Moyer, *Seventeenth Pennsylvania Cavalry*, pp. 49–50, 329.

*26. Barker, *Riding with Hampton*, pp. 52–3.

*27. *OR*, I, p. 27, pt. 2: pp. 334–5; Lee, *Memoirs*, 2: pp. 498–502.

28. Coddington, *Gettysburg Campaign*, pp. 264–5; Calef, "Gettysburg Notes: The Opening Gun," p. 48; Fuller, "Who Fired the First Shot at the Battle of Gettysburg?" pp. 793–4.

*29. Prentiss and Perry, *From Manassas to Manila Bay*, pp. 361–4.

*30. Carter R. Powell, *Carolina Cavaliers: The Civil War Career of the First North Carolina Cavalry, 1861–1863* (Durham, NC, 1972), p. 198.

*31. *OR*, I, p. 27, pt. 1: pp. 567–8; pt. 3: pp. 1112, 1115, 1118–9. Following his hospitalization in Washington, D.C., Buford appeared to recover from his wound but took a turn for the worse in September. When told he could not survive, he supposedly alluded to the outcome at Reading and remarked: "I don't care to live now, anyway." See Peter Penn Gaskell, *Service under Buford, Gregg, and Pleasanton* [sic] (Elizabeth, NJ, 1869), p. 47.

32. Cheney, *Ninth New York Cavalry*, pp. 109–12; Moyer, *Seventeenth Pennsylvania Cavalry*, pp. 63–5.

*33. *OR*, I, 27, pt. 2: p. 819; Prentiss and Perry, *From Manassas to Manila Bay*, p. 380.

*34. James Lee Coates, *Gettysburg: The Beginning of the End* (Boston, 1959), pp. 314–21.

*35. *Ibid.*, pp. 326–33.

*36. *Ibid.*

*37. David Yellin, *Debacle at Pipe Creek* (Garden City, NY, 1977), pp. 311–26. A revisionist account of the combat of July 15 is Bruce D. Venter, *Kilpatrick the Superb* (Shippensburg, PA, 2003), pp. 217–20, 454 and note.

*38. Lafayette McLaws, "The Pipe Creek Campaign, July 5–30, 1863," in Markham and Royce, *Campaigns and Commanders*, 4: pp. 609–18.

*39. Yellin, *Debacle at Pipe Creek*, pp. 374–7; Richard Krauthamel, ed., "A 'High Old Time' on the Susquehanna: The Journal of Capt. G. W. Albritton, 3d Virginia Cavalry," *Military Annals of Pennsylvania* 7 (May 1938): pp. 116–7.

*40. McLaws, "Pipe Creek Campaign," in Markham and Royce, *Campaigns and Commanders*, pp. 629–35; Charles O. Stambaugh, ed., *Philadelphia and the Crisis of '63: Eyewitness Accounts* (Philadelphia, 1913), pp. 354–67. Historians almost universally condemn Meade for his timidity and vacillation throughout the operations of July and August. For a more sympathetic view, see Ted Zeman, *Meade: Soldier, Savior, Scapegoat* (Baton Rouge, LA, 2002) and Zeman's "The Snapping Turtle Snaps: George G. Meade in the Pipe Creek Campaign," in Russell F. Weigley and Richard J. Sommers, eds., *New Directions in American Military History* (Bloomington, Ind, 2003), pp. 114–52.

*41. The literature on the fighting in Berks County is voluminous. The most recent book-length treatment is Donald M. Lawless and Corinne Jacobs Lawless, *Climax at Reading* (New York, 2002), although nearly 50 years after its publication, the standard account remains that of the British historian C.J.T. Howlett-Pryce, *Glory's Last Stand: The Battle of Reading, September 10–11, 1863* (London and New York, 1956). See also: Gary Gallagher, ed., *Even More Essays on the Battle of Reading*, September 10–11, 1863 (Kent, Ohio, 1998).

*42. Lee, *Memoirs*, 2: p. 603.

7

"MOVES TO GREAT ADVANTAGE"
Longstreet vs. Grant in the West

John D. Burtt

> "I desire to go to the west because there seems to be opportunities for all
> kinds of moves to great advantage."
> *General James Longstreet to Senator Louis Wigfall, February 4, 1863*

Dawn broke clear and cold in the northern Georgia forest on Monday,
September 21, 1863. The acrid smell of smoke from smoldering brushfires
drifted through the trees, only slightly masking the stench of death that
permeated the area. Out of sight of the clearing lay the detritus of war:
shattered trees, abandoned cannon, rifles and haversacks, dead horses and
the Union and Confederate casualties from two days of savage fighting. The
toll would ultimately reach over 34,000. Chickamauga Creek had indeed
been a "River of Death."

Confederate Lieutenant General James Longstreet, commander of the Left
Wing of Braxton Bragg's Army of Tennessee, stood talking to his aides,
Colonels Moxley Sorrel and Payton Manning, about his plans for continuing
the battle when a staff officer rode up and saluted.

"General Longstreet, sir! General Bragg's compliments, sir, and would
you attend him at his headquarters immediately."

"My compliment to General Bragg," replied Longstreet. "I fear I cannot
leave my troops with the enemy still at my front. Please inform the general
I will attend him as soon as the situation has cleared."

Instead of saluting and riding back, the major leaned over his horse's neck
and spoke more urgently, "General Bragg has been wounded, sir. We, the
army, need you to come now."

Frowning, Longstreet turned to Sorrel and issued several orders to go to
his division commanders. Then he and Manning mounted and followed the
aide to Bragg's headquarters near Thedford's Ford.

General Braxton Bragg tried sitting up in his ambulance when Longstreet appeared, but his doctor kept him still. Bragg had looked sickly and haggard to Longstreet when Longstreet had arrived late on September 19. Now the bloody bandages wrapping his right side accentuated his physical frailty, but had not mellowed the man's irascible personality.

"My condolences on your wounds," Longstreet began.

"My wounds don't matter, sir," Bragg snapped. "The army does. You are in command now, sir. The Army is yours."

Startled, Longstreet suppressed a smile. "Surely, one of the others, sir. I have just arrived."

"And done more than THEY ever did," Bragg interrupted, pushing up from his cot. He sagged back. "Hill and Polk... worthless. Couldn't get their troops going. This," he gestured to his bloody side, "from having to give the orders myself. Whole plan lost, another battle lost. You are senior, sir, thank God, and you will command."

Longstreet walked out of the tent a few minutes later. Awaiting him were the other commanders, Lieutenant Generals Leonidas Polk and his old friend, Daniel Harvey Hill, plus Major General Simon Buckner. He looked at them and said quietly, "Bragg has placed me in command of the Army."

Buckner and Hill nodded; Polk hesitated, and Longstreet knew he was comparing seniority of rank. Then the Bishop smiled and said, "Good. While I wish wounds on no man, I cannot help feeling grateful to that Yankee ball." He turned and gestured north. "Liddell[1] put skirmishers out this morning. The Yankees are gone. Forrest[2] is looking for them as well."

Longstreet nodded. "See to your men, gentlemen. If the enemy is gone from these woods we need to find him."

"And when we do?" Hill asked.

"We finish this fight."[3]

The Situation

For the fledgling Confederate States of America, the summer of 1863 had not been a good one.

Fresh from defeating Major General Joseph Hooker and the Union Army of the Potomac at Chancellorsville, General Robert E. Lee led his Army of Northern Virginia into Pennsylvania in June. Lee and Confederate President Jefferson Davis hoped that the invasion would spur on anti-war sentiment in the North and possibly bring foreign assistance to the Confederacy from France and Great Britain. The invasion led to the three-day battle at Gettysburg, where, after success on the first day, Lee's soldiers tried to dislodge the Union Army, now led by Major General George Meade, from strong positions south of town. On July 3, Meade's troops repulsed a massed charge by Major General George Pickett's division and supporting units with nearly half of the 12,000 troops in the attack cut down. Lee retreated the following day leaving fully a third of his army on the field as casualties.

In the west, after four months of floundering in the marshes and swamps around the Mississippi River fortress of Vicksburg, Union Major General Ulysses S. Grant cut loose from his lines of supply and communication and took his army across the river south of the fortress on May 1, 1863. In the next two weeks, his troops traveled nearly 180 miles, fought five battles and pinned 32,000 Confederate troops in Vicksburg. Seven weeks of siege ended with the surrender of the fortress on July 4, 1863. Although paroled, over 60 percent of Vicksburg's defenders simply deserted the Cause.

Finally, after six months of inactivity following the hard fought victory at Stones River (Murfreesboro, Tennessee) on December 31, 1862—January 2, 1863, Major General William Rosecrans's Army of the Cumberland moved against General Braxton Bragg's Confederate Army of Tennessee. While feinting a direct assault toward Bragg's base at Tullahoma, Rosecrans maneuvered the bulk of his army onto Bragg's flank, threatening his lines of communication with the rest of the Confederacy. The move forced Bragg to withdraw from his fortifications and evacuate Middle Tennessee. At the cost of only 560 casualties and ten days, the Army of the Cumberland captured Tennessee's most productive region.

Despite these successes, war weariness was striking hard above the Mason-Dixon Line, as well as below, after two bloody years of war. In the North, the anti-war faction of the Democratic Party, titled Copperheads by their Republican opponents, pushed hard against the war. Clement L. Vallandigham, a Peace Democrat from Ohio, stated the problem clearly when asking, "What has this wicked war accomplished?" He became so effective at drumming up opposition that the military commander of Ohio had him arrested and convicted of treason. The arrest and trial embarrassed Lincoln and his administration so much that he commuted the sentence and had Vallandigham simply deported to the Confederacy.

New draft laws that required all men from ages 20 to 45 to enroll added fuel to the peace effort. Any congressional district that failed to meet troop quotas through volunteers could use the lottery draft to fill the ranks. However, the law allowed draftees to "buy" a replacement soldier, leading to the Democratic charge that Lincoln waged a poor man's war. Draft riots broke out in Northern cities with the worst being a four-day reign of destruction in New York City.

In the South, draft laws also caused considerable hardship, but inflation and food shortages hurt far worse. Prices for staples like sugar and salt rose 9,000 percent—when they were available at all. The exhilaration from the early 1863 successes crashed heavily with the losses at Gettysburg, Vicksburg and Tullahoma. Southern governors all screamed for troops to protect their states, and the Confederate military leadership was in shambles. President Davis remained locked in a feud with General Joe Johnston over the loss of Vicksburg; Bragg was feuding with virtually all of his subordinates.

After the disasters, Davis had to reassess Confederate options. His focus on the East had led to Gettysburg. Other opinions pointed to Middle Tennessee as a viable option for a Confederate counterstroke. General P.T. Beauregard, former commander of the Army of Tennessee, suggested combining Johnston's Mississippi troops, Simon Buckner's Eastern Tennessee troops and reinforcement's from Lee's Army with Bragg to attack Rosecrans. Lee's top subordinate, James Longstreet, seconded the idea, which would leave Lee on the defensive in Virginia while he took an independent command to Georgia. Davis finally conceded to that option and ordered Longstreet to take two divisions of his First Corps troops to join with Bragg. Unfortunately, it took another Confederate disaster to force the decision. For, while Davis and his advisors argued, the Union moved first.

In mid-August, Rosecrans put his troops in motion again in a complicated maneuver aimed at the vital city of Chattanooga. William Starke Rosecrans, a 43-year-old Ohioan, had graduated from West Point in 1842. He had missed the Mexican War, but had performed well under McClellan in West Virginia and under Grant in Mississippi. Best known for his defense of Corinth when attacked by Earl Van Dorn's Rebel army, he replaced Don Carlos Buell as the head of what became the Army of the Cumberland in November 1862. A month later he clashed with Bragg at Stones River.

Rosecrans's August target, Chattanooga, was one of the Confederacy's most important cities for a variety of strategic reasons. First, it held the junction of three key railroad companies' systems whose lines radiated out in virtually all directions. Second, it sat as one of the few centers for heavy industry in the South; coal and copper were mined in the nearby mountains and sent throughout the Confederacy. Third, its location allowed access to Knoxville in East Tennessee, and the backdoor of Virginia as well as Georgia and the Deep South. Important strategically, Chattanooga took on an even more important morale role for the battered Confederacy, especially after the loss of Vicksburg. Union leaders knew this well. Abraham Lincoln noted to General-in-Chief Henry Halleck that, if the Union took Chattanooga, "the rebellion can only eke out a short and feeble existence, as an animal sometimes may with a thorn in its vitals."[4]

For his maneuver, Rosecrans's Army of the Cumberland consisted of 13 divisions split into four corps. The largest corps, the XIV Corps under Major General George Thomas, consisted of four divisions and 16,000 troops. XX Corps and XXI Corps, under Major Generals Alexander McCook and Thomas Crittenden, each had three divisions and 10,500 and 13,900 respectively. Rosecran's Reserve Corps, under Gordon Granger, technically held three divisions and 11,600 men, but a full division stayed in Nashville to guard that important city. Finally, the Army of the Cumberland fielded some 10,000 cavalry. One significant part of the cavalry was Colonel John T. Wilder's Lightning Brigade of mounted infantry. Ostensibly, part of Fourth

Division/XIV Corps (4/XIV),[5] Wilder's troopers, armed with Spencer repeating rifles, acted as an independent cavalry brigade most of the time.

At the same time that Rosecrans began moving toward Chattanooga, Major General Ambrose Burnside attacked through the Cumberland Gap into East Tennessee toward Buckner's troops in Knoxville. On September 2, the Union took Knoxville as Buckner withdrew his forces to join Bragg. On September 9, Chattanooga fell. The loss of the two cities forced Davis to order Longstreet's troops to move west, but now their journey went the long way through Atlanta to reach Bragg, doubling the distance they had to travel.

Under the mistaken impression that he faced a demoralized Army of Tennessee, Rosecrans continued his risky maneuver, with his corps becoming increasingly separated and vulnerable to an attack by a reinforced Bragg. In sharp contrast to Rosecrans's beliefs, Bragg was preparing to attack his opponent and defeat the separate columns in detail.

With the belated concurrence of Jefferson Davis, Braxton Bragg's Army swelled with reinforcements from all over the Confederacy. He ultimately controlled some nine divisions split into corps under Buckner, Polk, D.H. Hill, and Major General William H.T. Walker. Longstreet would add two more divisions when he arrived. Unfortunately for the Confederacy, the status of command in Bragg's Army, riddled with dissension and bitterness, rendered reinforcement nearly moot. Most of Bragg's subordinates felt that any order from Bragg was automatically wrong and obedience therefore discretionary. In two separate instances, on September 11 at McLemore's Cove and on September 13 at Lee and Gordon's Mill, subordinates bungled attack orders from Bragg or simply disobeyed them. The Union troops escaped the traps, and Rosecrans started to concentrate his army.

Bragg decided he could wait no longer to attack, despite the fact that all of his reinforcements had yet to arrive. He fielded more than 60,000 troops and for the first time actually outnumbered his Union foe, although he did not know it. He maneuvered to attack on September 18 to interpose his army between Rosecrans and Chattanooga. The attack was only partially successful, with several bridges over Chickamauga Creek captured against a stubborn defense by Union cavalry and Wilder's mounted infantry. The added delay allowed Rosecrans's scattered troops to close up and Bragg faced a much larger, more difficult battle the next day.

Fighting on September 19 became confused in the forests as opposing units blundered into frontal assaults or onto enemy flanks. Both sides fell exhausted by the end of the day. That night Longstreet himself arrived with more troops, bringing Bragg's army to some 68,000 men minus the day's casualties. Bragg gave the new arrival command of the army's Left Wing, a change in command structure that threw more confusion into the Rebel ranks. A dawn attack by Leonidas Polk's Right Wing fell victim to the confusion and got underway late. Polk's troops struck hard at the dug-in

Union brigades but lost heavily despite the occasional success at finding an exposed flank.

Fate stepped in on the side of the Confederacy toward noon. In an effort to close a non-existent gap in his lines, Rosecrans ordered a division to fill it, inadvertently creating a real gap. Longstreet's massed wing struck this real gap around 11.00 a.m., and shattered half the Union army, sending it reeling back toward Chattanooga. George H. Thomas, commander of the Union XIV Corps, averted total disaster, however, by calmly rallying Union troops on Snodgrass Hill and repulsing everything the Confederates threw at him until late in the afternoon. When September 20 drew to a close, Thomas withdrew toward Chattanooga, leaving the battered, but victorious Rebels in possession of the field. Their victory, however, had cost them almost 25 percent of their strength.

Longstreet in Command

Frustrated, James Longstreet stood on Missionary Ridge overlooking Chattanooga, watching Rosecrans's defeated Union troops preparing to defend the town. Ironically the Confederates had built many of the city's fortifications themselves when they had hoped to defend it. Minor skirmishing over the past two days had pushed the Union troops out of Rossville and off Lookout Mountain, but the new commander of the Army of Tennessee could see that the initial reports that Rosecrans planned to evacuate the town had been false.

Longstreet's initial plan had been to take his army across the Tennessee River north of the city and envelop it from the rear. But his plan proved impossible for a variety of logistical reasons. First, there had been the question of food—his army had little. The railroad from Atlanta was fragile and broke down far too often, delaying the delivery of rations. In addition, the movement of his own troops from Virginia had obstructed food deliveries. Four more of his brigades had just arrived, with one brigade and his artillery train still coming. The second problem was one of transport off the rail. His army was seriously short of wagons to transport supplies forward. Again, his movement from Virginia had magnified the problem because his troops had not brought wagons with them. Finally, the army had no pontoon train, limiting their river crossing points to easily defended fords.

However, the state of his forces after the bloodbath along Chickamauga Creek worried Longstreet more than anything else. The Army of Tennessee had suffered over 18,000 casualties. Twenty-five of the 33 brigades engaged had lost more than a third of their men. Division commanders John Bell Hood and Thomas Hindeman, plus eight brigade and nearly half of the regimental commanders had been killed or wounded in the fighting. Physically exhausted, the army now needed rest, replenishment and reorganization. He had some 46,000 troops to take on a Union army that, based on Bragg's intelligence figures, outnumbered him.

Despite the losses, morale was high, especially with a new commander in charge. Longstreet had visited each of the divisions in the past two days and seen troops ready and willing to finish the fight. The army, used to seeing its top leaders dissolve into petty feuds and squabbles after each battle, felt they had a leader they could follow, but Longstreet had to find a plan to lead them and soon—already word had reached him of substantial Union reinforcements on their way to Rosecrans.

As he studied the Union positions below, he discarded the idea of a direct attack. He had witnessed such attacks virtually destroy the Union Army of the Potomac at Fredericksburg and Pickett's division at Gettysburg. He did not want to make the same mistake if he could avoid it. Logistics eliminated a large-scale move across the Tennessee. That left some sort of siege.

A static siege would be difficult. While the Union remained entrenched in a line some three miles long around Chattanooga, Confederate lines stretched across seven miles from the foot of Lookout Mountain to Missionary Ridge then north toward the river. Extending both flanks to the river pushed his lines out two miles further on both sides.

Cutting Rosecrans off from his supply would not be easy. According to his cavalry commanders, there were five routes that stretched from the Union supply depot at Bridgeport to Chattanooga. Two were already cut off: the burned bridge at Bridgeport cut the Nashville and Chattanooga Railroad and the Tennessee River itself remained too low for supply boats due to drought. The third route, a wagon route that ran parallel to the railroad on the south shore of the Tennessee, could be easily interdicted by Confederate troops and artillery. Sharpshooters and artillery could also interdict the fourth route, another wagon route on the north shore of the Tennessee. The final route was a trail that went up the Sequatchie Valley, then turned off to go over Walden's Ridge. This 60-mile route had poor roads, little water and very little forage for mules, but it was open and currently out of reach of Confederate troops.

In thinking over his options, Longstreet drew back to the chokepoint of the Union system—Bridgeport, through which all of Rosecrans's supplies had to pass. By the time he met with his corps commanders, his idea had gelled. To Polk and Hill, with their four divisions, fell the chore of keeping Rosecrans bottled up in Chattanooga. Simon Buckner, still the commander of the East Tennessee Department, was ordered to begin moving back toward Knoxville with Major General Alexander P. Stewart's and Brigadier General William Preston's divisions, plus a division under Liddell. Buckner's threat would keep Burnside pinned away from the siege. To Major General Lafayette McLaws, newly arrived from Virginia, Longstreet gave Wofford's, Bryan's and Jenkins's fresh brigades, plus Humphreys's from Hood's division, and ordered him to move toward Bridgeport, screened by Forrest's cavalry. Forrest would reconnoiter Bridgeport and determine if the supply depot could be captured, then cooperate with the infantry in doing so. Wheeler's cavalry moved northeast with Buckner with orders to find a crossing point over the Tennessee and raid into the Union rear. Hood's old division and a provisional division commanded by States Rights Gist,[6] remained in reserve.

In Chattanooga, Rosecrans waited impatiently, worried and nearly overwhelmed by the disaster of Chickamauga. He had only some 35,000 effectives left in his army, and about ten days rations. His infantry's morale remained high, despite the loss, and they were determined to hold the town. Union cavalry patrolled potential crossing points. Washington informed him that Joe Hooker and four divisions from XI and XII Corps, some 14,000 troops, would be sent immediately from the Army of the Potomac. In addition, four divisions from XV and XVII Corps, another 17,000 men, would be transferred under Major General William Sherman toward the town. Finally, Washington ordered Ambrose Burnside to leave Knoxville and combine with Rosecrans. Burnside telegraphed he would comply, but ultimately did not move from his headquarters.

Political wrangling behind the scenes added to the discomfiture of the Union forces. The key figure in this wrangling was Assistant Secretary of War Charles A. Dana. Dana was acting as the eyes and ears in the field for Secretary of War Edwin Stanton. Although his written introduction to Rosecrans stated he was there to improve communications with the War Department, most officers saw Dana as a spy out to destroy their general. His dispatches from the field and Chattanooga stirred up major discussion about the leaders of the Army of the Cumberland. Two of Dana's targets were Alexander McCook and Thomas Crittenden, commanders of XX and XXI Corps who had retreated back to Chattanooga following Longstreet's devastating charge at Chickamauga.[7] But Rosecrans stood as Dana's primary target. The Assistant Secretary warned Washington that Rosecrans would blame the administration for the defeat, and appeared "greatly lacking in firmness and steadiness of will."[8] Later his attacks became sharper; he called Rosecrans a "dazed and mazy commander [who] cannot perceive the catastrophe that is close upon us, nor fix his mind upon the means of preventing it. I never saw anything which seemed so lamentable and hopeless."[9] However, Lincoln and his staff, though concerned about Dana's reports, hesitated to remove Rosecrans for fear of a Peace Democratic backlash against one of Ohio's favorite sons.

The Fall of Chattanooga

By September 28, Forrest's reconnaissance of Bridgeport had been completed and he met McLaws's infantry, who had marched to within five miles of the crossing. The cavalry leader judged that weaknesses in the Union defenses gave the attackers a fair chance of achieving surprise. Although the

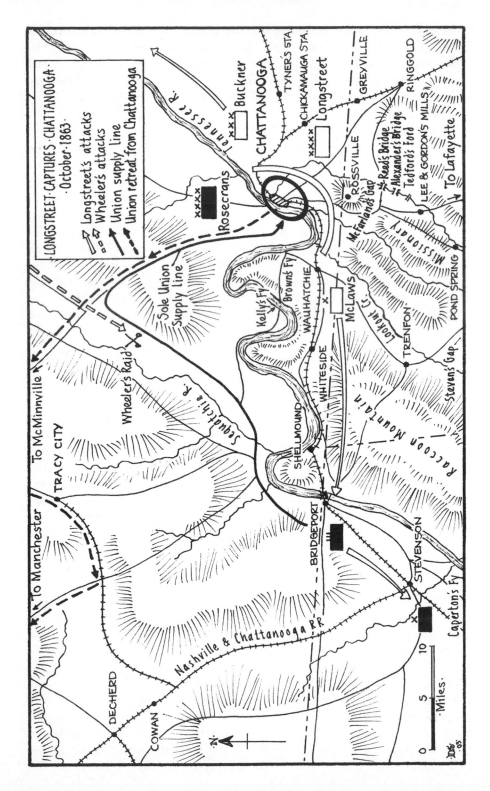

railroad trestle bridge had been destroyed, the Union had connected the Tennessee River's north and south shore by two pontoon bridges. From the north shore the bridge crossed to Bridgeport Island, a three mile by half mile wooded isle in the middle of the river. A road crossed the island to the second portion of the bridge that finished the crossing onto the south shore. A small blockhouse, garrisoned by a single company of infantry, guarded the southern end of the bridge. A small number of cavalry vedettes were also present, but Forrest shrugged off their abilities. In Bridgeport itself, civilian sources informed him that three infantry regiments and three cavalry units, numbering 1,000–2,000 troops, garrisoned the town.[10] Two more brigades, some 2,500 men, were stationed five miles southeast in Stevenson, Alabama.

Forrest suggested taking the blockhouse by surprise assault, then using the southern pontoon boats to ferry troops across the river to form a lodgment. A brigade could be stationed on the island itself before cutting the pontoons free to help with the assault on the town. McLaws liked the idea and assigned Brigadier General Micah Jenkins's brigade to take the blockhouse and stand ready on the island. Brigadier General William T. Wofford's brigade would cross first, followed by Brigadier General Benjamin G. Humphreys and Brigadier General Goode Bryan. Forrest's cavalry would take care of the vedettes.

Just after midnight, September 30, 1863, Jenkins attacked. Rifles unloaded and bayonets fixed, he fell upon the small Union garrison, Company B, 10th Illinois, and in a brief struggle captured the post. The Union soldiers had no warning of the attack. Only a few shots were fired in defense of the post, but one was costly, striking Jenkins himself in the groin. While one regiment took care of their new prisoners, the rest of the brigade crossed to Bridgeport Island.

Some 41 boats were cut loose and made available for the crossing and, under cover of cloudy darkness, McLaws sent his troops to the north shore. Union security was abysmal and nearly all of Wofford's brigade and most of Humphreys's were across before a Union courier, coming from Stevenson, blundered into the landing and escaped to Bridgeport. The alarm there sent the small garrison scrambling. Colonel R.F. Smith, commander of 1/2/RES and the commandant of the town, rousted his troops while a company of cavalry scouted out the enemy landing. They were driven off, but not before gaining a view of the force opposing them. Outnumbered, Smith sent cavalry in all directions to inform Rosecrans and other Union forces of the Confederate incursion. While some of his men worked with teamsters to get as much of the stockpiled supplies as possible away from the town, his other troops began barricading the streets. But the Rebels gave them precious little time.

Wofford, following the alarm, put his Georgians into line and advanced. Brushing aside the cavalry, he fell upon Smith's troops as dawn broke. A sharp exchange of fire heralded the start of the small battle. Smith's defenders held their ground for almost an hour, aided by a section of artillery, before more Confederates from the landing site arrived and began maneuvering onto his flank. His withdrawal became a rout when Jenkins's brigade, howling the name of their fallen leader, crossed the bridge. By full light the town sat in Rebel hands, along with much of the Union supply dump and, more importantly, over 300 wagons that had not been able to escape.

Union Brigadier General James Morgan, brought the rest of 1/2/RES and his whole Third Brigade up from Stevenson, but found McLaws ready for him. The Rebel commander advanced with three of his brigades, leaving Jenkins's men in Bridgeport to hold the town and rebuild the southern bridge. Morgan's outnumbered troops put up a stiff fight for several hours; but with no reinforcements nearby, he finally withdrew back to Stevenson, then north after setting fires in the Union supply depot. McLaws let him go, deeming saving supplies to be more important.

In Chattanooga, an elated William Rosecrans had been celebrating the news that the advance troops from XI Corps were in Cincinnati and would be in Bridgeport in two days. Thus, the news of the town's capture stunned him. More bad news followed. On October 1, his cavalry reported that Wheeler's Confederate cavalry had crossed the Tennessee River north of the city. The same day he received a report from "reliable" spies that the Rebels under Longstreet now numbered 100,000 infantry and 30,000 cavalry.[11]

Rosecrans received the final blow the following day as he and his commanders sat and discussed their options. Wheeler had attacked an 800-wagon train, destroying half and scattering the rest. Absorbing the news, Rosecrans told his commanders it was either retreat or surrender; with the scarce supplies on hand dwindling, their supply depot gone, and outnumbered 3:1, there were no other choices. McCook and Crittenden stayed quiet, but Thomas stated, "The Army will not surrender. We march."[12] Assistant Secretary Dana immediately protested, emphasizing the orders from Washington to hold Chattanooga. But the politician advanced no constructive suggestions and could not contact Washington for more instructions—Rebel cavalry had destroyed the telegraph lines into the town.

On the night of October 3, 1863, McCook and Crittenden led their two corps out of Chattanooga toward Walden Ridge in the pouring rain. Thomas and the men of XIV Corps held the fortifications and endeavored to show the activity level of twice their number. The following night XIV Corps crossed the river. Thomas left Wilder and his brigade to hold the town as long as they could before withdrawing and destroying the bridge and the town.

Confederate reaction was slow. Longstreet had put Hood's old division, now under Evander Law, in motion toward Bridgeport to reinforce that vital point and both D.H. Hill and Polk failed to recognize what had occurred in Chattanooga. It was nearing noon on October 5 when a civilian from the town reported that most of the Union troops had left. Hill ordered Major

General Patrick Cleburne's division to confirm the report. The Irishman's advance triggered a short battle with Wilder's troops. Wilder's repeating rifles easily repulsed the first advance but Cleburne stretched his line to work around the troopers and Wilder decided he had done enough. By 3.00 p.m., explosions were roaring through Chattanooga as the bridge and buildings went up in smoke.

Pursuit and Regrouping

The march from Chattanooga became a nightmare for the Federal troops. Rain had turned the Walden Ridge trail into a muddy quagmire. Although they took no wagons, starving animals had tremendous difficulty dragging the Army's guns, forcing exhausted men to help. One survivor remembered being "wet to the skin and mud to the knees, while it was with difficulty I could lift my feet out of the deep mud. We prayed we would not fall and perish by the wayside."[13] The troops had endured a similar ordeal during the June Tullahoma campaign, but this mud march felt worse because they were retreating.

Aside from the weather and some cavalry, the Confederates did not pursue aggressively. Forrest's men attacked the Union rearguard at Jasper, but the defenders put up a stout fight and Forrest withdrew his exhausted troopers. Wheeler continued his rampage ahead of the retreating Union Army, attacking McMinnville, then trying Murfreesboro. However, Union cavalry from Brigadier General George Crook's division intervened, cutting up those Rebel cavalry units burdened by loot taken from destroyed wagon trains— looted liquor proved particularly effective in slowing down some of the Rebels. Wheeler finally recrossed the Tennessee on October 9, still hounded by Union horsemen. His raid had been a devastating success. In addition to convincing Rosecrans to evacuate Chattanooga, he had destroyed some 1,000 wagons, killed or captured hundreds of horses and mules, and destroyed various trains and bridges, all for the cost of under 200 men.

By October 10, the Army of the Cumberland had reached safety and its supplies. XX and XXI Corps stayed at McMinnville, while Rosecrans, Thomas and XIV Corps stood down at Manchester. Almost as soon as the exhausted troops collapsed into a brief rest, the political uproar stirred up by their retreat broke over them. Rosecrans was relieved of command, as were McCook and Crittenden. Their two corps were reorganized into a single formation, retitled IV Corps, under Gordon Granger. George Thomas was named interim Army Commander on the basis of Dana's reports and his stalwart stand at Chickamauga.

For overall command Lincoln sent for Ulysses S. Grant, hero of Vicksburg, and gave him command of the Military Division of Mississippi, a field command encompassing Sherman's Army of Mississippi, Thomas's Army of the Cumberland and Burnside's Army of Ohio. But even as Grant traveled to Nashville to take over, the Federal government received its second grievous shock.

Following the battle of Chickamauga, Ambrose Burnside had withdrawn his troops back from the Tennessee and dug in at Knoxville, ignoring all entreaties by Rosecrans, Halleck and Lincoln to move to Chattanooga's aid. His cavalry kept him informed, however, of the forces moving against him. From Chattanooga, Buckner approached with four divisions; from Virginia, Sam Jones marched with 5,000 men. Knowing he would soon be surrounded, Burnside abandoned Knoxville—without orders—and pulled back through the Cumberland Gap. His retreat erased all of the Union gains of the past two months and dealt the Lincoln administration a severe political blow.

The Confederacy rejoiced in the sudden turn of its fortunes and sought to keep the initiative. In Virginia, Lee left his Rapidan River defenses and maneuvered to turn the Army of Potomac's right flank the way he had done at Second Manassas. Meade's troops responded rapidly and dealt Lee several sharp blows but the Union counterattack petered out when Meade refused to assault Lee's new fortifications at Mine Run.

In Tennessee, Longstreet began pushing his rejuvenated troops forward in an effort to gain as much ground as possible. His two Virginia divisions probed the defenses at the Union depot at Decherd where Hooker stood with two of his divisions. Longstreet ordered Polk to bring up his troops to aid in a coordinated attack, but, in typical Polk fashion, the Bishop decided instead to dig in below Tracy City. Longstreet attacked alone and Hooker easily held him off, but in the fighting Major General O.O. Howard, commander of Hooker's XI Corps, was killed.

In Nashville, Grant had arrived to assume his new command and was faced with some hard choices. Thomas's army lay safe but exhausted and incapable of operations. Hooker's troops remained fresh, but exposed to the encroaching Confederates. Sherman's troops were still weeks away from joining up. Grant authorized Hooker to pull back from Decherd to Tullahoma after destroying the railroad and any supplies he could not get out. After further discussions, the pull back continued to Murfreesboro. At Thomas's suggestion, entrenched Union divisions were left in the four gaps that breached the Highland Ridge to hold the positions.[14] Longstreet moved into the vacated areas and went into winter quarters, with his primary goal the repair of his railroad supply line.

Winter Strategic Planning

For the South, the latter part of 1863 had seen a tremendous change in fortune. From the depths of despair resulting from Lee's defeat at Gettysburg and the losses of Vicksburg, Knoxville and Chattanooga, the victory at Chickamauga and the retaking of East and Middle Tennessee brought the Confederacy back to life. For the army, the benefits were more than just higher morale—desertions fell off dramatically, especially in Mississippi. Initially, only some 11,000 of Vicksburg's defenders (40 percent) had showed up in parole camps; by January 1864 that number had jumped to nearly 25,000.

Just after the New Year, Longstreet traveled to Richmond to meet with President Davis, Secretary of War James Seddon and General Lee to plan strategy for 1864. General Joe Johnston, although invited, declined to attend, citing new Union activity at his front.

Johnston's position was one of the awkward situations that Davis had to resolve. Ostensibly, Johnston remained the theater commander and thus, Longstreet's immediate superior. However, he had also been Bragg's superior and had done nothing to wield his authority; in fact at one point he had informed Davis that he "had not considered himself commanding in Tennessee"[15] after moving to Mississippi to lead the relief army to Vicksburg's aid. The fall of the Mississippi fortress had initiated a sharp and divisive exchange of letters between Johnston and Davis that kept both men preoccupied to the detriment of their country. Johnston had answered the call for reinforcements to Bragg, but had added, "This is a loan to be promptly returned."[16] Longstreet's success following Chickamauga had eclipsed Johnston's protest. Davis decided to handle the sticky command situation by simply ignoring it. Johnston made it far easier by not requesting further clarification from his president and by not traveling to Chattanooga to assume command. He stayed in Mississippi and sulked.

Seddon began the meeting by suggesting a massive move north into Kentucky, similar to the invasion that Bragg had initiated in 1862. Such a move, he felt, would outflank Nashville, force Grant out of Tennessee altogether and into a battle where he could be defeated. Once Grant had been dealt with, Longstreet could take all of Kentucky, opening the state for supply and recruits, and threaten Ohio, identical goals to Bragg's purposes the previous year.[17] The politician even suggested crossing into the Union state.

Longstreet objected, citing the problems Bragg had encountered in Kentucky and the lack of support for the South in the Bluegrass State. He also pointed out that Grant was no Don Carlos Buell. Longstreet knew Grant very well—they had been best friends at West Point and had served together in the Mexican War. "We cannot afford to underestimate him," he told the others, "He will fight us every day and every hour until the end of the war."[18] He felt that Grant would be more likely to dig in and threaten his supply line than pull up stakes and follow. The others had to agree with Longstreet's logic. Grant's tenacity in overcoming obstacles and multiple failures finally to succeed in taking Vicksburg worried them.

Robert E. Lee concurred with his former subordinate, stating that the Confederacy was in no condition to take and hold new territory, especially hostile or even neutral ground. Citing massive Union manpower, he reminded Davis that over 120,000 militia had been mustered in July 1863 when John Morgan's small force had invaded Indiana and Ohio. However, he felt the initiative had to be theirs. The Confederate forces should "alarm and embarrass [the enemy] to some extent and thus prevent his undertaking anything of magnitude against us."[19]

The plan resulting from the meeting called for Longstreet to pre-empt any Union move by feinting an advance into Kentucky to disguise the real goal of flanking and taking Nashville. For that purpose, he received two more divisions from Johnston. In addition to the reinforcements, Longstreet, soured by Polk's failure near Decherd, asked that William Hardee come back east with the new troops to replace Polk. Forrest's command also went to Mississippi at that general's request after he argued that he could be more effective there. More to the point, though, he did not get along with his cavalry "superior" Joe Wheeler.

As spring approached, Longstreet had essentially four corps and eleven divisions. Hardee commanded the divisions of Major Generals Benjamin F. Cheatham, Thomas C. Hindman and A.P. Stewart (17,000 men) at Shelbyville. Hood commanded the divisions of McLaws, Brigadier General Evander M. Law and Walker (19,500 troops) at Wartrace. D.H. Hill commanded the divisions of Major General John C. Breckinridge, Cleburne and Liddell (16,500 men) at Manchester. Major Generals Carter L. Stevenson's and William W. Loring's divisions stayed with Longstreet in Tullahoma. On either flank was one of Wheeler's cavalry divisions, each with about 3,500 horsemen.

For the Union, the winter of 1863–64 was a time of reassessment as well. Reversals in Tennessee had muted the euphoria of the mid-year advances and victories. Just when it looked like the South might be collapsing, Longstreet's advance showed that expectation to be premature. It gave Lincoln's political opponents more ammunition.

Lincoln's overall goals had not changed: build up loyal governments, arm freed Southern slaves, and defeat the south politically and psychologically with military and economic pressure.[20] But one immediate political requirement focused on East Tennessee. The Unionists in the region had emerged when Burnside's forces took Knoxville and the surrounding territory. In fact they had emerged with a vengeance against their pro-Confederacy neighbors who had subjugated them for three years. Burnside's retreat and the return of Confederate forces had turned the tables and a fratricidal bloodbath resulted. Lincoln had pledged much of his political future on restoring East Tennessee and its loyal inhabitants to the Union and he meant to see that pledge upheld.

With the political necessities identified, Grant and Meade met with General-in-Chief Henry Halleck to discuss their plans. Both field commanders were experienced enough to accept the limitations they were facing. First, they operated on exterior lines, making coordination slower than for their opponent, who would be able to shift troops by rail. Second, annihilating an enemy army in battle appeared to be nearly impossible because of the power of the defensive and the constraints of moving at the same speed as a retreating enemy—slower if the railroads had to be repaired. Grant's success in smashing Pemberton's army at Vicksburg stood more as a function of the Southern mistake of being trapped against a river than Grant's maneuvers. With these factors in mind, Grant favored a strategy of destroying the South's logistical base with simultaneous advances on several fronts to stretch the Rebel resources. Any Confederate troop shift would weaken their lines somewhere, allowing the Union to advance. Even if a Union army was pushed back, the destruction it left in its wake would be beneficial to the Union cause. His recommendations stressed this approach.

Halleck disagreed, stating that they had not been able to defeat a Southern army completely as yet and would not be able to if they spread their resources. He told both men to concentrate on defeating their opposing armies.

Meade's responsibility would be Lee's army, along with the security of Washington and Maryland. He would try to maneuver to advantage and hurt the Army of Northern Virginia if at all possible. He had 100,000 men, organized in three corps, in his Army of the Potomac to work with.

Grant had Longstreet's army as his primary target, along with responsibility to support Major General James Schofield, who replaced the cashiered Burnside, in his bid to retake East Tennessee. Schofield's XXIII and IX Corps consisted of 30,000 troops, with 3,000 cavalry. Under his direct command, Grant had his favorite lieutenant, William Sherman and three corps of the Army of the Tennessee. Major General John Logan commanded four divisions of XV Corps (12,200 men); Major General Greenville Dodge commanded XVI Corps with two divisions and 10,700 men and Major General Frank Blair commanded XVII Corps with two divisions and 8,700 men. Most of these troops were stationed near Columbia, Tennessee, on the Duck River, threatening Longstreet's left flank.

Grant also commanded Thomas's Army of the Cumberland. The two generals did not particularly like one another, a strained relationship stemming from the Mississippi campaigns when Halleck played the two against each other. Their personalities were far different as well. While both stood solid on defense, Thomas tended to be slower and more methodical than Grant in offensive operations. Grant improvised with whatever he had on hand to do the job. Thomas would decide what was needed to do the job and would not budge until he had it. Grant had been in favor of removing Thomas as well as Rosecrans from command following the retreat from Chattanooga, but he realized the depths of the army's admiration for their Rock of a general who had "saved" them at Chickamauga.[21]

Under Grant, Thomas commanded three corps: Major General John M. Palmer's XIV Corps with three divisions and 22,700 men, Major General

Gordon Granger's IV Corps with three divisions and 20,500 men, and Hooker's XX Corps with three divisions and 20,600 men. These three corps spread out with divisions covering the important gaps. Nearly 9,000 cavalry supported both Sherman and Thomas. Major General John Buford arrived in late winter after recovering from pneumonia to assume command of the three cavalry divisions. He had proved his worth on the first day at Gettysburg when his division stopped Lee long enough for Union infantry to close up.

The Dance Begins

Union troops opened the ball early in February with a raid into Mississippi, targeting the town of Meridian. In early March, another 40,000 Union troops began moving up the Red River in Louisiana, supported by naval forces, with the goal of capturing cotton. Confederate forces attacked the vanguard at Mansfield, and despite numerical superiority the Union withdrew. And on May 4, 1864, Meade sent his Army of the Potomac across the Rapidan River and into the dense and tangled woods known as the Wilderness. Lee's hard marching troops met him there and held on against multiple assaults. Over the next week marches and counter-marches, interspersed with bitter clashes, failed to break through the Confederates. The armies suffered another 30,000 combined casualties during the battle.

In the west, Grant had planned to coordinate his advance with Meade's movement forward. His plan: pin Longstreet's troops (and attention) to the Highland Rim Gaps and move Sherman's troops against the Confederate left from Columbia. But Longstreet moved first.

On May 1, 1864, D.H. Hill began moving his corps from Manchester toward McMinnville, while Hood's corps replaced him. To cover Hood's redeployment, Longstreet moved onto the Wartrace lines with Stevenson's division. Wheeler moved north with Martin's cavalry division with the goal of advancing through Sparta and on to Carthage. Longstreet hoped Wheeler's troopers would make Grant think he was attempting a major flanking attack on Nashville. Grant did in fact delay his response when word of the Confederate troop movements reached him.

A week later battle erupted in various locales. Hardee sent Cheatham's division against the Union defenders at Guy's Gap in a spirited demonstration. The battle got out of hand, though, when the Confederates actually broke through into the fortifications, only to have the Union reserves counterattack heavily. Caught on the wrong side of the fortifications, Brigadier General George Maney's brigade was savaged before it could withdraw. Further east, Law's division demonstrated against Hoover Gap, but neither side suffered much in a very controlled fight.

To the north Wheeler charged through Carthage, raising havoc in the town and generating panicked telegraph signals of a "massive Reb attack" going out to other stations in Tennessee and Kentucky. Confederate sympathizers soon warned Wheeler about Union cavalry approaching. Wheeler traded charge and counter-charge with Brigadier General Kenner Garrard's cavalry division, but ran afoul of Wilder's Lightning Brigade. The brigade's repeating rifles shredded Wheeler's charge, wounding the Confederate leader and killing division commander William Martin. The arrival of John Buford and Brigadier General Edward M. McCook's division of cavalry sealed the fight and sent Wheeler's decimated troopers into flight.

But D.H. Hill emerged from the wooded hills of the Highland Rim to surround the village of Smithville and caught its garrison, the 52d Indiana Volunteer Regiment, by surprise. Clearly outnumbered, the 52d's commander, Colonel Zalmon S. Main, did what he could to delay the Confederates by arguing surrender terms with Hill. Cavalry vedettes spurred outward to warn Grant and the rest of the Union force.

Grant reacted by moving two divisions from Granger's corps northward to extend his line and cover the eastern approach toward Nashville. News of the attacks at Carthage and Smithville made him assume that Nashville was indeed the target. He also saw an opportunity in the Confederate action and sent Sherman orders to start moving toward Shelbyville.

However, Longstreet had no real intention of attacking Nashville, as tempting a political target as it might be. Sympathizers had given him detailed information on its fortifications and he realized the city was too strong for him to attack directly. So, after taking Smithville and sending Breckinridge's division toward Alexandria to continue the diversion, Hill turned with Liddell's and Cleburne's troops southwest toward Woodville, where Granger's remaining division, the 1/IV under Brigadier General William Grose, guarded the McMinnville road. Hood with two of his three divisions moved on the lone division as well. When the two forces joined up, they would attack toward Murfreesboro, flanking and uncovering the Gap defenses as they went and allowing more Confederate troops to join them. Longstreet reasoned if he could get into Murfreesboro and destroy the supplies there, any Union move would be severely disrupted.

Unfortunately, terrain and weather delayed Hood's march over the rugged terrain so Hill arrived first and began skirmishing with Grose's troops. Outnumbered already, the Union general started his withdrawal before Hood joined up. The division pulled back and joined Hooker's 1/XX under Brigadier General Alpheus S. Williams, digging in near Peak's Hill, ten miles east of Murfreesboro.

George Thomas arrived to take command of the two divisions, intending to slow the Confederates and buy time for Grant to concentrate more forces. On May 17, Hill and Hood, now with Longstreet in direct command, launched their attack, pitting 20,000 troops against the Union's 13,000. Hood's troops were tired from their arduous march, which disrupted the coordination of the attack and allowed Thomas's troops to hold throughout the day. The 2/1/IV's epic stand on the Union left aided the defense by

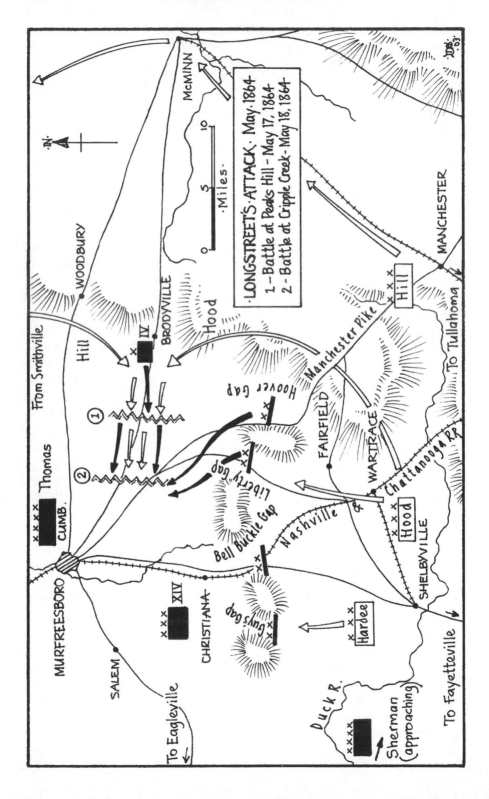

·LONGSTREET'S·ATTACK· May·1864
1 – Battle at Peaks Hill – May 17, 1864
2 – Battle at Cripple Creek – May 18, 1864

holding off Cleburne's whole division.[22] As dusk fell, Confederate numbers began to tell and the two Union divisions fell back toward their supply depot.

Impatiently, Longstreet ordered his two corps out of their post-battle camps early to press the enemy hard the next day. At mid-morning, May 18, the four Confederate divisions, now numbering less than 18,000, ran headlong into the new Union line along Cripple Creek. Thomas had been busy, reinforcing the 1/XX and 1/IV and their remaining 10,000 troops with the 3/XX under Major General Daniel Butterfield, pulled out of Hoover Gap, and the 2/XIV, under a Union brigadier general named Jefferson Davis. The two new units added 14,000 troops to the Union total. Longstreet's initial attack was stopped and he did not press the assault, knowing full well, he had no men to spare. But Davis's fresh troops, screaming the battle cry of "Chattanooga!" did not let him disengage cleanly. The Union counterattack forced the Confederates back, but suffered heavy casualties in doing so. Fighting raged until night fell.

To the north of the battle site, Granger's two divisions had engaged Breckinridge, who held a line along the Clear Fork to the east of Alexandria. Grant himself ordered Granger to attack. Inexplicably, the corps commander got himself fully involved in the preliminary artillery barrage, even going so far as to take charge of a single cannon and direct its fire while two divisions of infantry stood idle. Grant waited for something to happen, then rode to find out the source of the delay. Finding Granger at his gun, the commander snapped, "If you will leave that gun to its captain and take command of your Corps, it will be better for all of us."[23]

Once it got moving, the Union attack by Brigadier General John Newton's and Thomas J. Wood's divisions pushed Breckinridge back easily despite the terrain. The Kentuckian withdrew and moved south, marching through the night to rejoin Longstreet. The arrival of Breckinridge let the Confederate commander know he faced two more Union divisions on his flank and he made the sensible decision to withdraw from the battlefield. When the Union forces stood to the following morning, it was to face abandoned Confederate breastworks.

Grant, joining Thomas at noon, ordered a pursuit, but Thomas took his time to sort his troops out and get them in motion. By the time he approached the Gaps, Longstreet had withdrawn through them, leaving a division at Woodbury and at Hoover Gap to hold the Union out. Thomas decided not to attempt to force the issue but Grant ordered an attack anyway. Hooker's 3/XX moved forward and ran into defenders commanded by Patrick Cleburne. In two hours of fighting, Butterfield's troops made no headway while losing more that 500 men in the process. Cleburne's losses were fewer than 200.

With the abortive action at Hoover Gap on May 19, Longstreet's offensive and what came to be called the Second Battle of Murfreesboro drew to a close. He had failed to take the Union supply depot, but had disrupted Grant's plans for an advance. Both sides lost heavily; Longstreet some 11,000 of his 53,000 and Thomas's Army of the Cumberland, 14,000 of 63,000. But the respite gained by disrupting Grant proved minimal. Elsewhere Union forces stayed on the move. The following day, as Cleburne was holding off Hooker, Longstreet had to dispatch Stevenson's division from Wartrace and Loring's from Tullahoma to aid Simon Buckner in East Tennessee.

Reinforcing Buckner created a major gamble for Longstreet because, while he engaged Thomas and Grant, Sherman's Army of the Tennessee had advanced from Columbia toward Longstreet's left flank, opposed only by John Kelly's Rebel cavalry. The western troops advanced to within 20 miles of Hardee's headquarters at Shelbyville. Fortunately, Sherman was not advancing along a railroad, which limited his supply to vulnerable wagon trains. Confederate cavalry and guerrillas did their best to impede the advance. Grant finally halted Sherman at Lewisburg while Thomas reformed his army after their battles.

The Battle of the Gaps

A frustrated and impatient U.S. Grant finally saw his advance against Longstreet begin on June 20. Despite repeated urgings, George Thomas did not begin moving until he believed the Army of the Cumberland ready, which included replacing all the casualties incurred during Longstreet's May attacks. All in all some 90,000 Union troops prepared to move. Longstreet could muster some 49,000, having made up only half his losses.

Grant's plan stayed similar to the one that he had chosen in May. Buford's cavalry would attack from the north, moving with a single division from IV Corps toward McMinnville. The rest of IV Corps, now commanded by Major General David Stanley, would demonstrate against the Confederate line in Hoover Gap. Hooker's XX Corps would also feint against Liberty Gap to make Longstreet think the attack from the north was the main assault. Once those attacks began to develop, Sherman would advance on Shelbyville with Palmer's full XIV Corps assaulting out of Guy's Gap against Hardee's flank. Grant fully expected Sherman's and Palmer's 50,000 troops to take Shelbyville and roll up the Confederate line. Longstreet held Liberty and Hoover Gaps with brigades in multiple lines and erected fortifications at the exits of Bell Buckle and Guy's Gap to contain any Union excursion. He had no real reserve for this battle—Stevenson and Loring were still in East Tennessee with Buckner.

The attack opened as planned with good weather aiding the marching Federals. Buford skirmished with Wheeler's troopers, who fell back with delaying tactics. John Newton's division (2/IV) moved in to McMinnville with almost no resistance. Further west T.J. Wood's division (3/IV) led the demonstration against Hoover Gap, massing the divisional artillery for a

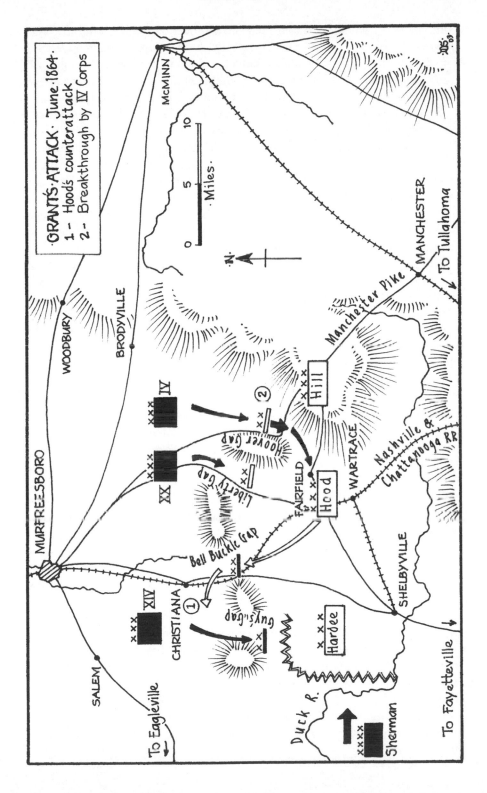

GRANT'S ATTACK · June · 1864 ·
1 – Hood's counterattack
2 – Breakthrough by IV Corps

bombardment. Wood made two small-scale probes of the lines but only half-heartedly—his men knew they were only a diversion. Brigadier General Edward C. Walthall's brigade of Liddell's division defended the line and easily stopped the probes. Brigadier General Patton Anderson's brigade of Law's division in Liberty held off similar probes from Hooker's men.

Sherman and Palmer opened up the main Union assault the following day. Sherman attacked Hindman and Stewart in the fortifications, while Cheatham's division held the line against Palmer. Guy's Gap only allowed a single division to deploy effectively, so Palmer could not bring the full weight of his corps against Cheatham. Sherman nearly overlapped Hardee's line, but the timely arrival of Walker's division, dispatched by Hood, shored up the defenses. By the end of June 23, little had been accomplished except casualties. Grant ordered the attacks to continue, with more strength against the gaps to pull troops away from in front of Sherman.

Longstreet faced some hard choices on the night of June 23. His left flank had held but suffered for it. Since the gaps had held easily, he chose to mass his troops on the left to beat Sherman's assault, leaving the gap defenders without backup. He ordered Hill to leave Liddell's division to defend Hoover Gap and move his other two divisions west toward Wartrace. Hood would keep Anderson in Liberty Gap, but would assault with McLaws and the rest of Law's division through Bell Buckle Gap along the rail line to take the Union troops at Guy's Gap from the rear. Hardee's three divisions, plus Walker, would defend in place.

Hood's attack went better than expected. Hooker had withdrawn all but one brigade, Brigadier General Thomas Ruger's 2/1/XX, from Bell Buckle to support a stronger attack against Liberty. Ruger's men were overwhelmed and, when dawn broke, Palmer's rearmost division, Brigadier General Absalom Baird's 3/XIV, found itself nearly surprised in its camps. A vicious fight broke out. Palmer withdrew Jeff Davis's 2/XIV out of the Gap to help Baird's hard pressed men. With Palmer fully involved with Hood, Sherman again went alone against Hardee and again suffered heavy casualties.

Longstreet's gamble at Bell Buckle seemed to mark the demise of Grant's planned advance, but fate took a hand in a different direction. T.J. Wood's men had been demonstrating against Walthall for two days, taking casualties for no apparent purpose. Frustrated by the casualties, and the emphasis Grant placed on Sherman's troops, the Cumberlanders, without orders, began to assault forward. The surge caught the Confederates in the middle of switching out front-line regiments and the attack broke through the front line. Wood's screaming men pursued the Rebels as they tried to withdraw to their second line, which could not open fire without hitting their own men. The Hoover Gap line collapsed as the Union overran Walthall's brigade.

Grose's division came hard on the heels of Wood's troops. They emerged from the Gap in time to see McNair's and Wilson's brigades scrambling to get into line. But Liddell's remaining troops had little time to prepare for the onslaught and cracked under the Cumberland battle cry of "Chattanooga!"

Liddell's disaster placed Longstreet's right flank in jeopardy and he had to send Hill's troops back the way they had just marched to stem the tide. North of Bell Buckle, Hood's attack had run its course by early afternoon, having savaged two of Palmer's divisions. But the seven Confederate brigades had been hurt, too, and now faced fresh Union troops as Hooker's divisions moved in from the east. Hood withdrew back through Bell Buckle.

The two-day Battle of the Gaps had cost the Union some 19,000 casualties, mostly in Sherman's army and Palmer's XIV Corps. Longstreet had lost nearly 11,000 troops, including virtually all of Liddell's division.[24] While his defenses at Guy's Gap and Shelbyville had bent, they remained strong; but he had lost his right and Grant could cut him off from Chattanooga. He fell back onto his supply line and centered his defenses on the fortifications at Tullahoma. Grant followed slowly while his forces regrouped from their battle.

The Political Scene

By mid-July, the military stalemate and heavy casualties had sparked intense debate in the North, just months before a presidential election. Meade and Grant had lost close to 80,000 men and had little to show for it. East Tennessee remained in Confederate hands after Early's corps moved in from the Shenandoah to stop another drive by Schofield.

In August, the Democratic Party held its presidential nominating convention. While the two wings of the party had many areas of disagreement, all could agree on one proposition: "After four years of failure to restore the Union by experiment of war, justice, humanity, liberty and public welfare demand that immediate efforts be made for the cessation of hostilities." The party nominated George B. McClellan, former General-in-Chief of the Union Armies, as its candidate.

McClellan was an awkward choice to spearhead a peace platform. As a Union general, he remained as committed to restoring the Union as Lincoln, including doing so by war if necessary. But the two men differed in the details. Lincoln demanded emancipation of the slaves as part of the Union while McClellan believed such a requirement an impediment to peace and a social decision for states to make. Little Mac, as the army knew him, felt strongly that, without the emancipation issue, peace parties in the Confederacy would rise up and demand reunification. This left him uncomfortable and embarrassed with a policy that could only be described as peace at any price. His running mate, George H. Pendleton of Ohio, an ardent Copperhead, had less trouble with that policy. Together they ran a campaign that stressed the war's failure, the unconstitutional attempt to free the slaves by what they termed abolitionist fanatics, the economic chaos war had created and, finally, the Lincoln Administration's abuse of power, such as the suspension of Habeas Corpus, political arrests, and conscription.

In the South, peace was a priority for Davis and his government as well— Union resources were exerting enormous pressure and, despite the successes of Lee, Longstreet and Buckner in holding off the blue tide, he knew it was just a matter of time. Peace feelers to the North had been made, but stumbled on the emancipation issue, as McClellan had thought. However, the Democratic candidate was wrong in thinking it was the only issue. The desire for independence remained strong in the South. Davis had, in fact, broached the subject of emancipation in return for foreign recognition of the Confederacy to both Britain and France.

Lincoln and his Republican Party worried about the coming election. With the war stalemated, other issues generated bad party morale. Lincoln and the Congress were at odds about how to handle the South once the war had been won. The Secretary of the Treasury, Salmon Chase, resigned from the Cabinet because of the economic mess the war created. Party officials met secretly to discuss *not* nominating Lincoln, but failed to reach an accord. As the election drew near and the news grew worse, Lincoln resigned himself to defeat and promised to support the new president immediately. The Republican campaign stayed a negative one, stressing McClellan's war record and dedication to the Union. In the meantime, Lincoln pushed his generals to do something to show positive progress in the war effort. Meade suggested a version of McClellan's Peninsula Campaign, moving the Army south by boat and attacking Petersburg to sever Richmond from the rest of the Confederacy. Halleck refused to consider it, believing Lee would simply move north and attack Washington. Grant put his armies in motion to try and flank Longstreet out of Tullahoma, but the Confederates held off each attempt. In October Forrest returned to create havoc along the Union supply lines.

When the voters went to the polls that November, historians agreed that it was Lincoln who lost the election, rather than McClellan who won it.

The Final Acts

Although he had several months in office left, Lincoln, as promised, chose to allow McClellan to take command of the country and its military immediately. McClellan ordered a cease fire in place and requested talks with Davis. He announced that the emancipation proclamation was void. This news caused some rioting among the colored troops in the Union Army as false rumors made them believe they were to be returned to slavery.

The Confederate president, a crafty negotiator, replied that negotiations while Confederate territory remained occupied were fruitless. He hinted that a pullback would make it easier to convince his state governors that union was a good choice. President-elect McClellan began to realize the war had moved from the country to the conference table.

The Reality

In reality, Braxton Bragg did not fall wounded at Chickamauga and stayed in command of the Army of Tennessee while it invested Rosecrans in Chattanooga. However, as he had done after all his battles, Bragg's attention turned toward his own commanders rather than the enemy, starting a feud that resulted in nothing getting done. President Jefferson Davis made a personal appearance to quell the dissension, but ultimately left Bragg in charge. Bragg drove both Polk and Hill out and the army was reorganized to break up anti-Bragg power bases, further demoralizing the rank and file. Longstreet, disgusted with Bragg—and with Davis for allowing the irascible commander to remain—did little constructive during the period. Ultimately, Bragg sent him off against Knoxville.

While the Army of Tennessee disintegrated from within, the Union reinforced the Army of the Cumberland in and around Chattanooga. Grant took over as overall commander and he immediately sacked Rosecrans, installing Thomas in his place. In November 1863, after Sherman's troops from Mississippi arrived, a massed assault broke Bragg's line at Missionary Ridge, sending it reeling southward. The victory took Grant to Washington as the Union General-in-Chief and set the stage for Sherman's march to Atlanta. The taking of that city in September 1864 sealed the re-election of Abraham Lincoln to a second term in the White House and the continuance of the war until the complete destruction of the Confederacy. The political discussion, except for the election's outcome, is historical.

Much has been made of Longstreet's poor performance following Chickamauga and has led many historians to feel he was incapable of successful independent command. Such a view would make this alternate history seem beyond the realm of believability. Longstreet's desire for a top command was his reason for pushing for a transfer to the West. His poor performance after not getting it was in part due to his disgust with Bragg and in part his disappointment at not getting what he wanted. In this version of history, he did, in fact get what he wanted, thus much of the reason for his historical sulky behavior is absent.

Longstreet has also been considered more comfortable on tactical defense than on the attack; thus his actions at Second Murfreesboro and the Gaps may seem out of character, but his opponent has to be considered. Much of Robert E. Lee's success was due to his out-generaling Northern opponents like McClellan, Pope, Burnside and Hooker. Longstreet was facing Grant, someone he knew very well. His decisions would have taken Grant's known aggressiveness and tenacity into consideration, thus I believe he would have attacked in Tennessee rather than stayed on the defensive.

Two additional historical notes: first, Longstreet's chief of artillery, E. Porter Alexander, was the real author of the plan for the attack on Bridgeport. Alexander reconnoitered the town himself in mid-October 1863 and recommended the plan, which his boss took to Bragg. Nothing came of it. Since Hooker's two divisions of XI Corps had arrived there in early October, such an attack at that point would have probably failed. Second, the Longstreet counterattack through Bell Buckle Gap was actually Bragg's plan to thwart any Union move against him at Tullahoma in June 1863. The plan came to naught due primarily to Polk's refusal to consider the move.

Bibliography

Alexander, E. Porter, (ed.Gary Gallagher), *Fighting for the Confederacy: The Personal Recollections of General Edward Porter Alexander* (University of North Carolina Press, Chapel Hill, NC, 1989).

Cozzens, Peter, *This Terrible Sound: the Battle of Chickamauga* (University of Illinois Press, Urbana, IL, 1992).

Cozzens, Peter, *The Shipwreck of their Hopes: The Battles for Chattanooga* (University of Illinois Press,Urbana, IL, 1992).

Lamers, William M., *The Edge of Glory: A Biography of General William S. Rosecrans, U.S.A.* (Harcourt, Brace & World, New York, 1961).

Longstreet, James, *From Manassas to Appomatox: Memoirs of the Civil War in America* (J. B. Lippincott, Philadelphia, PA, 1896).

McKenney, Francis, *Education in Violence: The Life of George H. Thomas and the History of the Army of the Cumberland* (Americana House, Chicago, 1991).

Woodworth, Steven E., *Jefferson Davis and his Generals: The Failure of Confederate Command in the West* (University Press of Kansas, Lawrence, 1990).

The War of the Rebellion: A Compilation of the Official Records of the Union and Confederate Armies. Volumes XXX parts 1-4 and XXXII, Part 3. (U.S. Government Printing Office, Washington D.C., 1880–1901); cited below as *OR*.

Notes

1. Brigadier General St John R. Liddell was a division commander in Walker's Reserve Corps of Polk's Right Wing.
2. Nathan Bedford Forrest was one of the South's most celebrated cavalry leaders.
*3. The description of Bragg's meeting comes from General Payton Manning's memoir *With Longstreet* (Neal Publishing Company, New York, 1905)
4. *OR*, Volume XXX, Part 2, p. 148
5. Union and Confederate nomenclature for military units differed. The Union used numbers for corps, the divisions within corps, and the brigades within the divisions. Thus the Second Brigade of the First Division of XIV Corps was designated 2/1/XIV. The Confederates generally named units after their commanders (and occasionally after the original commanders). For example Brigadier Micah Jenkins commanded Jenkins's Brigade of Pickett's Division of Longstreet's Corps. After the loss of Stonewall Jackson at Chancellorsville, however, General Lee reorganized the Army of Northern Virginia and used numbers. Thus A.P. Hill's Corps was also known as Third Corps.
6. States Rights was his actual name—his father was making a strong political statement when his son was born.
7. Ironically, Dana himself was part of the Chickamauga disaster. Shortly after Longstreet's devastating attack, Dana intercepted Wilder's Lightning Brigade and demanded escort back to Chattanooga. Wilder had just struck the exposed left flank of the Confederate charge, driven off one brigade, and could have easily disrupted the rest of the attack with the power of his repeating rifles.

8. *OR*, Volume XXX, Part 1, p. 202

9. *Ibid.*, p. 217.

10. The infantry units were the 10th Illinois, 16th Illinois and 60th Illinois Volunteers, all from 1/2/RES. The cavalry units were the 2d Indiana, 4th Indiana, and 1st Wisconsin cavalry.

11. *OR*, Volume XXX, Part 4, pp. 13–14. The two spies, Mr. Roberts and Mr. Lumpkins, also reported that Wheeler would cross the Tennessee at Washington and raid into the Sequatchie Valley. Wheeler's crossing convinced Rosecrans that the numerical report was accurate.

*12. William M Lamars, *The Edge of Glory* (Harcourt, Brace & World, New York, 1961) p. 376.

*13. Second Lieutenant Charles C. Briant, Company K, quoted in *History of the 6th Indiana Volunteer Infantry: To Chattanooga and back with Rosy.*

14. Hoover, Liberty, Bell Buckle and Guy's Gaps. It was through these poorly defended gaps that Rosecrans had maneuvered his troops to lever Bragg out of Tullahoma in June 1863.

15. *OR*, Volume XXIV, part 1, p. 226.

16. *OR*, Volume XXX, part 4, p. 539.

*17. Henry Hathaway and Archibald Smith, *How the North Lost*, p. 260. The goals of the 1862 Kentucky invasion were to 1) draw Don Carlos Buell and his Union army away from Chattanooga, 2) defeat him in battle, and 3) "liberate" Kentucky into the Confederacy. It succeeded only in drawing Buell away. A southern tactical success between portions of the opposing armies at Perryville ended up negated by Bragg's retreat back into Tennessee sans supplies and Kentucky recruits.

*18. Manning, *With Longstreet*, p. 266.

19. *OR*, Volume XXXII, Part 3, pp. 494–5.

*20. Hathaway and Smith, *How the North Lost*, p. 486.

21. Francis McKenney, *Education in Violence*, p. 273. Another factor that swayed Grant's decision to keep Thomas was probably the letter that he carried from Union Secretary of War Edwin M. Stanton. The letter thanked Thomas for his magnificent behavior at Chickamauga and said in part, "You stood like a Rock and that stand gives you fame... You will be rewarded by the country and by the Department."

*22. Hathaway and Smith, *How the North Lost*, p. 426. The brigade, under Brigadier General W.C. Whitaker, suffered nearly 65 percent casualties in repulsing every attack Cleburne threw at it. The casualties included the survivors of the 35th Indiana under Major John P. Dufficy Jr., who acted as the rearguard as the brigade withdrew at dusk .

*23. Benjamin Cousins, *Changes of Vast Moment: the Battle of the Tennessee Gaps* (University of Illinois Press, Urbana, 1994) p. 248.

*24. *Ibid.*, p. 377. Sherman's Army of Mississippi lost nearly 9,600 men in their frontal assaults on Hardee's line. Palmer lost over 5,000 in their battles. Hardee's Corps, including Walker, lost about 4,000—half of Sherman's losses. Kershaw and Law lost about 3,500 in their Bell Buckle attack. Hill lost virtually Liddell's whole division, 4,000 of 4,700.

8
CONFEDERATE BLACK AND GRAY
A Revolution in the Minds of Men

Peter G. Tsouras

Richmond, Virginia, June 2, 1868

The crack of the gavel echoed through the new marble chamber of the Confederate States Congress. The chairman called the committee to order and invited the first witness to approach and take the oath.

The witness strode down the aisle past adoring spectators like the Confederate Mars that he was. Though in middle age he moved with the grace and coiled strength of a leopard among cows. He placed his hand on the Bible and swore the oath and sat down.

The chairman was all graciousness. "General Forrest, this committee thanks you for your assistance in this matter."

"I am glad to be of service, Sir."

"General Forrest, I believe you are familiar with the issue with which this committee has been dealing, one of some controversy in our young republic—the amendment to the Veterans' Pension Bill of 1866 respecting the Confederate States Colored Troops.

"Yes, I am, Mr. Chairman."

"Well, then, General, in your opinion should the pensions for former slaves be set lower than for free Negroes who enlisted voluntarily?"

> "Mr. Chairman, let me illustrate my position by relating my own experience with both slaves and free Negroes under arms. At the beginning of the war, I said to the 45 colored fellows on my plantation that I was going into the army; and that if they would go with me, if we got whipped they would be free anyhow, and that if we succeeded and slavery was perpetuated, if they would act faithfully with me to the end of the war, I would set them free. Eighteen months before the end of the war closed I was satisfied... "

And here he paused and then emphasized the next three words,

> "*at the time*, that we were going to be defeated, and I gave those 45, or
> 44 of them, their free papers for fear I might be called.
>
> They fought as faithfully and courageously before manumission as
> after it. I led men, gentlemen. Slave and free they all bled the same deep
> red for the Confederacy. And I trust this committee will give equal
> treatment under the law to ALL veterans of the Confederate States
> Colored Troops who served honorably in the late war."[1]

January 1864

The war was eating the South alive. Not even the most diehard Southern
secessionist could have imagined the train of events unleashed by the
decision to fire upon Fort Sumter in Charleston Harbor on that dreadful day
in 1861. Since then the South had poured out a torrent of blood and treasure
to stave off the increasing might of the Union armies and the flood of
material that sustained them. But to no avail. The borders of the
Confederacy burned ever southward despite every sacrifice.

The South was financially exhausted and had tapped the bottom of its
white manpower barrel despite a draconian conscription effort. Yet, as the
South grew weaker, the North grew stronger. Its already huge 3:1
manpower advantage in its white population was now further increased by
the large scale enlistment of foreign immigrants, Northern blacks, and
runaway Southern slaves in the Union Army. The Northern cause was
strengthened by this by more than the numerical increase in its order-of-
battle. Much of the population of the North and an even larger part of its
fighting men had been radicalized by the revolutionary nature of the war
itself.

Had the Federal Government appealed to the Northern man to enlist to
suppress slavery after Fort Sumter, the South would quickly have received its
independence. The idea of fighting for black emancipation was not a popular
idea in the North outside of trouble-making Massachusetts which had been
a thorn in everyone's side since it broke the King's Peace in Boston in 1774.
No, the Northern man fought for the honor of the flag and for the very
precious idea that his own liberties were inextricably bound with the survival
of the Union. The failure of the Union was the failure of the democratic
experiment. Dictators would plant themselves on the ruins of the Union.

But war has a mind of its own and is never constrained by those who pick
up the sword. Such was the course of the Civil War. By early 1863, Northern
recruitment of white volunteers was drying up as the war stalemated.
Southern valor in all its fury had fought Northern courage and numbers to
a standstill. Imperceptibly, though, the war had become a revolutionary
process, unleashing new passions and experiences. As the Union armies
penetrated deeper into the Confederacy, the reality of slavery became a first
hand experience for the Union soldier. The idea of making soldiers of black

men had been firmly suppressed at the beginning of the war. As the death
toll mounted, the Union soldier began to make the altogether common-
sense conclusion that this wonderful liberty he was fighting for might be
worth sharing. He also had a practical motive, typified in the statement that
"A black man can stop a bullet as well as a white man." Those thoughts were
also occurring in the South.

Confederate representatives in Europe early in 1863 were already
discussing the possibility of negating Lincoln's Emancipation Proclamation
by freeing slaves to fight in the Confederate Army. Undoubtedly, they were
influenced by the strong European anti-slavery opinions. Despite the South's
many friends in Europe, these envoys could make no headway. Always it was
slavery, like a bone in the throat, that strangled their every effort to secure
European assistance for the Confederacy. The irony was that the South had
many friends in Europe among the elites who did not wish the Union's
infectious experiment in democracy to succeed. That success would give new
power to the thrust toward democracy in states where it was making
headway or in those where reform had been frustrated. There was a palpable
tension in the issue as well as opportunity. In September of that year a rumor
swept through London that the South would free a half million slaves and
conscript them for military service. The Confederate representative in
London sent a secret dispatch to the Secretary of State, Judah Benjamin,
urging the adoption of just such a course. Other contemporary
communications to Benjamin within the Confederacy also urged the same
action. Benjamin rejected them as impractical but left the door open by
replying that the subject was one "which has awakened attention in several
quarters lately."[2] None of these conversations was made public. No one had
the nerve to bell the cat.

HQ, Army of Tennessee, Dalton, Georgia, January 2, 1864

The corps and division commanders of the Army of Tennessee had no idea
why they had been ordered to attend a meeting at General Johnston's
headquarters. They were surprised when Lieutenant General William "Old
Reliable" Hardee addressed them, stating that Major General Pat Cleburne,
one of his division commanders, had prepared a paper on an "important
subject."[3] Not a pin dropped as Cleburne read his manifesto to the assembled
corps and division commanders of the Army of Tennessee on that cold night
in January 1864. Cleburne's educated Irish accent was still a novelty in a sea
of liquid Southern English. They gave him their complete attention because
they had already given him their complete respect as the finest division
commander in the army. Already some, including Jefferson Davis, called him
the Stonewall of the West.

The 36-year-old Patrick Ronayne Cleburne was a gentleman and a natural
soldier through and through—spare, distant, taciturn, just, and exacting—

he lived as purely as a blue flame. He truly was a *chevalier sans peur et sans reproche*—a knight without fear or stain on his honor.

He was by birth an Anglo-Irishman, a Protestant, his father a prosperous physician in County Cork. The British Isles in the budding of the Victorian era hammered out men in the forge of empire. Among the middle and professional classes, the bar was set high indeed with a Protestant severity matched only in clanking Prussia. His family expected him to follow his father's profession, for which he had no passion. So when young Cleburne failed Greek and Latin in the entrance examinations for Trinity College in 1846, his shame drove him to enlist into the brutal oblivion of the British Army as a common soldier.

Yet whatever weakness had caused his failure burned away in the harsh but professional routine of garrison life in Ireland. If nothing else, a man learned to soldier in a British infantry regiment. Luckily he had joined a good regiment, the 41st Foot (the Welsh Regiment). By all accounts, Cleburne became an exemplary soldier and was promoted corporal before buying himself out in 1849. The man who hung up his red coat was not the boy who had run away to hide in it. There was a quiet seriousness in him and clarity of purpose:

> "He had learned useful lessons in the army, to apply in later life: patience, a disciplined cool nature, self-control, and an austere life style of self-denial. More importantly, he came to appreciate the position of those at the mercy of authority."[4]

As he left the army, Ireland was writhing in the worst of the potato famine, a land without hope and without a future. Cleburne, with a brother and sister, joined the countless Irish, Catholic and Protestant, who fled the stricken land for America. He made his way to Helena, Arkansas, on the Mississippi River, and fell passionately in love with his adopted country. By 1860, he was a pillar of his new community, a lawyer, and a man who would back a friend in a gun fight without question and with a steely coolness that met the highest standards of Southern male expectations.

With civil war on the horizon the local counties formed a militia company, the Yell Rifles. Cleburne was the first to enlist, as a private, and was quickly elected its captain. His reputation for leadership was clear, but it helped that he was the only man with any military experience, a quality in short supply in the young Confederacy. To its great good fortune, the young army in gray had found more than a good corporal drill master. Experience, maturity, and natural talent now all combined to produce a superlative leader of men and master of the battlefield.

> "Cleburne knew not the meaning of fear and so compelling was his personality and so dynamic his leadership that he was able to impress his gallantry and dauntlessness on those whom he commanded."[5]

In less than two short years of intense effort and fighting, the former British corporal rose to Confederate major general by December 1862.[6] Truly, at that moment in time, careers were open to talent.

From the beginning he was in the thick of the fighting—Shiloh, Richmond (Kentucky), and Perryville. As major general he commanded the 2d Division of Hardee's Corps, turning it into one of the great fighting formations in American history, North and South. Such was the reputation of his division that it was the only one allowed to keep its original colors when the Confederate battle flag was issued to the army to replace the previous regimental colors. The men in blue would have cause to fear whenever they saw the blue flag with a centered white moon and "crossed cannons inverted" appear on the field. He led the division at Stone's River, Chickamauga, and Chattanooga. In the army's desperate retreat after its defeat at Chattanooga, Cleburne and the 2d Division saved the artillery and trains by inflicting a stinging reverse on Hooker's pursuing corps at Ringgold's Gap. It was the only bright spot in the dismal, near disastrous campaign that had begun so brightly with the victory at Chickamauga. For retrieving the honor of the Army of Tennessee, Cleburne received the singular reward of the official thanks of the Congress and President.

Now in 1864 that valor and skill shown on so many battlefields had earned him the attention of the senior officers of the Army of Tennessee. In stark words he described the deterioration of the morale of the army that came from shrinking numbers as the ranks of the enemy swelled.

> "Our soldiers can see no end to this state of affairs except in our own exhaustion; hence, instead of rising to the occasion, they are sinking into a fatal apathy, growing weary of hardships and slaughters which promise no results."

The consequences were obvious:

> "If this state continues much longer we must be subjugated. Every man should endeavor to understand the meaning of subjugation before it is too late. We can give but a faint idea when we say it means the loss of all we now hold most sacred—slaves and all other personal property, lands, homesteads, liberty, justice, safety, pride, manhood. It means the history of our heroic struggle will be written by the enemy."

In addition the reasons for the impending disaster were plain.

> "We can see three great causes operating to destroy us: First, the inferiority of our armies to those of the enemy in point of numbers; second, the poverty of our single source of supply in comparison with his several sources; third, the fact that slavery, from being one of our chief sources of strength at the commencement of the war, has now become, in a military point of view, one of our chief sources of weakness."[7]

The solution was equally plain.

> "We propose... that we immediately commence training a large reserve
> of the most courageous of our slaves, and further that we guarantee
> freedom within a reasonable time to every slave in the South who shall
> remain true to the Confederacy in this war. As between the loss of
> independence and the loss of slavery, we assume that every patriot will
> freely give up the latter—give up the negro slaves rather than be a slave
> himself."[8]

It was a fool's hope, he explained, that Britain, after freeing its own slaves,
would aid the Confederacy to retain its human chattels, such was the
intensity of anti-slavery feeling in that country as well as elsewhere in
Europe. The conclusion was as simple as it was earthshaking. The South
could not have both slavery and independence. It must choose. And as
slavery was of lesser importance than independence, it must be sacrificed to
achieve the greater goal. Enroll slaves in the Confederate Army and reward
faithful service with freedom for themselves and their families. Then Britain
and other countries would no longer be hindered by the stigma of slavery in
coming to the South's aid. Then the wind would be taken out of the North's
moral crusade and black enlistments in the Union Army would dry up.

The clarity of Cleburne's proposal was stunning. He would destroy the
Old South to save it. The Old South was doomed in any case, he could see.
A New South would be born and, for the sake of liberty, the Southern people
must give it birth, not a vengeful North. That made all the difference in the
world. Cleburne's clarity came from seeing the problem with different eyes.
Although an adopted Southerner, he still had a different perspective, shaped
in another society. Cleburne was no slave holder; nor did he have any special
abolitionist feelings for the Southern slaves. If anything, he stated once that
he was indifferent to the fate of the blacks in the South. But he valued liberty
above all for it had given him a chance in life. He also remembered the
wanton cruelty of the Famine and how it had destroyed his homeland. Above
all, Cleburne displayed the gift of the master strategist for he had identified
slavery as the South's negative center of gravity. All issues were increasingly
controlled for ill by it in some fashion. It hung like a growing dead weight
on the back of the Confederacy. Yet, unlike Cleburne, the Southern people
and leadership were prisoners of their own history. They had grown up in the
system that was like second nature to them.

Cleburne recognized this as he urged the greatest of sacrifices:

> "It would remove forever all selfish taint from our cause and place
> independence above any question of property. The very magnitude of
> the sacrifice itself, such as no nation has ever voluntarily made before,
> would appall our enemies, destroy his spirit and finances, and fill our
> hearts with a pride and singleness which would clothe us with new
> strength in battle. Apart from all other aspects of the questions, the

necessity for more fighting men is upon us. We can only get a sufficiency by making the negro share the danger and hardships of the war. If we arm and train him and make him fight for the country in her hour of dire distress, every consideration of principle and policy demands that we should set him and his whole race who side with us free.

It is a first principle with mankind that he who offers his life in defense of the State should receive from her in return his freedom and happiness, and we believe in the acknowledgement of this principle... For many years, ever since the agitation on the subject of slavery commenced, the negro has been dreaming of freedom, and his vivid imagination has surrounded that condition with so many gratifications that is has become the paradise of his hopes. To attain it he will tempt dangers and difficulties not exceeded by the bravest soldiers in the field. The hope of freedom is perhaps the only moral incentive that can be applied to him in his present condition. It would be preposterous then to expect him to fight against it with any degree of enthusiasm, therefore we must bind him to our cause by no doubtful bonds; we must leave no possible loophole for treachery to creep in. The slaves are dangerous now, but armed, trained, and collected in an army they would be a thousand fold more dangerous; therefore, when we make soldiers of them we make free men of them beyond all question, and thus enlist their sympathies also. We can do this more effectually than the North can now do, for we can give the negro not only his own freedom, but that of his wife and child, and can secure it to him in his old home. To do this we must immediately make his marriage and parental relation sacred in the eyes of the law and forbid their sale. The past legislation of the South concedes that a large free middle class of negro blood, between master and slave, must sooner or later destroy the institution. If, then, we touch the institution at all, we would do best to make the most of it, and by emancipating the whole race upon reasonable terms and within such reasonable time as will prepare both races for the change, secure to ourselves all the advantages, and to our enemies all the disadvantages that can arise, both at home and abroad, from such a sacrifice. Satisfy the negro that, if he faithfully adheres to our standard during the war, he shall receive his freedom and that of his race. Give him as an earnest of our intentions such immediate immunities as will impress him with our sincerity and be in keeping with his new conditions, enroll a portion of his class as soldiers of the Confederacy, and we can change the race from a dreaded weakness to a position of strength."[9]

"Will the slaves fight?" he asked rhetorically. Yes was the answer he drew from numerous examples—he reached deep into history to single out the helots of Sparta, and the galley slaves at Lepanto. Then, more boldly, he cited the examples of the slaves of Haiti, who won their freedom from their white masters and maintained it against a French army, and of the Maroons of Jamaica:

> "... and the experience of this war has been that so far that half-trained negroes have fought as bravely as many other half-trained Yankees. If, contrary to the training of a lifetime they can be made to face and fight bravely against their former masters, how much more probable is it that with the allurement of higher reward, and led by those masters, they would submit to discipline and face dangers."[10]

In ending, Cleburne read the names of a number of his senior subordinates who had signed the manifesto. The moment he finished and looked up from the paper, a commotion erupted from his audience. The content of the manifesto had come as a complete shock to most of the generals. Cleburne had had time to discuss the issue with his own officers and had been able to talk many of them around and obtain their signatures. His own corps commander, Hardee, and his good friend, Major General Thomas Hindman, who were already familiar with the document, supported it. His peers, however, largely failed to give him the same support. The rest were non-committal or hostile. Among the non-committal was the army commander, General Joseph E. Johnston, who declined to forward it to the government as it was more of a political than a military document.

An exception to the near unanimous support of Cleburne's staff was Major Calhoun Benham who remained so angry that he had attended the general officer to read his own dissent to the plan. More dangerous than Benham, who was open with his opposition, was Major General William Walker. He wrote to Cleburne the next day declaring the paper to be dangerous and "incendiary" and, stating he would poll their fellow general officers on the subject, asked boldly for a copy to forward to President Davis. Cleburne promptly agreed with equal boldness, thinking that would put the document just where he wanted it. He did not count on the venomous gloss Walker would put on it with his own letter. Being a gentleman, he did not realize that Walker's polling of the other officers was a fishing trip for support for what he considered borderline treasonous conduct. Here Walker miscalculated. No officer would give him a written statement. Hindman, whose life Cleburne had saved seven years before in Helena, threw the request back at Walker with the cutting reply, "I do not choose to admit any inquisitorial rights in you." He informed the army commander of the correspondence, and stated he was ready to call Walker out over the matter.

Undeterred, Walker wrote to Johnston that he, in effect, was stooping to violate military protocol in a way that Cleburne had not, by forwarding the manifesto to Davis because "the magnitude of the issues involved" and "strong convictions that the further agitation of such sentiments and propositions would ruin the efficacy of our army and involve our cause in ruin and disgrace."[11] Johnston played a passive role in the entire matter. The manifesto that he would not forward officially to the President, he would allow Walker to send. It was not one of his more attractive moments as a commanding general. On January 12, Walker dispatched the copy of the manifesto to Richmond.

Cleburne had made more enemies than just Walker. Major General Patton Anderson wrote to Lieutenant General Leonidas Polk:

> "Yes, sir; this plain, but in my view monstrous proposition was calmly submitted to the generals of this army for their sanction and adoption with the avowed purpose of carrying it to the rank and file. I will not attempt to describe my feelings on being confronted by a project so startling in its character—may I say so revolting to the Southern sentiment, Southern pride, and Southern honor. And not the least painful of the emotions awakened by it was the consciousness which forced itself upon me that it was met with favor by other beside the author in high station then present."[12]

More to the point, Major General Joe Wheeler, commander of the cavalry of the Army of Tennessee, picked up Walker's line and suggested that Cleburne's loyalty was suspect and the fit subject for investigation. The Irishman's many wounds and victories were forgotten as Wheeler insinuated that Cleburne's ten years in the country were insufficient proof of his fidelity to the Confederacy. Going further, he stated that the citizens of Helena would have lynched him had he ever made such a proposal to them.[13]

As the poisonous accusations flew through the army, Cleburne was in Mobile on much-deserved leave. There he discussed his proposal with powerful men in the state and received a generally favorable response. On his return, he stopped in Atlanta, and was visited by Colonel A.S. Colyar, a Congressman from Tennessee, who would record Cleburne's comment: "If we take this step now, we can mold the relations, for all time to come, between the white and colored races."[14] Clearly Cleburne was thinking deeply into the future. Just as clearly, he had aroused the enmity of many who would lash themselves to a dying past.

The White House of the Confederacy, January 19, 1864

"The President will see you now, General Lee." The servant opened the door to the study, and Lee entered. Davis left his desk to meet Lee as warmly as his stiff personality would allow. Lee matched him with a courteous formality. For all that, both men worked well together, one of the more successful civil-military relationships in American history. It worked because Lee had no ambitions to be anything more than he was—commander of the Army of Northern Virginia, shield of his beloved Commonwealth. It also worked well because Davis, who considered himself something of a military genius, was shrewd enough to allow Lee his scope within those virtuous ambitions.

Nevertheless, Davis valued Lee's unsolicited advice, not just on matters concerning the Army of Northern Virginia and the eastern theater of war, but on military matters in general. After all, Lee had been his chief military advisor before he had assumed command of the Army of Northern Virginia. As long as Davis was doing the asking, he was willing to listen. Now, he waved a sheaf of papers and dropped them on his desk with disdain. "From General Walker in Johnston's army. He forwards an outrageous proposal by Cleburne that we actually free slaves to fight for the Confederacy. I would not survive the political storm if word leaked out that I even considered it. I have instructed the Secretary of War to order it suppressed."

Lee replied, "May I read it, Sir? I have heard nothing but good reports about General Cleburne. His action at Ringgold Gap was by all accounts superb. And your official thanks and that of the Congress most fitting."

"Of course, General." He handed the manifesto to Lee and paused. "If you are staying in Richmond tonight, I would appreciate your comments tomorrow." His every instinct told him to bury the manifesto deep and to blast the author. But, but... he did not lightly discard Lee's words. And there had been real admiration in Lee's voice, and his normally reserved countenance had visibly brightened as he complimented Cleburne. Perhaps the Secretary of War's letter could wait another day or two.

Lee spent the night with his family in the house he had rented in Richmond. A family man to the core, Lee treasured the few opportunities to lose himself in the love of his wife and daughters. After dinner, though, he tore himself away from the feminine delights of hearth and home, and retired to his study with his aide, Major Charles Taylor, to read the manifesto. He read it twice, then handed it to Taylor. "Read it, Major." The young man was quick off the mark and not intimidated by general officer correspondence. Lee watched the expressions of astonishment race across his face. When he had finished, Lee rose to stand in front of the red glow of the fireplace.

> "Shortly before I resigned my commission in the United States Army, I stated clearly that I thought slavery a great evil not only for the negro but for the white man as well. If I had it in my power, I would abolish it. But that was merely an idle posturing without ability to execute. I did not turn my back on a lifetime's work for slavery, Major. I did it for Virginia."

His brown eyes lost their focus as he seemed to look far into the distance:

> "Perhaps, it is not so idle a posture after all."[15]

White House of the Confederacy, January 20, 1864

Lee rode into a sea of pandemonium outside the White House. Smoke filled the street as fire poured from a basement window of the building. Firemen were rushing into the house as servants were rushing out of it, their arms full of what they could save. Everyone seemed to be shouting or screaming. Lee scanned the crowd around the building and found Davis actively directing the operation, much to the obvious annoyance of the local fire chief. Lee knew better than to interrupt a busy man. He leaned forward to pat Traveler on the neck, speaking softly, "We've seen worse, haven't we, old boy?" The horse snorted and shook its head as if emphatically to agree.

"General Lee, General Lee!" Lee turned to see the source of the shout. It was Judah Benjamin in his carriage waving him over. He trotted over and touched his fingers to his hat.

"Mr. Secretary, good morning, Sir."

Benjamin waved towards Davis. "It seems our President is in his executive element."

Lee suppressed a smile. The Secretary looked up and said, "The Cleburne matter, General?

"Yes. The President asked for my comments. I spent the night with it."

"Indeed, General, it is enough to keep one up *through* the night."

A dapper military aide, in a new uniform cleaner than any Lee had seen in months, appeared and saluted. "Gentlemen, the President asks that you wait until the fire is put out." It was an hour or so until the aide returned to invite them into the President's office. Davis was not the man to let chaos and rooms full of smoke interrupt his duties. It had not been wasted time, though. Lee and Benjamin had had much to discuss.

Davis may have been a slave to duty, but he was obviously upset. It was not the fire itself but who set it. Two of his house servants, a slave named Jim Pemberton and a free black woman, Mary Elizabeth Bowers, had set fire to the house and fled North.[16] Davis was nothing if not self-controlled, but the sense of betrayal was bitter beyond measure. It was made plain by his uncharacteristic reference to the matter in his guests' presence. A Southern gentleman rarely discussed such "family problems" with others.

"The Cleburne manifesto, Gentlemen. I was wrong to entertain it even momentarily. All we could expect is servile ingratitude made disastrous by putting weapons into their hands."

Benjamin waited until Davis had worked out his anger. "Mr. President, I would suggest that this incident supports rather than confounds Cleburne's contentions."

Davis was visibly taken aback. Before he could speak, Benjamin continued. "The lure of freedom is too great, Sir. If it can sunder even your own household, it can appear anywhere. And it has and will at an increasingly debilitating rate until the institution we thought was such a valuable resource when this war started is transformed into a weapon by our enemies."

"We have not reached that extremity that would admit of this as a solution," Davis said.

"But we have, Mr. President," Lee stated clearly.

"Cleburne's statements about the deleterious effects on our army is true beyond doubt. He could have been describing the Army of Northern Virginia and not just the Army of Tennessee. We will be inexorably ground down, Sir. Waiting until *extremis* forces us to grasp this nettle will ensure we do it too late. We must resolve to do it while we have the strength to take advantage of it."[17]

"I am not convinced they would fight well," Davis retorted.

"I can attest that they do, indeed, fight well, Mr. President. You yourself are the perfect example of the effectiveness of well-led negroes in a fight."

Davis looked surprised, and then forced a smile. Yes, before the war he had armed the black men of his estate and led them to hunt down a band of white desperados. He was hoist on his own petard, for it was a story he had relished telling for years.

Lee went on:

"In my opinion, the negroes, under proper circumstances, will make efficient soldiers... Under good officers, and good instructions, I do not see why they should not become soldiers. They possess all the physical qualifications, and their habits of obedience constitute a good foundation for discipline. They furnish a more promising material than many armies of which we read in history.

Fifteen percent of the strength of my army is black, but they fill the same roles as an equal number of white soldiers do for the enemy. The army could not peel a potato or shoe a horse without them. Cooks, teamsters, musicians, and body servants have frequently found their way into the firing line. They are regularly armed. I could not have brought 5,000 Union prisoners south after Gettysburg without armed black guards. You may not be aware, but the first Union soldier killed in battle in this war was shot by one of our negro snipers at Big Bethel."[18]

"Even if I granted that they can fight, how would we compensate their owners? We are penniless. It would ruin the country if we could do it, and for that reason, it would be politically impossible even to touch."

Benjamin saw his opening. He realized the issue was in play when Davis essentially conceded the viability issue of black men in arms. "Mr. President," he said as he drew papers from his briefcase:

"I have here the secret letter from our very able agent in London, Henry Hotze. He discussed the sensation made in London by the very rumor of our freeing the slaves and making them soldiers. He personally completely endorses the idea. Mr. President, his finger is on the pulse of European, and particularly, British opinion. He further says that this position represents the opinion of those circles in Britain most friendly to our cause.

Mr. President, this is the key to our survival. Our friends in Britain and Europe look only for an excuse to come to our aid. Follow Cleburne's plan, but tie the emancipation to the large loans we must have to compensate the owners. The British spent hundreds of millions of pounds compensating the owners of their slaves when they abolished the institution. They will understand this. With the slavery issue nullified, our British friends will not face the domestic opposition to aiding us in even more substantial ways that they do now."[19]

Davis's sunken cheeks never seemed so starkly outlined as at that moment; he rose stiffly and thanked his guests. That night he did not sleep. The household could hear his footsteps across the long wooden floor of the study as he paced back and forth through the night.

The next morning Benjamin received instructions to order Hotze in London and other agents in Europe to put it squarely to the Confederacy's friends at the highest levels that emancipation was being considered but required loans to see it through. It was a clever way to put the ball in the British court. Another message went to the Secretary of War instructing him to take no action on the Cleburne Manifesto. Rather, Cleburne was to be summoned to Richmond for a personal interview with the President.

The White House, Washington, D.C., February 24, 1864

The Confederate proposal hit official London like a bomb. Even the anti-slavery parties, usually pro-Union, voiced guarded support of the idea. It did not take long for the events in London to whipsaw back across the Atlantic to Washington where the reaction was even more explosive as rumors spread throughout the Union. Lincoln sent for Frederick Douglass, the great black abolitionist.

Douglass was one of the few men Abraham Lincoln admired through and through. More than that madman John Brown, he resembled an *Old Testament* prophet with a strong dose of Roman senator thrown in. For his part, Douglass returned the admiration. Lincoln was, he would write, "the first great man that I talked with in the Unites States freely who in no single instance reminded me of the difference between himself and myself, of the difference of color."[20]

"Douglass, read this." Lincoln handed him the report from the Union's ambassador in London, Charles Adams. As Douglass read, Lincoln stared out the window with his hands clasped behind him.

Douglass was instantly alarmed as the import of the report became obvious. If both the North and the South offered emancipation and the honor of bearing arms to slaves, what advantage did the North have to counter the great Confederate advantage that the South was their home? The black man's growing allegiance to the Union was directly related to emancipation. Northern racism had come as a shock to many slaves who expected the land of their dreams to be all milk and honey. But freedom kept them coming, abuse or no. His own sources reported the wild rumors that crossed the lines. They spoke of Union officers selling off escaped slaves to Cuba. These rumors and others of Northern abuse were rampant through the South and had contributed to a marked fall off in the number of escaping slaves.

As he put down the paper, Lincoln turned around to face him. "If this is true, Douglass, they have checked us. The Democrats will be braying at my heels now. This is a godsend to them."

"The land, Mr. President, the land is the key. Surely this ploy will be found wanting as the enemy hedge their promises. But the promise of land bounties would be the one thing the South could not, would not trump."[21]

"Is that what it has come to, Douglass, bidding for the support of men in bondage?" His gangly shoulders seemed to slump. "We do not have much time, should this come to pass. Grant will be moving in a few months. He must win before the ground falls out beneath us."

HQ, Army of the Potomac, Petersburg, Virginia, July 30, 1864

Grant's visage was harder than usual as the bad news kept rolling in. Major General George G. Meade, the army commander, was briefing the General-in-Chief of the armies of the Union, on that day's bloody failure. At great expense a mine had been secretly driven beneath the Confederate works and exploded. The formidable earthwork had disappeared in a mighty blast that sent dirt, logs, guns, and men hurtling through the air. Into the breach a black division had been thrown. Unfortunately, the attack had been badly planned, and the troops had been trapped inside the crater without any means to scale its sheer earthen walls. As they milled about, the enemy had regained his wits and rushed reinforcements forward to ring the crater's edge. Hundreds of rifles pointed downward into the milling black mass.

"It was a slaughter, General," Meade said. "The *Rebs* [and he emphasized the word harshly] included one of Lee's new black regiments."

"Well, Meade, we know now if blacks will fight blacks. Shouldn't surprise us, should it? Why should whites have a monopoly on that? Yes, yes, we have North and South set them at *liberty* to kill each other."[22]

Grant spat out the stub of his cigar. "Lee is being reinforced almost as fast as I am. They call me a butcher because I was willing to spend lives to end this war quickly. In doing so I would save more lives." He went on to say that he had suspended the cartel for exchanging prisoners because the enemy just kept putting the released men back into the army.[23] Attrition had seemed a useful strategy given Southern tenacity and skill on the battlefield. Only it had lost much of its utility in the last few months. He had fought Lee back from the Wilderness to Petersburg, the last shield before Richmond. Both armies had left an enormous blood trail following their struggle southward, but the losses of the men in blue had been twice that of the men in gray and butternut. That was the cost of always attacking a formidable foe.

Sherman had faced the same problem in Georgia and had now been stalled at Kenesaw Mountain for over a month. He had come perilously close to disaster at the hands of Lieutenant General Cleburne and his corps— aggressive and skillful that Irishman, like that little bantam Sheridan. Cleburne had been promoted and given the command of the corps made up of the divisions Hindman, Stevenson, and Stewart.[24] There was alarming intelligence that Davis was looking for a new commander for the Army of Tennessee. Grant hoped it would not be Cleburne. He would then truly have to worry about Sherman for the first time.

Attrition would have worked in spite of the cost had not the Confederacy turned the tables on the North and issued its own Emancipation Proclamation on March 13, flush with British pounds and French francs to pay off the slave owners. Lee had augmented his force by enrolling blacks already in the army in non-combat roles. "Can't blame him for wanting to get a head start," Grant was quoted as saying, "but what a damned sharp stick in the eye."[25] Not only had the calculations upon which he had based his attrition strategy been foiled, but the Southern emancipation had severely demoralized a large part of the Union Army. The white Northern soldier had been incredulous on the occasions before emancipation when he came across instances of blacks bearing arms for the South. The incredulity usually had been mixed with a painful sting as well. The black men had fought uncommonly well. Now that sting was spread by personal experience and by rumor through the main Union armies in Virginia and Georgia.

Grant ruminated on the increasing disaffection within his own ranks. The occasional black deserter from the other side was more than canceled out by the open and near-mutinous rumbles from the ranks of his white regiments. One old soldier had brazenly accosted Grant and demanded to know, "Why are we fighting if the nigger has already been freed? Let the Rebs keep them."[26] More dangerous had been the loss of morale within his own black regiments. The desertions were going the other way as Southern-born men were seduced by appeals to home and freedom.

Near the Crater, Petersburg, Virginia, July 30, 1864

Lee had maintained a position 500 yards from the Crater for much of the fighting. Now that the crisis had passed, he watched as the lines of black Union prisoners from the Crater were marched to the rear past the jeering ranks of the 9th South Carolina Colored, the regiment that had been one of the first to rush to the breach. Two of its sister regiments, the 19th and 22d South Carolina, had been decimated by the explosion, leaving only the 17th and the 9th S.C. Colored to fight it out until regiments from other brigades had arrived to trap the in-rushing Union forces within the 30-foot-high walls. Lee had been heartened by the performance of the South Carolinians of both races.

He turned to Brigadier General William "Little Billy" Mahone whose brigade had led the attack that had cleared the Crater. He promoted him on the spot. It was a suitable moment to make another point. The 17th and 9th S.C. Colored were being withdrawn, all that was left of their shattered brigade. As the first black rank passed, Lee doffed his hat with a broad wave of his hand. The troops, exhausted by the day's fighting, quickly squared their shoulders and dressed their ranks. Their white officers drew their swords to return the salute. And the band struck up *Dixie*.

Lee's open and enthusiastic backing of the emancipation had carried the army and much of the Southern public along with the idea. The Army of Northern Virginia had taken the change calmly, all things considered. There were no greater realists in the South, save perhaps in Johnston's Army of Tennessee. Facing the sharp end of the stick had focused them on what was essential. Lee's prestige, almost godlike in the deference and trust it inspired, had carried the issue. In many cases there was downright enthusiasm within the army for arming blacks. Georgia regiments in Lee's army petitioned the government, stating that the cause of "glorious independence" demanded black participation. Officers of the 49th Georgia suggested to Lee that men be sent to their home counties to recruit blacks.[27]

A wave of enthusiasm for arming the black man swept across the South. The desperation of the moment was a sharp spur. In their enthusiasm, though, white Southerners took comfort in the comfortable assumption that they would remain in control after the war. Only the opponents of the measure were talking of consequences, and they were drowned out. The planter aristocracy came out in force for the measure. Twenty three of the largest slave owners in Roanoke County, Virginia, came out in favor of emancipation tied to military service. The *Sentinel* of Virginia boldly pronounced that: "None... will deny that our servants are more worthy of respect than the motley hordes which come against us." It urged whites not to be too jealous of the honor of killing Yankees. It thundered that the guarantees of freedom must be "redeemed with the most scrupulous fidelity and at all hazards... bad faith must be avoided as an indelible dishonor."[28]

It was not as if Southern racism had suddenly evaporated, but the essential biracial nature of Southern society meant that these men, black and white, had lived together for 200 years. You could not separate the one from the other. Whether they liked each other or not, they were part of the same communities in a way blacks and whites in the North had never been. It was, after all, a Southern solution to a Southern problem. The thousands of blacks in the Army of Northern Virginia before emancipation had been more fully integrated into the life of the army and suffered less cruelty and abuse than did their counterparts in the North. One historian of slavery would write that, "Blacks retained a strong sense of local identity and a bittersweet affinity for the land of their birth." Moreover, the motives that led to their willing military service were complex and varied.

"Some sided with the South, and some with the North, but the majority were loyal to themselves and their families, and tried to do what was best for themselves without recourse to abstract political causes. One recalled that he had fought for both North and South, 'but I neber fought for the Yankees till dey captured me and put me in a corral and said, "Nigger, you fought for de South; now you can fight for the North."'"

Another prisoner, a free black volunteer, was questioned by a Northern officer about his allegiance to the South and replied:

"I had as much right to fight for my native state as you had to fight for your'n, and a blame sight more right tan your furriners, what's got no homes."[29]

Before the first drafts of new men had arrived at their camps, Lee encouraged those body servants and other blacks in support positions within the army to be voluntarily enrolled within the regiments they already served. There were at least 20–30 body servants alone per Southern regiment. This gave the Army of Northern Virginia an immediate increase of over 5,000 men in strength, the equivalent of a division. The original idea had been to incorporate the new regiments into brigades, but Lee recognized that time would not allow this step. When the new regiments began arriving from Camp Lee, he simply incorporated them into existing white brigades. That served a two-fold purpose by ensuring the green units would be brigaded with veterans while at the same time providing a watch on their actions. The policy also meant that black regiments were appearing all down the line.

The black regiments were all organized as Confederate States Colored Troops (C.S.C.T.), officially with no state affiliation. There were two large complexes of training camps for the eastern and western theaters. Those regiments training in the Richmond camps numbered 1–50; those training outside Atlanta were numbered 51–100. By the Battle of the Crater, eight C.S.C.T. regiments had already joined the Army of Northern Virginia. Inevitably, though, as the drafts by state were trained together at the large training ground at Camp Lee west of Richmond, they took on affiliations of not only their states but their counties as well. Lee was sure to brigade the new regiments with white regiments from the same state and counties, where possible. Thus a new recruit from Virginia would officially be enrolled in the 1st Regiment C.S.C.T., but would quickly learn to call his unit the 1st Virginia Colored Infantry. Johnston was following much the same policy in Georgia with the new C.S.C.T. regiments pouring out the training camps around Atlanta. This gave the Confederates an advantage the Union Army did not have with its own United States Colored Infantry. When a new

C.S.C.T. regiment joined its brigade, inevitably it found itself among neighbors and even family from home. There was something particularly Southern about both races; neither could abide the taint of cowardice in the presence of men who would carry word of their shame back home.

It was the Virginia brigades that were augmented first, simply because Virginia was the main battleground and because one-sixth of all the slaves in the Confederacy were in that state according to the 1860 Census. The Superintendent of the Census in Washington had hurriedly calculated that 236,990 Afro-Virginians (12,475 free blacks and 224,515 slaves) were of the right age groups for military service. Already about 48 percent of the white male population was in the army; a similar ratio for blacks would give the Confederates another 113,755 men from the black population.[30]

After the Crater, Lee's aggressive nature found its scope again. His counterattacks began to beat upon Grant's forces with growing strength.

Second Battle of Kenesaw Mountain; Georgia, August 5, 1864

Sherman pitched out his saddle as if he had been picked up and thrown. He was dead before he hit the ground, a bloody bundle of blue rags. The shell that killed him killed his horse and two of his staff as well. Sherman had been everywhere that day trying to stem the fury of Cleburne's assault which had led Joe Johnston's unexpected attack. Bedford Forrest's raids had so often interrupted Sherman's supply lines that he had not been able to mass the men and supplies for further offensive operations. Both armies had therefore settled down to position warfare, but after holding the Federals in place for over a month with a steadily strengthening army, Johnston had finally gone over to the attack, to Sherman's great surprise.[31]

Confederate infantry swept over the corpses and beyond. A black soldier stopped to pull off the fancy swordbelt from Sherman's body. It would be presented to Cleburne that night. His corps had broken the Union center with one hard punch after another. The point of the attack was Gilgal Church which the troops had nicknamed "Golgotha". Now Cleburne was directing his divisions to the right and left to exploit the advantage. The neighboring blue corps were vulnerable, fixed by the rest of the Army of Tennessee. The news of "Uncle Billy's" death had raced through the ranks. No army had had more confidence in a commander than this one. The news of his death while they were in the most desperate fight of their experience unnerved them. Units bolted to the rear, and soon the army had collapsed as a living thing. Men said it was Chickamauga all over again. This time there was no staying the pursuit.

Epilogue

Sherman's death at Golgotha unleashed the floodtide of Union disaster. Although officially the Second Battle of Kenesaw Mountain, Southerners would always prefer the biblically resonant name, "A Place Called Golgotha."

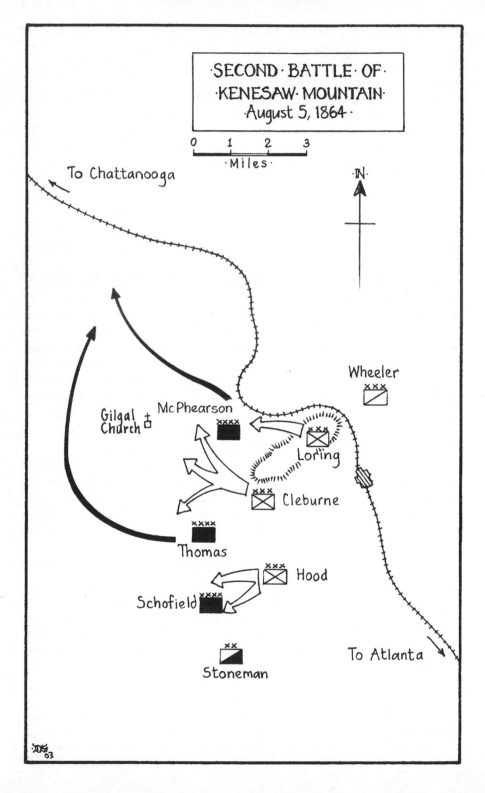

SECOND · BATTLE · OF ·
· KENESAW · MOUNTAIN ·
· August 5, 1864 ·

0   1   2   3
· Miles ·

· N ·

To Chattanooga

Wheeler

Gilgal
Church

McPhearson

Loring

Cleburne

Thomas

Hood

Schofield

Stoneman

To Atlanta

Sherman's most gifted subordinate, Major General William McPhearson, fought his way back to Chattanooga through Forrest's cavalry with most of his Army of the Tennessee (not to be confused with the Confederate Army of Tennessee). Major General Schofield's Army of Ohio was shattered, and most of its men killed or captured. It fell to Major General George Thomas, the "Rock of Chickamauga" to play again the thankless rearguard role.

Johnston's attack had not been entirely out of the blue; once resolved to attack he coordinated his assault with Lee. The same morning that Sherman died, Lee attacked Grant, unleashing the Battle of Petersburg, the last great bloodbath of the war. The armies grappled for two days amid the trenches of Petersburg. Lee's men twice broke through the Union defenses only to be beaten back by Grant's ruthless use of reserves. A third time the Confederates could not be dislodged. Lee quickly reinforced their lodgment and thereby made a large stretch of the Union siege works untenable. Grant was forced to pull back several miles. It was a tactical victory for Lee. The news of Kenesaw Mountain magnified Grant's reverse, and both coming together sent a shock wave through the North. The South rejoiced that the two battles were a fitting revenge for Gettysburg and Vicksburg.

The twin disasters sank the Lincoln Administration. Going into the 1864 election campaign with nothing but bad news, Lincoln was swept from office by former Major General George B. McClellan and the Peace Democrats. McClellan promptly recognized the independence of the South and turned his hand to dictatorship. It was a brief attempt, and his vice-president served out his term.[32]

The Confederate Government kept its word about emancipation. That was the start of troubles. For the most part, prewar social relationships reasserted themselves at first, but, to the South's surprise, the word "suffrage" followed emancipation as surely as the day follows the night. Surprisingly, the United Confederate Volunteers became a leading exponent of the black franchise. The bonds of shared hardships and danger had altered many attitudes. As honorary president of the Volunteers, Lee was instrumental in the adoption of a policy of gradual suffrage based on education. His influence, however, ensured that all black veterans were guaranteed the right to vote by act of Congress. Full suffrage arrived finally with the Voting Rights Bill of 1896. That had been made inevitable with the growing political and financial power of black Southerners. Although social patterns had initially reverted to prewar forms, the disappearance of slavery made it economically inefficient so support so many people on the land. Many blacks drifted to the new industries created by Northern and European investments and became skilled industrial workers and entrepreneurs.[33]

The Reality

The events surrounding the presentation of Cleburne's Manifesto are historically accurate. Instead of seizing this opportunity, Jefferson Davis, after receiving a copy from Walker, ordered that the document be suppressed. There was no fortunate meeting with Lee in Richmond in January. Davis's slaves did set fire to his house on January 20. Lee would confer with Davis in February. Davis's argument was that the South was not in such extreme danger that it had to resort to such a drastic measure. The irony, though, is that by the time such a state of danger was recognized, remedies were too late.

That is exactly where Davis found himself by the fall of 1864 when he finally accepted the necessity for change. Lee's support carried the argument and a bill was passed on March 13, 1865, authorizing the enrollment of blacks in the Confederate armies, but leaving to the states the matter of manumission. This measure and the resulting surge in public and military support that followed I have placed one year earlier in an effort to demonstrate that timing is everything. What might have saved the Confederacy in early 1864 was too little, too late, in early 1865. Grant himself stated in his memoirs that:

> "Anything that could have prolonged the war a year beyond the time that it did finally close, would probably have exhausted the North to such an extent that they might then have abandoned the contest and agreed to a separation."[34]

Pat Cleburne's career was driven into eclipse by his boldness. He had been manifestly the most able and successful of the division commanders of the Army of Tennessee. He was clearly in line for a promotion and a corps command before he read his manifesto. Instead, on two occasions in 1864, he was passed over in favor of lesser contemporaries as punishment for his vision and courage.

The most intriguing thought to come out of the slavery issue in the Civil War is the concept that it lighted a fire in the minds of men by the revolutionary process of the war itself. A major if not primary pillar of secession was the South's "peculiar institution." For the Northern man, abolition was at first a hateful idea as well. He had no use for the black man as slave—but did not want him as a neighbor either. But the bloody revolution of war broke down these attitudes until both sides arrived at the abolition of slavery and the arming of the black man as essentials to victory. History enjoys her jokes, barbs and all.

Bibliography

Barrow, Charles Kelly, *et. al.*, eds., *Black Confederates* (Pelican Publishing, Gretna, LA, 1995).

Buck, Irvin A., *Cleburne and His Command* (Broadfoot Publishing, Wilmington, NC, 1995).

Grant, U.S., *U.S. Grant's Personal Memoirs* (Applegate Publishers, Philadephia, 1874).

Grooms, Robert M., "Dixie's Censored Subject: Black Slaveowners," *The Barnes Review, 1997*, cited at http://americancivilwar.com/authors/black_slaveowners.htm.

Jordan, Ervin L., Jr., *Black Confederates and Afro-Yankees in Civil War Virginia* (University Press of Virginia, Charlottesville, VA, 1995).

Joslyn, Mauriel Phillips, ed., *A Meteor Shining Brightly: Essays on Maj. Gen. Patrick R. Cleburne* (Terrill House, Milledgeville, GA, 1999).

Oates, Stephen B., *With Malice Toward None: A Life of Abraham Lincoln* (HarperPerenial, New York, 1994).

Purdue, Howell and Elizabeth, *Pat Cleburne: Confederate General* (Hill Jr. College Press, Hillsboro, TX, 1973).

Rollins, Richard, ed., *Black Southerners in Gray: Essays on Afro-Americans in Confederate Armies* (Rank and File Publications, Redondo Beach, CA, 1994).

U.S. War Department, *The War of the Rebellion: A Compilation of the Official Records of the Union and Confederate Armies*, 4 series in 70 volumes in 128 books (Government Printing Office, Washington, D.C., 1880–1901) (referred to as *OR* for *Official Records*).

Notes

*1. Testimony of General Nathan Bedford Forrest before the Finance Committee of the Confederate States House of Representatives, June 22, 1868, *Congressional Record*, Vol. 13, p. 1037.

2. Purdue, *Pat Cleburne: Confederate General*, pp. 268–9.

3. Mark M. Hill, "Concerning the Emancipation of the Slaves," in Joslyn, *A Meteor Shining Brightly: Essays on Maj. Gen. Patrick R. Cleburne*, p. 150.

4. Mauriel Phillips Joslyn, "Irish Beginnings," in Joslyn, *ibid.*, pp. 22–3.

5. Bell Irvin Wiley, in foreword to Buck, *Cleburne and His Command*, p. 8.

6. When this author related Cleburne's military experience to a British officer, the latter remarked good-naturedly, "British corporal, American major-general—a proper equivalence."

7. *OR*, Ser. I, Vol. LII, pt. 2, pp. 586–92.

8. *Ibid.*

9. *Ibid.*

10. *Ibid.*

11. *OR, Ibid.*, p. 594.

12. *OR, Ibid.*, p. 598.

13. *OR, Ibid.*, p. 599.

14. Cited in Purdue, *Pat Cleburne: Confederate General*, p. 273.

*15. Walter Herron Taylor, *General Lee and His Colored Regiments* (University Press of Virginia, Charlottesville, 1906), p. 42.

16. Jordan, *Black Confederates and Afro-Yankees in Civil War Virginia* (University Press of Virginia, Charlottesville, 1995), p. 195.

*17. Taylor, *General Lee and His Colored Regiments*, p. 73.

18. Rollins, *Black Southerners in Gray*, p.16. "The first Northern officer killed was Major Theodore Winthrop, member of an old, distinguished New England abolitionist family, shot by an unnamed black sniper at Big Bethel. He was a member of the Wythe Rifles of Hampton, Virginia, whose Captain had told him that the 'Yankees would take you to Cuba and sell you. If you wish to stay with your wife and children, drive them out of Virginia.'"

*19. Judah Benjamin, *Diplomacy of the War Years* (Tendley and Sons, London, 1879) p. 439.

20. Stephen B. Oates, *With Malice Toward None: A Life of Abraham Lincoln*, p. 357.

21. Jordan, *Black Confederates and Afro-Yankees in Civil War Virginia*, p. 237.

*22. Henry Martin Tyler, *Black on Black Combat in the Civil War* (Applegate Books, Philadelphia, 1993) p. 298.

23. The cartel was the system of prisoner exchange established between the belligerents. Prisoners were exchanged on the basis of man for man of equal rank. Exchanged prisoners were returned to active duty.

*24. Davis, Jefferson, *The Southern Emancipation* (Bartlett Publishers, Richmond and New York, 1876), p. 274. Major General John Bell Hood was recovering in a Richmond hospital from the loss of his leg at Gettysburg at this time. It had been Davis's intention to award Hood with the promotion and corps command that he actually gave to Cleburne. Had it not been for the affair of the manifesto, Hood would have commanded the Army of Tennessee. It is anyone's guess how this aggressive but uncounselable officer would have done with such a critical command.

*25. John Rawlins, *My Service With Grant* (Winslow House, New York, 1880) p. 334.

26. Grant, *U.S. Grant's Personal Memoirs*, vol. 2, p. 542.

27. Jordan, *Black Confederates and Afro-Yankees in Civil War Virginia*, p. 244

*28. *Richmond Sentinel*, March 23, 1864.

29. Rollins, *Black Southerners in Gray*, p. 5.

30. Jordon, *Black Confederates and Afro-Yankees in Civil War Virginia*, pp. 246–7.

*31. Patrick R. Cleburne, *The Road to Golgotha* (Stoddard, Richmond, 1872), p. 95. Cleburne describes his arguments that persuaded Johnston to take the uncharacteristic decision to attack.

*32. Archibald Cummings, *The McClellan Dictatorship* (Levi and Sons, New York, 1923), pp. 344–9. McClellan had made enough indiscreet comments about the country needing a dictator while he had commanded the Army of the Potomac to have given anyone who cared to examine his character the warning that his ego would attempt to transform the presidency into just such an instrument of power. It took an entirely constitutional bill of impeachment backed by troops of the Regular Army to depose McClellan. He was sent off to Europe with a warning not to come back for ten years.

*33. John T. Towes, *Black Capital and the Industrialization of the Confederacy* (Hampton Publishers, New York, 1926) p. 333.

34. Grant, *Personal Memoirs of U.S. Grant*, vol. 2, p. 345.

9

DECISION IN THE WEST
Turning Point in the Trans-Mississippi Confederacy

Cyril M. Lagvanec

Alexandria, Louisiana, May 6, 1864

From a window on the second floor of the Burgoyne Plantation, Major Forrest Arnondin of the 28th Louisiana Infantry Regiment watched through his binoculars as a spectacle unfolded before him. Down on the Red River, below Alexandria, Commander David Dixon Porter's Mississippi Squadron of eight ironclads, two tinclads and numerous transports and supply ships, were afire. Periodically one exploded with such fury that the plantation's windows rattled. Major Arnondin lamented the fact that such a grand pyrotechnic display could not fall on the Fourth of July. Little did the major know that by that date, two months hence, the Confederacy would have much to celebrate. The scuttling of Porter's squadron marked the scuttling of the Red River campaign and prepared the way for greater endeavors to the north.[1]

Many Motivations, Foul and Fair, 1863–64

The Red River campaign originated in the Federal halls of power the previous year. There existed the overwhelming desire to capture the bales of cotton that were stockpiled along the banks of the river. The accepted estimate was 105,000 bales, worth approximately $35 million. Not only would this windfall benefit the Northern economy in general, and the New England textile mills in particular, but it was hoped that the purchase or seizure of the cotton would beggar the Trans-Mississippi Department and demoralize or corrupt Confederate officials.

However, more than mere cotton motivated the Federal leadership. There existed a great desire to encourage and succor the supposedly strong Unionist sentiment in Louisiana and Texas. Reconstruction was already underway in Louisiana with elections being held, and from Brownsville to Matagorda Bay, the North had secured several lodgments on the Texas coast. In September 1863, the Federals attempted an amphibious invasion at Sabine Pass, but four gunboats and 5,000 infantry were repulsed by the Jeff Davis Guards: 47 men manning seven cannon emplaced in a mudwalled fort. The following month, a corps of Yankees moved across southern Louisiana to reach Texas via the lower Sabine River. This enterprise, too, came to grief at the hands of unexpectedly fierce Rebel resistance. In both cases, it was the rather luckless Brigadier General William B. Franklin leading the Federal forces.

Other benefits to a campaign up the Red River Valley would be the salutary influence a Union success would have on the French designs in Mexico and the damage that could be done to the Confederate Trans-Mississippi Department, especially with the fall of Shreveport, the departmental headquarters and the center of much military production and political activity.

The plan originated with General-in-Chief, Henry W. Halleck, and he did all in his power to win support for it. President Abraham Lincoln approved of the idea, as did Generals William T. Sherman and Nathaniel P. Banks. In fact, the only sustained dissent amongst the Union high command came from Ulysses S. Grant, and his concerns came not from a fear of failure, but rather from a worry that such an effort would divert men and material away from more important theaters. Nevertheless Halleck, after months of preparation, saw all the pieces fall into place. To lead the expedition, Halleck settled upon Banks, and he represented a sound choice for several reasons. A consummate politician, Banks had resigned as the Republican governor of Massachusetts to join the army, and he certainly possessed the skills to encourage further the development of any Unionist sentiment in the region. In addition, as the "Bobbin Boy of Waltham," Banks enjoyed an intimate connection with the textile mills in his state. He always showed himself to be personally honest, which would help prevent any corruption arising from cotton procurement, and, finally, Banks was no coward. In practically every way, Banks fit Halleck's bill, save one: Banks was not a particularly good general. Into his hands would pass the command of this most ambitious enterprise.

As the North made its plans, in the Trans-Mississippi Department the Confederates awaited the spring, which heralded warm weather, rising waters, swarms of mosquitoes and hordes of Yankees. The departmental commander was General Edmund Kirby Smith. A West Pointer and veteran of both the war with Mexico and numerous Indian fights, Kirby Smith stood as the perfect example of the professional soldier faced with the quandaries of divided loyalties. Born in Saint Augustine, Florida, in 1824, Kirby Smith had resigned his commission in the U.S. Army after receiving news of his home state's secession and after he had seen to the safe evacuation of his command, Company B, 2d United States Cavalry, from Texas. Quickly gaining promotion in the Confederate forces, his martial skills, genius for organization and his deep-seated antipathy towards General Braxton Bragg led to Kirby Smith's posting to the Trans-Mississippi Department in March of 1863. In 12 months' time, Kirby Smith reinvigorated the department and brought efficiency, productivity and, in consequence, higher morale to the region. Also, he could call upon some of the finest fighting generals in the Confederate Army, such as the cavalry brigadiers J.O. Shelby of Kentucky and Tom Green of Texas. There was also the fire-eating Richard Taylor of Louisiana. Son of President Zachary Taylor, he was classically educated but a complete novice in the ways of war. He took to it with a will, eventually earned the rank of lieutenant general and always showed himself one of the best infantry commanders of the war. This proved fortuitous for Kirby Smith, for while his men were properly armed and equipped, they would also be heavily outnumbered, and it would require smart, aggressive leadership to overcome such odds.

The Opening Guns, March 1864

After much deliberation in the highest echelons of Federal command, Banks began to collect his troops in the New Orleans area. His force comprised two infantry corps, the XVI Corps, under Brigadier General Andrew Jackson Smith and the XIX Corps led by Franklin. Some 11,000 tough Western veterans filled the ranks of the former while 14,000 Easterners made up the latter formation. In addition, Brigadier General Albert L. Lee led a division of nearly 5,000 Federal horsemen divided into four brigades. To all of this, Banks could add 90 artillery pieces and a mammoth wagon train. To escort the army up the Red River, Porter's Mississippi Squadron of some two dozen warships boasted over 200 cannon.

However, Banks's army and Porter's squadron represented only one half of the Yankee plan. Major General Frederick Steele, with his corps of 11,000 men, prepared in Little Rock for a drive south to Shreveport in conjunction with Banks's thrust up the Red. However, Steele displayed no enthusiasm for the project. Bad roads, lack of forage and bands of Rebel partisan rangers all threatened to plague his efforts. Steele complained to Grant that he must also first attend to local elections held under the auspices of presidential reconstruction. Without his soldiers at the polls, murder and mayhem were sure to mark the political scene in Arkansas. Eventually Steele offered to mount a demonstration southwards, but Grant, who had replaced Halleck as General-in-Chief, scotched the suggestion and ordered "full cooperation" with Banks. In fairness to Steele, Banks could rely upon the Red River for the transport of his supplies while Steele would have to make do with wagon trains. Banks, however, also faced political concerns. He delayed opening his campaign in order to participate in the inauguration of Louisiana's Unionist governor, Michael Hahn. Although ready by the beginning of the month, it was not until March 7 that Lee's cavalry division trotted down the road to Alexandria, and it was not until the 12th that

Banks's infantry began disembarking from river transports at Simmesport, 40 miles southeast of Alexandria.

The powerful, if ponderous, Federal advance met with an immediate Confederate response. As early as January 4, Kirby Smith predicted such a move when the river rose in the springtime. Nevertheless, he questioned the wisdom of a campaign in the Trans-Mississippi while the "future of our weal or woe" lay in the East. He confided to Taylor "that the enemy cannot be so infatuated as to occupy a large force in this department." Whatever the level of Yankee infatuation with the Red River Valley, the Rebels prepared to receive the invaders. Kirby Smith ordered the concentration of his forces and Taylor organized a number of magazines which would guarantee the Southerners a steady stream of supplies.

With the Federals on the march and the Confederates readying to meet them, the Red River campaign began. It opened hopefully for Banks when, on March 14, after a well-planned assault, Union infantry stormed and took Fort De Russy. Located at a sharp bend in the river, its garrison of 300 put up a good fight, but it was over quickly and the Yankee advance upriver continued. A week later Banks enjoyed another success, when, on the night of the 21st, a brigade of infantry and a brigade of cavalry overwhelmed a regiment of Rebel horse at Henderson's Hill. Normally this would have proven only a minor setback as the department suffered from a surfeit of cavalry. Unfortunately for Taylor, this was his only mounted regiment at the time, and its loss left him blind.

These early successes provided Banks with great encouragement, but his satisfaction soon faded. Several worries dogged him. The pace of his army could only be described as plodding. On March 20, Lee's troopers rode into Alexandria, but the infantry did not arrive until the 25th. Banks landed by steamer on the 24th, and two days later received word from Grant that he had until the end of April to complete his conquest of the Red River Valley. After that date, the bulk of the infantry would transfer to the East. An even more pressing concern met Banks when he stepped off his headquarters ship, the *Black Hawk*. He discovered to his dismay, that Porter and his sailors were every bit as adept at thievery as they were at fighting. Equipped with stencils that read "C.S.A." and "U.S.N.", Porter's men roamed the countryside and marked cotton bales with the first and then with the second. The confiscated cotton would then fetch prize money in Northern courts. Word spread of the depredations, and much of the white gold was burned by the Southerners to prevent its capture. Whether Confederate, Unionist, or neutral in sympathies, all suffered at the hands of the sailors, and wags remarked that "C.S.A./U.S.N." stood for the "Cotton Stealing Association of the United States Navy."

The situation horrified Banks. He wanted a much more orderly, efficient and honest collection of the cotton, especially with the idea of cultivating the goodwill of the local population. This was all swiftly slipping away. His protestations and counter-orders fell uselessly into the inter-service gap and, while Porter enriched himself, a major goal of the Red River campaign receded into oblivion. While at Alexandria, Banks attempted to hold elections, but only 300 Unionists bothered to participate, and many of those did so in an effort to protect their bales of cotton.

Disgusted and despairing of halting the Navy's plunderings, Banks turned his attention back to the military aspects of the campaign. Spurred by Grant's communiqué, Banks sent out Lee's division on March 26. Its destination was Natchitoches, 80 miles northwest of Alexandria, and the last major town upriver before Shreveport. Franklin's XIX Corps followed and reached the town after some very hard marching. Natchitoches was a pretty and prosperous town and the oldest settlement in the state. The Federals had never reached this far up the Red before, and they met a cold reception. Banks ignored the antagonized populace and kept pushing his army to the northwest.

It was at Grand Ecore, an inconsequential village four miles upriver from Natchitoches, that Banks faced his first great strategic quandary. Banks's guide, a river pilot with the impossibly Dickensian name of Wellington W. Withenbury, presented the general with a dilemma. To continue using the river for supplies and communication, and to enjoy the security provided by the guns of Porter's squadron, the army would have to cross the Red in order to have access to a road that ran along the riverside. This represented a laborious endeavor and Shreveport lay on the western side of the river, so at some point the army would have to recross as it approached the city. To remain on the western side of the Red, Banks would have to follow a road that led inland, relying on his supply train and leaving Porter's warships behind. In reality, the river road on the west bank began again a few miles above Grand Ecore, but Withenbury was either a Confederate agent or, most likely, he hoped to move the Yankees away from his own cotton stocks. Faced with only these choices, on April 6, Banks directed his army out of Grand Ecore and onto the western trail away from the Red River.

In the meantime, Kirby Smith and Taylor had not been idle. At the town of Mansfield, some 40 miles due south of Shreveport, Taylor collected approximately 7,000 men. There was Texan cavalry under the command of Tom Green, who as a young boy had served in the artillery at San Jacinto in 1836. Brigadier General Jean J.A.A. Mouton led a division of Louisiana infantry and Major General John George Walker commanded a division of Texas infantry. All the Rebel infantry divisions were equal in size to a Union brigade. Taylor also had Brigadier General S.B. Maxey's independent cavalry brigade that featured several regiments from the Indian Nations. With divisions of Missouri and Arkansas infantry in Shreveport, the entire Trans-Mississippi Department was represented in the defense of its headquarters. Kirby Smith held the troops at Shreveport for they needed to be resupplied with ammunition and because he contemplated a move against Steele's corps in southern Arkansas if Banks slowed his advance. On the other hand, Taylor strained to lunge at the detested Yankees despoiling his home state and, with Banks's army advancing at a steady pace, Taylor soon got his chance.

On April 7, at Wilson's Farm, Lee's cavalry found itself charged by Green's Texans. The Rebel horse were veterans, but Lee called up his reserves and pushed Green back. The sharpness of the skirmish convinced Lee that the Confederates were before him in force. He foresaw a fight coming, but his fellow officers scoffed at the suggestion of a battle unfolding before they reached the outskirts of Shreveport. Vindication for the Union Cassandra proved bittersweet.

Mansfield and Pleasant Hill

Taylor decided to stand at Mansfield because, after that town, the road directed Banks back to the river and Porter's squadron. In any case, Taylor burned to avenge his beloved Louisiana and he held his opponent in contempt. In the Shenandoah Valley campaign of 1862, Taylor had led a brigade of infantry under the command of Major General Stonewall Jackson and witnessed first-hand Banks's defeat and his subsequent earning of the nickname "Commissary" Banks for all of the captured supplies he unwillingly provided the Rebels. As Banks's army approached, Taylor vowed to Brigadier General Camille A.J.M., Prince de Polignac, one of Mouton's subordinates, that he would "fight Banks if he has a million men." Fortunately for Taylor, Banks possessed only 30,000 men, yet that still substantially outnumbered the 8,800 that the Rebels massed for the fight. To Colonel Henry Gray's brigade of Louisiana infantry, Taylor gave the privilege of drawing first blood. As a coiled spring, the Confederates awaited battle.

While Banks might enjoy a nearly four-to-one superiority, this was entirely negated because his army was in a line of march, and it was but the head of the column which deployed at Mansfield. In the center stood Colonel William J. Landram's infantry division, 2,400 strong, while Lee posted a thousand horsemen on each flank. The Federal line was in place by 3.30 p.m. on April 8, and then a quiet descended upon the field. Taylor held his men in check as he expected a Federal assault. Banks wished to accommodate the Rebels, but he was not on the scene and Lee balked at attacking a numerically superior enemy. He rode to meet Banks and explained that the Union soldiers "could not advance ten minutes without a general engagement, in which we should be most gloriously flogged." Such expostulations took Banks aback, and he delayed the attack until he could bring more infantry into the line. The problem for the Federal army commander lay in the fact that Taylor's patience deserted him.

At 4.00 p.m., Taylor ordered in his troops. They attacked in echelon, with Mouton's division going in first, followed by Walker's Texans. The

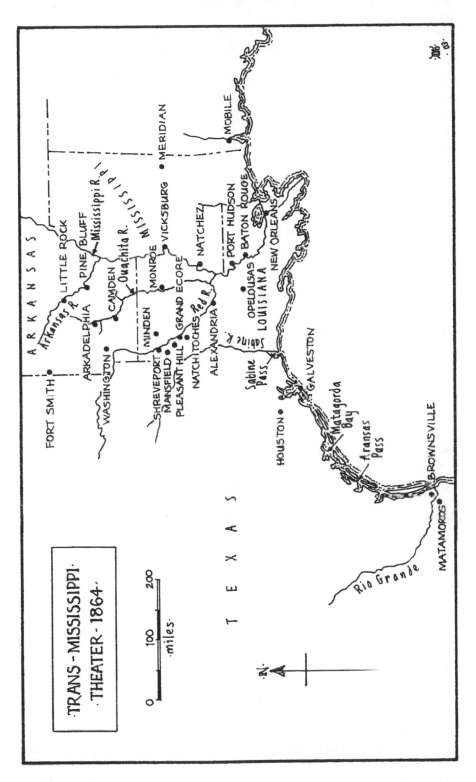

TRANS-MISSISSIPPI·THEATER·1864·

fighting proved hot and the Louisianans lost many men, including the beloved Mouton, but the Federals suffered heavily, too. Then the Texans, "yelling like infuriated demons" hit the Union line "like a cyclone." Outnumbered, outfought and outflanked on both ends of the line, the Federals folded. Infantry, cavalry, and what guns could be saved streamed back down the road that had brought them to the battle. In some places they retreated in good order, but elsewhere poor morale, scant experience or shoddy leadership generated a rout. The Rebels added to the Northerners' torment by turning captured guns on the fleeing Federals. Franklin arrived with another division of infantry and deployed them across the road but, after an hour of fighting, this line also found itself flanked and overborne. The rout continued.

The soldiers of Franklin's XIX Corps streamed down the road, a mass of men and animals. The wagons of the cavalry division's train lined the way and added to the confusion. Lee had requested earlier that his supply wagons join the rest of the train at the rear of the army, but he was told to keep them up front. Now the teamsters, unable to turn their wagons around, cut the mules from their traces and ran. Banks, never wanting in personal courage, rode through the mass of men and plaintively pleaded, "I know you will not desert me." If he had not faced his horse about he would have been alone amongst the Rebels.

As Banks trotted away from the carnage, he sent word to Brevet Major General William H. Emory from the XIX Corps to hurry forward his infantry division and shore up the front. At Pleasant Grove, about two miles from Mansfield, Emory's soldiers deployed and survivors of the battle either fell in with, or found refuge behind, their line. The Confederates were soon upon them. Despite the lure of 150 wagons, Taylor's men did not stop to plunder the supply train. Their blood was up and twice now they had put the Yankees to rout. They hit Emory's line with the same expectations but with a good deal less fury. Although tired and disorganized, the Southerners almost broke Emory's division, but exhaustion and the setting sun ended the affair.

To his credit, Banks intended to make a stand at Pleasant Grove, but a lack of water and the fact that most of those who fought at Mansfield ended their retreat at Pleasant Hill led him to pull back to there. For fewer than 1,000 casualties, the Confederates inflicted 2,200 losses on the North and captured 20 guns, the wagon train and numerous stand of firearms. Once more, Confederate soldiery offered their gratitude to "Commissary" Banks. The physical losses, though severe, perhaps did not represent the most grievous damage inflicted on the Federal forces. Most of the formations in Franklin's XIX Corps and Lee's cavalry division were not just decimated, but terribly shaken. The XIX Corps could muster at most 2,000 effectives. The 130th Illinois Regiment consisted of one skinny youth in a coonskin cap. While they still maintained a quantitative advantage, the morale of the army had drained away. With the exception of the hardened veterans of the XVI Corps, most of the enlisted men quickly lost any confidence they held in the highest ranks of command. The XVI Corps' commander, A.J. Smith, still enjoyed his men's trust, but the campaign soon became identified as merely a cotton-grabbing exercise. The soldiers sang improvised songs deriding Banks, and E.R.S. Canby, a major general in the United States Army, claimed that the cotton speculators "follow in the tracks of the army, traffic in its blood and barter the cause for which it is fighting, with all the baseness of Judas Iscariot, but without his remorse." Between the Confederate Army and the Union Navy, Banks's Red River campaign seemed saddled with failure.

A.J. Smith assembled his corps at Pleasant Hill. Even though he expected the Rebels forthwith, he inexplicably laid out his troops in a most haphazard fashion. Four brigades of infantry were scattered about the ground before the village of Pleasant Hill, with the brigade of Colonel William T. Shaw particularly far forward and exposed. The rest of Smith's corps lay behind Pleasant Hill, more than a mile away from Shaw's line. Perhaps worst of all for Smith's men was not their deployment, but rather the knowledge that the army's supply train was retreating towards Grand Ecore, guarded by most of the XIX Corps and the cavalry. This event signalled the turning point in the campaign.

The Confederates knew something of this. Green's Texan horse harried the Federals all the way back to Pleasant Hill, where at 9.00 a.m. on the 9th they halted before Smith's corps. Aware of the units retreating to Grand Ecore, Taylor had not expected the Yankees to make a stand at Pleasant Hill. In response to this development, Kirby Smith was already hastening forward the infantry divisions of Brigadier Generals James C. Tappan and Mosby M. Parsons. Tappan's Arkansans and Parsons's Missourians force-marched 45 miles in a day and a half to reach Taylor and, while the divisions were in reality little more than reinforced brigades, they doubled Taylor's infantry command. After the hard fighting at Mansfield, the whole Southern group was jaded. Taylor collected them before Pleasant Hill, his hopes rising as the Federals seemed in no hurry to quit the place.

By 3.00 p.m. on April 9, the combative Louisianan had gotten his men into line and even allowed them two hours of rest. Most of the Rebel cavalry deployed to the left flank, while Taylor posted one brigade on the right. The Louisiana infantry, now under the command of Polignac, was held in reserve. To their right stood Walker's Texans, and to the right and ahead of the Texans, were the divisions of Tappan and Parsons under the combined command of Brigadier General Thomas J. Churchill. Overall, the Confederate line took the shape of a giant ladle.

The battle opened with a Confederate bombardment by what Taylor half-jokingly referred to as his "petite-grand battery."[2] Consisting of all of the Rebel guns, they soon silenced the battery assigned to Shaw and then proceeded to punish the hapless brigade. After three-quarters of an hour, Walker, Tappan and Parsons all moved out with their divisions. The cavalry kept pace and secured the flanks but stayed out of the fight. Polignac and the petite-grand battery followed the Texans up the road that led into Pleasant Hill.

From here the battle developed in two distinct stages. This general advance was the first stage. The fighting at this point proved sharp, short and decisive. Shaw's men represented the best of the tough Western soldiery, but no troops could have stood up to the pummelling bombardment and the divisional assault that overtook them. As Shaw's brigade simply disintegrated, the folly of A.J. Smith's haphazard deployment bore its bitter fruit. None of the other three brigades could provide effective support for Shaw, or to each other. A tide of gray and butternut uniforms swamped the Federal infantry and drove towards Smith's second line behind Pleasant Hill.

Here the Union defense crystallized. Nine regiments of solid Western soldiers, backed by three batteries, and all well-placed, met the Rebel attack and stopped it cold. Taylor's men reformed while he brought up Polignac and the artillery. In addition, Green's two cavalry brigades, under the command of Brigadier Generals James P. Major and Hamilton P. Bee, swung out far to the left and rode to a position threatening Smith's right flank. The first stage closed with the Confederates readying for a renewed effort. Polignac assumed the left end of the line and unlimbered the petite-grand battery where his Louisianans met with Walker's Texans.

It took the better part of two hours from the first shots until Taylor finished his preparations for the final attack. In the meantime, Banks left the retreat to Grand Ecore and rode to the sound of the guns. Once again he rode through the milling humanity of broken troops. His spirits rose when he came upon Smith's line. Finding Smith, he congratulated the corps commander, "God bless you general, you have saved the army." Smith wisely cautioned against any such premature praise.

The second stage of the battle began with another artillery duel, and this time the Federal guns more than held their own. Nevertheless, the fight unfolded much like the earlier actions. The Confederates pressed home their assault with great determination and once more a Union flank was turned. The 5th Minnesota and the 8th Wisconsin anchored Smith's right flank, and now these two regiments found themselves overlapped by Polignac's infantry. Major Arnondin noted that the Yankees fought with a white hot fury, but their "blue coats disappeared in a sea of gray and brown."[3] The French prince pivoted his men to the right and began to roll up the rest of Smith's line like a rug. At this juncture, the world crashed in on Banks. Smith rode forward with his staff to rally his men and almost immediately fell from the saddle with a grievous wound to his chest by a musket ball. Pressed from front and flank, the other seven Federal regiments routed from the field. The best Banks could do was see to the safe removal of Smith from the action. Green's troopers then made their appearance to the right and rear of the Union mob and finished the work. None of the Northern cannon made it to safety, and very few of the infantry ever reached Grand Ecore. Only a few mounted officers and the cavalry, which were conspicuous only in their ineffectiveness, escaped the net. The well-educated Taylor later greeted Green, hailing him as the "Murat of Texas."[4]

Retreat and Surrender

The Federal retreat to Grand Ecore turned into a nightmare. As the survivors of Pleasant Hill streamed to the southeast, they began to overtake the army wagon train and its guard. As word spread throughout the remainder of Banks's army, a rot set in and the morale of the Easterners and the discipline of the Westerners disappeared. The former deserted or surrendered while the latter engaged in an orgy of vandalism and brigandage. Green's cavalry added to the growing disarray with a series of raids and strikes until the Yankees reached the relative safety of Grand Ecore, where they had earlier constructed rudimentary fieldworks secured by the river. Here Banks took stock and blanched at the audit of war. Out of some 25,000 infantry and cannoneers, he could marshal approximately two-thirds of that original number, and from 90 pieces of artillery, he could now count 34 muzzles. Most of the cavalry remained, and this left Banks with about 20,000 men with which to face Taylor's force of less than 10,000. The issue, however, concerned not relative numbers, but rather the state of the soldiers' spirits. While the Johnny Rebs knew they could not be beaten, the Billy Yanks wondered if their generals would ever lead them to victory. In the early morning hours of April 10, Banks's best general, A.J. Smith, succumbed to his wound, but not before imploring Franklin to arrest Banks and take command.

Adding to Banks's misery was the absence of Porter and his Mississippi Squadron. On April 7, the naval commander had taken his ships upriver to support Banks for the final push on Shreveport. By the 10th, the squadron had reached its destination, the mouth of Loggy Bayou, site of the expected rendezvous with Banks's victorious army. Instead, a mile above the bayou, the navy discovered a nasty surprise waiting for them. The *New Falls City*, an extremely large steamer, lay transversely across the Red River, with 15 feet of her bow and stern lying on each shoreline, her back broken in the middle and resting on a sandbar. Draped across the wreck, a banner in large letters invited the Federals to a ball to be held in Shreveport. Even before Porter could contemplate removing the impressive obstacle, a tinclad gunboat arrived on the scene with news of the defeat at Mansfield and the disaster at Pleasant Hill. Porter decided to turn about and ordered the laborious process begun. Already the river was falling and most of the ships' keels were dragging on the bottom, especially that of the massive *Eastport*.

Porter had always bragged that he could steam wherever the sand was damp. It looked as if he would finally get the chance to back up that boast.

On April 12, Porter returned to Grand Ecore and the magnitude of the defeat became obvious to him. That night at a grim council of war, Banks, Franklin, Porter, Emory, who had replaced Smith, and all of the divisional commanders weighed their options. The one bright spot in the proceedings came from the repulse of a general assault ordered by Taylor the day before. After bringing up his infantry and his ever-growing artillery park, Taylor, anxious to carry on with the impetus of victory, assured Kirby Smith that one more determined attack would bag the Yankee host once and for all. Following a heavy cannonade that played havoc with the chevaux-de-frise, the Confederate infantry went in and suffered a terrible rebuff. The Federals fought with a determination borne of desperation and the defensive works conferred an advantage not to be conquered by Southern elan. Taylor concluded that he must wait "for the hedgehog to unfold itself again."[5]

The council of war settled upon a retreat following the river road downstream to the Mississippi, and then to Baton Rouge. Half of the land force would lead the way for the immense wagon train, while the remainder of the army would serve as the rearguard. Porter's ships would parallel the line of retreat and it was expected that the navy's heavy guns would contribute much towards dissuading Rebel aggressiveness. Inexplicably, Porter refused to dump his cargo of cotton to ease the navigation of the rapidly dwindling Red River. Banks entertained no such compunction and saw to the transporting of the wounded first. Porter's overarching greed presaged the doom awaiting downriver.

At first, all went according to plan, as the Union retreat easily pushed through the stretched Rebel cordon. Taylor and his men quickly regained their equilibrium, however, and set off in pursuit. While the infantry and artillery followed closely on the heels of Banks's rearguard, most of Green's horsemen rode inland and then ahead of the Federal host to harass and impede its progress. At the same time, Green dispatched Maxey's brigade of cavalry from Texas, and the Arizona and Indian Territories across the river with several batteries of horse artillery. With no Union forces to contend with on the east bank, Maxey's men ranged up and down the Red bedevilling Federal ships with artillery ambushes and sharpshooter sniping. More than once individual, or small groups of, warships, transports and packets found themselves under heavy fire and taking serious losses. Only under the cover of the massed firepower of the squadron could the Yankees find any relief. As the pressure on the retreating Federals increased, so did the tempo of the withdrawal and the pursuit. The Union forces grew more and more anxious as the Confederates offered no respite. The Rebels pressed home their exertions, especially as they came upon scene after scene of the wanton destruction inflicted on the civilian population. Blood begat more blood and the Louisiana troops vowed to save Natchitoches from the "Vandals."[6]

The Southerners' desire to put a halt to the depredations spurred their pursuit. Several times they roughly handled the Northern rearguard and many Yankee "foraging parties" fell captive. In one case, an enraged captain of cavalry, a certain Robert Martin, gave a half a dozen Federal marauders a drumhead court martial and an equally summary execution as an example for others. Whether word of this incident spread or the Rebel pursuit simply proved too energetic, looting and pillaging dropped off as the Federals neared Alexandria. By far the most successful intervention on the part of the Southerners occurred at Natchitoches. It was here that Bee's brigade of horse thundered down the main avenue and caught several hundred Union cavalry in the process of firing the town. While the numbers were about equal, Bee's troopers, flushed with victory, drawn up in a strike column and mad with rage scoured the streets of Natchitoches. The disorganized Yankees either scattered or were captured, and any caught with incendiary materials were shot on the spot.

From Natchitoches, Banks's army force-marched down the river road towards Alexandria. Men fell out, animals collapsed and more and more wagons, caissons, equipment and even a few spiked artillery pieces added to the detritus of war. As Taylor compared Green to Marshal Joachim Murat, William B. Franklin, now commander of the amalgamated XVI and XIX Corps, likened the retreat to Napoleon's disastrous rout from Russia in the winter of 1812–13. He wondered if he would throw the last of the muskets into the Mississippi River. However, Banks enjoyed two advantages over Napoleon: the sunny weather and the protective guns of the Mississippi Squadron. The warships generally kept the Rebels away from the main body of the army.

In this way the Federals reached Alexandria five days after leaving Natchitoches, as the Confederates continued to torment their movements. At Alexandria the Yankees found security within a series of fieldworks thrown up on the outskirts of the town. The relief proved temporary. The steadily dropping river demanded another anguished war council. Banks wanted to rest his men and await a new delivery of supplies via steamer. Porter, deeply concerned for the fate of his squadron, insisted on a hasty departure. At Alexandria a series of underwater sandstone obstacles and the dangerous channels they created threatened the Navy's ships. By this time, it was not known if the larger ships could still navigate the falls in the river. At the council, Franklin introduced Lieutenant Colonel Joseph Bailey of Wisconsin. Bailey proposed building a temporary dam to raise the river's water level and float the squadron over the falls. Bailey had originally proffered the idea to Porter, who ignored it, and it took Franklin, another engineer by training, to appreciate and sponsor the plan.

As the Confederates began to collect in the vicinity of Alexandria, Banks ordered the construction to begin on April 22. The Union soldiers took to the task with a will, while the navy slipped into lethargy. There were no efforts made to lighten the ships by removing armor, guns or stores, and especially not the precious bales of cotton. After eight days, the water level rose and only then did work to divest the ships of armor and guns begin. Porter would not allow any cotton to be unloaded and, in addition, he decided to send his largest warship, the *Eastport*, through the passage first even though it had already suffered grounding problems on the river. Perhaps with cannon and armor off-loaded and shipped down-river by wagon, the *Eastport* might have successfully made its way over the falls. Unfortunately for the United States Navy, Porter seemed to believe his own boasts concerning his ability to navigate across damp sand.

Still loaded down with cotton, on April 30 the *Eastport* headed for the passage between two stone crib dams that extended from each bank of the river. The ship drew too much water and her keel caught on an underwater obstacle. Efforts to free the *Eastport* added more stress and strain until the hull buckled and the ship took on water. The pilot could not keep the *Eastport* under control and the massive ironclad swung to starboard in the current, smashed into the right-hand crib dam and partially dislocated it. Lodged on the crib dam, the vessel quickly settled upright in the river, the decks awash and the hold packed with sodden cotton. Even worse, the broken dam allowed too much water to escape, so not only did the *Eastport*'s bulk block the middle passage, the water level immediately began to drop. Bailey watched in horror as all of his endeavors came to naught. Porter looked out on the death knell of his squadron.

By the following day, a dolorous scene greeted the ill-starred Banks. The Mississippi Squadron, partially unarmored and unarmed, had collected in knots of three or four ships in a long column that stretched down the center of the river. This was the only way to take advantage of the deepest part of the Red. The problem lay in the fact that this pushed some of the ships so far upriver they were beyond the support of the army in Alexandria. As dawn broke, sections of newly captured 3-inch rifles and Parrott guns started to pepper the hapless ships. Holed by roundshot and gutted by shells, three transports, a tug and most damaging of all, the tinclad *Cricket*, all succumbed to the cannonade and sank at various points along the river during the course of the day.

That night Banks called for one more council of war. While a few advised surrender, most of the officers supported Banks in his decision to break out of the Confederate cordon and fight their way to the Mississippi River. The last communiqué Banks had received spoke of a relief force headed upriver. The great unanswered question was how far upriver could this group proceed in the face of mounting Rebel resistance? Whatever the distance, Banks's army, now reduced to the size of a weak corps, must fight its way free. Supplies were dwindling and no more were expected. During all of the discussion, Porter drew within himself and found deep and abiding solicitude in a bottle of looted cognac. He understood that, when the army left, it would leave with a brigade of bluejackets shouldering arms and manning a few field pieces. To prevent capture, his whole squadron would have to be burned.

As the noose tightened around the Federals, Taylor moved heaven and earth to finish off the hated Yankee invaders. Although Kirby Smith possessed no further reinforcements to send from Shreveport, the lull had allowed Taylor to collect stragglers, reclaim the lightly wounded, organize his artillery park and raise approximately 2,000 state militia and equip them with captured small arms. Rebel cavalry freely roamed the east bank of the Red and long range guns sniped at the trapped ships. The bulk of the infantry and artillery encircled the town of Alexandria, and in the intervening days, the Southerners built their own rudimentary fieldworks, especially along the river road southeast of the town. Downriver, a number of blockships rested on the bottom and the cavalry brigades of Major and Maxey watched for any relief efforts while felling trees and burning bridges to delay any there might be. Taylor understood full well that the supply situation put time on his side. With preparations complete and troops in place, he merely waited.

For a fourth and final time, Banks summoned his council of war. Meeting in the home of Brian Camp, a local impresario, a grimly resolute Banks explained to his subordinates his plan. He announced to all in the room that the army would form up in an assault column and break through the part of the Confederate defenses that secured the river road. Porter began to interrupt with a pointed inquiry concerning his stranded squadron, but Banks, at the end of his patience with the greedy, sodden braggart, cut Porter off. "Spike your guns, burn your ships and add your men to the assault or wait for the next patch of damp sand and steam for New Orleans," Banks curtly told Porter and thus closed the matter.[7]

Throughout the night, the Federals prepared for the attack and the ships were readied to be fired. With the first light of morning on May 4, two divisional columns under Emory and Brigadier General Thomas E.G. Ransom emerged from the defenses of Alexandria. Emory's left flank hugged the river bank and Ransom's right was secured by Lee's cavalry. An *ad hoc* brigade of bluejackets remained in reserve. A short, sharp bombardment by Banks's remaining guns preceded the attack. Initially, the Rebel defenders displayed no small amount of confusion, but Polignac's Louisianans held that portion of the line and, although outnumbered, they hunkered down behind breastworks and abatis. Taylor had also placed the lion's share of his artillery along this section of the Confederate position. Although displaying desperate courage, the Federal infantry could not pierce the defenses. The attack foundered against the resolve of Polignac's men and the storm of shot and shell from the Rebel guns.

As the assault fell apart, Banks sent an order for Lee to disengage from a skirmish with Green's Texans and ride for freedom. Lee did not ask for a confirmation, but sent his command, led by the troopers of Brigadier General N.A.M. "Gold Lace" Dudley, from the current combat towards the more open country directly west of the town. Since the region due west of Alexandria was far removed from the river or any road net, Taylor had only covered this area with a cavalry screen. By hard riding, some hard fighting and foraging off the land, Lee and his men rode into Simmesport on May 7, where they met forces organizing for the relief of Banks. It fell to Lee to inform those present that the opportunity had passed.

Back at Alexandria, Banks met his men as they straggled back to the environs of the town. He understood full well his worsening supply situation and, while a citizen-soldier and an amateur who had learned his profession on the job, Banks clearly saw that his army was played out. Turning to his chief of staff, he directed Brigadier General Charles P. Stone to ride out under a flag of truce and discuss terms. Taylor, upon meeting with Stone, immediately gave his answer: unconditional surrender. Taylor relished the thought of Grant in northern Virginia receiving the news of the surrender and the appropriation of his defining phrase. Banks delayed responding for a full day, but an impatient Taylor threatened a bombardment and Banks promised an answer on the next morning. On May 6, the remnants of Banks's army left Alexandria and entered into captivity. As the last of the soldiers and sailors cleared the town, picked crews set torches to the ships of the Mississippi Squadron. As the tinclad *Fort Hindman* went up in a towering explosion, soldiers and civilians alike made for cover. Few, if any, windows survived the concussive waves and the explosions were heard and felt miles away. Far from the scene, Major Arnondin understood that the smoke and the noise "signalled the end of the Yankee invasion and all of their cotton-stealing schemes."[8]

Thus the Red River expedition ended in ignominy and failure. Two corps, more than 25,000 men, and all 90 guns were captured. Only Lee's horsemen, slightly fewer than 4,000, escaped the net. All of the major warships, many more auxiliary craft and their whole complements, were lost, too. Banks, his staff and his officers went into captivity with their men to do their utmost to ameliorate the worst aspects of the surrender. Porter slipped downriver via a packet boat the night before and arrived in New Orleans well ahead of news of the debacle.

Taylor revelled in his victory, but he was not one to rest upon his laurels. With the destruction of Banks's army and Porter's squadron, Taylor envisioned a grand march through the sugar parishes, redeeming his state and eventually appearing in Algiers, a town across the river from New Orleans. From there, the city would fall to him and thus close the

Mississippi River to the detested Yankees. The problem for Taylor's grandiose scheme lay in the fact that he possessed no means for crossing the mightiest river in North America. Even as he put forth his idea to Kirby Smith, the departmental commander faced another threat, and in consequence, another opportunity.

Steele's March into Oblivion

Some 120 miles to the northeast of Shreveport, at the town of Camden, Arkansas, Major General Frederick Steele sat with 11,000 men. Back on March 23, Steele had moved out of Little Rock with his corps. He had delayed his departure to oversee local elections and in part because his heart was not really committed to the enterprise. His complaints to Grant concerning poor roads, little fodder, strained logistics and Rebel partisan rangers made no impression on the commanding general. Steele was to threaten Shreveport from the north and divert men and material away from Banks. In this, Steele conspicuously failed. His progress proved glacial, although this was more from the difficult going he predicted to Grant rather than from his own incapabilities. His men marched on half-rations and the road to Camden turned out to be a bottomless track of mud that often required a corduroy carpet of logs. Steele informed Grant that, "our supplies are nearly exhausted and so is the country. We are obliged to forage from five to fifteen miles on either side of the road to keep our stock alive." Perhaps the only source of comfort for Steele came from his men maintaining their march discipline and generally refraining from looting.

In response to this Union move, Kirby Smith mobilized five small brigades of cavalry and put them under the command of Brigadier General John Sappington Marmaduke. With some 3,000 troopers, Marmaduke set about the task of harassing and delaying Steele's advance. In this endeavor he succeeded admirably. The mobility of his force and his soldiers' intimate knowledge of the terrain gave the Confederates a nearly insuperable advantage. Steele's two brigades of horse could neither outride nor outfight Marmaduke's division and Steele moved southward with only the vaguest notion of what to expect. Kirby Smith counted on the habitual caution of Steele and calculated that cavalry alone would suffice to slow, if not halt, the Federal commander. A cavalryman himself, Kirby Smith fully appreciated his mounted arm's potential. While the infantry of the department converged against Banks, Kirby Smith contented himself with sending only the cavalry of Colonels Richard M. Gano and Tandy Walker to Marmaduke. Gano's Texans and Walker's Choctaws would soon add to Steele's discomfiture.

It was on the evening of April 13 that the first Yankee horsemen rode into Camden, three weeks after the opening of the campaign. Camden put Steele's corps halfway betwixt Little Rock and Shreveport, and here Steele hesitated about his next move. His supply situation grew more precarious with each mile marched southward, and Shreveport still lay many miles away. At one point, he even began to contemplate a retreat but, whatever discouragements or difficulties troubled Steele, a rising urgency pressed him hard. Word began to filter in at his headquarters of the battles southeast of Shreveport and the perilous state of Banks's army. Grant and others implored Steele to do all in his power to succor Banks. Trapped between the Scylla and Charybdis of advance or retreat, Steele did neither.

As these events unfolded in Arkansas, the denouement in Louisiana played itself out. With Banks's surrender, Kirby Smith immediately turned his attention towards Steele. He directed Taylor to detach the infantry divisions of Walker, Churchill and Parsons and the large artillery park and send them posthaste to Shreveport for service in Arkansas. Polignac's Louisianans would remain with Taylor, as would the Texan horse that had fought so well. At first, Taylor became absolutely apoplectic over Kirby Smith's order. He wanted to redeem New Orleans, but Kirby Smith seemed intent on denying Taylor his ultimate glory: a triumphal entry into the Crescent City. At first, Taylor refused, but eventually the impasse broke when Kirby Smith dispatched Colonel Michael F. Labranche, a most capable and trusted staff officer, to reiterate the order. A scion from an old south Louisiana family, Labranche, a native of New Orleans, explained the futility of the proposed river crossing to Taylor. Early the next morning, the infantry and artillery headed for Shreveport.[9]

With Churchill serving in the role of a corps commander, the Rebel force made swift progress and, upon reaching the capital of Confederate Louisiana, they found plenty of supplies stockpiled for their use. While he showed himself a most competent battlefield general, Edmund Kirby Smith also possessed a positive genius for military administration. His effective and efficient governance resulted in the Trans-Mississippi Department being labelled "Kirbysmithdom." At Shreveport Kirby Smith assumed command and sent his more than 6,000 infantry and 66 guns north, to a rendezvous with Marmaduke's cavalry. While Steele pondered his next move, Kirby Smith hurried to tighten the noose he had extended around Camden. His instructions to Marmaduke called for the Rebel horse to fix Steele in Camden with raids, probes and feints. This they did with great success, especially as Steele's cavalry began to suffer from a want of fodder. When the Yankees did ride, it was usually as guards to supply trains that found it harder and harder to reach Camden from Little Rock. Even as Kirby Smith maneuvered his infantry into blocking positions around Camden, the Confederate cavalry struck the telling blows of the campaign.

On April 28, 3,000 troopers under Marmaduke set upon a Union supply train of 200 wagons some 14 miles northwest of Camden at the ominously named Poison Spring. The Rebels quickly overcame the guard of 800 foot, 300 horse and a 4-gun battery. The fight was short and brutal with incidents of atrocities perpetrated against the black troops present. That little quarter was shown surprised no one, as Tandy Walker's Choctaws faced the men of Brigadier General John M. Thayer, whom in earlier actions had despoiled the Choctaw lands and inflicted unspeakable horrors on the civilian populace. In addition, many of the captured wagons revealed much in the way of goods looted from Arkansas farmsteads. Only after a portion of the defeated Federal cavalry made it into Camden, did Steele learn of the setback. The infantry, the battery, and worst of all, the supplies, were totally lost. With the news, Steele prepared for an evacuation and retreat to Little Rock. A very large supply train of over 300 wagons was on its way, and Steele needed to bring it in safely to Camden before he left. His animals desperately required the fodder, and in consequence he sent out 1,200 infantry, 250 cavalry and five cannon to escort the train to Camden.

Reports from Marmaduke spurred Kirby Smith and his men to greater efforts. Command of the cavalry was transferred to Brigadier General James F. Fagan, after Marmaduke had suffered a fairly serious wound to his leg at Poison Spring. Like his predecessor, Fagan intended to isolate Steele and, when word arrived of the latest Yankee wagon train winding its way to Camden, Fagan moved to intercept it. Twelve days after the action at Poison Spring, 2,500 Confederate cavalry under Fagan caught the Union supply train at Mark's Mill, little more than 20 miles due east of Camden. Although the numbers were much closer this time, the same result followed. The Rebel troopers washed over the Federals like a tidal wave. In a very brief time, most of the Union soldiers were prisoners and all of the wagons and guns were taken. Fewer than 100 officers and men on horseback reached the relative safety of Camden. The trap was closing around Steele.

With the defeat at Mark's Mill, Steele realized that he must form up his corps and fight his way free to Little Rock. Unfortunately for the beleaguered general, the Confederates had no intention of allowing that to come to pass. To the north and east, Fagan's seven cavalry brigades, supported by several batteries of horse artillery and the nine captured Federal pieces blocked the most direct route to the state capital. Also, this direction necessitated the crossing of the Ouachita River, swollen by spring rains and guarded by the enemy. To avoid such a daunting task, Steele could march northwards with the river on his right and head for Arkadelphia, 50 miles above Camden, or head west towards Washington, 60 miles northwest from Camden. While these routes offered greater promise, especially the road to Arkadelphia, Kirby Smith fully appreciated their strategic import, too. As Steele prevaricated, Kirby Smith placed Churchill's Arkansans across the north road and Parsons's Missourians blocked the western road. Walker's Texans deployed between the two as a reserve. Kirby Smith also liberally distributed his sizable artillery park along the cordon. As he waited his men dug fieldworks.

After conferring with his officers, Steele settled upon a drive due north with the intention of shoving Churchill's division aside and bolting for Arkadelphia. It was a bold plan and the Federals would bring more men to the point of attack. Nevertheless, numerous problems conspired to thwart Steele's undertaking. The losses from Poison Spring and Mark's Mill, coupled with the lack of forage, deprived the Northerners of any effective cavalry. Also, there were simply not enough healthy horses and mules to move what wagons and artillery they needed for the retreat. What Steele possessed was two divisions of infantry, who had been on half-rations for more than a month, supported by a decimated artillery arm. On the morning of May 13, the date set for the breakout assault, Steele and his staff rode forward to reconnoiter the ground. Through their field glasses they saw 2,000 Rebel soldiers, backed by several dozen guns ensconced in formidable defensive works. Steele's heart sank at the sight. He had never approved of the march on Shreveport, nor the insistence by his superiors that he execute it. Now his command, reduced by defeat and tormented by want, faced a surely insurmountable challenge. While he could bring to the field 6,000 infantry, Steele would have to guard his left flank (his right was screened by the Ouachita) and provide a rearguard in the town. In addition, even with a victory, most of the wagons, artillery and worst of all, the ambulances, would remain behind. The thought of leaving his wounded to the Rebels proved particularly galling.

As a pall descended over Steele's spirits, word came that an envoy from the Confederate camp had arrived in Camden. Steele and his staff returned to town at a trot. There they found the ubiquitous Colonel Labranche. Under a flag of truce, Labranche now proffered fairly generous terms of surrender. Parole was out of the question, but the Southerners promised good treatment for all, medical care for the wounded and proper food, clothing and shelter in a prisoner of war camp at Marshall, Texas. Aware of the terrible rumors emanating out of Andersonville, Georgia, Kirby Smith had made sure that the longhorn cattle and cotton harvests of the Trans-Mississippi Department would keep such infamy east of the mighty river. Steele asked for 24 hours to consider the offer and, knowing that time favored the Rebels, Labranche cheerfully consented. That afternoon, following a spartan lunch, Steele conferred with his divisional and brigade commanders. While none advocated surrendering, none spoke convincingly for launching the assault. Unfortunately for Steele, the decision lay entirely with him. After a sleepless night, he sent out an aide-de-camp who met with Labranche and at noon, on May 14, at the Alan Halphen farmstead north of Camden, Steele surrendered his corps. Slightly fewer than 10,000 Federals went into captivity.

Missouri in the Balance

For Kirby Smith, the capitulation of Steele's corps opened a wide vista of opportunities. Even as his quartermasters saw to cataloging and pressing into service all the captured Union equipment, Kirby Smith marshalled his forces and pointed them northwards. Nary a Federal soldier remained in Arkansas. Harris Flanagin, the Confederate governor in exile, urged the departmental commander to march on Little Rock, for both understood the value of redeeming the state from the Yankees. Kirby Smith needed no prodding. Among his many talents were his political skills and his ability to work with civilian leadership. To take Little Rock and restore Confederate authority in Arkansas would set a precedent and severely damage the Lincoln administration's reputation. As the newly named Army of Arkansas moved north, Kirby Smith sent out J.O. Shelby's Iron Brigade to enforce the conscription laws. There would be no want of weapons to arm the new recruits.

In Washington, D.C., the reports piled up the grim news. By the second week of May, 35,000 Federal soldiers had been killed or captured and, coupled to this, the North had lost over 125 cannon and more than 1,000 wagons and ambulances. Additionally, the entire Mississippi Squadron lay at the bottom of the Red River. These losses had led to the Union relinquishing all of Louisiana west of the Mississippi River and all of Arkansas save for a garrison established behind entrenchments at Helena. One of Sherman's corps had been transferred to New Orleans and Grant now sent a reinforced corps to St Louis while other troops rushed to Memphis. These redeployments played havoc with the Northern spring offensives in Virginia and Georgia. General Joseph E. Johnston penned Sherman in the northwestern corner of Georgia and Grant could not sustain his war of attrition, especially after the bloody reverse at the Wilderness.

On May 23, after a series of rousing speeches and an artillery salute from a battery comprised entirely of captured pieces, Governor Flanagin re-established Confederate governance in Arkansas. Meanwhile, Kirby Smith kept pushing his Army of Arkansas forward. Shelby's recruiting proved particularly effective, as he informed the men of the state that not joining in the fight left their lives and property at risk. In short order, Kirby Smith could count another infantry division of more than 4,000 amongst his order of battle. While some of the recruits harbored Unionist sentiments or simply wished to be left alone, many were veterans of Pea Ridge, Prairie Grove and Vicksburg and looked to avenge the depredations inflicted upon their homes. With 8,000 infantry, 4,000 cavalry and nearly 100 cannon, Kirby Smith marched into Missouri to deliver the *coup de grâce* of the Confederate campaign.

For the Federal Military Division of West Mississippi, the crisis was coming to a head. Reinforcements sent from the east had to help secure all of the great cities on the eastern side of the river and St Louis on the western bank. Most of Major General Edward R.S. Canby's men knew little of combat beyond garrison duty, pursuing Rebel raiders or brutalizing the secessionist elements in Missouri. To flesh out his forces, Canby called up the home guard units but, outside of their county of origin, they proved next to useless. Even worse for Canby, the Confederate advance emboldened the Missouri bushwhackers and their strikes grew in frequency and strength. As the Army of Arkansas crossed into Missouri, another 2,000 flocked to Kirby Smith's banner and the partisan rangers ran rampant. An old warrior, Canby steeled himself to meet the threat. With approximately 25,000 men evenly divided into two corps, Canby marched out of St Louis intent on keeping Missouri in the Union.

Missouri's secession loomed large in Kirby Smith's thoughts. One of the general's entourage was Thomas C. Reynolds, the Confederate governor of Missouri. Reynolds enjoyed a very cordial relationship with Kirby Smith, and always vigorously supported the commander's efforts to administer the Trans-Mississippi Department. Now Reynolds made a persuasive case for seizing Jefferson City, calling a convention and voting on an ordinance of secession. Coupled with the loss of Arkansas, this would ensure that the Lincoln administration would stagger into the election of 1864. It was a bold plan, and boldness had already carried the Confederates far. Also, the Missouri troops of Parsons and Shelby had already performed prodigies of valor as a regular course of action and now, back in their home state, their morale knew no limits. From Fayetteville, Arkansas, Kirby Smith led his corps-sized army to Springfield, Missouri, confident in his men's spirits. Since his days with the Army of the Shenandoah, Kirby Smith never doubted his soldiers' resolve and never wavered when it came to sending them into battle.

Canby's general staff finished the arrangements for a move from St Louis, and on June 11, the same day that Kirby Smith left Springfield, Canby's army marched out to meet the enemy. The Union commander especially wished to prevent a Rebel entry into Jefferson City. The Yankee host made a direct course for Rolla, a town that lay 60 miles southeast of the capital and 100 miles southwest of St Louis. Any Confederate thrust at the state capital must proceed through Rolla. Canby planned to bring the Army of Arkansas to battle at Rolla, and Kirby Smith displayed no hesitation for a contest of arms.

As the two armies closed, both sides could claim certain advantages and both faced serious drawbacks. For the Confederates, their problems were twofold. The most glaring lay in the fact that the Federals outnumbered the Southerners 25,000 to 15,000. Also, the burden of the attack rested squarely on Kirby Smith's shoulders, with all of its attendant risks and higher casualties. Despite such considerations, Kirby Smith knew that his force, with the exception of one division of Arkansas infantry, was comprised of battle-tested veterans. His cavalry was keeping the Union horse at bay, depriving Canby of accurate reconnaissance and, because of all the battlefield captures, the Rebel artillery park surpassed its Northern counterpart. For Canby, his larger force and defensive posture held him in good stead. Yet, he also labored under dangerous handicaps. Most of the Missouri bushwhackers did not ride in and join the Army of Arkansas. Rather, they ranged far and wide, striking at isolated garrisons and breaking Canby's supply line to St Louis. Even before the battle was joined, Canby had detached two brigades, one of infantry and one of cavalry, to secure his line of communications. More troubling, much of his infantry were either garrison troops or home guard units. For Canby, the Army of the Missouri was blue on the outside and green on the inside.

On the morning of June 18, the two armies drew themselves up near the John Flettrich Plantation, approximately two miles south of Rolla. Only a few buildings and fences broke up the landscape, and it was here that Canby meant to stop the Rebels once and for all. Kirby Smith deployed his cavalry in equal parts on both wings with his veteran infantry in the center, backed by most of the artillery. The recruit division he placed in reserve. Canby matched his opponent's dispositions and, while his superior numbers in infantry allowed for a longer line, Canby's men suffered in terms of morale and experience. A military career built on burning down the farmsteads of families of suspected bushwhackers inculcated poor discipline and fleeting courage. While spreading out his infantry extended his line, it also led Canby to broadcast his batteries up and down the army's frontage. Already outgunned, the move robbed the Federals of any concentrated artillery fire.

At 10.00 a.m., Kirby Smith ordered his guns to open up on the Army of the Missouri. The Yankee cannoneers soon replied. Kirby Smith's chief of artillery, Brigadier General Peter Van Wooten, a Scottish engineer and soldier of fortune, brought practically all of his guns to bear on the center of Canby's line. Here they did a terrible execution, to the point where the Union commander ordered forward half of his reserves to bolster the line. Confederate counter-battery fire also silenced many of the Federal guns on this section of the front. For an hour and a half the guns roared, until bugles sounded and drums rolled and the whole of the Rebel infantry advanced. Walker's Texans took the left and Churchill's Arkansans were on the right. Both marched in echelon to protect the flanks and to allow Parsons's Missourians in the center to serve as the spearpoint of the assault. As Taylor did with Gray's Louisianans at Mansfield, Kirby Smith gave the Missourians the honor of drawing first blood on their native soil. The reserve, the artillery and the cavalry all supported the attack.

The Federal soldiers braced for the shock. The infantry, inexperienced and unnerved, discharged ragged musket volleys and many of the cannon were already silenced. As the Confederates closed to within a hundred paces, they halted, fired one volley and then with a Rebel yell charged at the double quick. Once more in the campaigns of the Trans-Mississippi Department,

elan and impetus carried the day over superior numbers. The center of
Canby's position gave way in one huge surge. The remainder of Canby's
reserve, a brigade of infantry, melted away at the sight of the carnage before
them. Within a quarter of an hour, the Army of the Missouri was streaming
back up the road towards St Louis. Shelby, Fagan and the other cavalry
officers then took up the pursuit, granting the Yankees no respite and
bagging nearly 3,000 prisoners and practically every cannon, wagon and
ambulance in the Northern army. The Southern horse finally drew off after
many days of giving chase brought them to the outskirts of the defenses of
St Louis.

From St Louis, Canby telegraphed Washington with the black news,
while simultaneously requesting reinforcements and resigning his
commission. In the meantime, Kirby Smith turned his army to the
northeast and marched on Jefferson City. Even though it was but a short
distance to the capital from Rolla, several thousand recruits joined the Army
of Arkansas in its victorious progress, and each received a newly captured
Springfield musket. On June 21, three days after the rout at Flettrich's
Farm, the Iron Brigade, 600 Missourian troopers accompanied by two
batteries of horse artillery, trotted into Jefferson City. Since the brigade
lacked a national banner, the 5th Missouri Regiment volunteered its colors,
which were run up over the capital building.

The following day, the Army of Arkansas trooped into town and 36 hours
later Governor Reynolds sent out the call for a convention to consider an
ordinance of secession. As the former government-in-exile assumed
authority and delegates arrived from the Missouri hinterland, Kirby Smith
took his army to the east. Leaving the new division of Missouri recruits to
train and dig fortifications, he rendezvoused with his cavalry eight miles due
east of St Louis at the town of Clayton. Recalling the debacle at Helena,
Arkansas, the prior July, the Confederate commander entertained no notion
of assaulting Yankees dug in with their backs to the river and supported by
the big guns of the United States Navy. His men could accomplish the
difficult, but not what he deemed the impossible. In any case, Canby, whose
resignation was denied, could not hope to leave his defenses and challenge
Confederate hegemony in the state. On July 23, the secession convention
met and in an overwhelming vote Missouri left the Union.

Victory and Independence

While no one at the time recognized Missouri's secession as the turning
point in the war, such was the case. West of the Mississippi River, Union
forces confined themselves to the fortifications of St Louis and Helena. More
Federal troops dispatched from the East secured these two spots but the
Federal cantonments on the Texas coast were abandoned. A sizable portion
of the Northern reinforcements went to Minnesota to keep the Sioux
Nation in check. Missouri left the Union and with Arkansas redeemed, the

majority of neutral or Unionist tribes in the Indian Territory went over to the Confederacy. As spring gave way to summer, Grant's and Sherman's campaigns in Virginia and Georgia came to grief as the Federal leaders helplessly watched as entire corps left for the west. The shifting of troops robbed the Federal offensives of the weight of numbers needed to grind down the Rebels. Without such an advantage, their attacks quickly stalled, then stopped altogether. Against this depressing background, Lincoln went out to meet George B. McClellan in the election of 1864. Despite the questionable Republican machinations behind West Virginia and Nevada achieving statehood before the election, and the use of the "bayonet vote," the defeats and war weariness gave the Democrats the presidency and both houses of Congress. President-elect McClellan arranged an armistice for Christmas which held throughout the spring and summer of 1865 until the Treaty of Hamilton, signed in Bermuda on August 22 of that year, ended the war with complete independence for the Confederate States of America.

Victory did much to ease the ill will between Edmund Kirby Smith and Richard Taylor. Kirby Smith eschewed several opportunities to enter the political arena and instead accepted the post of superintendent at the newly established Southern Military Academy in Montgomery, Alabama. Taylor followed in his father's footsteps and, after sitting in the Confederate Senate, he became the Confederacy's third president, after Robert E. Lee's administration. The fates of the Union leadership in the west proved much less sanguine. No one's career or reputation survived intact, although Banks, Steele and Canby all penned exculpatory memoirs. Banks went back to politics and prospered well enough to return eventually to the United States House of Representatives for Massachusetts. Steele retired to his property in Connecticut, went into semi-seclusion and made his living as a gentleman farmer. Canby, who possessed more military acumen than good fortune, accepted a generalship in the army of the khedive of Egypt. He perished bravely with his men at the hands of the Mahdists in 1881 in the Sudan. Porter faced a court-martial which found his negligence only exceeded by his greed and ego. Stripped of his rank, fined into penury, within a year he was dead by his own hand in a bordello in Boston. The unforgiving Taylor summed up the news, that Porter died "without honor, without mourning and without his pants."[10]

Today the Confederacy observes its independence on February 8, the date it officially came into existence. Confederate Veterans' Day, however, falls on April 12, not only to commemorate the firing on Fort Sumter in 1861, but also to honor the victories along the Red River Valley in 1864 that set the stage for the eventual Southern triumph. It is a grateful nation that marks the contributions and leadership of Edmund Kirby Smith and Richard Taylor, two men who transformed a strategic backwater, the Trans-Mississippi Department, into the cockpit of the war.

The Reality

The Trans-Mississippi Department never became a theater of decision, but it possessed the potential. While there was little chance of the Confederates successfully projecting any real force across the Mississippi River, redeeming Louisiana, Arkansas or Missouri could have produced calamitous results for the North, especially on the eve of the election of 1864. As for the Red River and Camden campaigns, in both cases the Federals narrowly averted disaster. Porter nearly lost his entire squadron at Alexandria and the Union victory at Pleasant Hill was of the most limited tactical nature and still confirmed to Banks the wisdom of retreating. Finally, Steele came within a hair's breadth of surrendering his entire corps in the wilds of Arkansas. Such a loss would have left the state open to Rebel redemption. If the South had liberated a state capital in the spring of 1864, the dismay caused in the Republican ranks would have been overwhelming. As for raising new troops, War Department documents in the National Archives show that Shelby raised nearly 4,000 men during and after the Camden campaign, and this while Union occupation still remained. Indeed, all of the events leading up to the Battles at Pleasant Hill and Poison Spring are factual. The alternate history only appears with the sweeping Confederate victory at Pleasant Hill and an altered date for the action at Poison Spring.

Bibliography

Anders, Curt, *Disaster in Damp Sand: The Red River Expedition* (Guild Press of Indiana, Indianapolis, 1997).

Bearss, Edwin C., *Steele's Retreat from Camden and the Battle of Jenkins' Ferry* (Pioneer Press, Little Rock, 1967).

Brooksher, William Riley, *War along the Bayous: The 1864 Red River Campaign in Louisiana* (Brassey's, London, 1998).

Hollandsworth, James G., *Pretense of Glory: The Life of General Nathaniel P. Banks* (Louisiana State University Press, Baton Rouge, 1998).

Johnson, Ludwell H., *Red River Campaign: Politics and Cotton in the Civil War* (Johns Hopkins Press, Baltimore, 1958).

Joiner, Gary Dillard, *One Damn Blunder from Beginning to End: The Red River Campaign of 1864* (Scholarly Resources, Wilmington, Delaware, 2003).

Parks, Joseph H., *General Edmund Kirby Smith, C.S.A.* (Louisiana University Press, Baton Rouge, 1954).

Parrish, Michael T., *Richard Taylor: Soldier Prince of Dixie* (University of North Carolina Press, Chapel Hill, 1992).

Waugh, John C., *Sam Bell Maxey and the Confederate Indians* (Ryan Place Publishers, Fort Worth, 1995).

Winters, John D., *The Civil War in Louisiana* (Louisiana State University Press, Baton Rouge, 1963).

Notes

*1. Forrest Arnondin, *Honor, Duty, Country* (Crescent City Press, New Orleans, 1868), pp.137-38.

*2. Terrence Freygan, *Richard Taylor: Soldier-Statesman* (Innsmouth Press, Boston, 1929), p. 244.

*3. Arnondin, *Honor, Duty, Country*, p. 166.

*4. Freygan, *Richard Taylor,* p. 258.

*5. *Ibid.*, p. 266.

*6. Michael Palmer, *Beau Sabreur of the Confederacy: The Life and Times of Tom Green* (Freedom Press, Philadelphia, 1991), p. 723.

*7. Richard M. Doskey, *Memoirs of a Staff Officer* (Throne Press, New York, 1884), p. 822.

*8. Arnondin, *Honor, Duty, Country,* p. 137.

*9. Michael Labranche, *My Life as a Right Bower* (Pelican Press, Baton Rouge, 1888), p. 314

*10. Freygan, *Richard Taylor,* p. 758.

10
TERRIBLE AS AN ARMY WITH BANNERS
Jubal Early in the Shenandoah Valley

Kevin F. Kiley

"Arbitrary, cynical, with strong prejudices, he was personally disagreeable; he made few admirers or friends either by his manners or his habits. If he had a tender feeling, he endeavored to conceal it and acted as though he would be ashamed to be detected in doing a kindness; yet many will recall little acts of General Early which prove that his heart was naturally full of loyalty and tenderness."
Major Henry Kyd Douglas[1]

The Shenandoah Valley, June 13, 1864

The long, weary, hard-marching column of gray and butternut-clad infantry, heads and bodies bent forward under the weight of their equipment, trudged silently in the dark along the rutted country road to yet another killing ground. The only sounds that could be heard in the long infantry column in the moonlight were the rustle of equipment and the curses of men who tripped and fell in the ruts. Periodically, horses' shoes, of the few senior officers that were actually still mounted, would strike a rock and send off a few sparks, but that was not remarked upon, as these men were veterans, and a night march was just part of the drill.

The war had ground on for three years and many tens of thousands dead, the South's hopes getting grimmer by the month. Yet, these veteran infantry, dirty, ragged, and many barefoot, but with clean weapons and full ammunition pouches, were ready to continue the fight under veteran officers who had no quit in them. The rank and file did not either.

This was especially true of their commanding officer, Jubal Early. Hard, irascible, ascetic, this tobacco-chewing fighter had nothing of human kindness about him. Not popular, but trusted, he was tough as nails and twice as hard-headed. He was a proven commander and leader, disdainful of his peers and superiors, but known to take good care of his men. He now commanded the II Corps of the Army of Northern Virginia, Jackson's old command.

Early was still smarting from the disastrous defeat at Rappahannock Station the previous November. An expert night attack, the first successful one of the war, was launched by crack Federal brigades under Brigadier Generals David Russell and Emory Upton against Old Jube, and had caught him, and one of his brigades, on the defensive in an intricate system of trenches and redoubts protecting a bridgehead along the Rappahannock River. They were not ready, and the position was penetrated, overrun, and captured, along with most of the Confederate troops who could not get away. That included the famous Louisiana Brigade with the Army of Northern Virginia, and it had infuriated the already unfriendly Early, who had sworn vengeance against the hated Northerners.

Now, seated on his horse on a small rise with his staff, watching the battle-hardened, silent men of his command file past him with that swinging gait that could eat up 20 or 30 miles a day, he spat tobacco juice, nodding to one of his staff to be about his business. As the aide turned his horse and galloped off, Early spat again, raising his head to take the salute of a smart battery of horse artillery as it rumbled past their commander.

The artillerymen were as ragged as the infantry, but they had somehow kept their traditional red kepis, and all were wearing cavalry boots, acquired from heaven knows where. It was a smart outfit, well turned out and spoiling for a fight. The guns, vehicles, and horse harness were well maintained and clean, the harness gleaming in the moonlight. What was noteworthy was the fine state their horses were in. The good Lord only knew what their battery commander had done to keep their gun teams and mounts in such great condition. The horses were in better physical shape, and much better fed, than the men were, and that included their commanding officer. Their captain was old for his grade, a grizzled, much-wounded veteran, but, like his commander, tough as a cob. These gunners would give a good accounting of themselves, and they did not fear the Union superiority in artillery or the deadly efficiency with which the Yankee gunners practiced their art. They would serve their guns until hell froze over, and then fight on the ice. Early had only 40 guns in his little army, but maybe they could get more from the Yankees, perhaps even some of the excellent 3-inch ordnance rifles so especially prized by Southern artillerymen and the most accurate gun of the war.[2]

Summer of Crisis

The South was in a very bad way in the summer of 1864. Gettysburg the previous July had crippled the Army of Northern Virginia; the 25,000 casualties it had suffered could not be replaced, at least not any time soon. Grant had come east to take command of the Union armies, and his offensive at the beginning of the campaigning season of 1864 had been one continuous battle after another with Lee in the horrific terrain of Northern Virginia that was mostly forest and scrub, and truthfully dubbed the Wilderness.[3]

Unlike the other Union commanders that Lee had faced, this one did not quit after one defeat or draw, and continued the campaign without regard to losses or setbacks. Grant could replace the casualties suffered in the campaign, though perhaps not the experienced troops and officers, but Lee could only get weaker. The Confederacy was at the bottom of the manpower barrel, and it was beginning to tell in the field armies.

The Shenandoah Valley was, quite literally, the breadbasket of the South. It was also a sword pointed at Washington. It was a natural invasion route from the South into Northern territory, running southwest to northeast, but it was not a reciprocal route. Moving up the Valley towards Washington, any Southern force came out of the Valley in a position to do damage in a variety of strategic ways. A Northern force exiting the southern end of the Valley found itself in the middle of nowhere.

However, the Valley itself was a strategic prize to be controlled. Its fertile fields and harvests fed the Army of Northern Virginia and supplied food to the Southern populace. Whoever controlled it could control the destiny of the Confederacy. The North had tried it before in 1862, only to be defeated and its troops routed by the elusive, brilliant, and somewhat unorthodox Thomas Jackson, nicknamed Stonewall.[4] They would tried again in the summer of 1864 in order to support Grant and Meade against Lee.

The Southern commanders that summer in the Valley, led by tough, capable Major General John C. Breckinridge, though outnumbered, held the Yankees generally at bay, but Union numbers were beginning to tell. Breckinridge defeated the first Union force sent against him commanded by Major General Franz Sigel, a political general employed mainly for his ability to enlist German immigrants. A dedicated man, but an incompetent general, he was replaced by the department commander, Major General David Hunter, by Grant's order. Hunter ruthlessly and efficiently laid waste to the Valley, ably seconded by commanders such as Brigadier Generals George Crook and William Averell. They ranged down the Valley and generally had it their own way until the advent of Jubal Early and the II Corps of the Army of Northern Virginia, who chased them out, once again claiming the entire Shenandoah for the Confederacy.

Grant now sent one of his western generals, Phil Sheridan, the new commander of the newly-formed Cavalry Corps of the Army of the Potomac, into the Valley with enough cavalry and two infantry corps to clear the Valley and then to lay waste to it when the last Confederates were either killed, captured, or driven out. However, his primary mission was to find, fight, and destroy Jubal Early and his army.

Council Of War

Robert E. Lee had more up his sleeve than just sending Early into the Valley to help hold it for the South. He suggested to President Davis that there be a meeting of Davis, Joe Johnston, the Southern commander facing Sherman in Georgia, and himself in Richmond. Dangerous it might be, pulling commanders away from their armies in the middle of campaigns, but desperate times called for desperate measures. Besides, what do you have capable subordinates for anyway? Davis agreed, and ordered Johnston temporarily north.

As Early's veterans were tramping up the Valley to meet the Yankees, the three men met at the President's mansion in Richmond. What Lee proposed to the two men was this: It was obvious to all that Johnston could not stop Sherman and Lee would eventually lose to Grant and Meade. The odds were too long, and there were virtually no replacements left in the South. Davis and Johnston nodded agreement. What could be done, though, was to achieve local superiority in the Valley under Early, attempt to take Washington and influence the coming United States presidential election. It was the only chance they had of a negotiated peace. They could not match Northern industrial might and manpower on the battlefield any longer. They were bleeding to death.

It was decided to detach Major General Patrick Cleburne's division, plus supporting artillery and cavalry, from Johnston's army facing Sherman, and, as secretly as possible, send it north into the Valley to join Early. Cleburne was a more than capable commander, who was smart enough both to take care of himself and his command, and to do what the irascible Early wanted done. A competent, cantankerous Irishman, Cleburne was one of the most respected commanders in the western armies. Further, the currently unemployed General D.H. Hill, one of the best combat generals in the Confederate Army, would be attached to Early and given a command as the opportunity arose. With such fighting subordinates such as Hill, John Gordon (who was already in Early's command), and Cleburne, and the numerical superiority this transfer of troops from the west would give, the chance of a decisive victory in the Valley would increase. It was really their only hope.

This bold strategic decision would leave Johnston severely short of veteran troops. However, if they did not do something, they were going to lose for sure. It was a calculated risk all three men agreed was worth taking. It was akin to the decision Lee and Jackson came to at Chancellorsville the year before. Planning boldly, the three men knew this was the South's last chance. If it did not work, they were dead in the water. If it did, it could lead to a negotiated peace and independence. Johnston would have to fight and delay the best he could. Every effort would be made to scrape up every available man, horse, and gun to replace the veterans that Cleburne would take north, but north they would go. If they did not win in the Valley it would not matter what Johnston had, Sherman was going to beat him anyway and they all knew it.

Both Hill and Cleburne might have a problem working with and for Early. Hill had resigned after Antietam, both for health reasons and for feeling somewhat unappreciated by Lee. He had also been blamed for the famous "lost order" recovered by McClellan before Antietam, which could have been, and almost was, the undoing of the Army of Northern Virginia. Against a more aggressive commander than McClellan, it would have spelled disaster and quite possibly the end of the war. Bitter over his treatment and the promotion of officers he believed less capable than he, and with a *bona fide* physical problem (he had chronic, and sometimes severe back pain), Hill had resigned and gone home. Lee, realizing that Hill would be invaluable in the coming operation, both because he was one of the best combat generals in the army and he had operated in the Valley in 1862, would send a trusted officer to talk to him. The fate of his country, to use a well-worn cliché, definitely hung in the balance, and he would listen. Cleburne would be convinced to swallow his pride and get on with it. He had a hard time with his superiors, and he was as ambitious and aggressive as they came, but he was an outstanding combat leader who also took good care of his men. Early would have to be carefully handled, but, if necessary, Lee would talk to him personally, even though it would be difficult to get Early to come out of the Valley for a meeting. While Early had been a difficult subordinate all these years, he had always done as Lee had asked.

Lastly, word would be sent to John Mosby, the successful partisan, to cooperate fully with Early's army. Mosby could be very useful to Early, providing deep intelligence and raiding along the Federal line of communications and generally causing hate and discontent in the Union rear. The forces the Yankees would have to send to deal with Mosby, especially cavalry, would be much missed elsewhere. Additionally, garrisons along the line of communications and in Federal depots would have to be strengthened and established if necessary.[5]

The three grimly desperate men agreed to the plan, with the hope that the troop transfer would be complete by mid-July, if not sooner. If they could catch the Yankees napping on this one, perhaps they had a chance. If not, nothing would be lost anyway. The meeting broke up, the two generals hastened back to their commands, and Davis summoned his staff to issue the necessary orders. It appeared that the Yankees held all the cards—a full house, while Lee, Johnston, and Davis were betting on a pair of fives.

Into The Valley Of Death

While the plans for Early's reinforcement were being made, along with the orders to have the plans come to fruition, Old Jube was taking his small army up the Valley to search for and destroy the enemy. Hunter's troops, under such commanders as Crook and Averell, as well as the French cavalryman Brigadier General Alfred Napoleon Alexander Duffie and his talented artillery commander Captain Henry DuPont, of the wealthy DuPont family of Delaware, were making themselves decidedly unpopular amongst the population of the Shenandoah. Crook commanded the VIII Corps, Brigadier General William Emory the XIX Corps. Both of these able commanders were capable of thinking on their feet, but their superior, Hunter, was not. A thorough pedant and marplot, he was not a competent independent commander and definitely met his match in Jubal Early. However, the Confederates were badly outnumbered, and even the considerable skills of Breckinridge and the hard-bitten cavalryman John Imboden, could not make up for lack of numbers. Before Early's arival in the valley, the Confederates were scraping the bottom of the manpower barrel, having to field the cadets of the Virginia Military Institute who distinguished themselves at the Battle of New Market on May 15. By skillful fighting and maneuvering, Hunter, and such dubious subordinates as Franz Sigel, were kept from winning decisively, Hunter bumbling his way into obtuseness.[6]

The Southern commanders were generally successful against the likes of Sigel and Hunter, but the odds were just getting too long. They outmaneuvered and outfought them, and, thanks to Hunter's general gun-shyness, the Northerners gave the Valley up by default to the outnumbered, determined Confederates before Early made his presence felt.

Fort Stevens, Washington, D.C., July 11, 1864

Early and his little army had helped clear the Valley of Federal troops. Now he was at the outskirts of Washington, skirmishing with the units that had been rushed to defend the capital. Wright's VI Corps of the Army of the Potomac was disembarking from steamers at the Potomac docks and rushing into Washington's formidable defenses. Early was not strong enough to take and hold Washington, even though Cleburne's large division of 10,000 veterans, including 1,000 cavalry and 30 guns, was coming up the Valley as fast as Cleburne could drive his men.

While the outpost bickering was going on, President and Mrs Lincoln drove up to Fort Stevens and stopped to get out. The President wanted to see at least part of the war first hand. Dressed in a light colored linen coat and his familiar stove-pipe hat, Lincoln, ignoring the occasional, though constant, musket firing towards the fort, climbed up to the parapet to get a good look at the enemy and the Union troops that opposed them. Seemingly oblivious to the increasing rate of fire among the Confederate troops, Lincoln stood calmly on the parapet, ignoring the pleas of his wife to get down.

Finally, an exasperated Union officer turned around and shouted, "Get down, you damned fool, before you get shot!" An amused Lincoln looked at him and then a familiar, ugly sound echoed along the parapet. It sounded like an axe being sunk into a thick log, and as others soldiers on the parapet looked towards the sound, they saw a surprised look on the President's face and at the same time heard a shrieking scream from his wife. The President seemed to hang in mid-air for a moment, and then toppled over like a giant oak tree that had been felled by a lumberjack. He had been shot through the head and was dead before he hit the ground.

Officers rushed to the President's aid, but it was obvious that it was useless. Mrs Lincoln had toppled over in a dead faint, and the President's body was quickly removed to their carriage. General Wright was summoned, and he dispatched aides to the city to inform the Vice-President, and the Secretaries of War and State what had happened. This was a disaster of epic proportions, especially with the national election only months away.

On the other side of the fence, Early and his commanders had no idea what had happened. He held his army before Washington until dark, and then expertly slipped away back down the Valley to take up positions around Winchester and await both his reinforcements and whatever the Yankees were about to send against him. He would have to try against Washington again after Cleburne joined him. If not, he would have to destroy the Union forces in the field.

Sheridan

The North was in a political crisis of epic proportions. Lincoln was dead, the sitting vice-president Hannibal Hamlin had been sworn in as President, and the government was in a low state of panic and a very high state of complete uproar. Hamlin had no discernible political following outside of his home state, and had been chosen for precisely that reason. He was reliable and honest, but was not a viable candidate for the fall election for president. Not only was the election now in doubt, but the war effort itself was in danger of collapsing. Something had to be done quickly to seek a decision, and the Valley was now the center of attention, both militarily and politically. Early had to be dealt with and dealt with decisively.

Grant sent Sheridan with the entire Cavalry Corps of the Army of the Potomac, save one division, and Wright's VI Corps into the Valley to reinforce whatever troops could be salvaged or rallied to face Early. As reorganized, Sheridan's new command was composed of Wright's corps, his own cavalry corps, Crook's VIII Corps, and Emory's XIX Corps. Qualitatively it should be the equal of Early's veterans. Quantitatively, at about 35,000 men in all, it would outnumber the Confederates and be able to drive them down the Valley.[7] Sigel was relieved for cause, Hunter relieved of all responsibilities in the field, though he maintained his position as the nominal departmental commander. Sheridan was given complete autonomy in the Valley, reporting only to Grant.

Sheridan's orders from Grant were simple and succinct: First, find and defeat Early, destroy him if possible, but drive him from the Valley. Second, render the Valley incapable, by whatever means, of supporting the Confederate war effort with food, horses, cattle, or anything else. Then, rejoin the Army of the Potomac with the VI Corps and the cavalry, leaving the other two corps at the head of the Valley to protect Washington.

Unknown to Sheridan, Cleburne had finally joined Early after Early's return to the Valley in July. Early now outnumbered Sheridan. Mosby had kept Early informed as to Sheridan's movements, and he took up a defensive position at Winchester to entice the Federals to attack him there. Sheridan obliged him. Boldly planning a double envelopment of Early's position, Sheridan and his army were up and moving at 3.00 a.m. on September 19, anticipating an annihilating hammer blow to take control of the Shenandoah away from the Confederacy, once and for all.

Outside of Winchester Virginia, September 19, 1864

The Yankee horse artillery battery was in march column along the road waiting for the battery commander to come back from his reconnaissance of the gun position. Section chiefs and other NCOs were dismounted and walking along the column checking guns, harness, ammunition loads, and quietly talking to some of the gunners. This was a horse artillery battery, the elite of the service,[8] and each gunner was individually mounted. It was a sharp outfit, and the gunners were proud of their record. They belonged to Wright's VI Corps, which had been "Uncle John" Sedgwick's. He had been killed at Spotsylvania, though, and was gone. Wright was a good commander, but he was not Uncle John.

This was also a regular battery, and the gunners, their NCOs, and officers considered themselves a cut above the average volunteer outfit. They had trained hard between campaigns, and the 3-inch ordnance rifles[9] with which they were equipped were sweet-shooting guns that could knock the eye out of a squirrel at a mile distance. They had their battle honors on the battery guidon, which was at the head of the column, drooping on its staff in the cool, windless early morning air.

Horses were being fed by their riders during the halt, or silently cropping grass if they were not, and gunners were munching on hardtack. Some were dozing in their saddles, catching a little sleep, as most of the veterans did whenever they could. Some of the horses had actually dozed off, displaying that amazing characteristic of being able to sleep standing up and locking their knees as they slept. There was no coffee, as the battery first sergeant had forbidden any fires. They were going into the attack this morning, and the order had come down to be as quiet as possible with no lights or unnecessary noise.

Suddenly there was a pounding off to the left. Horses ears pricked up and they turned their heads to the sound long before their semi-alert riders heard it. Over a small rise about 200 yards away the battery commander and his trumpeter, mounted on a very visible dapple-gray, were galloping towards the battery. By their haste it was quite evident they were about to move on. NCOs hustled along the column, cuffing sleeping gunners and drivers awake, and then swinging into the saddle themselves. The battery commander and trumpeter reined in quickly, both horses sliding along the grass, slick with early morning dew. The trumpeter took his place at the head of the column with the guidon bearer, now awake and alert, the guidon staff in its bucket in the right stirrup, the staff straight to the sky.

The battery commander quickly conferred with his second-in-command, the only other officer in the unit. All of the gun sections were commanded by sergeants, the battery not having a full complement of officers due to heavy losses and promotions. Good artillery officers were hard to come by this late in the war. Section chiefs were summoned, and a few brief sentences served as the battery commander's march order. He had found an excellent gun position and, at his command, the NCOs rejoined their sections. He and the Executive Officer took their places in the column. The battery commander's hand and arm signal to move out was immediately obeyed by the first gun team, dutifully followed by each in succession, and the long, deadly column moved forward with only the creak of harness leather and rattle of trace chains to mark their passing.[10]

Winchester

Sheridan meant to bring Early's Confederates to a battle of annihilation as soon as possible. He was convinced that he had Early outnumbered, and he definitely had more cavalry and artillery. He had no idea that Cleburne had joined Early, giving Early numerical parity and over 70 guns. Early's cavalry arm had also been strengthened by almost 1,000 sabers. Early now had almost 40,000 men, many more than Sheridan expected and more than enough to have a good chance of victory in any fight.

Mosby hung almost out of sight and range on Sheridan's flanks. Sheridan did know he was there, but he could not quite pin the elusive "Gray Ghost" down, so that every day couriers galloped to Early informing him of Sheridan's every move. Early knew Sheridan's approximate strength in infantry and cavalry, he knew who Sheridan's subordinates were, and his artillery strength had been accurately counted down to the last gun, limber, and caisson. The only thing Early did not know was if Sheridan knew about Cleburne or not. Well, he would soon find out.

Early planned a trap. He understood how aggressive Sheridan was, and knew any attack by him would be hard-hitting but might also be impulsive. Early planned a defensive-offensive battle, wanting Sheridan to commit fully to an attack on the Confederates before unleashing his main blow.

Taking up position at Winchester, Early deployed only Rodes's infantry division in front of the town. Rodes had orders to hold until relieved by the Southern counterattack. Breckinridge was placed in echelon to Rodes's left, inviting an enveloping attack. Cleburne's division was placed under cover on the Confederate right, sheltered by the town itself and not visible to the Federal advance. Gordon was emplaced in position to support Rodes, who had to hold for the plan to succeed. Imboden's and Brigadier General Thomas Rosser's cavalry brigades covered the Confederate left. On the Confederate right flank, Major General Lunsford Lomax and Colonel William Jackson's (contemptuously nicknamed "Mudwall" in contrast to "Stonewall" Jackson) cavalry brigades were placed and assigned a similar mission.

The battlefield was bordered by two creeks, Redbud and Abraham's on the north and south, respectively. Sheridan's attack would come between these two obstacles, the Federals deploying for the attack directly from march column. Their three corps, Wright's VI, Emory's XIX, and Crook's VIII, in that order.

Sheridan planned a frontal assault to pin the Confederate center in position with Wright's VI Corps, while maneuvering Crook and Emory to the right for an enveloping attack. As planned, Emory would hit and engage Breckinridge's division, while Crook would hit deeper, enveloping Breckinridge and rolling up the Confederate left flank. Federal cavalry would cover both flanks, Wilson's cavalry division being placed on the Federal left to protect the flank and to be available for the pursuit. The Union cavalry divisions of Brigadier Generals Wesley Merritt and William Averell would take station on the Federal right flank.

Wright's attack broke on Rodes's division like an avalanche, blue doom coming on like a cresting tidal wave. The fighting was savage and desperate with the Confederates contesting every inch of ground, but being driven steadily back. Gordon had to be committed on Rodes's right sooner than expected, and Gordon had to take over command of both divisions after Rodes was killed. However, the front stabilized, and Union losses were very heavy. Russell was killed by a shell fragment that ripped through his chest, and Upton was wounded and put out of action.[11]

As the fight on what would become the Confederate left flank became general, and Wright was completely committed, Emory came into action smartly on the VI Corps' right flank, driving hard against Breckinridge, who was outnumbered. Emory's attack overlapped Breckinridge's left flank, which Breckinridge skillfully refused. In the middle of this slug-match, Crook was marching hard for Breckinridge's left flank to envelop it. He was held up slightly by marshy ground along Redbud run, but finally came into action at about 10.30.

Imboden's and Rosser's cavalry vainly sacrificed themselves to gain time for Breckinridge, but Merritt's and Averell's veteran Union cavalry drove the Confederate horsemen from the field. Breckinridge shifted what artillery he could to attempt to slow Crook's juggernaut and give time for him to disengage partially and form a new line. Fortunately for the Confederates, Gordon was holding his own and Wright's attack seemed spent.

Sheridan was up and down the length of his line, urging troops and their commanders forward, waving his personal battle flag. Despite heavy losses, the Union troops manfully shouldered forward into withering musket and cannon fire, only to be repeatedly stopped short of Gordon's line. Regimental commanders and officers of all grades recklessly exposed themselves, summoning their now-exhausted men for another effort, and officer casualties were very heavy. Sheridan, realizing that Wright had shot his bolt, galloped madly to the Union right flank, urging Crook and his troops forward, yelling above the crash and thunder of the battle that the fight was won if they merely advanced one last time. It very nearly was.

Jubal Early, Harvey Hill, and Patrick Cleburne watched the battle unfold as they had hoped it would. The Union army was fully committed. There were not any reserves to fall back on and rally in case of defeat. Sheridan had really shot his bolt and it was the time for the counterattack. Early, having heard of Rodes's fall, gave the division to Hill, who saluted and galloped forward to assume command and assist the heavily pressed Gordon. Then he looked at Cleburne, nodded and merely said, "Drive those people away." Cleburne saluted, turned his horse and hurried to his division. It was now around 11.30 a.m.

Envelopment

Cleburne rejoined his waiting division, his subordinate commanders fairly frothing at the mouth to get into action. He nodded to his artillery battalion commander, who galloped forward and led his guns at full speed to an enfilade position on Wright's left flank, generally unseen by the Union commanders. Lomax and Johnson, the two Confederate cavalry commanders on the Union right, who had been reinforced specifically for this mission, went after Wilson, who was soon embroiled in a large cavalry fight and out of the picture for the time being. That would not last too long.

As the Confederate artillery opened up on the Union line, taking Wright's entire force in enfilade with the fire of 30 guns, Cleburne's division came booming out of its positions in a howling assault, preceded by the dreaded "Rebel yell" that reminded Wright's veterans of Jackson's devastating flank attack at Chancellorsville the year before.

With two brigades leading in line, and one following in reserve, Cleburne's division hit the Yankee flank with such force that it shattered Wright's left wing units so badly they literally disintegrated. What had been a steady, but depleted, line of solid Union infantry, now degenerated into a mob of fugitives swept away by the fury of the Confederate assault.

Yankee artillery batteries either swung trails or attempted to redeploy to face the onslaught, but they, too, were caught up in the mess and rout, several batteries being overrun before they were able to limber up and displace out of the way of the attacking brigades. At the same time, Hill, who had by now assumed command of Rodes's former division, and Gordon counterattacked with every available man to complete the rout of the best corps in Sheridan's army.

Wright had the presence of mind to send runners and couriers to Emory and Sheridan, but it was too late for Emory. Early had joined Breckinridge and together they led a vicious counterattack that stopped Emory in his tracks. Sheridan quickly ordered Crook to pull back out of his attack and attempt to cover the Union withdrawal that was now necessary, but Crook was about to be faced by the entire Confederate army as Emory's corps fell apart under Cleburne's attack as badly as Wright's had.

Wilson saw the debacle before the courier reached him to tell him about it and "to act as he saw fit." He immediately disengaged from the cavalry fight behind his horse artillery and reserve regiment, the Confederate horse withdrawing as they were outnumbered and had no artillery. Wilson reformed his division and redeployed it to act as a rearguard and screen, behind which the wrecked corps of Wright and Emory could withdraw and rally.

Sheridan left Crook to get out of the mess as best he could, as he had to see to the rest of his army. Crook was in a horrible situation. Instead of enveloping Breckinridge, he was now about to be faced by the entire Confederate army and possible encirclement. Pulling back his attacking brigades, he reformed his corps to fight in three directions, and prepared an attack "in the other direction" that was the only hope of breaking out of the coming trap and rejoining the army.

To his rear, Merritt and Averell had defeated Imboden and the Confederate horse, killing Imboden in the process. As the Confederates were leaving the field in some disorder, the two Union cavalry commanders saw the jaws of the trap closing on Crook. The quick-witted Merritt ordered his troopers into a column of regiments in line, conformed to by Averell, and the two cavalrymen charged the Confederate infantry about to encircle Crook. What followed was an action of cavalry against rifle-armed infantry that had not yet been seen in the war.[12]

Sabers flashing in the sunlight and trumpets blaring the charge, the two Union cavalry divisions burst out of the smoke and noise on the unsuspecting Confederate infantry, overrunning one of Cleburne's brigades and forcing the other two to stop their converging attack on Crook. Spent by the initial attack, Merritt withdrew his command to reorganize, but Averell continued to advance, hurting Gordon badly before being stopped for good by D.H. Hill.

In the respite, Crook gathered up his bleeding regiments and attacked "to the rear" breaking out of the impending Confederate trap and saving most of his corps, though his corps artillery was lost to the Confederate assault. What had been planned as an annihilating hammer-blow by Sheridan had been turned into a rout by Early's careful planning and the ace he had up his sleeve—Cleburne's division.

There was no pursuit, an omission which left Early in a fit of fury. However, Imboden was dead and his cavalry wrecked. The remaining

Confederate cavalry under Rosser were following the Union retreat, but at a respectful distance, for Wilson was alive and alert, and he had enough artillery for a Confederate division. Gordon and Hill were fought out. Breckinridge was picking up the pieces of his hard-used division, and Cleburne, for all the fury of his decisive assault, was at the end of his tether. One of his brigades had suffered heavily to Union cavalry, and the other two were disorganized somewhat by the flank assault.

Casualties on both sides were heavy, the Federals, however, losing twice as many as the Confederates, especially in prisoners. Early's casualties were 5,500 killed and wounded and almost none captured. Sheridan lost 11,971, including 2,500 prisoners plus horses and guns captured, two of his artillery batteries being overrun in the last stages of the fighting. The one advantage to this was that Sheridan could replace his losses, Early could not.

Sheridan was furious. Why had they not known about the other Confederate units with Early? He was much stronger than expected, with more artillery and cavalry than had been reported. This was not over by a damned sight, and there would definitely be another day. Time before November, and the fateful national election, however, was running out.

Plans

Sheridan withdrew northwest to Charlestown where he set about assessing his position and reorganizing his command. His losses in officers had been especially damaging. He wrote to Grant informing him in very blunt terms what had happened ("We were whipped badly, but it was a very close thing."). Without waiting for a reply, he set about refurbishing his command, no excuses, none tolerated, and waited for a chance to get at Early's army just one more time.

Grant took his subordinate's accurate report with deep regret, yet he had not lost faith in Phil Sheridan. He ordered more troops out of the Washington garrison to the Valley, and resupplies and more artillery, to replace guns lost at Winchester, were hurriedly rushed to railheads and sent to Charlestown. Sheridan maintained his three corps organizations as well as the corps commanders. All had done well, but Wright was furious at what had happened to him and his VI Corps. The entire army was still full of fight and burning for revenge.

Early, Hill, and Cleburne planned boldly. Mosby ranged the upper Valley, looking for signs of movement. What Early wanted to do was entice the aggressive Sheridan to attack him again, at least to move against him in force. He wanted the Union Army in his pocket, not to retreat and regroup. If he could destroy Sheridan, the election in November might go to the Democrats, giving the Confederacy a chance for a negotiated peace and perhaps independence.

After cleaning up the battlefield, taking care of the wounded and prisoners, Early withdrew down the Valley to the vicinity of Woodstock, an unforaged area that could and would feed his army. Prisoners were sent south, the wounded to follow, and the army moved out on September 22, gingerly followed by Wilson, sent back to the Valley to keep an eye on Early. Reaching Woodstock the next day, Early put his army into a cantonment area prepared for defense and waited for Sheridan's next move, his troops living in unaccustomed, for them, luxury while his cavalry ranged the Valley to the north, keeping contact with both the Federals and the ever-present Mosby.

Finding out from Wilson that Early was curiously withdrawing down the Valley, Sheridan sent all of his available cavalry under Wilson, Custer, and Merritt down the Valley to find out as much as they could. As soon as the hard-used infantry was fit to move, they followed, starting at the beginning of October. Sheridan's army had reached Middletown, on Cedar Creek, by the second week of October. With Grant's admonishments and instructions still ringing in his ears, and no movement at all from Early's army, Sheridan went into a cantonment area a little northwest of Middletown.

Sheridan placed his infantry facing down the valley in their camps, the cavalry cantonments to the rear. His artillery was liberally placed throughout the area, ready for instant use. He knew numbers were about equal in infantry, artillery, and cavalry with Early, and he wanted to entice Early to attack, which might actually fool the Confederate. What he did not know was that Early was already planning to oblige him.

On the morning of October 15, Sheridan was summoned by courier to Washington for a conference with the President, the Secretary of War, and General Grant. Reluctantly leaving his army, he and a small escort left at breakneck speed for Washington. He could not have left at a worse time.

Cedar Creek

The Confederate army was on the move. They were moving north to attack Sheridan in his camp at Cedar Creek. Early planned to catch the Yankees napping, and envelop and trap them before they knew what had hit them. Thanks to Mosby, he knew that Sheridan was probably absent and, without their driving, fiery commander present, Early was positive that he could catch them unawares and destroy the last Union force of any size in the Valley. The Union general election was in a little over three weeks.

In Sheridan's absence, the local security of the camp at Cedar Creek became somewhat lax. Early moved up undetected during the night of October 18–19, crossing Cedar Creek at 3.00 a.m. on the 19th and forming in line of battle by 4.30. Early's army was now organized into three divisions commanded by Gordon, Cleburne, and D.H. Hill, Breckinridge had been badly wounded at Winchester, and had been sent home The cavalry was now commanded by Rosser, reorganized as a single division and reinforced with captured Federal horse artillery. It was sent deep into the battlefield on the right to be ready to take care of any intervention by the Union cavalry.

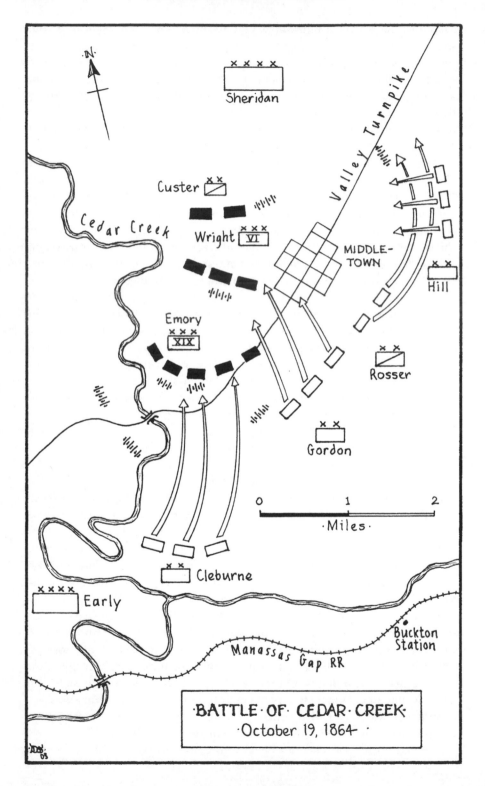

BATTLE·OF·CEDAR·CREEK·
·October 19, 1864·

Cleburne was to make a direct frontal assault on the Union encampment, which was lightly fortified. Gordon was to bypass to the right, enveloping the camp, Hill to envelop even deeper on the right flank in order to encircle and pocket the Union army against Cedar Creek. The signal for the attack was to be a three-gun salvo from the Confederate artillery positioned on the friendly side of Cedar Creek on Cleburne's left flank.

By 5.00 a.m. both Cleburne and Gordon were in position. Hill was not, as he had the furthest to go, but Early decided to launch the assault at 5.15 as planned anyway. He wanted to hit the Yankees at the time of the morning when they would be the least alert. Hill would just have to catch up. If he knew Harvey Hill, he would be furious that the attack had begun without him and would bust a gut to get to his assigned position and start his enveloping move.

The attack burst like a sudden thunderstorm on the Union positions. Men were asleep and pickets were dozing. The eager Confederate infantry came out of the gloom like gray doom, hitting the Northern picket line just at that time of day when the human body is at its lowest ebb. Cleburne met Emory's corps just as it was attempting to form up and overran its artillery and lead units, Confederates streamed past surrendering and running Federals, shooting up any of Emory's units that attempted a stand.

Gordon went in hard, breaking through the more professionally organized picket line of Wright's corps, overrunning Wright's command post and almost capturing Wright. Wright's divisions managed to form a line of battle through which Emory's men ran, and they finally stopped Gordon 500 yards behind their encampment.

Suddenly, the almost irresistible Southern attack slowed and nearly stopped. Famished infantrymen, who had lived on hard, scanty rations for quite some time, stopped to loot the Northern camps, eating food that was still cooking over slow fires. This respite allowed both Wright and Emory to disengage and re-form their units in a position behind both camps. The Union cavalry had hastily mounted and moved out, not allowing itself to be trapped in the mess. Their horse artillery moved with them, and most of Wright's artillery got out, but Emory had lost his, and his corps had lost almost 50 percent of its strength. However, a line of battle had been formed by 8.00, and the attacks by Gordon and Cleburne were effectively stopped. They were not beaten, but needed to reorganize to continue the attack.

Harvey Hill was damning and urging his men forward on their movement to get into position. Ahead of them, they were being screened by Rosser's cavalry, and they could hear the firing slackening to their left. Behind them, a courier was pounding up the road to them, a bandage over his left eye, and a bullet hole in his kepi. He reined up next to Hill and gave him a message from Early, "For God's sake, hurry up and attack, we're stalled and need the support. The enemy is formed in line of battle behind their camps. We will continue our attack presently." Nodding to the messenger, Hill ordered his subordinates to turn the command to the left and into line. By 7.45 a.m. he was ready to go.

Sheridan's Ride

Sheridan, accompanied by his faithful aide, Lieutenant Colonel Forsyth, and his escort were making their way down the Valley at an easy gait. Off in the distance, they heard a growing crescendo of firing, getting louder by the minute. What they were hearing was Gordon's men over-running the Federal camp. The time was 6.00 a.m. Knowing that he and his army were in trouble, Sheridan sunk spur and bolted down the turnpike, followed by Forsyth and his escort. Sheridan rode like a man possessed. He knew if he lost to Early, the Valley would go and probably the national election. He drove himself and his escort to the limit, finally encountering Yankee cavalry and wounded infantrymen on the road and in the fields to either side of the turnpike.

'Turn around! Go the other way! We can still beat them boys! Form up! Form up!'

Sheridan's horse ate up the distance to Cedar Creek, and the troops were beginning to stop in ones and two, and small clumps of them were starting to form up, spurred on by his enthusiasm and the fact that he was present among them. Sheridan was a force of nature when leading troops, and it never shone more clearly than in the cluttered mess along the road to Cedar Creek. Tough clumps of veterans were gathering around their regimental colors; officers were shouting through the retreat and rout for the troops to rally, and NCOs were cuffing recalcitrant troops back into line. Then the gods stopped smiling at Phil Sheridan.

With a whoop and a holler, and the familiar Rebel yell, Confederate cavalry burst on the little party like the hounds of hell. Sheridan's escorts turned to fight, but were almost instantaneously overwhelmed. Sheridan drew a pistol, but was shot from the saddle by a Confederate sergeant, and he hit the ground hard on his shoulder. Sitting up, holding his side, he was instantly made a prisoner, his guards dead or captured, along with Lieutenant Colonel Forsyth.

At the same time that Sheridan was wounded and taken, Hill's assault broke on the left flank of the new Union line. The shock was terrific, the left flank brigade being almost instantly destroyed, and with no time to refuse its flank, an entire division of Emory's corps was overrun. At almost the same time, Cleburne and Gordon attacked again and the entire Union line collapsed. Fugitives streamed to the rear, Wright and his staff were captured this time, and Emory was killed, being blown out of the saddle by three simultaneous wounds. He was dead before he hit the ground.

The Yankee cavalry gallantly sacrificed itself trying to cover the retreat and rout, but over half of the infantry and all of the corps artillery was lost.

It was as complete a victory as Jubal Early might have wanted, with the added bonus of taking Sheridan prisoner.

Early's victory was overwhelming. Wright's veteran corps was virtually destroyed. Emory and Crook both lost over half of their commands, and all the artillery of the army was lost. The only intact units that survived were in the cavalry corps, and they, too, had been badly hurt. Total losses were over 20,000, including 5,000 taken prisoner. Early's army had also lost heavily, with 7,500 killed and wounded, and another 1,500 missing. But he held the Valley, as well as Sheridan, and the immense booty taken from the Yankees. It was the most lopsided victory of the war, Sheridan's army being destroyed as a cohesive fighting unit.

Aftermath

Lincoln's untimely death and Sheridan's defeat and capture did become the decisive event of 1864 and of the entire war. These two incidents entirely changed the picture both at home and abroad, canceling out the earlier, seemingly overwhelming, Northern victories of 1863: Gettysburg, Vicksburg, and Chattanooga. The Republicans could not field a candidate of suitable stature and prestige, though Secretary of State Seward manfully stepped up to the plate and tried. The Democrats and McClellan were the winners in the fall election, even though the military vote went overwhelmingly for Seward. The Northern soldiers did not want to give up all that they had achieved and definitely did not want the Union to be dissolved but, as soon as McClellan had been inaugurated, peace feelers went South and a cease fire was agreed to between the combatants. Britain and France, having no objection to the creation of a much-weakened United States, immediately offered to mediate between the two sides. The shooting stopped in all theaters, and the Union blockade of Southern ports was lifted. A much-disputed peace treaty was negotiated and signed in the summer of 1865, granting the South its independence, though without the provision of war indemnities from the North. The Confederacy was granted all territory that had seceded in 1861, though West Virginia was recognized as a Northern state. The so-called "border states" stayed as part of the United States and the Emancipation Proclamation was enforced in those areas still under the control of the United States.

Slavery was maintained as an institution by the Confederacy, at least temporarily, but an immediate infusion of European investment capital quickly dried up when cotton became a glut on the market. "King Cotton" became a liability to the South, as European markets had found alternate, and cheaper, sources of cotton to substitute for the blockaded Southern product. The underpinnings of slavery were manifestly creaking when Virginia abolished the institution in 1870. By the turn of the century, it was gone. The Southern economy never fully recovered from the devastation of three years of brutal warfare. The United States never recovered its political stability from the cult of the leader established by President McClellan. It sullenly refused to help its Southern neighbor, and the border between the two nations remained hostile for decades.

The Reality

Jubal Early's small Confederate army did enter the Shenandoah Valley in June 1864 to support the Confederate forces there and to keep the Valley, the South's breadbasket, as a supply center for food for the Confederacy. Initially successful, Early drove to the outskirts of Washington outside of Fort Stevens. Troops (Wright's VI Corps) were rushed from the Army of the Potomac to protect Washington, but there was little fighting, though President Lincoln, standing on the parapet of Fort Stevens, was under fire for a little while. Lieutenant Colonel Oliver Wendell Holmes, later chief justice of the Supreme Court did, in fact, tell him "get down you damned fool!" which Lincoln reluctantly did. (Holmes did not realize who it was until after he had said it. The much-wounded Holmes was no doubt suitably embarrassed, but the fact that the comment was obeyed says much for its common sense.) However, Lincoln was not harmed and won the national election that November. Lincoln defeated the anti-war Democrats and their somewhat reluctant candidate George McClellan, who was a twice-failed commander of the Army of the Potomac. Interestingly, the military vote went heavily for Lincoln.

There was no council of war with Lee, Davis, and Johnston. Johnston was soon relieved by Davis, being replaced unwisely by John Bell Hood, who wrecked what was left of the Southern forces in the Deep South at Franklin and Nashville. A competent division commander for Longstreet, Hood was in over his head commanding an army.

Lee, though admired as the "marble model," and the epitome of an army commander, really did not grasp the strategic situation for the Confederacy. His concern was for Virginia. He defended it well, was an excellent tactician and counter-puncher, but as he doggedly held on in Northern Virginia in 1864–65, the South fell apart behind him.

By mid-July 1864 Early and his small army did control the Valley. Union forces under the department commander David Hunter had been defeated and outmaneuvered. Sheridan arrived in late July and the situation changed. He defeated Early at Winchester and unwisely figured the Southerners were done. Early and his resilient troops did conduct a savage attack at Cedar Creek, which initially swept all before it, but Sheridan's timely arrival from Washington reversed the situation.

Phil Sheridan completed his famous ride on his black horse Rienzi, rallied the defeated troops of his army and counter-attacked, defeating and routing Early's outnumbered army. Early was no longer a threat, and Sheridan's army went on down the Valley to comply with his instructions to render it incapable of providing food and fodder for the Confederate armies, especially

Lee's Army of Northern Virginia which was then besieged at Petersburg, outside of Richmond. It was another nail in the coffin of Southern hopes for a successful conclusion to the war. The Union noose was tightening. In actuality, with Lincoln's re-election, Grant's dogged determination not to give Lee any breathing space, and Sherman's ruthless march to Atlanta and then Savannah, it was all over but the shouting.

Bibliography

Bridges, Hal, *Lee's Maverick General, Daniel Harvey Hill* (University of Nebraska Press, Lincoln, 1961).

Catton, Bruce, *A Stillness at Appomattox* (Doubleday, New York, 1953).

Davis, William C., *Death in the Trenches* (Time-Life Books, Alexandria, VA, 1986).

Downey, Fairfax, *The Guns at Gettysburg* (David McKay, New York, reprinted 1987).

Elting, John R., *The Superstrategists* (Scribner's and Sons, New York, 1985).

Elting, John R., *American Army Life* (Charles Scribner's Sons, New York, 1982).

Esposito, Vincent J., ed., *The West Point Atlas of American Wars*, Volume I, (Praeger, New York, 1959).

Lewis, Thomas, A., *The Shenandoah in Flames* (Time-Life Books, Alexandria, VA, 1987).

Martin, Jane A., and Ross, Jeremy, Associate Editors, *Spies, Scouts, and Raiders* (Time Life Books, Alexandria, VA, 1985).

Naisawald, L. Vanloan, *Grape and Canister* (Oxford University Press, New York, 1960).

Notes

1. Thomas A. Lewis, *The Shenandoah in Flames*, p. 53.

*2. This battery would distinguish itself both at Cedar Creek and Winchester.

3. The command relationship between Grant, commander-in-chief of the Union armies, and Meade, Commander of the Army of the Potomac from Gettysburg to the end of the war, was interesting. Contrary to many accounts, Grant was never the commander of the Army of the Potomac, he and his staff merely accompanied it for the duration as Grant saw that Northern Virginia, and Lee's army, was the decisive theater. Odd as it was, the relationship worked.

4. The old story about Jackson's acquisition of the name "Stonewall" is probably apocryphal. He did stand like a stone wall as General Bernard Bee emphatically, and undoubtedly profanely, stated. However, Bee may not have used the term because of Jackson's steadiness under fire, but for his tardiness in supporting Bee and his troops, who were going through a very bad time. Unfortunately, Bee was killed, and we will never know the truth of the story.

5. A portion of the Shenandoah Valley became known as "Mosby's Confederacy" for the impunity with which Mosby and his troopers operated in that general area. Mosby was the ideal partisan chief—intelligent, quick-witted, and hard-hitting.

6. The Northern volunteer units were raised by the state governors, not the Federal Government. Since this was the mass of the troops that fought the Civil War, this gave the Northern governors immense political influence. It also was, as the old saying goes, one hell of a way to run a railroad. There were two great faults of the system: first, except for Wisconsin, the "replacement" method most favored by the state governors was to raise new units, not replace

casualties in veteran ones. Hence, officers in new units, especially senior field grade ones, were inexperienced and outranked veteran captains and majors who commanded the small, veteran volunteer units and knew much more of warfare. This led to more mistakes and high casualties. Second, the governors had politicians and hacks commissioned as general officers, most of whom were found to be incompetent. Both Sigel and Hunter were of this ilk, though at least Sigel tried. Hunter is infamous as the officer who ordered the Virginia Military Institute to be burned.

7. Wright and his VI Corps were probably the best choice for the Valley Campaign. Wright was more than competent, and the VI Corps, which had been commanded by "Uncle John" Sedgwick until he was killed by a Confederate sniper at Spotsylvania, was a veteran unit, inured to hardship and the rigors of campaigning. It became the linch-pin of Sheridan's army. Two of its senior officers, David Russell and Emory Upton, were outstanding up-and-comers. They had organized, planned, and led the first successful night assault of the war at Rappahannock Station in November 1864, capturing the fortified position and most of the famed Louisiana Brigade, part of Jubal Early's command.

8. Yankee horse artillery was considered a true elite arm of the service. See Fairfax Downey, *The Guns at Gettysburg*, p. 15.

9. The 3-inch ordnance rifle was considered to be the best field piece of the Civil War. Light, durable and accurate, it was much prized by its crews and was the ideal horse artillery weapon.

*10. This tough, veteran battery, commanded by Captain Samuel Fallon, was one of the few units to extricate itself intact from the disaster at Winchester. Fallon later rose to be chief of artillery.

11. Emory Upton has been described as "something of a northern Stonewall Jackson" and arguably the best tactician the Civil War produced. His tactics were adopted by Grant at the Muleshoe Salient at Spotsylvania.

12. The fighting in the Valley saw sabre-wielding Yankee cavalry in massed formation charge and overrun formed Confederate infantry in the open. It is little known and studied, but the hard-riding Northern cavalry under such commanders as James Wilson was a highly capable, well-led weapon that had finally come of age in the last two years of the war.